IRELAND AND THE EU
POST BREXIT

IRELAND AND THE EU POST BREXIT

Ray Bassett

© Ray Bassett, 2020

Published by Grangeland Ventures Ltd (2020)
        Castleknock
        Dublin
        D15V 3KT

A CIP catalogue record for this book is available from the British Library.

ISBN 978-1-8380397-0-7

Book layout and cover design by Clare Brayshaw

Prepared and printed by:

York Publishing Services Ltd
64 Hallfield Road
Layerthorpe
York YO31 7ZQ

Tel: 01904 431213

Website: www.yps-publishing.co.uk

Contents

About the Author

Dr Ray Bassett is the Senior Research Fellow in European Affairs with Britain's leading Think Tank, Policy Exchange. He has held that position since 2017. He has also worked with Politeia, another leading Think Tank in London.

Bassett is a former senior Irish diplomat and served as Ireland's Ambassador to Canada, Jamaica and the Bahamas 2010-2016. Dr Bassett holds a PhD from Trinity College Dublin in biochemistry (on Folic Acid).

Dr Bassett spent most of his career working for the Irish Government on the Northern Ireland Troubles and conflict resolution. He was part of the Irish Talks Team to the Good Friday Negotiations(1998), including at the final session at Castle Buildings in Stormont, Belfast. He subsequently became the Irish Government's representative in Belfast 2001-2005 and part of the Good Friday Agreement's Implementation team.

Other posts held by Dr Bassett include head of the Irish Consular Service 2005-2010 and the senior official in charge of Ireland's relations with its Diaspora. He has had other postings in Ottawa, Belfast (twice), London, Canberra and Copenhagen.

Dr Bassett has been a regular commentator on Irish, British and EU matters since he left the Irish Diplomatic Service in 2016. He was a columnist on the Sunday Business Post (Dublin) and appears regularly on radio and TV current affairs programmes in Dublin, Belfast and London. He has also published articles in the Irish Times, the Irish Sun, the London Telegraph, the Daily Mail, the Belfast Newsletter, the Irish Echo (Sydney), the Globe and Mail (Toronto), the Derry News, An Phoblacht (Irish Republican Publication), Conservative Home News, Brexit Central and the Irish Trade Union Publication, Liberty.

In 2019, Bassett was awarded a Poynter Fellowship in journalism in Yale University, Connecticut, USA.

The views in this book are entirely his own.

Acknowledgements

This book is dedicated to the memory of Dermot Gallagher and Sheamus Howlin, two outstanding and special people who departed this world far too early.

I would like to acknowledge the help and assistance of my family and especially my wife Patricia, as well as our adult children Mark, David, Paul, Jennifer and Kevin. Without their support and their constructive suggestions and criticism, I would not have been able to complete this work.

I would also like to mention, with deep gratitude, the assistance I received from Michael Clarke, who did trojan work on the manuscript.

I would also like to take this opportunity to thank Dean Godson and the staff of Policy Exchange in London for the opportunities that they have afforded me in the last three years. Also, to Sheila Lawlor of Politeia, much appreciation for your support and more importantly your friendship. Also, a big thanks to Dr Bonnie Weir of Yale University. It has been a pleasure and a privilege to work with her over the years.

Also, I want to acknowledge the assistance of the wisest man I know, Pat McArt, whom I always turn to for a second and wiser opinion. To my good friend Tim Pat Coogan, who keeps me sound on all important matters, many thanks. To Liam Halligan my sincere thanks for his steadfast and constant support.

I would also like to include a special word of appreciation for Hermann Kelly, who is a steadfast defender of national sovereignty in Ireland as is Edward Spalton of the Campaign for an Independent Britain (CIB) on our neighbouring island. Also, thanks to Gerry Staunton and John Kennedy who constantly challenge my views and prejudices and in so doing are invaluable sounding boards. Martin Kinsella, Frank Donnelly, Noel Gallagher and Jim Brogan are great allies and friends.

To Tony Coughlan thanks for keeping the flame of Irish self determination alive through many difficult years. Our country owes you a debt of gratitude.

PART I

Chapter 1 – Introduction

The Last Refuge of Scoundrels

"If it's a Yes we will say on we go, and if it's a No we will say we continue."

Jean-Claude Juncker

The first question that must be asked about any book is what is the point of this publication and even more importantly, what is the motivation of the writer?

I can honestly answer that I have set out to help redress an imbalance, which I believe is long overdue. There is a paucity of books on Ireland, which challenge the accepted wisdom that the European Union and Ireland are an ideal match. In fact, there has never been much of a fundamental debate on European issues inside the country. This has been the position from its accession to the European Economic Community (EEC) in 1973. I would like to contribute towards changing that deplorable situation.

I believe that a more balanced environment would be beneficial for the country, as I am convinced that the lack of exposure to counterarguments, has impacted adversely on our decision makers. That has caused the country harm in the recent past and has the potential to do further damage, unless corrected, as we enter the post-Brexit era.

The whole Brexit process in Britain has thrown up serious challenges which require adroit handling and strategic vision from the authorities in Dublin. Now that the UK has formally left the EU, there is a need for a fundamental re-examination of our own position. Unfortunately, from my experiences within the Irish Civil Service, I have little confidence that there will be any serious commitment to vigorously road test our current EU policy in the near future.

Towards the end of my time in the Irish Government's service, I had become seriously concerned about the determination of that Government, both elected politicians and the permanent officials, to pursue what I considered to be a blinkered eurocentric policy on Brexit, regardless of the consequences. This included the potential negative effect on relations within the island of Ireland, and between Ireland and Britain. I questioned the wisdom of completely casting our lot in with the Eurozone, a failing economic and political project, well removed from what Ireland originally signed up to in 1973 in the EEC, and which I believe is not in tune with the Irish people's longer-term interests.

Getting started

Although I had harboured concerns about the Irish authorities' subservient devotion to Brussels for some time, at a personal level I never had any intention of getting involved publicly in the Brexit debate as it developed in Ireland in 2016. It was only close to my departure from the Department of Foreign Affairs and Trade in Dublin in the summer of that year, and after I noted, with growing alarm, the content and tone of internal discussions on the issue, including some very naïve position papers, that I became concerned enough to begin to commit my own thoughts to paper. At that time among officials, with whom I had informal discussions, there was no real or deep appreciation of the dangers that Brexit represented to the delicate balance of relationships in these islands. Events would later shake them out of their misplaced complacency. When I suggested that we should be acutely aware that the Dublin/London axis was vital to preserving and developing the Good Friday Agreement (GFA), this was politely dismissed. It was pointed out forthrightly that Ireland's future lay largely with the remaining 26 Member States and that the old emphasis on British/Irish links would not enjoy its former prominence in future Irish foreign policy. It was clear that my views were not welcomed, and that the Brussels centric view would prevail over all other considerations.

The UK and the EU would be going their separate ways, and in those circumstances, I strongly felt we needed to act as a bridge between them, so as to avoid damaging the foundations of the GFA. There was no sympathy for that policy line. In fact, quite the contrary. We would be true Europeans and the UK must be made to suffer for their heretical views. The strength and vehemence of the opinions expressed reminded me of religious fervour. Perhaps there were echoes of the Inquisition and determined efforts to stamp out the Reformation, or in its modern manifestation, euroscepticism. It was then that I began to realise that the Irish official approach was prepared, in effect, to sacrifice the GFA in order to appease Brussels, the new Holy See.

I felt that this was a myopic view of Brexit, which needed to be challenged. However, it was pervasive throughout official and political circles in Dublin. It had all the classic hallmarks of groupthink, coupled with the herd instinct, and had the potential to cause huge damage to my country.

It was also clear that there was no further point pushing my views internally. The officials involved in European matters inside the Government system had a proprietorial attitude and resented input from those outside their own immediate circle, even sometimes from politicians. Only the caste of euro high priests could really understand the detail and complexity of the EU. Those on the outside should not interfere. Also, my views were outside the accepted norm for the system. Dissenters were most definitely not welcomed.

From the moment that British Prime Minister, David Cameron, agreed to hold a Brexit referendum, I felt that there were potentially huge negative implications for Ireland. Therefore, I personally was opposed to Brexit and wanted Cameron to win the referendum. This was not out of any great love for the current arrangements in the EU. I simply feared for the consequences of Brexit on Ireland and also that the departure of the UK would greatly weaken those inside the EU, who wanted to see democratic reform and the abandonment of the idea of an ever-closer Union. I felt that official Ireland, at that time, greatly underestimated the possible damage that a Brexit could do to our national interest. However, this was a purely selfish Irish position. If I had been British, I would have strongly supported Brexit, as a means of regaining the country's national sovereignty and escaping from the economic straitjacket of the EU.

In Ireland, because of the country's recent good economic performance, there is little awareness of the overall Eurozone's poor record in this area. The Eurozone economic performance, relative to North America and Asia, has been dreadful over the last twenty years[1]. It has even been poor relative to the EU countries which stayed out of the new currency[2].

In many ways, the Brexit debate had thrown up questions, which require a serious re-examination of Ireland's best interests. While the UK remained inside the EU, the balance of advantage seemed to lie with our continued membership. This did not include the usual Irish uncritical support for further transference of powers and competences to the EU institutions. However, a post-Brexit EU greatly altered the political and economic landscape for Ireland in a way, that certainly required deep discussion and reassessment. In the circumstances, the least that could be expected was a series of far reaching policy papers which would examine all possible scenarios. Unfortunately, nothing like this occurred in Ireland, which lemming-like rushed to embrace Brussels even more enthusiastically. It was a sobering and dispiriting experience listening to the internal discussions. The outlook that predominated was one of total devotion to the EU and lacked any long-term strategic vision or creativity.

Once I formally left the Irish diplomatic service, I shared my thoughts with my friend, the economist David McWilliams, who suggested I give them to the then editor of the *Sunday Business Post*, Ian Kehoe. Ian was enthusiastic about including it in his newspaper. After a career, deep within Government, I was naturally reluctant to air my dissenting views in public. However, I felt that the issue was important enough to break cover. After some agonising, I agreed to let it go forward for publication on 1 January 2017[3]. I had expected some misgivings from my former colleagues but did not foresee the level of antagonism that my first article engendered, including a text from a senior official asking that I refrain from ever using the title of ex-Ambassador. It was clear that I was no longer welcome back in my old workplace because I had broken a sacred taboo. I had questioned the Irish blind devotion to Brussels and did so publicly.

However, if I managed, even marginally, to promote a real debate, then it was a small price to pay. To show I was concerned, I refused any payment for that and subsequent articles in the *Business Post*. I was

4

grateful to the *Post* for giving me a platform, even if this platform was later largely withdrawn when Ian left as editor. I subsequently wrote for the British Think Tanks, Policy Exchange and Politeia, as well as a number of publications, including the Telegraph and BrexitCentral in London. These further writings only seemed to exasperate relations with my old Department. I felt I should use all platforms, available to me, to publicly air a different perspective on Ireland and the EU. I also used these platforms to urge Ireland to adopt a more conciliatory approach to Brexit, in our own national interests. There were very few others taking on a similar role at that time. I do not believe that differences in policy should lead to personal animosity but unfortunately this is what transpired. I also contributed articles to *Liberty*, the Irish Trade Union paper; and to *An Phoblacht*, the Irish Republican publication, on other topics. I strongly believe in speaking to all shades of opinion, not just to those with whom I agree or are somehow deemed acceptable to the conservative consensus in Dublin.

Motivation

I have been very lucky in life. The Irish State had educated me, without any fees and with maintenance grants, up to the level of a PhD in biochemistry in Ireland's most prestigious university, Trinity College. I was one of the Donogh O'Malley generation, which had benefited hugely from the educational reforms of the 1960s[(4)]. O'Malley was the Minister who had introduced free post-primary education in the Republic.

Neither of my parents nor none of their immediate families had gone much beyond basic primary education. I had a very fulfilling career in the public service and had been privileged to have participated in many worthwhile and valuable events, including being part of the Irish Government delegation to the Good Friday negotiations. Therefore, I felt I could not stay silent, if I believed a major error was being committed. I owed a great deal to the country which had been so good to me. It would, of course, have been much more comfortable and profitable to have stayed with the crowd and rowed in with the prevailing narrative.

In one way, the decision to go public had become easier. The Department, where I had worked, had been personally and professionally very supportive to me throughout the many years I spent there. However, it was changing, both in personnel and in its strategic aims. Its primary focus when I served was in securing the Peace in the North. The emphasis had now switched to Brussels.

There had also been a huge loss of institutional memory in Irish Government circles since the days of the GFA Talks and its implementation. There were virtually no politicians or officials, who had been directly involved in the GFA Talks in Castle Buildings, still serving in Dublin. Casual remarks among my colleagues on Brexit about the relative unimportance of our bilateral relations with Britain, and a complete blank when it came to the potential fragility of peace on the island of Ireland, only compounded my concern. At that time, the political leadership in Dublin was personified in the Taoiseach, Enda Kenny, a well-meaning and genial individual. His only answer seemed to be to follow the EU line on everything. His constant changing of position on the Irish border; first there would be no border, then a frictionless border, as frictionless as possible, a technological border, etc., seemed to encapsulate a mental confusion at the time about the way forward.

Kenny and his advisors had set Ireland on the wrong course, right from the beginning of the Brexit process. It was a knee jerk reaction to commit ourselves completely to the EU. Kenny did not emphasise enough that Ireland's connections with the UK were of a different magnitude to those in other EU countries. What we needed was a special new arrangement with both the EU and Britain, should Brexit occur. We needed some new imaginative solutions, not to be hogtied into the rigid EU framework.

The Irish political class had never really come to terms with Brexit. It never countenanced that the Brexit referendum would be carried in the first place. In fact, there was widespread disbelief that the British were actually going to give their citizens a choice on future membership. Even so, there was a general assumption that the referendum might produce a close result but that the Remainers would carry the day. When the then Prime Minister, David Cameron, went to Brussels seeking renegotiation and new terms for British continued membership of the EU, Ireland was not even slightly sympathetic. There was a determination to show our European credentials. It was even mused that we should be among the hardest against any meaningful concessions to Cameron, lest we be accused of being soft on the British.

We were the country with the most to lose, should the referendum go wrong. Hence, logic demanded that Ireland would do its best to ensure that Cameron would be provided with enough substance to justify the UK's continued membership of the EU. This led to the suspicion in Brussels that we might actually act in our own national interest. The EU elite need not have worried. Under Enda Kenny, there was no possibility of any show of independence from Brussels. Anyway our "experts" in the Taoiseach and Foreign Affairs Departments had assured the Government that there was little or no chance of a majority in favour of Brexit. Better to take the opportunity to keep in with Brussels. It was a bad error of judgement.

Hence, there was initial confusion in Dublin after the vote, as the Irish Government apparatus scrambled to come to terms with the unexpected outcome. There was hope that the result could be somehow ignored or even rapidly reversed. In 2005, Jean-Claude Juncker, then the Prime Minister of Luxembourg, stated the EU position on the forthcoming French referendum on the EU Constitution. Juncker said, "If it's a Yes we will say on we go, and if it's a No we will say we continue."[5] Juncker was now President of the EU Commission, the premier position in Brussels, then surely, he would now follow the same course? Dublin did not need to worry unduly; they had such confidence in the EU and Juncker. In the circumstances, it was difficult for me to maintain silence when our interests were being blatantly disregarded by the powers that be.

Events don't go to plan

But, perplexing to official Ireland it soon seemed that this was not the way things were going. The amicable and malleable David Cameron was replaced by the dour Home Secretary Theresa May, who at the outset wanted to doggedly pursue the policy of giving effect to the democratic result of the British people. Mrs May, a clergyman's daughter and a former Remainer, seemed to believe that her sacred mission in public life was to deliver a Brexit[6] and simply ploughed on in the face of many difficulties. She had been a Remainer and wanted to keep the UK as close as possible to the EU, but she did not try the old method of forcing the British to vote again until they got the correct result. I know this caused severe irritation in Brussels and in the capitals. This had not been in the script. However, there was still a much-desired hope, as the Charles Dickens character Wilkins Micawber put it in *David Copperfield*, that "something will turn up" to save Ireland and avoid facing the consequences of Brexit. This was a classic example of the whistling past the graveyard phenomenon, because thinking about the possible dangers is just too great to contemplate. There was also hope that the Remainers in London would be able to destroy the Brexit process either by a complete reversal or by making the whole undertaking as messy as possible with delays and procedural wrangles.

Theresa May proved to be a very poor Prime Minister, but she was prepared to be reasonable in the Brexit negotiations, probably too reasonable. Unfortunately, this was not reciprocated on the EU and indeed Irish Government side. They pushed May into accepting a wholly unequal Withdrawal Agreement which essentially ended her Premiership. There was no way the House of Commons was going to accept it. The EU side had pushed too far and destroyed their moderate interlocutor.

During the Good Friday Talks, the SDLP politician, Seamus Mallon, was fond of advising all and sundry not to push too far, saying it was important that everybody "got up from the table with their trousers on." The EU, with Dublin's active participation, did not seem to realise that May was their valuable partner in delivering a sensible Brexit. Instead of destroying her through excessive demands, they should have assisted her by being reasonable. This was especially important for Ireland. Instead she was handed something she could not deliver, and the EU and Ireland just watched her period in office come to an unsatisfactory end.

As May fell from grace, Dublin watched while its Brexit policy fell asunder. The Taoiseach Leo Varadkar warned of dangerous times ahead[7] as May's political career came to an inglorious end, but with no admission of Ireland's key role in her demise. It was the cumulation of a number of miscalculations.

Irish Reactions to the Brexit vote

In the Republic of Ireland, one of the immediate reactions to the Brexit vote was to instruct all Irish Ambassadors around the world to put out the clear and unambiguous message that Ireland was "sticking with Team EU", regardless of the outcome of any subsequent EU negotiations with the British[8]. There could be no ambiguity about Ireland's devotion and subservience to Brussels. In retrospect, this put us on the wrong road right from the outset. It essentially advertised that Ireland had no bottom or Red Lines in the discussions on the future relationship, other than to follow the EU's interests. Ireland's big brother, the EU would do Ireland's negotiations for it, as simply one part of a united 27 remaining countries. This in no way reflected Ireland's special relationship with the United Kingdom. Our announcement that we would accept whatever the EU would tell us, was also difficult to understand.

The only similar example of a Government stating in advance that it would commit itself to accepting the outcome of impending negotiations that I can think of was David Cameron in his attempts to get the UK a new arrangement with Brussels. Cameron asked for little, he got even less but he had pre-committed himself to campaign against Brexit. This was a disastrous approach to safeguarding a country's interests and it naturally rebounded heavily against him in the subsequent Brexit referendum. The "concessions" he had obtained from Brussels were treated by the two sides in the referendum debate as irrelevant[9].

The Irish Government's relaxed attitude to the possibility of a negative result in the Brexit referendum was not confined to south of the Irish border. Complacency about the outcome extended to the Nationalist community in the North, where there was no serious effort to mobilise an anti-Brexit vote. The view was that the whole Brexit issue was a row within the Tory party and need not concern Ireland. They also surmised that, in the end, the Remainers would carry the day and local Nationalist politicians were not going to waste their resources in securing a big anti-Brexit vote. Hence, there was a low turnout in Nationalist areas of the North, with less than 50% of the electorate in West Belfast even bothering to exercise the franchise, the lowest in the UK. In Derry, a city which would be hugely affected by a decision to leave the EU, only 57.18% voted, compared to a UK average of 72.2%. In fact, no constituency in Northern Ireland even reached the UK average. The overall result was a defeat for Brexit, 56% to 44%[10].

If a determined effort had been made, particularly if backed by a strong Irish Government commitment and cooperation with local parties, a pro-EU vote in Northern Ireland of well over 60 % may well have been obtained. However, under Enda Kenny, the Republic's role in the North had visibly withered away through benign neglect. There was no close cooperation, at that time, with the leadership of Northern Nationalism in Sinn Féin. When the Brexit referendum came around, the Dublin Government had no real desire or ability to energise an effective anti-Brexit campaign in Northern Ireland. I would like to acknowledge that recently both Taoiseach Leo Varadkar and Tánaiste Simon Coveney have shown much greater commitment to developing links with Nationalist representatives in the North.

When the Brexit result became known, anxiety spread in the Nationalist community, subsequently inducing big numbers to turn out in the last Assembly election, partly in a belated attempt to recover the position. Although anger with the Democratic Unionist Party (DUP) also played a big role. The perceived abuse by the DUP in Stormont of the requirements for cross community support, to the point of causing gridlock there, also played a major part.

On the Unionist side of the community, the picture was more mixed. While the Nationalists were essentially united against Brexit, though complacent about the outcome, the Unionists were divided but much more engaged in the process. The DUP, alone among the main Northern parties, supported the pro-Brexit campaign and unexpectedly found itself on the winning UK side, though losing the vote in Northern Ireland. The DUP were always at the margins of UK politics, with their extreme views on issues such as gay rights, abortion, a strong creationist element, hostility to the indigenous Irish language and culture of the region, etc. However, the UK general election on 8 June 2017, gave the DUP an enhanced role at Westminster. The DUP, while pro-Brexit, wants to avoid the complications that a physical border in Ireland would bring[11]. The party also does not want anything that could lead to a differentiation between Northern Ireland and the rest of the UK. Their supporters' recoil from the prospect of any enhanced security or customs at British ports/airports for arrivals from Northern Ireland or any disruption to trade across the Irish Sea or to North/South business links on the island of Ireland.

Hence, the Johnson EU Withdrawal Agreement in October 2019 came as an unpleasant shock to Unionists, and especially DUP members. The price of getting the Backstop removed was a clear distinction between the treatment of Northern Ireland with that of GB. Despite the stated intention of Prime Minister Boris Johnson to change that arrangement in the future trade agreement, Unionists remained deeply alienated. The DUP reaction greatly assisted Taoiseach Leo Varadkar to make a political U-turn and accept a much more limited guarantee on a frictionless border.

Now all shades of political opinion in Ireland face a difficult dilemma as the practical implications of Brexit are becoming clearer and they don't make for comforting reading. On all sides, events have taken a course which has contained nasty surprises.

Ireland in an isolated position, post Brexit

The policy of placing all the Irish eggs in one basket (the EU) is making less sense every day. Leaving it to Brussels seems so out of place with the national interest that it begs the question as to why the Irish are so determined to hold on to the EU apron strings. The answer lies in the way that the European Union has worked with Irish political and public service leadership over the years. Constant meetings in Brussels, involving Ministers and senior officials, have made these groups much more eurocentric than the population at large. This is particularly true for those who served in the Departments of the Taoiseach and Foreign Affairs. Irish politicians and officials value their seats at the EU table, even if they carry only just over 1% of the voting power there. A similar pro-EU effect was evident among UK officials leading up to the referendum. A compliant and generally supportive media, especially the influential *Irish Times*, has helped give the impression of a very pro-EU country. In some official circles the *Irish Times* is mockingly described as the Department of Foreign Affairs' house journal. It is so supportive of the Government's pro-EU line.

This eurocentric view, however, does not permeate deep into the general population. During the banking crisis and the subsequent deep recession in Ireland, young people, North and South, headed for the old emigrant destinations – Britain, USA, Canada, Australia and New Zealand. While a small number went to mainland Europe, the vast majority of those who migrated did so to Anglophone countries, much as their forbearers did in times of past crises. It was a formidable demonstration of where the Irish felt culturally more at home.

While Ireland was benefitting financially from EU transfers, there was a general acceptance that the country and its citizens needed to be classified as good Europeans. However, there was never any deep ideological pro-European identification – the connection was essentially based on material gain and not on any emotional or symbolic attachment. The sight of the then Taoiseach, Albert Reynolds, returning from the fractious Edinburgh Summit in 1992, claiming that he had obtained £(Irl)8bn support in structural funding, encapsulated Ireland's attachment to the EU at that time[12].

Once Ireland became wealthier and eventually a net contributor to the EU budget, attitudes became more measured.

In addition, Ireland, apart from the United Kingdom, does not have any natural allies in the EU, "no kith and kin." It is not active in many of the international groupings. Even within the EU, most countries belong to separate interest groups, such as the Nordic Council, the Commonwealth, Francophonie, Visegárd, Arctic Council, NATO, Benelux, etc. (Table 1). Ireland is not an active participant in any of these groups. This lack of participation in other international fora means there is a tendency in Dublin to think in very narrow EU terms, often guided to a position by the EU Commission. Hence, the instinctive response is to take on the Commission's view on new proposals unless there is a public outcry back home. The lack of natural allies for Ireland was starkly illustrated when Taoiseach Leo Varadkar announced that the country would seek observer status in La Francophonie, the French version of the Commonwealth[13]. What Ireland will add to an organisation catering for promoting French culture and language, is a matter for conjecture. It is another glaring example of the Irish elite's blind devotion to the concept that everything in mainland Europe is good, despite the clear irrelevance of La Francophonie to Ireland. It also shows that Ireland does not have any natural allies inside the EU, once Britain departs. We are seeking to become an appendage to groups, with which we do not have strong linguistic or ethnic connections.

The Brexit process and its outcome represents a catastrophic failure for Irish Government policy. There was an astonishing lack of a wider vision or appreciation of the need to support David Cameron during his attempted renegotiation. While it is debatable, whether Ireland could have made much difference to the eventual outcome, the country's national interests cried out for a proactive response and for Ireland to act as an intermediary between the Cameron Government and the EU. Again, the hard-line approach to Theresa May's attempts at a conciliatory approach backfired and resulted in the virtual elimination of the pro-EU section of the Tory Party.

Despite these huge errors of judgement, the authorities in Dublin carried out no post-mortem in the aftermath of the referendum; nobody was hauled over the coals, there were no political resignations, no officials cast out into the wilderness and the Irish official line in Brussels continued as before, namely strict adherence to Team EU. In fact, there was an air of self-congratulation within the upper levels of the Irish Civil Service at that time. In retrospect, it is hard to fathom the reason for such sentiment.

Lack of strategic thinking

The starting point for any consideration of Ireland's reaction to Brexit should have been the Good Friday, or Belfast, Agreement (GFA)[14]. This Agreement was built around a close and cooperative relationship between the two sovereign Governments in Dublin and London; the concept of parity of esteem for both communities in the North; the principle of consent for any Constitutional change to Northern Ireland; a partnership arrangement in Stormont; new all Ireland institutions; and a strong commitment to human rights throughout the island of Ireland. The preservation and development of the GFA is the yardstick against which our policies should be judged. Could anybody honestly state that the actions of the Irish Government over the last three years have measured up to that criterion?

I had the enormous privilege and pleasure to be part of the Irish Government Talks Team on that occasion. The GFA was designed to underpin the Peace Process, and in so doing to usher in a new era of reconciliation between people living in the North of Ireland; between the pro-Union community there and the majority on the island of Ireland; and between the Irish and British peoples. It is the foundation on which I have built my views on Brexit and the future of Ireland's relationship with the European Union.

However, I sincerely believe that the reality of the present Irish Government policy is that it has been prepared to jettison its responsibilities under Good Friday in order to appease Brussels. It has claimed the opposite, namely that it is guaranteeing the Agreement, but the effect of its actions have been to place much of what has been achieved over a generation in jeopardy. I consider that to be a fundamental error and not in the interest of either the Irish or British people.

I do not think it is an exaggeration to state that the GFA transformed relations between Britain and Ireland, not just at State and diplomatic levels, but also had a very beneficial effect on the relationship between the two peoples. It ushered in a period of relative peace and reconciliation. The large Irish community in Britain greatly benefitted from the changed atmosphere.

I feared that the Irish Government, with its hard-line anti-British stance on Brexit, was reacting in a way which was endangering the close Anglo-Irish cooperation that is needed to sustain the GFA. As the Brexit process developed, I came to the conclusion that the Irish Government was in serious breach of its commitments under that Agreement. I felt I had to speak out.

The two Governments had committed themselves in the GFA "to develop still further the unique relationship between their peoples and the close co-operation between their countries as friendly neighbours." They also agreed to treat both communities in the North with parity of esteem. I did not believe that Ireland was fulfilling these obligations, when Britain badly needed friends inside the EU during the Brexit negotiations. In the longer term, this approach is likely to destroy the trust needed to sustain the GFA. The constant Dublin demand in the Backstop for the removal of the North from the economic management of London, and a border in the Irish Sea[15] smacked of failing to understand, either the principle of consent or the need to treat both communities in Northern Ireland, including their identity and interests, with equal respect. This was done while rightly strongly decrying any attempt to put a border on land.

Instead, the Irish Government has regularly stated that no matter what the final outcome of the Brexit process and the future trade arrangements, Ireland will be sticking with Europe. I feel that this blind devotion to Brussels needs to be challenged. The savage treatment of Greece by the institutions of the European Union, shamefully supported latterly by Ireland[16], along with our own experience of the Brussels-imposed financial Bailout, should have sounded cautionary alarm bells in any small nation thinking of placing its complete reliance, and indeed its future, on the good will of Brussels. In the final analysis, the EU has its own interests and theology, which over time may be at serious variance with Ireland's own concerns. In such a case, there will be only one winner and it will not be Ireland.

In addition, I had concerns about the lack of respect for the democratic process among the pro-EU elite. I had worked for the Government in Ireland when two referenda on European Treaties, Nice and Lisbon, had been rejected by the Irish electorate. I saw, at close quarters, the absolute determination of the Irish Civil Service to overturn those results, while paying lip service to respecting the outcome. It was soon clear that a similar operation was underway in Britain among those who refused to reconcile themselves with the result of the 2016 referendum. I simply could not support the Irish Government's strenuous efforts to assist in that campaign.

This was in no way to excuse or whitewash the incompetent and blundering performance of the then British Prime Minister, Theresa May, and her team in the Brexit discussions. They made serious mistake after mistake and moved all over the place in policy terms. I fully accept that the Conservatives in Government over the last nine years have shown very little interest in Irish issues and that the decision to enter into a confidence and supply arrangement with the DUP, had the effect of casting serious and legitimate doubts about the impartiality of London in Northern Ireland matters.

However, Ireland should not have let the temporary loss of vision and competence in Westminster, deflect it from guarding our own long-term interests. Elements in Dublin have vied with each other to pour scorn on the British for their performance, without in any way assisting them at a difficult time, despite our obligations under the GFA.

Throughout the first stage of the Brexit negotiations, the Irish concern over a return of a hard border on the island of Ireland was used as an effective weapon against the British desire to leave. The EU, ably assisted by diehard Remainer elements in the British establishment, used the border issue to pressure the British into staying within the orbit of Brussels. The EU and the Irish Government were, in essence, interfering in the internal political discourse in Britain by colluding to thwart the outcome of the referendum on membership of the EU. I believe that the Irish/EU policy in this regard could have long term deleterious effects on British/Irish relations.

I fully supported the Irish Government's desire to ensure that the Nationalist community should not have to endure a land border with their fellow citizens to the South. However, there seemed to be no recognition in the corridors of power in Dublin of a similar need for Unionists not to be cut off from those whom they regard as their fellow citizens in Britain, by a sea border. The reality that Britain is the main external market for products from Northern Ireland[17] was also ignored. This lack of sensitivity has undone many years of improving relations between the Irish Government and the Unionist community in the North (see Chapter 4). Even pro-Remain Unionists felt alienated by the present Irish Government's strident approach.

Regardless of the outcome of the Brexit process, geography has ensured that the Irish and British peoples will have to live alongside each other. The current anti-Brexit policy of the Irish Government could sour our bilateral relations well into the future. We are huge net beneficiaries of the current British/Irish relationship, none more so than with the Common Travel Area (CTA). The Memorandum of Understanding (MOU) signed between the two Governments on 8 May 2019[18] on the CTA is a welcome step forward but is no long-term guarantee against changes by future, and more hostile, UK administrations. Our current policy carries too high a risk premium for the long-term relations with our neighbouring island. Britain is, by far and away, the country that plays host to the largest Irish born resident population of any overseas location. We, in Ireland, as well as our fellow Irish who are resident in Britain, have much to lose from a worsening of relations.

I fully agree and support the consent principle, as outlined in the GFA and that the Constitutional status of Northern Ireland can only be settled by means of a simple majority in a referendum. To argue anything else is not democratic and is a repudiation of a central tenet of the GFA. It carries the implication that a Nationalist vote in the North does not carry the same weight as a Unionist vote. Could anything be more contrary to the concept of parity of esteem? However, it is important to think also in strategic terms.

With demographic changes in the North of Ireland meaning that the whole Constitutional question is becoming much more into play, the actions of the Irish Government in alienating the pro-Union community in Northern Ireland and demonstrating that the United Kingdom cannot rely on Ireland, as an ally and partner, when it is needed most, would seem to me to be wholly short-sighted. Constitutional change involving the reunification of Ireland, should it be carried in a referendum in the North, will inevitably need the active cooperation of the authorities in London. It would also be a lot easier for the Unionists, if they could be assured that their interests, including their Britishness, was genuinely respected by Dublin. The present policy of the Irish Government is the antithesis of that approach.

EU losing its attraction

Although we did so with enthusiasm, it should be admitted that we only entered the then European Economic Community (EEC), because we had no choice in the matter. We were so economically tied to our neighbour, the United Kingdom, that we did not have a viable alternative. This was reflected in the entry referendum in May 1972, which was carried with the support of 83% of those voting at the time[19]. Ireland essentially entered into the EEC on the UK's coattails. If the UK had changed its mind at the time, Ireland could not have become a member of the EEC in 1973. This was demonstrated starkly with our withdrawn applications, when French President Charles de Gaulle vetoed the British applications for membership in 1963 and 1967.

Much has changed for the better for Ireland over the last four decades, including lessening our economic dependence on the UK. That process had been well underway before our accession to the EEC, but membership greatly accelerated its development. As the Irish Free State came into existence, well over 95% of its external trade(1923) was with the United Kingdom[20]. By 1973, this had been almost halved to just over 50%[21]. The 1960s were a period of strong economic growth in Ireland, just prior to entry into the "Common Market".

Ireland is obviously a much more successful country today than in 1972 and that success was in no small degree dependent on the opportunities afforded by our membership of the EEC, later when it was called the European Community (EC) and more recently the European Union (EU). However, while Ireland has undoubtedly changed for the better, I am not sure there would be universal agreement that the European project has likewise evolved in as positive a direction. The current EU is a long way from the organisation, the EEC or more colloquially the Common Market, which we joined in 1973.

However, it would be very churlish not to acknowledge the beneficial influence, which the EEC has had over the years on the country. The Ireland of the 1960s and early 70s was a very insular place and was still recovering from its diplomatic isolation, after pursuing a policy of neutrality during the Second World War. This isolation was exacerbated by the Irish State's sudden withdrawal from the Commonwealth in 1949, an organisation where Ireland had particularly close ethnic and political ties with Canada, Britain, South Africa, Australia and New Zealand. These connections suffered in the aftermath of our departure. The net result was that, at that time, Ireland had very few opportunities to "take its place among the nations of the Earth", a position to which the patriot Robert Emmet had aspired. The United Nations, which Ireland joined in 1955[22], following an initiative by the Canadian Government and after enduring a ten year wait and successive vetoes by the Soviet Union, was one of the few international organisations in which Ireland was an active member.

Therefore, membership of the EEC in 1973 was a boom for a country, which lacked self-confidence and an international profile. That psychological boost of being part of an exclusive western European club was very much of its time and place. In addition, funding from the EU, and in particular the Common Agricultural Policy (CAP), no doubt helped to stimulate economic development.

Today, Ireland is a much more self-confident country and Irish industry, sport and culture are very strong and vibrant. Irish people have been successful all over the world in many capacities and the country does not need the approval of its EU partners, in the way it needed outside endorsement in the past. Ireland is now a net contributor to the EU budget. In 2019, that net contribution approached €1bn (Chapter 6). Ireland has come of age as a State. I have no time for those who believe that the country cannot have a successful future without being subsumed into the new European Superstate that the ongoing EU integration process seeks to bring about.

With the departure of our closest neighbour, Britain, with which we share so much history, culture and economic ties, and the changing nature of the EU itself, I believe the time has come to consider whether the overall balance of advantage for Ireland will continue to lie in full membership of the EU. Or whether we need to consider a different type of relationship with our European neighbours, that is formally outside the Union. However, the avalanche of one-sided propaganda on the EU over the years, has not properly prepared the country for that type of debate.

The departure of the UK from the EU is clearly a development which greatly reduces the attractiveness to us of EU membership. In addition, the business model, on which Ireland has built its economic development inside the EU, is now under serious challenge (Chapter 7).

Much of our success, in recent years, has been based on our unequivocal embrace of globalisation, and especially on attracting large amounts of mobile American Foreign Direct Investment (FDI) to our shores. This was achieved in some respects by our strong linkage to our huge Diaspora, but much more importantly, by means of what we euphemistically call a competitive corporate tax rate, while others have characterised the policy as essentially one of facilitating corporate tax avoidance on a grand scale. Regardless of the nomenclature used, the international climate in which Ireland operates its aggressive pursuit of multinational companies, especially the digital giants, has become much less permissive. These digital giants have come under strong adverse criticism over their failure to pay a reasonable tax level in the countries where they operate.

The protectionist mood in the United States and elsewhere has already resulted in a global slow-down in FDI flows[23]. International FDI has fallen heavily since a peak in 2015, especially into Europe. In Ireland, we will need to reflect on the changing external environment in our plans for future prosperity. Hence, the need for reflection. However, there has to be doubts on whether that debate would be welcomed in official quarters in Ireland.

Reaction to Brexit in the Irish media

The Brexit negotiations, and the UK's subsequent departure, has received massive coverage in Ireland and the interest that the whole controversy has engendered is an ideal starting point for such a debate. If Brexit does not spark a reflective examination of Ireland's place in the world, it is hard to imagine what would. It is badly needed.

Ireland was singularly and psychologically unprepared for Brexit. Whatever the eventual outcome of the withdrawal process, Ireland will be profoundly affected. Yet, beforehand there was no deep knowledge or appreciation of what was driving the Brexit process in our nearest neighbour. Irish public representatives and media never really "got Brexit", as there was no real or deep understanding of the nature of the European project itself, outside a small very pro-EU elite in Dublin. The Irish media essentially ignored the impulses that were driving Brexit and similar manifestations of discontent throughout the EU.

This was in contrast with many of our neighbours, especially Britain, where there has been a healthy debate over the future of the EU, and the relative balance of advantage of membership for individual Member States, for many years.

I am not sure why we have been so poor at long-term strategic thinking, but it may be something deeply embedded in our culture. We do not have a strong tradition of challenging accepted norms, within our Government system. The dissenting tradition has been particularly weak in Southern Ireland. Perhaps this is a legacy of our authoritarian Catholic past, but one thing is certain, contrarian views are rarely welcomed by the Irish establishment. The hierarchical nature of Irish Catholicism demanded communal group loyalty and groupthink. Woe betide those who questioned the official dogma. This was especially unwelcomed from, what was then termed, lapsed Catholics, who were perceived as having betrayed the tribe.

This form of groupthink has served Ireland very poorly in the past. There was a lack of serious challenges by officials to the prevailing economic orthodoxy, during the stagnation years in the immediate post World War Two period. It was heavily influential also in protecting the banks in the lead up to the financial crash in 2008 and the subsequent economic damage inflicted on the Irish people. Today, that type of groupthink is in evidence in official attitudes to the EU. Irish society is often more comfortable with an echo chamber rather than serious debate. Irish mainstream media, especially television is very conservative and risk adverse.

The bulk of publications on the EU in Ireland are unashamedly propagandist. They concentrate on the positive side of membership of the EU and shy clear of any of the negatives. Much of this material is actually funded by the EU itself, in a remarkably egotistical exercise. These propaganda pieces, when not published by the EU itself, are often written by people who have a vested and selfish interest in promoting the objectives of the Brussels establishment. Yet they rarely openly declare that they have benefited personally from taking this line. Hence, it is rare in Ireland to ask fundamental questions on Europe, yet many of the issues and fears, which gave rise to Brexit in the United Kingdom, are relevant to Ireland.

Scepticism of the EU is still regarded by official Ireland as almost traitorous. There is a tendency to paint those who seek to preserve Ireland's sovereignty and its place in the world as a separate, independent nation, as people trying to return the country to the old days of British domination. It is a perverse phenomenon and unworthy of those sheltering behind it. It is often used to avoid reasoned argument and discussion.

Samuel Johnson is widely reputed to be the originator of the phrase "Patriotism is the last refuge of a scoundrel." However, as his biographer Boswell makes clear, Johnson was only referring to false patriotism. On the Brexit debate in Ireland, Johnson would have found ample examples to vindicate his assertion. Yet there is a crying need for a true national debate which looks at all issues in a reasoned and rational manner.

Some of the mainstream Irish media have had the equivalent of a nervous breakdown over Brexit. Hysterical calls to revive old feelings of Anglophobia have even surfaced. One of Ireland's leading "intellectuals" Fintan O'Toole, kept up a barrage of bizarre anti-English articles in the "liberal" *Irish Times*. He followed this with a quixotic book, entitled *Heroic Failure*[24], which is so OTT that it is almost a self-parody. There have been other articles in the Irish media which, if written by English authors on Ireland, would be credibly described as racist. However, as Boris Johnson tightened his grip on power in the UK, the smugness of the Irish media began slowly to dissipate.

Coming to terms with Brexit

With the Irish establishment confused and perplexed by Brexit, they have trashed around for an explanation. Hence, there is a huge desire among the Dublin elite to ascribe the Brexit phenomenon to perverse motivations, such as racism, English nationalism, a desire to return to the Empire days, etc. This is not to say that there were not some elements of the above-mentioned present in Brexit. However, some of the issues raised by the Brexiteers, such as national sovereignty; a desire to tailor domestic policies in Britain to suit its own national interests, control of immigration, and a desire to return Britain to the status of a fully independent State; are summarily dismissed as a smoke screen. There is a desire among the Irish establishment to avoid conferring any legitimacy to Brexit, lest it have implications for Ireland's attitude to Europe. This has clouded their judgement and their ability to make dispassionate calls.

The overwhelming initial response by the political establishment in Dublin was to believe that this dreadful episode was a bad dream and that the British would wake up some morning and cancel the whole thing. If that did not happen than the all-powerful EU would simply force the Brits to recant. The bulk of politicians and media figures with whom I discussed Brexit in Ireland over the last three years, were privately completely convinced that it would never happen and therefore it was a waste of time to make serious preparations for a No Deal or a Clean Brexit. I admit that the situation changed gradually as the realisation dawned that this was not something that was going to disappear easily. The resignation of Theresa May and her replacement by Boris Johnson as British Prime Minister finally brought them to the realisation that there was a clear danger that a real Brexit would take place.

The Irish establishment have done well out of their European connections and Brexit threatens that cosy arrangement. Hence the fury and intransigence evident in their response, while retaining a special wrath for those locally who would upset the gravy train by questioning the status quo. We are Britain's next-door neighbour and heaven forbid that the Brexit "disease" should cross the Irish Sea and infect the natives on this island.

It is a paradox of modern society that the level of intolerance and authoritarianism is much more pronounced among the so-called liberal elements, than those who were traditionally accused of these vices in the past. This is particularly in evidence when it comes to EU attitudes in Ireland. I have seen at first hand the reactions of some senior politicians and officials to any suggestion of scepticism or even mildly questioning about Europe.

In all my time as a public servant, I have never come across the level of intolerance displayed by official Ireland to those who disagree with slavishly following the Brussels line. Throughout the Troubles in the North, there were always officials, and influential outsiders, who had problems with the Irish Government line, but these people were listened to and often regarded as valuable in providing a different perspective. To anyway question the EU in the Irish public service is regarded as close to career threatening. This is extremely unhealthy and highly unlikely to produce balanced considerations of policy options.

In Ireland, Brexit negotiations are often portrayed as part of Ireland's long historic struggle for independence from the British. This has ensured that the Irish focus has been directed at the shortcomings of London and there has been little criticism of Brussels. Yet these discussions are taking place at a time when the EU has never faced such serious challenges to its own legitimacy. It seems a strange time to totally commit your future to an enterprise, which is rapidly losing its popular appeal.

National elections in the Member States are proving very inconvenient to those in Brussels, who are committed to the doctrine of ever closer union with a Federation as the final objective. The citizens in the Member States are increasingly voting for strong nationalist parties which openly challenge the whole basis on which EU policy has been built and demand much greater autonomy for the Nation States. This has been largely absent in Ireland because the Brexit issue is often seen through the prism of an Anglo-Irish dispute.

Fianna Fáil, the long dominant Irish political party and one which was historically associated with Irish Republicanism, regularly speaks about Ireland sharing its sovereignty with the countries of Europe. In any sharing arrangement, it is a two-way process, whereby something offered can be taken back. In the EU the process is a one-way street. No power or function has been repatriated. Fianna Fáil, because of its history, does not like to speak of Ireland's surrendering of its hard-won sovereignty, better to use the euphemism, sharing, even if it is obviously a sham.

Meanwhile the political map of Europe is being rewritten, with the traditional centre left parties facing an increasingly uncertain future. The traditional left has deserted its old base among industrial workers, and the coping classes, to champion the causes of gender, identity politics and social liberalism. The centre left has also become identified with extreme europhilia. The old concerns for everyday issues, such as people's take-home pay, housing affordability, national sovereignty and job security, have been suborned to the new causes. The result has been nothing short of an electoral disaster for these left-wing parties.

At the same time, the parties of the extreme right have moved in on the old issues that the left were identified with in the past and particularly so on the matter of national identity and communal solidarity. During the 1960s when I was growing up, the left championed national liberation movements and nationalist causes but now they have a new liberal agenda and doctrine, which only denigrates sovereignty issues and sneers at ordinary people's concerns, describing them as pandering to populism. The Left in Europe has espoused the cause of ever closer union, despite being its main opponent in the past, with people like Britain's Tony Benn etc. It has paid a very heavy price for that volte face.

Against that background, I was often told that it is simply "unthinkable" for Ireland to consider leaving the EU. However, I always believed that the absence of thinking was a poor preparation for any policy decision. There is very little, if any, strategic planning underway in official Ireland on alternatives to the present policy, should our relationship with the EU turn sour. Any official who even suggested it would be a brave soul.

Breaking away from the consensus: A new approach needed

This is a pity. As I have outlined in the following sections, there is a very strong case for alternative courses post-Brexit. My own preference would be to opt to remain with the United Kingdom in a customs and free trade area, while negotiating, as favourable as possible, trade and investment terms with the remaining 26-Member States, possibly through continued membership of the European Economic Area (EEA). This is very close to what has been described as the Norway model. Every new trade deal is essentially a bespoke one and given Ireland's long standing pro-European attitudes and its constructive engagement with the EU institutions for decades, a new Irish/EU economic and trade agreement, post any Irexit, should be attainable on reasonable terms.

Liberal access to the Single European Market need not be synonymous with full membership of the EU. There are a number of arrangements with Third Countries which illustrate this point. In addition, the EU itself is facing huge internal problems and the future direction of that body is hard to predict and, though uncertain, it is unlikely to be to Ireland's taste or in its interests. Even if Ireland stayed within the EU, it should be pressing for special post-Brexit arrangements, given its deep links with the UK.

It is overwhelmingly in the country's interest that the UK obtain a generous deal on its future trading arrangements with the EU. Ireland needs a good Brexit outcome for its own national interests, as well as being in line with our GFA commitment to act as a partner to the UK. This puts it at loggerheads with the long-term interests of the EU Commission in Brussels. To the international civil servants, who have devoted their careers to the "European Project", Brexit represents nothing less than an existential threat to the EU and their life's work. In addition, their extraordinarily generous salaries, pensions and other perks depend long term on the success of the "European project". Under no circumstances can the Brits be rewarded for their treacherous decision to leave. Therefore, logically given our different perspectives for a post-Brexit world, there should be undercurrents of tension between Dublin and Brussels, which may become more apparent as the negotiations on future trading arrangements progress.

Why has this not manifested itself to date? Simply because the single most prominent interest of Ireland in the Brexit negotiations so far has been the Border. Here both Ireland and the UK, as the only two signatories of the GFA, have a huge common interest in maintaining arrangements as close as possible to the present status quo, namely keeping it invisible to the naked eye and the cross-border traveller. Sometimes it is hard to get across to people in Dublin that the UK genuinely, and for its own self- interest, has a huge stake in a frictionless border. One of the chief difficulties in achieving this is the European Union's strict Red Line that any arrangements on the island of Ireland, post-Brexit, "must respect the integrity of the Union's Legal Order."[25]

I have said on a number of occasions, and in particular in my columns in the *Sunday Business Post*[26], that it was a bad mistake for Ireland to accept that Red Line. It greatly restricted the number of potential solutions to ensuring the absence of a hard border.

The departure of the UK from the EU is an unprecedented event and the complicated and overlapping identities on the island of Ireland, overladen with centuries of history and conflict, do not lend itself to simple Red Lines of the type loved by Brussels.

The Irish Government, in its excessive europhile zeal and with a touch of old-fashioned Anglophobia and faux patriotism, put all its eggs on the so-called Backstop in the Brussels basket. The EU, anxious to maintain the UK within its economic orbit, seized on the Irish border as its best lever to pressurise Britain. During the phase one part of the negotiations, the British Government, under former PM May, agreed reluctantly to the Northern Ireland Backstop Option as a last resort on the Border Issue, though contesting the Irish interpretation of its meaning and then extending it to cover the entire United Kingdom[27] to avoid a customs border in the Irish Sea.

In a speech to a conference on Brexit in the Irish border town of Dundalk on 30 April 2018, the EU's chief negotiator Michel Barnier was reported as saying, "The Backstop is needed in order to respect the integrity of the Single Market and the EU's Customs Union."[28] The EU was not anxious to allow for any deviation from its own theology. Anything else, or any other goal, was secondary to that fundamental principle, including Ireland's own national interest. As time moved on and the UK Parliament refused to accept the Backstop, it was noticeable that there was markedly less emphasis in remarks from Irish Government Ministers on maintaining a frictionless border and more on preserving the rules of the EU's Single Market. Eventually the Taoiseach Leo Varadkar, with the prospect of a No Deal looming, dropped the Backstop. The figment was cast aside.

During the lead up to the GFA, various international settlements, and conflict resolution models, such as South Tyrol, Transylvania, Hungarian minorities in neighbouring countries, Aland islands in Finland, etc. were studied for possible lessons for Northern Ireland. Although much was learned, none, in the end, were suitable. It needed a new more radical approach. That was achieved by the British side accepting that the Irish Government had a major and legitimate role in the North, and the Irish Government accepting the need for Constitutional change in the Republic, to reflect the principle of consent. Both Governments agreed that the Constitutional status of Northern Ireland was to be decided by a simple majority of the people living there, not by Governments in Dublin or London.

There are very few similar examples around the world, where two Governments were prepared to slaughter their "sacred cows". If we had accepted the conventional wisdom and the Red Lines on sovereignty then, there would have been no GFA. In the same way, we need to move away from "respecting the integrity of the Union's Legal Order" mantra, so we can get a workable long-term solution. The present frameworks are too restrictive.

For Ireland, which never wanted Brexit in the first place, the UK staying in the European Union would have been, in theory, a good outcome. However, that would have required regime change in London and caused huge bitterness and instability. It would have required an abject surrender by the British. It would have left a bitter legacy, particularly in the Conservative Party there.

In our efforts to thwart Brexit, we may have forfeited, in the longer run, a lot of good will in our most important bilateral relationship, soured community relations in the North, made future North/South cooperation more problematic, and committed ourselves to the EU, at a time when everywhere else the trends are in the opposite direction. In addition, the Eurozone moves from one crisis to another and certainly does not want a post-Brexit Britain to be an economic success.

In such circumstances, an Irish Government might be tempted to ramp up the patriotic theme and seek the refuge of the scoundrel, rather than admit that it made a huge mistake in seeking to derail Brexit by demanding the Backstop, which was always undeliverable.

Ireland is therefore in a huge quandary. The ruling elite and much of the population have been subject to unremitting pro-EU propaganda for decades, coupled with a false nationalism and find the present situation hard to comprehend.

There are some well-meaning people in Ireland, who share much of my criticism of the EU, but believe that it should be reformed, rather than contemplate a more drastic solution, an Irexit. However, I believe that this is naïve, as the institutions of the EU have been designed to resist any fundamental reversal of the seepage of powers away from the democratically elected national Parliaments, to a centralised Brussels. The advocates of reform are unable to explain how any meaningful change can be actually achieved, while the most powerful body inside the EU, the unelected Commission, retains an effective monopoly on the initiation of new legislation. Brussels and the national capitals are packed with individuals and organisations that have everything to lose from a dismantling of the current arrangements and will, in their own self-interests, resist change. The odds, unfortunately, do not favour a reformist approach. A more fundamental change of direction by Ireland is needed, meaning an Irexit.

Table 1

EU Member States in other Organisations(2018)

NATO	Nordic Council	Arctic Council
Belgium	Denmark	Denmark – Member
Bulgaria	Finland	Finland – Member
Croatia	Sweden	Sweden – Member
Czech Republic		France – Observer
Denmark		Germany – Observer
Estonia		Italy – Observer
France		Netherlands – Observer
Germany		Poland – Observer
Greece		Spain – Observer
Hungary		UK – Observer
Italy		
Latvia		
Lithuania		
Luxemburg		
Netherlands		
Poland		
Portugal		
Romania		
Slovakia		
Slovenia		
Spain		
UK		

Francophonie

Belgium – Member

Bulgaria – Member

France – Member

Luxembourg – Member

Romania – Member

Cyprus – Ass Member

Commonwealth

Cyprus

Malta

UK

Lusophone Community

Portugal

Visegárd

Czech Republic

Hungary

Slovakia

Poland

Benelux

Netherlands

Belgium

Luxembourg

References

1. Ashoka Mody *"Euro tragedy"* p127–130.

2. Joseph E Stiglitz *"The Euro and its threat to the future of Europe"* p 46

3. Ray Bassett *"We can't wash our hands of Britain"*, *Sunday Business Post* 1 January 2019 *https://www.businesspost.ie/opinion/cant-wash-hands-britain-374708*. Retrieved 10 May 2019

4. *Mary Hanafin "O'Malley's vision for education still inspires" Irish Times,* 11 September 2006, https://www.irishtimes.com/opinion/o-malley-s-vision-for-education-still-inspires. Retrieved 10 May 2019

5. Christopher Booker and Richard North *The Great Deception* p 540

6. Lancaster House speech by Prime Minister Theresa May *"The Government's negotiating objectives for exiting the EU"* 17 January 2017. https://www.gov.uk/.../the-governments-negotiating-objectives-for-exiting-the-eu-pm-speech

7. Ben O'Brien and Daniel McConnell *"Taoiseach warns of dangerous period ahead for Ireland after May's departure"*, *Irish Examiner*, 24 May 2019. *https://www.irishexaminer.com/breakingnews/ireland/taoiseach-warns-of-dangerous-period-ahead-for-ireland-after-mays-departure-926500.html.* Retrieved 7 December 2019

8. *"Ireland is Team EU in the Brexit Talks"*, *Irish Examiner.* 29 March 2017. *https://www.irishexaminer.com/breakingnews/ireland/foreign-affairs-minister-ireland-is-team-in-the Brexit-talks.* Retrieved 13 May 2019

9. Andrew Glencross *"The Great Miscalculation: David Cameron's renegotiation and the EU referendum Campaign" https://www.referendumanalysis.eu/eu-referendum-analysis-2016/section-1-context/the-great-miscalculation-david-camerons-renegotiation-and-the-eu-referendum-campaign/* Retrieved 13 May 2019.

10. *"EU referendum: Northern Ireland votes to Remain"* BBC NI News. *https://www.bbc.com/news/uk-northern-ireland-36614443.* Retrieved 13 May 2019

11. Arlene Foster *"No one wants a hard border"* *Irish News*, Belfast 27 April 2017. *http://www.irishnews.com/news/2017/04/27/news/platform-arlene-foster-on-brexit-negotiations-1008829/* Retrieved 13 May 2019

12. Alan Murdock *"EU Summit, Luck of the Irish lifts Reynolds"* *The London Independent* 14 December 1992. *https://www.independent.co.uk/news/world/europe/ec-summit-luck-of-the-irish-lifts-reynolds-1563464.html.* Retrieved 13 May 2019

13. Ruadhán Mac Cormaic *"Why Ireland wants to join Francophonie; Brexit has shone an unflattering light on Dublin's relationship building skills"* Irish Times 2 December 2017. Retrieved 13 May 2019.

14. *"Agreement reached in the Multi Party Talks"*, commonly referred to as the Good Friday or Belfast Agreement, published by the Government of Ireland.

15. Karl McDonald *"If Britain insists on a hard border, Ireland wants it to be in the sea"* Inews 28 July 2017, *https://inews.co.uk/news/politics/britain-insists-hard-border-ireland-wants-sea-522260.* Retrieved 29 April 2019

16. Ashoka Mody *"EuroTragedy"* p 424

17. The Northern Ireland Statistics and Research Agency (NISRA) stated that in 2017, external sales for NI to the Republic were £3.9bn, while GB accounted for £11.3bn. *https://www.nisra.gov.uk/statistics/eu-exit-analysis/eu-exit-trade.* Retrieved 9 May 2019.

18. Memorandum of Understanding between the Government of the United Kingdom of Great Britain and Northern Ireland and the Government of Ireland concerning the Common Travel Area and associated reciprocal rights and privileges, 8 May 2019 *https://*www.gov.uk/*government/publications/*common-travel-area. Retrieved 13 May 2019.

19. *"Ireland and the EU; Joining the European Community"*, EU Commission, Representation in Ireland Office, *https://ec.europa.eu/ireland/about-us/ireland-in-eu_.* Retrieved 13 May 2109

20. The Trade Statistics for the Irish Free State in 1924. Retrieved 9 May 2019 www.tara.tcd.ie/bitstream/handle/2262/21200/jssisiVolXIv.

21. "Ireland and the EU 1973-2003" Central Statistics Office. Retrieved 9 May 2019. *www.cso.ie/.../documents/statisticalyearbook/2004/ireland&theeu.pdf.*

22. *"Ireland 60 Years at the United Nations 1955 -2015"* published by the Department of Foreign Affairs and Trade *Dublin https://www.dfa.ie/.../Ireland---60-Years-at-the-United-Nations.pdf*

23. *"Foreign direct investment (FDI) – FDI flows – OECD Data"* Retrieved 9 May 2019 *https://data.oecd.org/fdi/fdi-flows.htm*

24. O'Toole Fintan 2018. *Heroic Failure, Brexit and the Politics of Pain,* published by Head of Zeus Ltd.

25. European Council (Article 50) Guidelines for Brexit Negotiations, section 11. Published by the European Union 29/April 2017. *https://www.consilium.europa.eu/en/press/press-releases/2017/04/29/euco-brexit-guidelines.* Retrieved 13 May 2019

26. Ray Bassett *"Brexit, Brussels and the Border" Sunday Business Post* 3 September 2017, retrieved 9 May 2109 *https://www.businesspost.ie/opinion/brexit*-brussels-*border-396948.*

27. Fiach Kelly *"Brexit Deal to cover all of UK" Irish Times*, 5 November 2018, *https://www.irishtimes.com/news/ireland/irish-news/brexit-backstop-deal-set-to-cover-all-of-uk-1.3686240.* Retrieved 9 May 2019

28. *"Barnier warns of risk of hard border return as he urges rapid movement on issue". Irish Examiner*, 30 April 2018, retrieved 9 May 2019. *https://www.irishexaminer.com/breakingnews/ireland/michel-barnier-begins-two-day-irish.*

Chapter 2

The Irish Bailout

*"At a time when businesses were shutting down and the ranks
of the unemployed were growing, the Irish taxpayer was
paying bankers and their creditors incredibly large sums."*

Ashoka Mody, International Monetary Fund

Apart from the damage our excessive europhilia is doing to the foundations of the GFA, the experience of the Bailout, has been the driving force in my own scepticism of Brussels. It was a devastating period for Ireland but particularly so for our young people.

Yet a curious feature of Irish society, which has been commented on by many overseas visitors, is the virtual absence in official Ireland of contemporary comments on that notorious EU Bailout in 2010. Given the gigantic nature of what occurred and the devastating effects it had on Ireland, one would imagine that it would be a major and recurring feature of Irish publications and thinking on the EU. No, it is something that has been swept under the carpet. Our establishment does not want to discuss it, as for them it only evokes shame. Yet, those in official Ireland suffered less than many in a crisis, which blighted the lives of hundreds of thousands of Irish people. The official narrative also only mentions, in passing, the financial costs; other costs such as the stress and mental anguish of pensioners, who lost everything in the destruction of assets, such as bank shares; families torn apart by forced emigration; huge levels of negative equity; marital discord, caused by loss of employment and company failures, financial distress, etc, are simply not listed. These costs were very real and devastated the lives of thousands of Irish citizens and can never be numerically calculated. Many lives were torn apart by the dictates of the EU and the European Central Bank (ECB).

There are echoes here of the country's experience with the Great Famine in the nineteenth century, which was unspoken of for decades after that disaster[1]. Again, as in the Famine, a bad situation was made infinitely worse by the callous policy of the foreign overlords. It too was a classic example of blaming the victim. Despite that lesson, today official Ireland behaves as if nothing exceptional happened in 2010. The danger of relying on the EU for support in troubled times goes unheeded.

Financial cost to Ireland

The overall cost to the Irish people of the financial collapse, including resources provided by the State to the Irish banks, is difficult to quantify, perhaps impossible. Various figures have been quoted whether it be the gross €64.6bn, or the lower net figure of €44.7bn, estimated by the Central Bank[2], including gobbling up Ireland's sovereign wealth fund. The calculations are complex, the costs not only involve the actual money provided but also the cost of servicing these debts, the collapse in taxation which the subsequent austerity programme caused, the loss of our reputation, increased welfare payments, the loss of economic participation by the hundreds of thousands forced to emigrate, etc. There is also the offset of the disposal of assets. In reality, nobody will be able to give a totally accurate picture, there are so many interacting factors. It was described by Patrick Honohan, the former Governor of the Irish Central Bank as "one of the most expensive bank crises in history."[3] There are a number of excellent publications, including Simon Carswell's book, *Anglo Republic: Inside the Bank that Broke Ireland*[4], which details the financial machinations that went on inside the banking system.

Whatever the details of the final bill, one thing is clear. What happened in Ireland was way out of proportion to what happened elsewhere in the EU. Even under the lowest net cost estimates, the crisis massively increased the debt burden on the Irish people. Also, it should be remembered that it was the private banks which ran up the debts, that sparked the collapse, unlike the position in some other EU countries, where it was State borrowing which had run out of control.

Also, it should be remembered that the Bailout costs are continuing to this day. The destruction of the construction industry which resulted in very few houses being built in the immediate years after the collapse, the emigration of thousands of skilled craftspeople, etc. all have led, as the economy recovered, to a severe housing crisis and a huge increase in asset property values and exorbitant rent costs. Ireland is paying large sums annually in debt servicing on its huge national debt, money which could go to improving public services. This money has to be raised in taxes which impacts directly on the take-home pay of the workforce. The legacy of the Bailout will haunt Irish people for many years to come. In 2017, the cost of debt servicing was €10.6bn or 16% of total Government expenditure[5].

While a case could be made for a rescue package for the pillar banks (those necessary for the smooth running of the economy), there was little or no merit in rescuing the dysfunctional and malignant Anglo-Irish Bank. The total cost to the taxpayer for this bank has been estimated at up to €34bn, although this figure will be reduced somewhat in the end by asset disposal. The decision to pay for this bank, which had only a tiny number of branches and, as former Minister for Finance Brian Lenihan stated in 2010, had no "intrinsic merit", [6] was not taken in Dublin but rather in Frankfurt and Brussels. The folly of a tiny few greedy bankers and hangers-on would have to be paid for by the average citizen. The foolish investors who had chased yield, and hence increased danger, would not have to pay for their stupidity and avarice. The whole issue of moral hazard was put aside when it suited the EU establishment. As Ashoka Mody of the IMF pointed out "At a time when businesses were shutting down and the ranks of the unemployed were growing, the Irish taxpayer was paying bankers and their creditors incredibly large sums."[7]

Frankfort and Brussels were only interested in stopping a repeat of the Lehman Brothers collapse in Europe. That event had sparked a wave of panic and hysteria in the United States, which had rocked the international banking system to its foundations. For the sake of the stability of the EU, this rogue institution, Anglo-Irish, would be saved and its huge liabilities would be covered by the Irish taxpayer. Irish Finance Minister Brian Lenihan desperately wanted to avoid, as far as possible, the Anglo-Irish bill landing on the taxpayer. He tried to introduce the concept that the banks' lenders had to share the burden. He had the subordinated debt holders in mind, who were legally the next in line to take losses after the holders of equity in the banks. The reaction was furious and in the face of huge opposition from Brussels/ Frankfort, Lenihan had to back down[8].

It was a horrific outcome, which could have totally sunk the Republic of Ireland. While the creditors to the bank would be saved for the sake of Europe, no help could be expected to the innocent taxpayer, only loans, at high rates of interest. The rate of interest on the Bailout loans was just shy of 6%[9], described rightly at the time, as an onerous burden that led to immediate accusations the Government had done a bad deal. In reality, they had no power to refuse.

The Bailout beneficiaries

To add insult to injury, some of our European partners, whose financial institutions had been saved huge commercial losses on their foolish loans to Irish banks, including Anglo-Irish, appeared to believe that the Irish should be grateful for being forced to accept Bailout loans at exorbitant rates of interest. These countries, of course, unlike Ireland, had the full backing of the ECB. It is particularly galling to meet Germans today who still believe that their country did Ireland a favour during that period, rather than Germany and its financial institutions being huge net beneficiaries from the Irish Bailout. However more recently, one of the German officials involved in the Bailout, Professor Christian Kastrop, a former aide to ex-German Finance Minister Wolfgang Schäuble, conceded that Ireland was hit with unnecessary harsh measures in the Bailout at Berlin's insistence[10]. I am not sure that sentiment has in any way sunk into the mindset of many Germans.

This attitude also extends to some British Tories who continue to talk about coming to Ireland's aid during the banking crisis. Of course, it was good of the UK to provide money for the Bailout when they had no obligation to do so. However, it is rarely remarked that the loan the UK provided to Ireland, namely £3.2bn in 2011, was to cover loans the Irish Government did not really want but were forced to take on by the EU Commission and the ECB. It should also be noted that the high interest rate on this loan, although later reduced by former British Chancellor George Osborne, has netted the UK a handsome profit. The *Irish Times* in April 2017[11] reported that Ireland had paid €428m (£358m) interest up to that date and that, every six months the Irish exchequer was paying the UK £42m interest. The interest rate being paid is well above the level that Ireland can obtain in the international bond markets. That newspaper further reported on September 7, 2017, that Ireland would incur a once off extra penalty of €200m if the UK debt was paid early. So much for those claiming an altruistic approach.

Deception around the Bailout

While still in the service of the State, I was shocked by the circumstances surrounding the Bailout. In Irish Embassies overseas as the financial storm raged, we had been requested to categorically assure all, especially our host Governments and major local financial interests, that Ireland would not enter an EU Bailout.

This was against a background of Irish Sovereign bond yields rapidly climbing as market sentiment turned sour. We now know that some of that negativity resulted from anonymous briefing provided to influential financial journalists by figures from inside the European Central Bank and the EU Commission. There was a determination within the EU establishment to force Ireland into a Bailout.

As Kevin Cardiff, the former civil servant and head of Ireland's Finance Department, stated to a Parliamentary Committee, Ireland was simply pushed into the Bailout by the EU and ECB briefing, in a determined effort to undermine the country's ability to withstand market pressure. He said, "We knew who was doing it, we knew what they were saying. In other cases, the pressure came indirectly via some misinformation, anonymous media briefings, reportedly coming from official sources, which acted to accelerate market pressure and create enormous pressure on Ireland to enter an EU/IMF programme quickly."[12]

At that time, I was in Canada, a G7 country which has a strong banking and financial services industry and hence huge interest in the crisis in the Eurozone. I, and other Irish Ambassadors around the world, were all given detailed data and speaking points which indicated that the Irish State could finance itself for a reasonable period, without having to go back to the international bond markets. Even at Cabinet level in the Republic, Ministers were kept in the dark.

A senior figure in the Cabinet, Dermot Ahern, who was an able and conscientious Minister, speaking on Radio Telefís Éireann (RTÉ) television on 13 November 2010, stated that no Bailout would be required. Presumably, Dermot was provided with the same briefing note as our overseas representatives. When asked about rumours to the contrary, he replied, "It is fiction, because what we want to do is get on with the business of bringing forward the four-year plan and that's where all our energies are. We have not applied, there are no negotiations going on. If there were, obviously Government would be aware of it, and we are not aware of it."

It is now clear that senior members of the Government were blindsided on what the EU had planned. However, others, outside of Ireland, all seemed to be only too well aware of developments. In reality, the official briefing notes we were working with, were fiction.

A good friend of mine, John Murphy, a proud native of Prince Edward Island who is an international bond dealer with Wood Gundy, a division of the Canadian bank CIBC, told me a week beforehand that the market fully expected Ireland to be forced by the ECB into a Bailout, on the basis of briefings they were hearing from Europe. I mistakenly, however, chose to believe in the official line. Yet there were other conflicting signals. Several of my EU Ambassador colleagues in Ottawa seemed to be aware, without any doubts, that Ireland would enter a Bailout. They were very well briefed and seemed incredulous that I was unaware of what was being planned in Frankfort. However, I continued to doggedly adhere to the Government line right up to the end, including at a meeting with senior bankers in Toronto where again there seemed to be general acceptance that we would have no choice on the matter. The ECB simply decided that an Irish Bailout was needed for the prectection of the euro.

Therefore, when the Bailout actually came, I was shocked, not just by the about-turn but by its conditions and the fact that Ireland as a State would have to take on the debts of the private banks, well above the basic level of the official State guarantees to depositors. The whole thinking behind this draconian imposition was that ordinary citizens were unimportant when compared to the welfare of European banks. German financial institutions were among the largest investors in Irish bank bonds during the pre-crisis period. As more of the details emerged later on, including the infamous letter from Jean-Claude Trichet,

President of the European Central Bank, to the Irish Government, the shameful exercise was exposed in all its unedifying glory (see Annex 1). Ireland ceased to exist as an independent State as the Troika took over the economic management of the country, with the overwhelming priority of looking after the interests of the common currency and the ECB. It was named the Troika because it was composed of representatives from three organisations: the European Commission, the European Central Bank and the International Monetary Fund. Hence no democratically elected component was included.

Reaction in Canada

I later had the opportunity of discussing the terms of the Bailout with the Canadian PM, Stephen Harper, when he was about to visit Ireland, and the Canadian Finance Minister Jim Flaherty. Both expressed private horror at what the EU had inflicted on Ireland. Flaherty simply said, "You were screwed," while Harper asked, "Are these people supposed to be your friends?" On hearing the extra percentage of GDP that would be added to our national debt, Harper winced visibly and said, "I feel your pain." Both he and Flaherty were very sympathetic and helpful, particularly in dealing with the International Monetary Fund, where Canada has a lot of influence. This was in marked contrast to our so-called EU friends. It also was in marked contrast to the attitude of the United States, where Treasury Secretary Tim Geithner lined up with the faceless officials of the ECB to pressure Ireland into the Bailout[13]. In addition, Flaherty a hugely influential and respected figure and Vice President of the World Bank, spoke repeatedly in public against the downgrading of Irish sovereign debt.

He was in regular contact with the then Irish Finance Minister, Brian Lenihan, and the two often spoke before and after key meetings of the G7, G20 and Eurozone Finance Ministers' meetings. I kept in contact with Flaherty during this period and he constantly asked how he could be of further help. Canada was doing everything it could to assist.

Later at a meeting in Farmleigh House (the official Irish State guest house) in Dublin in June 2013, which I attended, Harper and Flaherty promised the then Taoiseach Enda Kenny and Finance Minister Michael Noonan that Canada would work with the IMF to assist

Ireland when we were facing unfavourable changes in IMF regulations. It was a demonstration of practical friendship from a country with which we shared so much history and ethnic links. There was genuine commitment to helping us. I doubt if any of our fellow EU countries, were as committed to our welfare. Noonan and Flaherty also enjoyed a very good personal and professional relationship.

The Bailout shattered any lingering illusions I had about the benevolence of the EU. In stark terms the European Union, through the EU Commission and the ECB, had sacrificed Ireland to protect its own interests and those of Germany and France. Our Government and the Central Bank were completely helpless and hapless as the ECB threatened to strangle the country by cutting off support for the banks. Ireland had very foolishly given up its own currency in 2000 on entering the euro and could not legally print its own banknotes once the ECB threatened to shut off the normal supply of money. It was simply left defenceless.

While I could only watch and listen in Ottawa to the macroeconomic calculations of the crash, the more important human consequences, of what was happening in Ireland, were washing up on Canadian shores. People were getting desperate to leave Ireland and get a chance at a life overseas. Suddenly there was pressure to ease entry into Canada for Irish people.

As Irish Ambassador to Canada, I made the rounds of the Canadian Federal Cabinet Ministers, with Irish backgrounds, to literally beg for extra visas for young Irish people who stood no chance of getting employment in their own country. The job market in Ireland virtually disappeared overnight. The Canadian Finance Minister Jim Flaherty, who had become a good friend and a powerful ally, also promised to lobby informally for easier access for Irish citizens.

In particular, the then Canadian Immigration Minister, Jason Kenney, who had strong family ties to Ireland, came up trumps with a determination to assist as much as possible, as did the immigration authorities in various Canadian Provinces. These Canadian Provinces are very independent in many areas and have the power to operate separate immigration programmes to the Federal Government. Each Province is entitled to issue a specific number of its own immigration places, subject to Federal vetting on health and security grounds.

I travelled to meet immigration authorities, Irish community and business groups in Québec, Nova Scotia, Prince Edward Island, Saskatchewan, Alberta, British Columbia, Manitoba, New Brunswick, Newfoundland and Ontario, all the time asking for access for Irish citizens. My view was that it was much better to give our young people the opportunity to come to Canada and gain experience, rather than be left jobless in Ireland where the EU-induced austerity had wiped out their immediate prospects of employment. When better times returned to Ireland, then these young migrants would be much more equipped to make a contribution to the recovery. Everywhere I went with my begging bowl, I was greeted with sympathy and support. Canada was one of the few countries which, through very prudent policies directed by Flaherty and Bank of Canada Governor Mark Carney, had never given their banks licence to reign havoc on the real economy, unlike most of the rest of the western world. There was a huge skills shortage in many of the Provinces, especially the oil producing ones.

Newfoundland, with its oil reserves, was starting its first immigration programme and thankfully chose Ireland as its potential source of new migrants. Saskatchewan, through then Minister Rob Norris, was particularly enthusiastic about attracting Irish building workers. Several of the Provinces, including Alberta, B.C., Saskatchewan, Newfoundland, etc. organised special recruitment visits for employers to Ireland.

Minister Kenney made the biggest impact. At the Federal level, he opened up Canada, with the immigration quota for Irish citizens, under the International Experience Canada programme, going from 4,000 pa to 10,700 pa and increased these visas from one year to two, greatly assisting young Irish to get permanent residence. The new visas were snapped up within minutes of becoming available. Young Irish were appearing in Toronto, Vancouver, Calgary, etc. in large numbers, something that had not been seen for generations. I was personally delighted when Jason Kenney subsequently became Premier of Alberta in April 2019. I should also note that the Canadian Ambassador in Dublin, Loyola Hearn, was a huge support. Hearn is a former Fisheries Minister in the Canadian Federal Government, with an extensive network of contacts within the Conservative Party.

I never received any instructions from the authorities in Dublin to campaign for more visas for young Irish people. I felt that this was the one course of action open to me. I did report regularly back to HQ but never received any great feedback. I figured as long as they did not actively object, then I had clearance to plough ahead. It became my own and the Embassy's no 1 priority.

I argued forcibly with my own authorities that it was not sufficient to just lobby the Canadians for visas, the Irish Government needed to commit resources ourselves to assisting these new arrivals in Canada. I met with the representatives of several of the larger Irish organisations in Toronto about establishing an Irish Immigration Centre in the city. I had seen the outstanding work that this type of centre was undertaking in several US cities and was determined to get a similar operation underway in Canada.

The late Eamonn O'Loghlin, editor of *Irish Connections Canada*, became a strong ally and enthusiastically endorsed the idea. Eamon had been already working with the new arrivals. Everybody wanted to help, including the Ireland Fund of Canada and its Chair Oliver Murray and its Executive Director, Jane Noonan. It was an impressive display of the community coming together, just as the Irish community in Toronto, did during the huge wave of Irish arrivals during the Famine. Irish and Irish Canadian businesspeople, such as Robert Kearns and John Speers, could not have been more helpful. It would be impossible to list all who rallied to the cause.

Although it was a time of severe austerity on Irish Government finances, after several discussions with the authorities in Dublin I managed to get funding for a full-time Director for the Centre. The Director, Ontarian native Cathy Murphy, proved to be a huge asset, in support of the Irish Embassy, in advising young Irish of their rights, responsibilities and possible opportunities. The Embassy also secured some additional modest funding for Irish organisations, in places like Montreal, Vancouver, Edmonton, etc. so that they could have welcome nights for young Irish people forced to emigrate to Canada. At these events, the young immigrants were often introduced to potential employers. By meeting with settled Irish residents of Canada and also Irish Canadians, the process of integration into their new host society was speeded up.

The new Centre was formally opened in Toronto by Canadian Immigration Minister, Jason Kenney, and Irish Tánaiste and Minister for Foreign Affairs, Eamon Gilmore, on St Patrick's Day in 2012. Kenney had arranged with Canadian television that after the opening he and Gilmore would adjourn to the nearby iconic Irish pub, P J O'Brien's, which was chock-a-block with new Irish immigrants. He had planned that he and Gilmore would pour pints of Guinness and the event would be covered across Canada by national TV. However, Gilmore got cold feet and pulled out at the last minute, afraid to be associated with alcohol on Ireland's national holiday. In any event, as Ambassador I substituted as the Irish end of the pint pulling. It was a poor decision by Gilmore to the request from the Canadian Minister who had done so much to open Canada up to Irish migrants. Gilmore realised he had made an error when we all returned to our hotel in Toronto to view on TV then President Obama enjoying a pint of Guinness, with a distant Irish relation, in the Irish Times bar in Washington. Political correctness often makes Irish Ministers err on the extreme side of caution.

I must pay particular tribute to the Gaelic Athletic Association (GAA) throughout Canada who did a huge amount of work in helping the new arrivals and in particular the then Chair of the Canadian Board Brian Farmer, from The Moy in County Armagh and his able deputy, Tyrone native, Sean Harte. They were always there if I needed any support and also, they had a Canadian wide organisation behind them. I always felt we worked as a team and when I travelled throughout Canada, I made a point of calling to see the local GAA club. My own background and work with the GAA Overseas Committee in Croke Park, greatly assisted in building a very strong relationship with the Association throughout Canada. The late Sheamus Howlin, former head of the GAA Overseas Committee and Leinster Chairman, worked closely with me on the immigration issue. He was an invaluable support, as well as a close and loyal friend

In addition, many of the new arrivals had little or no interest in most existing Irish societies, especially the county associations which tended to have an older membership. The GAA in contrast was overwhelmingly a young person's organisation and attracted many of the newcomers, including those who had shown no interest in the GAA at home, even occasionally those from a Unionist background in the North. The GAA rapidly became the largest Irish organisation in Canada among those born in Ireland, both male and female, and a social outlet for those who had entered a new society. This development could be seen in other countries like the Gulf States, Europe, England, Australia, New Zealand and the USA.

Thousands of Irish poured into Canada, directly from Ireland and from places like the UK, Australia and the USA. This opening gave them a chance to get work and experience in their chosen profession. It was hard work for the Embassy but intensely satisfying to be in a position to assist. It was also terrific for the Irish Canadian community and revitalised many of the old Irish centres. However, I was deeply conscious that many were arriving directly as the result of a vicious insistence that banks on mainland Europe were more important than the future of these bright and wonderful young people. There have been many studies on the cost to the Irish economy of the Bailout but precious little about the devastation it had on families. Here in Canada we could see, at first hand the human costs of this huge displacement of people and the depopulation of much of rural Ireland. Every new arrival had a family in Ireland, many of whom did not want to see their children reared for export. I had children myself in the same age group as those new migrants to Canada and could readily identify with the angst being experienced by their parents.

In contrast to the mobilisation of help which we witnessed in Canada, there was a much colder attitude in Europe.

Reaction in Europe

Philippe Legrain, the former advisor to EU President, José Manuel Barroso, has admitted that the EU got it severely wrong in the Bailout. In his book, *Aftershock: Reshaping the World Economy After the Crisis* and *European Spring: Why Our Economies and Politics are in a Mess – and How to Put Them Right*, Legrain states that the EU acted solely in the selfish interests of the creditor nations to the detriment of those who found themselves in difficulties.

In the *Irish Independent* of 7 May 2014, Legrain described the treatment of Ireland in the following terms:

"It was outrageous of Germany, the European Commission and above all the European Central Bank to threaten to force Ireland out of the euro if it did not follow through with that foolish guarantee, lumbering Irish people, who had already suffered enough from collapsing house prices and a sinking economy with a €64bn bill to bail out bust banks," adding that, the bank guarantee had cost Ireland "€14,000 for every man, woman and child" – themselves in trouble and hence "greatly increased division."

The entire financial crash and the subsequent horrific Bailout cannot, of course, be laid solely at the door of the EU, but through its rigid ideological dogma and putting German interests first, it was a major participant. We in Ireland should never have left ourselves so open to this debacle.

It is now almost universally accepted that the EU's prescription of austerity is not only morally questionable by putting the burden of reform on the average citizen but also economically destructive. The EU should be the last organisation to claim credit for Ireland's subsequent economic revival which was due mainly to the hard work of ordinary Irish people and the inflow of large amounts of American FDI. The EU should desist calling Ireland the Poster Boy for its failed Bailout policies.

Shoot the messenger

The Irish authorities should of course take a rightful share of the blame, with their enthusiastic adherence to liberal economic policies, with "light touch regulation" of banks probably the worst mistake. However, the lack of strong opposition to that foolish approach, which is very similar to the situation regarding our present devotion to Brussels in the Brexit process, demonstrates a structural weakness in Irish public life. There is a crying need for really independent Think Tanks which challenge our sacred cows.

There was, of course, the occasional voice in the wilderness challenging the overwhelming orthodoxy of the economics that led to this terrible situation. University College Dublin Economics Professor Morgan Kelly, penned an article in the *Irish Times*, stating that Irish property values were heavily overpriced and were liable to a major fall[14]. He based his calculation on the experiences of Finland and the Netherlands that had lived through similar economic bubbles and subsequent crashes in the past. It was largely ignored. He submitted a second article to the *Irish Independent*, a cheerleader for the property developers, who formed a lucrative part of the paper's advertising revenue, but the article was never published. It also lay dormant when given to the *Sunday Business Post*. However, in September 2007, this long-delayed view was finally given the light of day, in the *Irish Times*. Kelly accurately predicted the demise of the Irish banks because of their lending practices[15]. He provoked nothing but hostility. In a tape recording of a conversation on 23 December 2008, between an executive of the rogue Anglo-Irish Bank and a stockbroker client, the latter shockingly suggested that Kelly be "incinerated" for rocking the boat[16]. On the same day, Kelly had accurately predicted in an article published in the *Irish Times*, that the Government's proposed investment of €1.5bn in Anglo-Irish Bank, which had just been announced, would "vaporise in months", followed by many billions more.

Later that year, Philip Ingram of Merrill Lynch produced a report which advised clients of the dangers of investing in Irish banking shares. After studying the situation over a period of time, Ingram rightly believed that the bubble was unsustainable. Just as with Kelly's prudent advice, Ingram was subjected to vicious criticism by the Irish banks. The report was withdrawn after heavy corporate pressure, and Ingram left Merrill Lynch by Christmas 2007[17].

The Irish establishment simply did not want to hear any contrary view to the prevailing wisdom. Commentators, academics and everybody in the public eye were expected to toe the party line. In an unfortunate outburst, the then Taoiseach Bertie Ahern, while addressing a conference of the Irish Congress of Trade Unions in Bundoran, county Donegal on 3 July 2007, was reported as saying[18] "Sitting on the sidelines, cribbing and moaning is a lost opportunity. I don't know how people who engage in that don't commit suicide because frankly the only thing that motivates me is being able to actively change something."

To be fair to Bertie, he quickly and sincerely apologised for his suicide remarks, but his statement was a reflection of the hostility in the higher levels of Irish society to anybody who questioned the prevailing economic wisdom. There was a constant requirement to "wear the green jersey," a euphemism for demanding conformity. It was wheeled out as a defence of Irish banks during the financial crisis and other occasions. I have been accused on a number of occasions by members of the Great and Good of Irish Society, of failing to wear the green jersey in the Brexit process, namely a demand for blind adherence to the official line.

Cliff Taylor put it well in his column, entitled – "The Green Jersey Merchants haven't gone Away" – in the *Irish Times* on 11 June 2016:

> The Ireland Inc creed continues to frown upon straight discussion of anything that might be seen not to be in the 'national interest'. My first experience of this was during the currency crisis of 1992–1993. Back then there was no euro and the Irish pound was tied to other currencies in a currency band, allowing limited fluctuations. The markets attacked and the pound was one of the currencies under pressure. Most of the banks and broking houses were 'onside' in saying the pound would not devalue, with a couple of notable exceptions. The media was put under constant pressure, with a barrage of what would today be called 'spin' from Government and the financial sector. In the end the inevitable happened and the pound devalued.

> It happened again as the financial crisis hit in 2008, when the message from 'Ireland Inc' was that everything was okay and the banks were well capitalised. There was a lack of plain talking as the crisis built up and immediately after it hit.

The same mentality is manifesting itself in the Brexit process. Any questioning of the basic policy is regarded as not wearing the green jersey, i.e. being unpatriotic. It is probably one of the most corrupting traits in Irish society and one which has been very destructive over the years.

This lack of realism can also be seen in subsequent dealings with the formation of the European Stability Mechanism (ESM). With much fanfare the then Taoiseach Enda Kenny, with the support of his Finance Minister, Michael Noonan, claimed that the Mechanism could be used to recoup some of the Government's support for the Irish pillar banks, namely the ones that were important to the real economy. Ireland through its efforts had helped save the European banking system and now it was time to help little Ireland. However, the answer from Berlin was a flat refusal. Germany had managed to pump billions into its weak banks via the Irish Bailout and the bill was left with the Irish taxpayer. Very neat work by the German authorities but it demonstrated the true nature of the European Union, the interests of small countries count for little when selfish German interest are involved.

The then Irish Minister for Finance Michael Noonan stated on Bloomberg TV in 2013:

> Part of the intervention which put the burden of the bank debt – 40 per cent of GDP – onto the shoulder of the taxpayer, while some of it was our own fault, a lot of the action was taken at the direction of the ECB to prevent contagion spreading to the European banking system.
>
> As Ronald Reagan used to say, 'We took one for the team.' And I think the team owes us now[19].

Michael Noonan was to be disappointed. In the final analysis, it counted for nothing. Therefore, it is touchingly naïve for the Irish authorities to place such trust in the EU establishment in Brussels and that it will look after Irish interests if it clashes with those of the bigger economies. It is certainly a great example of the triumph of hope over experience.

There is also a lack of recognition that the bank Bailout was largely the outcome of Ireland's foolish decision to join the euro. Those who advocated and campaigned for the Treaty of Maastricht and its destructive elements, have in retrospect to shoulder some of the blame for the Bailout. However, as the headlong rush to back Brussels continues, it seems no lessons have been learned. As the old adage states, "Fool me once, shame on you, fool me twice shame on me."

While it is only just to apportion the major blame for the Bailout on the EU institutions, our local politicians should not escape unscathed. As pointed out by Morgan Kelly, "Ireland went from getting 4-6 per cent of its national income from house building in the 1990s – the usual level for a developed country – to 15 percent at the peak of the bubble in 2006-07, with another 6 percent coming from other construction[20]."

Apart from the foolishness of relying on unsustainable levels of taxation from the construction industry, generations of Irish politicians had eroded the State's ability to manage its economic future by abandoning levers such as a separate currency, interest rates, control of capital flows, etc. They had ceded so much that it greatly affected our ability to mitigate the worst effects of the crisis for the Irish citizen. This is the context in which the Bailout took place and again there is little recognition of that pertinent fact in modern Ireland.

More help from Canada, Mark Carney to the Rescue

After the crisis had abated somewhat, Ireland found itself saddled with huge legacy debts, with penal rates of interest. The country badly needed a break so it could get on top of its repayments and start a virtuous circle rather than a spiral downwards similar to what happened to Greece. At an informal meeting in the Swiss resort of Davos between Irish Minister for Finance, Michael Noonan with Canadians; Finance Minister Jim Flaherty and Central Banker Mark Carney, a potential breakthrough was achieved. In what Noonan described as "back of an envelope calculation," Carney, using his expertise in international finance, suggested to the Irish Minister a different way of calculating interest on Ireland's promissory notes, essentially Governmental IOUs.

Carney's scheme would allow Ireland to pay less money upfront and give it a longer breathing space before it had to make heavy repayments. If accepted, it would be a major boost towards allowing the country time to recover.

When Ireland proposed the new calculations to the ECB, all the other countries, apart from Finland and Germany, agreed to offer Ireland support. Noonan was on good terms with the Finnish Finance Minister and asked her to speak to the Head of the Finnish Central Bank. The Finnish Minister agreed, and the Finnish objections were subsequently overcome. The Germans proved more resistant but Mark Carney, with his prominent role in the G20 reform of banks programme, approached the Head of the Bundesbank and asked as a personal favour could the Germans abstain on the Irish proposal. He reluctantly agreed and the new scheme went through. Ireland greatly benefitted from the respite. Again, it was our Diaspora, through Carney and Flaherty, who had come to our rescue. I was not present in Davos but listened to accounts of the Carney intervention from both Jim Flaherty in P J O'Brien's pub in Toronto and subsequently from Michael Noonan in the Canadian Embassy in Dublin.

IMF verdict on the Irish Bailout

The International Monetary Fund has been quite vocal on the role the European institutions played in the Irish Bailout. In popular folklore, the IMF, are normally portrayed as the heartless moneylender destroying local economies but in Ireland's case, they were the most sympathetic element of the Troika, in comparison to the EU Commission and the ECB.

Two former heads of the IMF mission to Ireland have commented negatively on the ECB's role. Ajai Chopra, decried the actions of ECB President Trichet in threatening the Irish Government, saying that threats should not play a part in such rescues. He further claimed that Trichet had exceeded his mandate in the ECB. Chopra confirmed that the IMF wanted to see the sharing of the burden of the Bailout by imposing haircuts on the senior unguaranteed bank bondholders but Trichet and ECB refused. Chopra said in an interview published by the IMF on 19 Dec 2013 that he hoped Ireland had learned its lesson but added that "the second lesson is that it is unfair to impose the burden of supporting banks primarily on domestic taxpayers while senior unguaranteed bondholders get paid out. This not only adds to sovereign debt, but it also creates political problems, making it harder to sustain fiscal adjustment."

Ashoka Mody, in his excellent book, *Euro Tragedy*, who also was head of the IMF mission to Ireland at one time, totally supported the criticism of the ECB and especially former President Trichet, whom he blamed for making the euro crisis much worse by his rigidity and obsession with assisting bankers. Mody reiterated that in the IMF view the ECB determination to impose severe austerity on Ireland was a major mistake

However, the ECB, which unlike the Fed in the USA has no political oversight, still appears to believe that it can act in a totally arbitrary manner. In a remarkably crass move, it was reported that the ECB wanted the Irish Government to legislate to phase out loss-making tracker mortgages over a five-year period in an effort to return banks to greater profitability. Tracker loans were costing Irish banks €700m pa.[21]. In plain talk, it wanted the Irish Government to allow the banks to renege on their legal obligations to their customers. The average citizen would again be sacrificed for the good of the bankers, who had done so much damage to the country. If any political party in Ireland even hinted at a similar proposal, it would be rightly subject to the harshest criticism. However, there is a different standard for EU institutions which appear to be immune from such judgements in the Irish mainstream media.

References

1. Tim Pat Coogan, *The Famine Plot* – p 3

2. Sean Whelan, *"It hasn't gone away you know... the cost of the bank bailout"* RTÉ website 24 Oct 2017. *https://www.rte.ie/news/business/2017/1023/914665-46-7-billion/* Retrieved 8 Dec 2019

3. Vincent Brown, *Irish Times* 6 April 2011. *"Let's own up to our part in burst bubble"*. *https://www.irishtimes.com/opinion/let-s-own-up-to-our-part-in-the-burst-bubble-1.564844*. Retrieved 8 December 2019

4. Simon Carswell. *Anglo Republic, Inside the Bank that Broke Ireland*, 2011. Penguin Publishing Dublin.

5. Fiona Redden, *"Budget 2018: Where does all your tax money go? Irish Times* Oct 5, 2017. *https://www.irishtimes.com/business/economy/budget-2018-where-does-all-your-tax-money-go-1.3245485.* Retrieved 6 December 2019

6. David Gardner and John Murray Brown, Interview with Brian Lenihan *Financial Times* 29 September 2010. *"Anglo failure would 'bring down' Ireland"*. *https://www.ft.com/content/025f321a-cbf5-11df-bd28-00144feab49a*. Retrieved 8 Dec 2018

7. Mody *EuroTragedy* p 272

8. Mody, *EuroTragedy* p 272

9. Arthur Beesley, *"Dark Days, Behind the Bailout"*, *Irish Times* 19 Nov 2011, *https://www.irishtimes.com/news/dark-days-behind-the-bailout-1.14049*. Retrieved 8 December 2019

10. Derek Scally "*Harsh austerity 'imposed on Ireland' by Berlin, says ex-official*" *Irish Times*, 26 November 2019. *https://www.irishtimes.com/business/economy/harsh-aus terity-imposed-on-ireland-by-berlin-says-ex-official-1.4094603*. Retrieved 8 December 2019

11. "*Ireland pays more than €400m in interest on UK bailout*" loan *Irish Times* April 19, 2017. *https://www.irishtimes.com/business/economy/ireland-pays-more-than-400m-in-interest-on-uk-bailout-loan-1.3053791*. Retrieved 8 December 2019.

12. BBC News website "*Irish banking crisis inquiry: Ireland was 'pushed' into bailout*", 18 June 2015. *https://www.bbc.com/news/world-europe-33185690*. Retrieved 8 December 2019

13. Arthur Beesley, "*Dark Days, Behind the Bailout*", *Irish Times* 19 Nov 2011. *https://www.irishtimes.com/news/dark-days-behind-the-bailout-1.14049.* Retrieved 8 December 2019

14. Morgan Kelly, *Irish Times* 28 Dec 2006. *https://www.irishtimes.com/business/how-the-housing-corner-stones-of-our-economy-could-go-into-rapid-free-fall-1.1042463, retrieved 29 February 2020.* Retrieved 8 December 2019

15. Morgan Kelly, *Irish Times* 7 September 2007. https://www.irishtimes.com/business/banking-on-very-shaky-foundations-1.960313. Retrieved 20 February 2020

16. Ronan Quinlan "*Incinerate Morgan Kelly – the most shocking Anglo tape yet*" *Irish Independent* 20 July 2014. *https://www.independent.ie/business/irish/anglo/incinerate-morgan-kelly-the-most-shocking-anglo-tape-yet-30444629*. Retrieved 8 December 2019.

17. Michael Lewis, "*When Irish eyes are crying*" *Vanity Fair*, 1 March 2011. *https://www.vanityfair.com/news/2011/03/michael-lewis-ireland-201103*. Retrieved 8 December 2019

18. "*Ahern sorry for suicide remark*" RTÉ website 30 Jun 2009 *https://www.rte.ie/news/business/2007/0704/90821-ictu/*. Retrieved 8 December 2019

19. "*Ireland took one for the team*" *Sunday Business Post* – 8 January 2013 *https://www.businesspost.ie/legacy/ireland-helped-french-by-taking-one-for-the-team-noonan-34b0e53b*. Retrieved 8 December 2019

20. Morgan Kelly. "*The Irish Credit Bubble*", 2009, Working Paper Series WP09/32

21. Cormac Lucey *Plan B* p 105

Chapter 3

The British Irish Relationship, Post Brexit

*"When it comes to exporting our racehorses – especially those
destined for the jumps market – there is no replacement market
for Britain and so unlike many other Brexit-hit sectors, we
simply cannot adapt our product to suit new markets… Royal
Ascot, Cheltenham, Aintree and Epsom cannot be replicated in
another country."*

Brian Kavanagh, CEO Horse Racing Board of Ireland,
June 2017

The post-Brexit relationship between Ireland and Britain is a conundrum, the eventual outcome of which is very difficult to predict. It is such a massive change from all the historical precedents. The two islands have been in a close embrace for centuries. It will be the biggest challenge facing any Irish administration in the near future. Given what transpired in phase 1 of the Brexit negotiations, I believe the onus will be very much on Dublin to undo the present impairment of bilateral relations.

Ireland only joined the EEC in 1973 because it was so intrinsically linked with Britain, it had no other option. Much has changed in the meantime, but it is not possible to change the past or indeed geographical reality, the two dominating factors in the relationship between the two islands.

Ireland now faces an existential moment in its history. If handled badly, and to date it has been very badly handled, it has the potential to damage economic, political and cultural ties that have, in some cases, lasted centuries. It is a pivotal moment in Irish history.

The decision of the Irish Government to adopt a tough, hard-line policy, which prioritised the country's europhilia over any assistance for London, will have serious long-term implications for the London–Dublin axis. It will also have consequences for relations between the Irish Government and the pro-Union part of the community in the North. Naturally it affects, by extension, the future of the GFA. The ramifications for Northern Ireland and intercommunity relations on the island of Ireland will be discussed in the next chapter.

Before we get too excited about supporting our Government's devotion to Brussels, we, in Ireland, should be very cognisant of what we could potentially be endangering in our relationship with our neighbours across the Irish Sea. We should also weigh up the likely future direction of the EU and see, if it still remains in our interests, to throw in our lot completely with Brussels.

With the departure of the UK from the EU, Ireland will be entering a totally new era in its relations with its neighbouring island and its most important economic, ethnic and cultural partner. The Brexit divorce process has been very painful, in some respects needlessly so. Old passions and, in particular, anti-English feeling, has been stirred up again in Ireland[1]. These are never buried too deep but in recent years have largely been confined to sporting rivalry in the Republic, less so in the North where Anglophobia is much stronger. In addition, there has been a revival of old-fashioned English resentment of Ireland[2] and a renewal of the old English accusation that Ireland will never miss an opportunity to stab Britain in the back. This is in neither country's interests.

Both countries will be anxious to stop the deterioration and to allow a new relationship, post-Brexit, to bed down. There will be complications in the new bilateral arrangements because the EU is pressing hard to take over responsibility for much of what was formally the preserve of the Nation States, particularly in the area of relations with third countries. The UK will be in that category, once Brexit is completed. However, it will be important that the Brussels influence is kept in check and not allowed to interfere with the healing process. The EU has no real interest in seeing the UK enjoy any bounce from Brexit and will be anxious not to be too helpful.

Despite the acrimony of the Brexit procedure and the EU's possible interference, there are firm Irish/British foundations on which to build future cooperation.

The Irish/British relationship is one of the closest between two sovereign countries. They share the Common Travel Area (CTA). Neither country regards its neighbour's citizens as foreigners. Both countries allow each other's citizens to vote in Parliamentary elections and immediately access social benefits in each other's jurisdictions. Both countries follow Common Law and the Westminster style Parliamentary form of Government. They have a strong bilateral Treaty, the Good Friday Agreement, which pledges each to be a partner and mutually supportive of the other. Our security services enjoy a huge level of cooperation and mutual trust.

This special relationship will not sit well with the ideologues in Brussels who are not comfortable with such close ties between a Member State and a third country. In the post-Brexit period, it is very likely that there will be increased strain on Dublin/Brussels relations, as their current common sparring partner, the UK, will be out of the immediate picture. Ireland's role in being the EU's leading cat's paw in the first part of the Brexit process will soon be forgotten in Brussels (but not by many Brexiteers in the UK). In such circumstances, Dublin will have to reassess its recent blinkered pro-EU policy and rebuild its links with London.

Of course, the age-old political relationship between Ireland and Britain has often been fraught and fractious. We had been joined in some form of political association for over 700 years. However, in recent times, the old animosities had started to die away, especially since the signing of the GFA, which largely settled the mechanisms whereby each country could bilaterally pursue its interests, as well as bringing the last round of civil disturbances in Northern Ireland to an end. The two Governments worked very closely and successfully with the political parties in the North to bring about that agreed settlement. There needs to be a return to that type of interaction between the two administrations.

Apart from working together on issues relating to peace and reconciliation in Northern Ireland, the common membership of the EU and its predecessor organisations, EEC and EC, played a crucial role[3]. This was not always the situation. When I first came into the Department of Foreign Affairs, there was a conscious policy in official meetings to emphasise our differences with the UK. It could occasionally take on a childish dimension. This was encapsulated by the practise of some senior Irish officials to speak in French in the European Political Cooperation (EPC) framework, when there was a choice to use either English or French at meetings, without any translation. It was a perverse practice and caused bemusement among other Member States.

However, as time passed and after working together in the same Ministerial Councils and official working groups for many years, it became increasingly clear that the interests of Ireland and the United Kingdom, more often than not, converged around policy in Brussels. This commonality of interest increased over the years.

Improving relations and then a reversal

The early Irish focus in Europe centred around the Common Agricultural Policy (CAP). Here the UK was regarded as a formidable opponent. At that stage, Ireland was a major net recipient of Brussels largesse, overwhelmingly to the agri-food area. Irish Governments often regarded the annual price setting discussions for CAP products inside the Agriculture Council as its number one priority in Europe. Mark Clinton, who was Irish Agriculture Minister 1973–77, very much set the tone in this regard. The UK in contrast wanted to reform the CAP, with its excesses visible to all, including its butter mountains and wine lakes. Those stark differences of approach changed over time. Once the CAP was brought under some control, the British–Irish divergences began to diminish. Also, the relative decline of agriculture as a proportion of the Irish economy, made it less of a divisive issue.

As Ireland's focus inside the EU moved away from an undue concentration on agricultural matters, the importance of abolishing barriers to free trade and the promotion of cross border services became much more pronounced. Here the UK was a staunch ally, along with the Netherlands. Ireland with its large multinational sector and the UK's traditional adherence to free trade ensured similar approaches from the two States. This contrasted with the more protectionist instincts of the French, Belgium and German Governments.

Even on budgetary matters inside the EU, the Irish and British national positions began to become more aligned. In 2013–14, Ireland moved from its traditional position of being a net recipient of EU funds to firstly a small contributor and then a much larger contributor on a per capita basis. Hence the previous Irish Government position of always lobbying for extra resources for Brussels, became more muted and started to shift gradually to a more conservative line on further budgetary transfers from the Member States to Brussels. This would see Ireland act in a similar manner to comparable States such as Denmark, Netherlands, Sweden, Austria, etc.

The personalities at the top of Government in Dublin and London assisted in the rapprochement. In the period of Bertie Ahern's time as Taoiseach and Tony Blair as British Prime Minister, Irish–British relations reached a level of cooperation and mutual trust which would have been unthinkable in the past. Regular bilateral meetings before European Councils were undertaken, phone conversations between the two heads of Government were a frequent occurrence on almost every issue. Even on matters relating to Northern Ireland, prior notice was given as to the content of replies to Parliamentary questions, draft speeches were often exchanged in advanced and there was the most detailed bilateral consideration at Civil Service level on draft legislation. It was an unprecedented period of harmony in Anglo-Irish relations. It was exactly what was envisaged in the GFA.

Ahern and Blair were greatly supported by US President Bill Clinton, with whom both had an excellent personal relationship. That US support continued under Clinton's successor, George W Bush, who proved to be very supportive of the GFA and the two Governments. The high calibre of his special envoy to Northern Ireland, Richard Haass, was a good example of the Bush administration's serious commitment.

Blair, in a move which symbolically encapsulated this new beginning, became the first British Prime Minister to address both Houses of the Irish Parliament when he spoke in Leinster House on 26 November 1998. In a similarly historically important occasion, Bertie Ahern addressed a joint sitting of the Houses of Parliament in Westminster on 15 May 2007. This was the first time an Irish Taoiseach had been accorded this honour.

Those events marked the high watermark in relations and there is no doubting the sharp decline of Dublin–London Governmental links in the meantime. This drift apart was apparent before Brexit, but the real damage occurred since the referendum. However, it is vital for the two countries, and especially for Ireland, that is the main beneficiary of the current bilateral arrangements, that we endeavour to get back to a good working relationship, based on trust. There is no doubt, but that trust has been severely lacking in some exchanges on Brexit. In September 2017, the then British Prime Minister, Theresa May, unwisely turned down an invitation to address the houses of the Irish Parliament, while on a visit to Dublin[4]. That would have been the first time a Conservative PM had been given this honour. It was also a good example of May's lack of appreciation of the need to develop good personal relations with EU leaders, in this case the newly elected Leo Varadkar. He only became Ireland's head of Government on 2 June of that year. Ireland was going to be a key player in the first phase of the Brexit negotiations.

Brexit and its fall out now threaten all the good work of the Good Friday period. Speeches by the Taoiseach Leo Varadkar and his deputy Simon Coveney have been needlessly provocative to the UK. There was press speculation that former Prime Minister May "loathed" Varadkar and asked her de facto deputy David Lidington to take over the Irish brief[5]. There was no denial from Downing Street of these reports and even Varadkar was unsure whether they were accurate[6]. Certainly, the body language between the two did not inspire confidence. However, it was very clear that neither leader had the natural people skills of Ahern or Blair. With a new Prime Minister at the helm in London, it is a good time to reset the relationship at head of Government level. Whatever criticism can be levelled at Boris Johnson, his ability to establish good relations, at a personal level, has never been in question.

There is no doubt but that Ireland's insistence on a Backstop for the North made negotiations for the original Withdrawal Agreement, and its subsequent acceptance by the House of Commons, hugely more difficult. The deterioration in the bilateral links are, of course, not solely due to Irish intransigence. The UK political parties, throughout the Brexit process, were wholly occupied in internecine civil war in Westminster and uninterested in the complicating Irish factors, until they were forced to confront the issue of the land border in Ireland.

The Backstop and British–Irish Relations

It is widely rumoured that the Backstop in its original format was drawn up by the Irish delegation in Brussels, with enthusiastic assistance from the EU Commission. However, confirmation of that story must await the eventual publication of the Irish State archives in a few decades. The Backstop was purported to be a position of last resort to maintain an open border on the island of Ireland, in the event of the UK leaving the EU, without an all-encompassing trade deal. In essence, it involved entirely detaching the North economically from the UK, should the British decide to operate an independent trade policy. It was later extended to cover the whole of the UK.

In reality, it was never about the border and the Peace Process. Essentially, the purpose of the Backstop was to keep the UK within the economic orbit of Brussels and to preserve the integrity of the Single Market. Given the poor economic performance of the Eurozone, it was important that the UK, post Brexit, could not adopt an alternative direction in trade matters, especially if that trade policy was to be successful. The Backstop was also enthusiastically supported by Remainers in London, who quickly identified the Border as a weapon to thwart Brexit. In many ways, it resembled the blanket bank guarantee, provided by the Irish Government, at the height of the financial crisis in 2008. The Irish Government's solution to that situation was a blanket guarantee for all the liabilities of its failing banks.

Initially the guarantee was regarded as an extremely clever move, which would put one over on other jurisdictions, stabilise the banking system and would never be called in. It resulted in an immediate and very temporary inflow of capital. Other European countries complained bitterly about it. It was tactically clever but strategically disastrous. It was based on a bluff and Ireland's bluff was called. Large deductions are still being made today from every pay-packet in Ireland to pay for this folly.

Again, the original Backstop, which only covered the North, was hailed as a smart manoeuvre, which gave Ireland and Brussels the whip hand in the Brexit discussions. Just like the initial stages of the bank guarantee, there was much self-congratulation and admiring of our own handiwork. Again, the early expectations that the Backstop would be a trump card began to fade as the House of Commons refused to stomach it. The British Government had it extended to cover the whole of the UK in the Withdrawal Agreement, but again it hit the rocks, despite all types of inducements and threats. In reality, it was never a runner, again tactical cleverness masking what proved to be, a major strategic error.

In is clear that the Backstop was a huge self-inflicted injury for Ireland. It scuppered the Prime Ministership of Theresa May. The damage is much more extensive, with the moderate pro-EU wing of the Conservative Party in total retreat. The party in the country is wholly pro-Brexit and became very annoyed at the failure by the Remainers and their EU allies to respect the outcome of the referendum. At the same time, the newly emerged Brexit Party threatened to inflict huge damage on both Conservative and Labour's traditional bases, outside of London. Because of the failure to deliver Brexit, the most preferred option, with the British public, became the No Deal outcome. In the circumstances, it was inevitable that Ireland and its use of the Backstop, would attract a large part of the blame.

The Irish and British authorities should have decided, at an early stage, to use direct bilateral discussions to resolve the border question. This could have been solved with a mixture of exemptions of the type allowed by the World Trade Organisation (WTO), together with enhanced use of technology[7]. The two Governments could, then, have gone to Brussels with a solution, not a problem. It would have required some flexibility from the EU, but that would have been difficult to refuse. Instead the Irish Government cooperated fully in the enterprise to use the sensitive border issue to maintain Brussels control. Much of the subsequent British Parliamentary mess can be traced back to that policy decision. In reality, the Irish Government had jettisoned its obligations under the GFA to display its euro credentials. As RTÉ's Brussels correspondent Tony Connelly outlined in his book, Ireland and Brexit, official Ireland gave no thought to any alternative approach.

The proposal to time-limit the Backstop was rejected out of hand by the Irish side, even though this would have probably secured the House of Commons assent to the Withdrawal Agreement, as shown by the passing of the so-called Brady amendment[8]. To agree a time limit would have allowed the UK to escape from the obligation to totally satisfy the EU in the trade discussions but as far as Brussels was concerned, that would have defeated the whole purpose of the Backstop.

In fact, the lack of knowledge on the European side was demonstrated in an interview with Claire Byrne on RTÉ on 9 April 2019, when Guy Verhofstadt, the European Parliament's lead on Brexit, claimed that the placing of even one "sensor" on the border, would endanger peace in Ireland, unaware that there are a considerable number of cameras already in place, and have been for years, monitoring traffic on the main Dublin-Belfast highway close to the border[9]. These installations have provoked no adverse response locally.

The failure of the Backstop placed Taoiseach Leo Varadkar in a very dangerous position. To his credit he reacted swiftly as the possibility of the UK falling out of the EU without a deal loomed large on the horizon. He did a dramatic U-turn. Suddenly dispensing with the EU embargo on direct negotiations with London on Brexit, he travelled to Thornton Manor Hotel in Cheshire to meet PM Johnson and while there agreed to drop the Backstop and support the UK demand to reopen the Theresa May Withdrawal Agreement[10]. The Irish volte face was breath taking after years of intransigence. However, the bitter reaction of the DUP to the probably temporary Northern Ireland specific measures in the new deal with the EU, saved Varadkar from adverse local reaction, as did the immediate avoidance of a No Deal outcome. It was widely believed in the Republic that the Irish State was in no way prepared for a No Deal scenario, with many of the country's ports several years away from being ready for such an outcome.

Varadkar was right to concede on the Backstop but the deafening silence from the media or any substantial analysis of what happened reflected badly again on the Fourth Estate and indeed the political Opposition in Leinster House. Better not delve too deeply as this might demonstrate the poverty of previous utterances.

Mutual interest, Ireland and Britain.
Despite the globalisation of the Irish economy, the United Kingdom is still by far Ireland's main trading partner, in recent years accounting for nearly 30%, by value, of the country's merchandised imports. It represents a much higher percentage in volume terms.

However, the real cornerstone of the British–Irish relationship is the connection between its peoples. Irish and British settlers have moved between the two islands for millennia and this continues to this day. The United Nations Migration report estimated that 9,664 Irish born people were resident in France in 2013, with 17,519 in Spain[11]; while the number of Irish born (from both North and South, all Irish citizens) in GB was in the region of 600,000. The number of Irish born in the USA was 143,571[12]. This means that more than 35 times the number of Irish born lived in Britain than in any other EU country, a powerful demonstration of the ethnic links between the two islands. Millions of Britons have at least one Irish grandparent, something the two football associations in Ireland (the Football Association of Ireland, FAI in the Republic; and the Irish Football Association, IFA in Northern Ireland) have been only too glad to exploit to strengthen their international teams with the so-called granny rule.

There is a huge commonality of citizenship as exemplified by the fact that many of England's most popular and successful football internationals, such as Harry Kane (Spurs), Wayne Rooney (Manchester United), Martin Keown (Arsenal), Declan Rice (West Ham), Michael Keane (Everton), Jack Grealish (Aston Villa), etc., could have also played for the Republic of Ireland, because of their Irish ancestry. After the Brexit referendum, many British people discovered that they could retain their EU citizenship by obtaining an Irish passport through a process called foreign birth registration, namely through descent. Applicant numbers for such passports soared in the post-Brexit period[13].

The former Irish Minister for Foreign Affairs, Charlie Flanagan, spoke on the BBC Newsnight programme about Ireland being part of the EU family and about our partnership with the UK. Given the pattern of historical migration, he appeared to get these descriptions wrong way round[14]. It is vital for Ireland that this intimate relationship with Britain is maintained and that Irish people are able to travel and work freely in Britain and vice versa in the longer run. The present ill feeling over the Backstop could impact in this area in the future.

Energy dependence

The trading relationship with the UK is particularly important in the energy sector, where Ireland is heavily dependent on UK energy supplies. In 2012, UK imports accounted for 92% of the total gas used in Ireland and 93% of refined oil products[15].

The Corrib gas field, which came online in 2015, has reduced but not eliminated the dependency on UK gas imports. In any case, production from the Corrib field will be short-lived – the total recoverable gas is thought to be 17 billion cubic metres, which equates to 3.5 years of total gas usage in Ireland. Once Corrib is depleted, Ireland will again become fully dependent on the transit of gas supplies via Britain.

Any disruption to gas supplies has the potential to cause significant disruption to the Irish economy. Research indicates that the cost of a natural gas outage (e.g. in the event of the gas interconnector failing) would result in an economic loss to the Irish economy of €350–€640 million per day[16]. Ireland's strategic 90-day reserve stocks of oil, operated by the National Oil Reserves Agency (NORA), are largely physically held in the UK, including at Cloghan Point in county Antrim[17]. After Brexit, there could be pressure on Ireland from the EU to change that situation[18].

The electricity industry in the Republic of Ireland is fully integrated with Northern Ireland in a single electricity market. Significant changes are being made to this market in order for it to conform to European Network Codes, which came into effect in 2018. There are significant benefits from these arrangements in terms of the overall efficiency of the system, particularly for Northern Ireland. Looked at in isolation, Northern Ireland has a significant electricity deficit. Disentangling the current set of arrangements following Brexit would be difficult, and highly undesirable for all parties involved[19].

Energy supply is a key strategic element in any economy. It will be important for Ireland that the UK is enabled to remain as close as possible to Ireland on energy supplies. It would be far better to keep as much of the present arrangements in place as possible. Here as right across the economic spectrum, Ireland needs to act in a way which facilitates EU–British cooperation on a mutually advantageous basis. The anti-British approach of Ireland to the Brexit process will have to be replaced by a much more constructive policy in the post-Brexit period. This is overwhelmingly in Ireland's interest.

Trade Links

While the USA has replaced the UK as the biggest single export market for Irish exports, it is the nature of Ireland's exports to the United Kingdom that causes the greatest concern in a post-Brexit situation. The country's small and medium-sized enterprises (SMEs), tourism and its food and drink sectors, all employment-rich areas, are the most heavily dependent on the UK. These companies are generally locally owned and source their raw materials in Ireland. Hence, their activities have a much bigger multiplier effect in the local economy than the more high-tech foreign direct investment (FDI) enterprises, mainly American, which are less dependent on the British market. The SME companies tend to be more regionally based and concentrated in less economically advantaged areas of the country, where alternative employment is not as readily available as it is in the affluent east coast belt around Dublin[20]. They are vital for the health and balance of the economy. It is in the area of agri-food where Ireland is most vulnerable to shocks in the post-Brexit situation.

In a hard Brexit environment, import duties on agricultural products under simple WTO rules could be up to 50% and would essentially end the centuries' old trade between Ireland and Britain in food.

The President of the Irish Farmers Association, Joe Healy, speaking on RTÉ on 19 January 2017 said, "The UK is an important trading partner for us. 40% of agri-food products go to the UK. That's worth about €5billion alone. We export 90% of our beef, with half going to the UK. Our dairy products that are exported to the UK have a value of slightly less than €1 billion."

He added that it was "almost impossible" to find markets where farmers would get the same returns as they currently do from the UK market. Irish Government figures show that approx. 280,000 tons of Irish beef are exported annually to the UK. Irish beef and veal represent 70% of UK imports of these products[21].

In 2016, 55% of Ireland's exports from the construction and timber sector went to the UK, as well as around half the country's exports of clean energy technology. The bulk of Ireland's exported small electrical goods go to the UK. Also, many of the Irish SMEs, which export to the

UK, lack the linguistic skills and international business experience to diversify into new markets on mainland Europe.

For Britain, any disruption of trade with the Republic would be serious, though of a lower order of magnitude than for the Irish side. Ireland is the UK's 5th largest export market, after the USA, Germany, France and the Netherlands[22] and is more important than China. It is the UK's largest market for food and drink exports and its second most important market for clothing, fashion and footwear. Because of its energy exports to Ireland, the UK enjoys a large trade surplus with the Republic, while seriously in deficit with the rest of the EU.

The Irish State, of course, will make laudable efforts to diversify export markets for Irish SMEs, using the good offices of Enterprise Ireland, the Irish State body which is tasked with the development of these businesses. This, however, will be simply impossible in areas like cheddar cheese, an essentially Irish–British food as there is little or no demand for exports of this product elsewhere in Europe. Ireland exports the bulk of its cheddar cheese production to the UK.

Another industry threatened with disaster is the thoroughbred horse industry. The links between Ireland, Britain and France are unique in Europe. The horse breeding industry is worth in the region of €1bn annually to the Irish economy. Speaking to a Senate committee in Dublin on 6 June 2017, the Chief Executive of Horse Racing Ireland, Brian Kavanagh, told the assembled Senators:

> "When it comes to exporting our racehorses – especially those destined for the jumps market – there is no replacement market for Britain and so unlike many other Brexit-hit sectors, we simply cannot adapt our product to suit new markets… Royal Ascot, Cheltenham, Aintree and Epsom cannot be replicated in another country."

He added that any disruption to the Irish–British links would be very damaging to the British racing industry and "catastrophic" for the Irish side.

Bilateral migration matters

Migration to the UK has traditionally been an option for Irish people in times of economic difficulties, often the only option. This has been a recurrent experience throughout Ireland's modern history. When I was growing up in Dublin in the 1950/60s, it seemed that every family had relations in England. In Dublin, there were huge family links, including in my own, with the city of Liverpool. There were tear-filled goodbyes, every evening on the North Wall on the Dublin quays, as the boats headed eastwards to Merseyside. At times of very little economic opportunity in Ireland for many working-class families, people were often very grateful for the chance to earn a decent living in places, such as Birmingham, Northampton, Coventry, Dagenham, etc.

If the EU and the UK Brexit negotiations result in leaving a sour taste, and possibly with long-term consequent effects on the Common Travel Area, then this centuries-old "safety valve" could be shut off. Where will young Irish people migrate to in such circumstances? No Irish Government would wish to see this connection disrupted. Mainland Europe is unlikely to be a viable alternative. There is a strong reluctance among Irish people to move in any great numbers to countries such as France, Germany, Netherlands, etc. This is not just because of a lack of linguistic skills but also, because of historical links; there is a much more attractive alternative in moving within the Anglosphere to Britain, and also to Australia, Canada, New Zealand, etc., where craft and professional training is very similar to Ireland. In addition, there are huge long-established Diaspora networks in these countries to assist incoming Irish migrants.

After the UK departs from the EU, Ireland will be the only English-speaking country left, apart from Malta, which also has English as one of its official languages. One of the main reasons why Britain attracts so many immigrants is its language; English is the main foreign language, taught in many eastern European countries. While Ireland will never attract the same number of arrivals, it is probable that Ireland will see a major increase in immigrants from eastern Europe, once their option of migrating to Britain is closed off. To date, there has been relatively little public opposition to immigration in Ireland, where, in general, it is still seen by the majority of the population as beneficial, if a bit too unregulated. However, a large unplanned increase in new arrivals could change the benign attitudes. In addition, the Economic and Social Research Institute (ESRI) found that antagonism to immigrants rose during the recent recession[23]. The immigration issue could become a major focus of discontent in a post-Brexit situation, especially where there is pressure on public services and housing availability.

Hopefully, the CTA, which is presently protected by Protocol 20 of the inelegantly named "Treaty on the Functioning of the EU" can continue indefinitely (Annex 2). The Treaty, specifically, recognises the right of the UK and Ireland to "make arrangements between themselves relating to the movement of persons between their territories" and this is retained in the Withdrawal Agreement. As mentioned earlier, the signing of a Memorandum of Understanding (MOU) between the Irish and British Governments on 8 May 2019, reaffirming the CTA and identifying the rights and privileges of Irish and UK citizens within the CTA area, is a welcome further commitment by both Governments to maintain the status quo. (It is a pity that a similar bilateral approach to the problems of the Irish border was not taken by Dublin.)

However, the CTA is dependent long term on the goodwill of both Governments and public acceptance. There is a danger that post Brexit, those seeking to immigrate illegally to the UK, may see Ireland and the land border with Northern Ireland, as a potentially weak link in the UK immigration control system. Unless this potential danger is tackled, it will have implications for the CTA in the longer run. It will require much deeper and much more public cooperation between immigration officials in both countries, including the positioning of UK immigration officials at Irish airports and seaports and similarly Irish officials at UK transport hubs. The Republic's authorities will be very anxious to ensure that the dreadful scenes from the "Jungle" refugee camp in Calais, are not repeated on the border outside Dundalk in county Louth.

Further Challenges

As the effects of Brexit finally take shape, Ireland will find itself on the extreme western fringe of the European Union. The centre of gravity of the Union will have shifted further eastwards. The Republic of Ireland will represent four fifths of an off-shore island, which is positioned behind a larger off-shore island, that is no longer a member of the European Union. Ireland will suffer from a major physical dislocation from the main centres of power and influence in the EU. Brussels is hoping for further expansion to the east (Ukraine and Turkey) and the south (Serbia, North Macedonia, Kosovo and Albania), thus placing greater influence on central Europe. It will become an increasingly peripheral environment for an Anglophone State on the extreme west of Europe. This will be evident even in the languages used in Brussels as the relative importance of English declines.

In recent years and particularly so since the admission of post-communist European States, the English language has become dominant within the EU, paradoxically the lingua franca. However, in a post-Brexit EU with only five million native English speakers in the Republic of Ireland, the English language will no longer have as strong a case to be the dominant language of the institutions. The French Government, no doubt, will have strong views on the matter. Former Commission President, Jean-Claude Juncker, was quoted at a Conference in Italy on 5 May 2017 as triumphantly claiming that already "English is losing importance in the EU", hardly a comforting thought for the linguistically challenged Irish politicians and officials[24].

This new enhanced peripherality post Brexit will also affect Irish trade with the remaining members of the EU. Irish trade with mainland Europe overwhelmingly travels through Britain via ports in western Britain and then through the English motorway system to the Channel ports. It arrives in mainland EU through Calais, Rotterdam, Antwerp, etc. In fact, two-thirds of Ireland's total exports by value (and a much higher percentage by volume) pass through the UK transport system[25].

Without a satisfactory trade deal, no Irish authority has yet indicated how this can be maintained without the threat of some disruption both at the point of entry into the UK, and later when the exports bound for mainland Europe, re-emerge into the EU Customs Union. Apart from the potential for huge time delays at either end, there could be extra costs on the administrative side. Also, there will have to be some inspections as no national custom regime can simply accept that goods travelling through its territory from a separate customs jurisdiction are completely safe from contraband, solely on the basis of enhanced technology. There will always be the need for on the spot human inspections, even if these occur well away from the ports themselves. This will disadvantage Irish trade and involve extra expense. Any special deal on customs clearance for Irish goods would not survive major infringements, a not impossible development.

Many of Ireland's seaports are not equipped to deal with cargo from outside the EU. The bulk of trade in our ports will now fall into that category. The change in the status of trade with the UK, Ireland's biggest trading partner, will therefore necessitate major change and new financial outlays at those ports. Some will be unable to cope and may have to cease operations.

Every level of society is linked

At every level of society, there are huge interconnections between the two countries. Having been joined together for so long in a single administrative unit, it would be extremely difficult to even enumerate the multiple linkages. The bulk of these connections are at a societal and communal level and dwarf comparable associations with any other country. Any impediment to these links, which touch every area, would be extremely disruptive and, given their scale, almost impossible to calculate.

Even with good cooperation, tensions can, and will arise. There was considerable annoyance in Dublin at what was regarded as unfair comments by the former Police Service of Northern Ireland (PSNI) Chief Constable, George Hamilton, that weaker immigration checks in the Republic could provide a route for international criminals to enter Britain[26]. Whatever the true situation, the national security implications of backdoor immigration into the UK from Ireland is bound to become an issue post-Brexit. A member of the Muslin community in Dublin, claimed that she met two of the London Bridge Jihadist attackers in Dublin, Khuram Butt and Rachid Redouane[27]. They had no difficulty travelling between Dublin and London. This emphasised the need for the closest possible cooperation in the public safety area.

As the Brexit debate took place in Britain, many in Ireland, particularly those in financial circles openly boasted about attracting many of the large financial, insurance and legal firms from London to Dublin. The

Department of Finance and Ireland's Industrial Development Authority (IDA Ireland), along with politicians and some pro-EU economic commentators in the media, were particularly vocal and triumphalist on the matter. However, as the process developed, these promised new large investment flows into Dublin have not yet materialised, at least not on the scale originally envisaged. These new jobs, it was hoped, would partially make up for the significant loss of Irish employment in other areas, especially in the agri-food sector.

The over enthusiasm of the Irish authorities was fanned by some of the most outrageous claims of what has been described as Project Fear in Britain. The Bank of England had claimed that in a worst-case scenario, the British capital could lose up to 75,000 jobs in the financial sector[28]. As with much more of the Project Fear scares, this has proved completely wrong. It is now estimated that any job losses will be relatively low, and Brexit will not seriously impair the City of London's status as the world capital for financial and insurance services[29].

For Ireland and its Financial Services Centre (IFSC), the presence of this global financial centre in London, together with the overall performance of the UK economy, the most dynamic economy in growth terms of the larger EU countries in recent years, has represented a major plus. The fact that the UK and the USA recovered much quicker and more comprehensively from the financial crisis greatly assisted Ireland's own bounce back from that period. These two Anglophone countries are Ireland's most important economic partners.

The Dublin–London air route is reputed to be the second busiest international inter-city air route[30], second only to Hong Kong to Taipei; a major testament to the commercial closeness of the two capitals. London's Heathrow and its huge network of air routes is often Ireland's gateway to Asian, Latin American and African cities. Ireland has a huge stake in the continued success of the UK's economy. To listen to Irish Ministers speaking about Brexit, this salient fact seems to have totally bypassed them. The Taoiseach's hyperbole about the UK facing "decades of economic decline" post-Brexit[31] is not in Ireland's long-term interest, apart from its wild assertion. It demonstrated a mindset which certainly was not focused on Ireland's own interests.

Future

The Brexit process has dealt a blow to the growing rapprochement across the Irish Sea that had been occurring for over twenty years. In a post-Brexit world how do these two island nations begin to rebuild their damaged relationship? I am sure at a political level strong personal ties will ensure that good communications remain but at the public level damage has been done, and it is only a matter of time before this affects official relations. It is simply impossible to insulate Government to Government links from the popular mood. Too many politicians believe that they can ignore that important fact.

The failure of Ireland to assist the UK at its time of need was a bad error. As mentioned earlier, the Irish Government could have rescued Theresa May's Withdrawal Agreement by simply agreeing to the insertion of a reasonable time limit on the Backstop. The influential former Chair of the Conservative Backbench 1922 Committee, Sir Graham Brady, personally assured me it would have allowed the original Withdrawal Agreement to pass[32]. He had managed earlier to steer the "Brady amendment" through the House of Commons which demanded a change in the Backstop.

An Irish concession on the Backstop, at that stage, would have been a magnanimous gesture to a neighbouring country. It would have been overwhelmingly in Ireland's long-term interests. However, that opportunity is long gone. In the end, when Taoiseach Leo Varadkar was forced to abandon the Backstop by the threat of a No Deal, it was far too late. The damaging of the Brexit process, using the Irish border, may have won the plaudits of the Remainers in the London establishment but it was a gamble which now, post Brexit, clearly did not pay off.

As already stated, the Conservative Party in Britain, at the grassroots level in the shires, became overwhelmingly pro-Brexit[33]. The landslide election victory in December 2019 reshaped the Parliamentary party in the image of its membership. The old Conservative Party, under former Prime Minister Ted Heath, were the enthusiastic pro-European cheerleaders of my youth. That element has been vanquished and unlikely to return in the future. Unfortunately, many Tories will remember with some bitterness the unhelpful part that Ireland played throughout the Brexit process. The British Conservatives have been the natural party of

Government in Britain for the last century and it does not make sense to make a long-term enemy of the vast majority of that party.

I am sure that some of the arch-Remainers in the Tory party, including some who held high office in the May administration, both encouraged and plotted with the Irish Government to try to thwart Brexit. This was still no excuse for Dublin trying openly to overthrow the democratic decision of the British people. Ireland has been cynically used by both establishment elements in London and Brussels. We should have seen this danger a mile away and shunned it.

The splits have not been confined to the Conservative Party. The British Labour Party was also divided, with the old Blairite remnants actively working against the leadership and seeking ways of thwarting Brexit. This cost them dear in the 2019 election. The Irish insistence on the Backstop, hugely unpopular even with pro-Irish elements in the Labour Party, even helped to facilitate a warming up of relations between that Party and the Unionist DUP[34].

Rebuilding of British-Irish institutions

Once Brexit is finally out of the way, Ireland needs to use the existing intergovernmental machinery to rebuild trust. The British Government will also need to give a much greater emphasis to its relations with Dublin than the present Conservative administration has, since coming into power in 2010. The two administrations regularly met during EU meetings and could routinely hold discussions en marge on these occasions. This allowed for easy exchanges. This will no longer be available to either Government.

Closer bilateral relations, post Brexit, between the Republic and the UK would help fill a void in our relations outside the EU. I believe that our lack of participation and serious engagement with organisations outside the Brussels bubble, means that our politicians and officials have become far too EU-centric. Regular consultations with a post-Brexit UK, and the various constituent parts of that State, would help broaden the experience and outlook of our administrators.

Upgrading the Good Friday Agreement mechanism

Therefore, there is a strong need to reactivate the mechanisms of the Good Friday Agreement. I am glad that the British and Irish Governments have agreed, in principle, to recommence meetings of the British Irish Intergovernmental Ministerial Conference (BIIGC)[35], which has been a neglected part of the GFA in recent years. I was Irish Joint Secretary of that ungainly named body(2001–05), when it was functioning well under the Fianna Fáil and British Labour administrations. It is a very useful forum where all matters of bilateral interest could be discussed (Annex 3). It should use its wide remit to meet in various sectoral formats, e.g. Transport Ministers, Social Welfare, Energy, Agriculture, etc. and not just Taoiseach/Prime Minister and Foreign Affairs/ Secretary of State for Northern Ireland.

While I believe that in the longer-term Ireland should leave the EU, unfortunately this is unlikely to take place in the short-term. The GFA could be used for close collaboration and consultation with the British Government on EU matters. Since it is very much in our interest that the UK continues in a close relationship with the EU, Ireland should consider itself a close ally and friend of the UK inside the Council of Ministers. This would help restore some of the trust lost in the Brexit process.

Hopefully we have now entered a better and more realistic period. Once we finish with the Transition Phase, detailed discussions could take place between the Irish and British Governments, under the GFA, to flesh out the details of avoiding any questions of a hard border. These would be informed by the wider EU/UK trade discussions.

All parties claim to be supporters of the GFA, and that Agreement commits both Governments to "come together to promote bilateral cooperation at all levels on all matters of mutual interest within the competence of both Governments." It is time to review the Agreement and amend it in a way that reflects the new situation. There is provision in the GFA for such a review of "the machinery and institutions established under it."[36]

A successful refurbished GFA could, no doubt, reset the Dublin–London relationship in a very positive and beneficial direction.

British Irish Council

Another institution which needs to be further energized is the British Irish Council (BIC). This body, created under Strand 3 of the GFA, brings together a novel set of administrations, the Irish and British Governments; the devolved administrations in Edinburgh, Belfast and Cardiff; along with the Crown dependencies of Isle of Mann and the Bailiwicks of Jersey and Guernsey (including Alderney and Sark). This is a total of eight different Governments. In addition, because of the emphasis on the preservation of minority languages, Cornwall now has observer status in the BIC since 2010.

It is a curious body but has greatly assisted in re-establishing relations right across these islands and among administrations, which would not otherwise have had cause to meet.

I remember the initial meeting of the Council which took place in Lancaster House in London. On the Irish side we were busy reading up on the various Constitutional arrangements of the smaller non-UK entities in the Channel Islands and the Isle of Mann. However, we were not alone in this respect. British Prime Minister Tony Blair confessed himself unsure as to why Jersey/Guernsey did not send MPs to the House of Commons. He enquired from the leader of the Guernsey delegation who promptly told Blair that it was because England and Jersey/Guernsey were on different sides in the Battle of Hastings in 1066. A bemused Blair reported back to the Irish and British delegations, stating that he was still none the wiser.

The concept of a Council was suggested by the Ulster Unionists during the Good Friday Talks, as a counterweight to the North/South Ministerial Council in Strand Two of the Agreement. In fact, most of those designated to be members of the Council were unaware of their inclusion, until well after the signing of the GFA. It never got the same powers as the North/South institution but in its own quiet way, it has built up strong links between Ireland and the devolved British administrations, especially Scotland. This has even caused its own little difficulties. At one stage, soon after Scottish devolution, Labour First Minister, the late Donald Dewar, felt that too many Scottish Ministers and Parliamentary Committees were heading to Dublin to establish links and he asked the Irish authorities to help slow down the process, in case it caused difficulties with London. The independently minded Scots were more interested in seeing how things were done in Dublin, rather than in other devolved administrations.

Perhaps there should be an initiative to strengthen the British Irish Council further. It has a permanent standing secretariat, which is based in the Scottish capital of Edinburgh.

British Irish Council/Parliamentary Assembly

The British-Irish Parliamentary Assembly is also a very useful body which includes 25 members each from the Irish and British Parliaments, as well as five members each from the Welsh Assembly, Scottish Parliament and the Northern Ireland Assembly, while the Isle of Mann, Jersey and Guernsey representative Assemblies have one each. Again, this body could be another vehicle for strengthening relations.

In promoting stronger Dublin–London links post Brexit, one issue which needs to be looked at seriously is Ireland's possible association with the Commonwealth. This is an extremely sensitive matter and any Irish Republican who raises the prospect is immediately labelled as a sell-out or worse a traitor. The link between the British Crown and the Commonwealth was the reason for Ireland's original departure and would remain a difficulty for many in Dublin/Belfast. However, it is something which would undoubtedly strengthen British Irish links at a time when these are badly in need of positive development. The issue of Ireland's relationship with the Commonwealth is discussed in more detail in Chapter 12 on the Anglophone world.

References

1.   Eilis O Hanlon, *"Ireland is again in the grip of Anglophobia"*, *The Daily Telegraph*, 31 January 2019. *https://www.telegraph.co.uk/opinion/2019/01/31/ireland-grip-anglophobia/*. Retrieved 10 December 2019

2.   Ronan McGreevy *"Irish ambassador to UK accuses British magazine of anti-Irish bias over Brexit"* *Irish Times* 12, April 2019. https://www.irishtimes.com/news/ireland/irish-*news/irish-ambassador-to-uk-accuses-british-magazine-of-anti-irish-bias-over-brexit-1.3858298*. Retrieved 10 December 2019

3. Irish Embassy London Website, accessed 27 April 2019

4. *Irish News "Theresa May declines invitation to address the Dáil", 25* January 2017. *http://www.irishnews.com/news/republicofirelandnews/2017/01/26/ news/theresa-may-declines-invitation-to-address-the-da-il-905270/.* Retrieved 11 December 2019

5. *"No10 at war over a new referendum: Theresa May's Deputy Prime Minister AND her Chief of Staff are both plotting for a second vote, infuriating Cabinet Brexiteers" Mail on Sunday*, 15 December 2018. *https://www. dailymail.co.uk/news/article-6500029/Theresa-Mays-Deputy-Prime-Minister-Chief-Staff-plotting-second-vote.html.* Retrieved 11 December 2019.

6. James Gant *"Varadkar unfazed by claims in English media PM 'loathes' him" Belfast Telegraph* 18, December 2018. *https://www.belfasttelegraph. co.uk/news/brexit/varadkar-unfazed-by-claims-in-english-media-pm-loathes-him-37636011.htm*l. Retrieved 12 December 2019

7. Bassett Ray, *"Brexit and the Border",* Politeia 2018. p 12

8. Stuart Greer *"What is the Brady Brexit amendment?"* MSN News 29 January 2019. *https://www.msn.com/en-gb/news/newsmanchester/what-is-the-brady-brexit-amendment/ar-BBSUfXR.* Retrieved 31 May 2019

9. Claire Byrne TV Live, 8 April 2019

10. Denis Staunton and Pat Leahy *"Brexit: Varadkar sees 'pathway to an agreement in coming weeks" Irish Times* 10 October 2019. *https:// www.irishtimes.com/news/politics/brexit-varadkar-sees-pathway-to-an-agreement-in-coming-weeks-1.4046312.* Retrieved 12 December 2019

11. Ciara Kenny Ciara Kenny, *"The global Irish: Where do they live?" Irish Times* 4 February 2015. *https://www.irishtimes.com/life-and-style/ generation-emigration/the-global-irish-where-do-they-live-1.2089347.* Retrieved 12 December 2019

12. Ibid.

13. Jack Power, *"Passport applications from UK almost double after Brexit vote", Irish Times*, 18 December 2017. *https://www.irishtimes.com/news/ social-affairs/passport-applications-from-uk-almost-double-after-brexit-vote-1.3331145.* Retrieved 12 December 2019.

14. BBC News website, 5 May 2017. *https://www.bing.com/videos/search?q =bbc+news+website+5+may+charlie+Flanagan+EU&view=detail&mid=61 C43A7D5B192B6FD96C61C43A7D5B192B6FD96C&FORM=VIRE.* Retrieved 25 April 2019

15. IEA Energy Supply Security 2014 report 2

16. *Scoping the Possible Economic Implications of Brexit on Ireland.* Policy Exchange document. "After Brexit will Ireland be next to Exit, July 2017" Ray Bassett July 2017.

17. Eimear McGovern *"Residents voice opposition to Cloghan Point oil facility expansion" Belfast Telegraph* 6 December 2019, *https://www. belfasttelegraph.co.uk/news/northern-ireland/residents-voice-opposition-to-cloghan-point-oil-facility-expansion-38759710.html.* Retrieved 12 December 2019.

18. Philip Ryan, *"Ireland set to remove oil reserves from Britain as Brexit Deadline looms closer", Irish Independent,* 15 July 2018. *https://www. independent.ie/business/brexit/ireland-set-to-remove-oil-reserves-from-britain-as-brexit-deadline-looms-closer-37119507.html* Retrieved 25 April 2019

19. Bassett Ray, *After Brexit, Will Ireland be next to Leave?* p 10

20. John Whelan, *"EU as a bigger home for Irish exports than the UK is a pipe dream" Irish Examiner* 2 January 2018. *https://www.irishexaminer.com/ breakingnews/business/eu-as-a-bigger-home-for-irish-exports-than-uk-is-a-pipe-dream-820899.html.* Retrieved 12 December 2019

21. Ciaran Moran, *"Irish beef exports to the UK up 7% in year to May" Farm Ireland,* 30 July 2018 *https://www.independent.ie/business/farming/beef/ beef-trade/irish-beef-exports-to-the-uk-up-7-in-year-to-may-37165347. html.* Retrieved 12 December 2019

22. UK Office of National Statistics 2019. In addition, trade with the Netherlands or Belgium is skewed by these countries' role as the warehouses of Europe. Much of the international trade, which is recorded with both, in fact is re-exported to other destinations. This is sometimes referred to as the "Rotterdam effect".

23. *The Economic and Social Review,* Vol. 48, No. 3, Autumn, 2017, pp. 253-279

24. BBC News website, Brexit: *"English language losing importance"* – EU's Juncker 5 May 2017, *https://www.bbc.com/news/world-europe-39816044.* Retrieved on 25 April 2019

25. Colm McKelpie *"British Land bridge to Europe for exports from the Republic of Ireland set to remain open" Belfast Telegraph* 7 Dec 2017, *https://www.belfasttelegraph.co.uk/business/northern-ireland/british-land-bridge-to-europe-for-exports-from-republic-of-ireland-set-to-remain-open-36385610.html.* Retrieved 12 December 2019

26. *"Criminals using weak border controls in Republic to enter UK, PSNI says"* PA report, *Irish Times*, December 14, 2016. *https://www.irishtimes.com/news/crime-and-law/criminals-using-weak-border-controls-in-republic-to-enter-uk-psni-says-1.2905783*. Retrieved 12 December 2019

27. Paul Williams *"Radicalised Irish woman claims she travelled Ireland with London Bridge attacker and says there are up to 150 Islamic extremists living here Irish"* *Independent* June 10, 2017. *https://www.independent.ie/irish-news/news/radicalised-irish-woman-claims-she-travelled-ireland-with-london-bridge-attacker-and-says-there-are-up-to-150-islamic-extremists-living-here-37349339.html*. Retrieved 12 December 2019

28. Kamal Ahmad *"Bank of England believes Brexit could cost 75,000 finance jobs"* BBC Website Oct 31, 2017. *https://www.bbc.com/news/business-41803604*. Retrieved 12 December 2019

29. Andrew MacAskill and Huw Jones "London's Brexit-Related Job Losses Will Be Fewer Than 1st Feared: Policy Chief", 19 January 2018. *https://www.insurancejournal.com/news/international/2018/01/19/477825.htm*. Retrieved 12 December 2019

30. Barry O Halloran *"Dublin–London second-busiest route in world"* *Irish Times* Jan 25 2016. *https://www.irishtimes.com/business/transport-and-tourism/dublin-london-second-busiest-route-in-world-1.2508617* Retrieved 12 December 2019

31. Richard Vaughan *"Leo Varadkar warns Brexit will bring UK 'decades of economic decline"* inews, 12 July 2019. *https://inews.co.uk/news/brexit/leo-varadkar-brexit-uk-economic-decline*. Retrieved 22 July 2019

32. This assurance was given at a Policy Exchange event en marge of the Conservative Party Conference in Manchester 29 September. I was an independent speaker at the PX meeting.

33. Jack Maidment, *The Daily* Telegraph *"Vast majority of Conservative Party members back clean Brexit while nine in ten oppose second EU referendum"*, 4 January 2018. *https://www.telegraph.co.uk/politics/2018/01/04/vast-majority-conservative-party-members-back-clean-brexit-nine/*. Retrieved 12 December 2019

34. Peter Hain, *"Shame on the Labour MPs who rejected the backstop"*, Labour List Daily email, 30 January 2019. *https://labourlist.org/2019/01/peter-hain-shame-on-labour-mps-who-rejected-the-backstop/*. Retrieved 12 December 2019

35. Bimpe Archer *"Agenda for first meeting of the British–Irish Intergovernmental Conference in decade shrouded in secrecy as Ministers*

gather in London". http://www.irishnews.com/paywall/tsb/irishnews/
irishnews/irishnews//news/northernirelandnews/2018/07/25/news/
agenda-for-first-meeting-of-the-british-irish-intergovernmental-
conference-in-a-decade-shrouded-in-secrecy-as-ministers-
gath-1390757/content.html. Retrieved 13 December 2019

36. GFA Strand 3, Section 9.

Chapter 4

Northern Ireland and the Peace Process

*"The position of countries has been violently altered. The modes
of thought of men, the whole outlook on affairs, the grouping
of parties, all have encountered violent and tremendous change
in the deluge of the world. But as the deluge subsides and the
waters fall short, we see the dreary steeples of Fermanagh and
Tyrone emerging once again. The integrity of their quarrel
is one of the few institutions that have been unaltered in the
cataclysm which has swept the world."*

Winston Churchill, 16 February 1922

Background

For most Irish people, the most neuralgic element in the Brexit Process
was always going to be its potential negative effect on Northern Ireland.
The GFA had achieved what many believed was not possible, a political
settlement which ushered in an era of relative peace. The Agreement
essentially recognised the conflicting identities and loyalties of the
different communities there. It proscribed a reasonable and fair balance
and was endorsed overwhelmingly in a referendum. This provided a good
basis for future Government. However, despite the noble sentiments in
the Agreement to "develop reconciliation and mutual respect between
and within communities and traditions," in reality, that aspiration to
promote a "culture of tolerance" did not extend to the political level. In
the institutions, established by the GFA, whether the Assembly or the
North/South Ministerial Council, partisan communal considerations
appeared to trump all other aspects. Hence, the divided society there was
vulnerable to any changes which altered the delicate balance achieved in
the region.

From the outset, Brexit challenged the status quo and introduced elements of uncertainty for both communities there, their relationships with each other; and in turn, how each would relate to the Republic of Ireland and Great Britain. The most immediate concern was the future of the Irish border and how it could be managed, without upsetting the delicate balances achieved in the GFA. That line of division cuts through the Irish countryside along its 310-mile(499 km) route, and under Brexit is destined to be the only land boundary between the UK and the EU. Prior to Brexit, the EU already had 8,000 miles of land borders with 19 non-EU countries and that experience offered no reassuring example or prototype of what could be constructed in Ireland to maintain the frictionless and free boundary, wanted by all sides. It was clear that there was no off the shelf precedent that could be used to solve that conundrum.

The GFA, at its core, is a bilateral intergovernmental Treaty between the British and Irish Governments. That is why only the signatures of the two heads of Government are on the actual document[1]. The accompanying multiparty Agreement, apart from the Strand One institutions, was essentially drafted by the two Governments, after extensive consultations with the individual parties, and issued to them through the Chair of the multiparty Talks, Senator George Mitchell. The parties were then given the simple option of accepting or rejecting it. This was annexed to the British/Irish section of the overall Agreement. Contrary to the public perception, none of the leaders of the political parties in the North actually signed the Treaty. History has clearly shown that unless the two Governments work together, then there is little likelihood of any progress there. This is especially true on difficult matters, like devising new arrangements on the border.

Hence, as indicated in the previous chapter, the British–Irish tensions thrown up by Brexit pose a direct threat to the foundations on which the GFA was built.

Therefore, it is no surprise that many on the island of Ireland believe that Brexit represents a real danger to the Peace Process and to the future of the GFA[2]. There has been a deluge of words written and spoken on this subject since. Much of it has been poppycock and offered by both Brexiteers and Remainers, who clearly had very little experience or understanding of this area.

The GFA has attained iconic status in Ireland and Britain. Therefore, all sides in the Brexit negotiations have claimed ownership of it, have vowed to defend it vigorously and accused those with whom they disagree of violating it. The two Sovereign Governments, Dublin and London, have loudly proclaimed that preserving its gains is a priority for them. In reality, neither the Irish nor British Governments can take on the mantle of the defender of the Agreement, as both have acted in ways that are contrary to its terms. Needless to add that many partisans of Leave and Remain have misused and misquoted the Agreement to bolster their own arguments. There has been almost no fact checking of the many statements that emerged and very little reference to the actual text of the Agreement. The myths have been more useful, and often many times more powerful, than the reality of what is actually contained within that Agreement.

Former First Minister of Northern Ireland and ex leader of the Ulster Unionist Party, David Trimble, commenced a legal action in the courts in London, claiming that the Backstop in the EU/UK draft Withdrawal Agreement was contrary to the terms of the GFA[3], despite the claim by Dublin that it was inserted to protect the Agreement. His judicial review, no doubt, would have run up against the natural reluctance of the judiciary to adjudicate on matters political but Trimble, a winner of the Nobel Peace Prize, certainly had an arguable case. I was approached myself to take a case in the UK on similar lines but felt uncomfortable about taking on my own Government, on a political issue, in a foreign court.

It should be remembered that the Agreement is not a nationalist or unionist document but a series of compromises and undertakings, essentially a balance, involving all shades of opinion on the island of Ireland. It is a complete misreading of the document for any side of the traditional divide in Ireland to claim exclusive ownership or special rights. In much of the public debate, the future of the GFA was reduced to a blame game over issues about custom controls.

The Brexit debate in Ireland was focused on the need to preserve a frictionless border on the island of Ireland. This is not surprising and is the product of our history. The partition of Ireland into two States and the subsequent violence and chaos that followed has shaped the debate on the matter. It has been corrosive right from the start.

In February 1923, Winston Churchill wrote, describing the aftermath of World War One and the changes that the Great War had wrought on the international scene, in the following way:

> The position of countries has been violently altered. The modes of thought of men, the whole outlook on affairs, the grouping of parties, all have encountered violent and tremendous change in the deluge of the world. But as the deluge subsides and the waters fall short, we see the dreary steeples of Fermanagh and Tyrone emerging once again. The integrity of their quarrel is one of the few institutions that have been unaltered in the cataclysm which has swept the world.[4]

These two Ulster counties, Tyrone and Fermanagh, had been forcibly incorporated into the new Northern Ireland State against the expressed wishes of the majority of their people. Local Government administration had to be suspended at the time[5]. The difficulty of drawing a border between the new Irish Free State and Northern Ireland was proving hugely difficult, even at that time.

Many of those who found themselves north of the new border, including districts in Derry, South Armagh and South Down, were bitterly resentful at their exclusion from the new Irish State. Periodic outbreaks of violence, followed by periods of uneasy peace, characterised much of the history of Northern Ireland. On 31 March 1923, the Irish Free State became a separate customs territory[6]. However, it was the Free State Government of William T Cosgrave who actually instigated a physical customs border in Ireland. Against the wishes of the PM of Northern Ireland, Sir James Craig, Edward Carson, the British Government and much of the Dublin business community, a new customs border was established on 1 April 1924[7]. The thinking behind this ill-conceived initiative was that it would force the UK authorities to move the border into the Irish Sea. Unlike the situation today, Belfast was the main business centre in Ireland at the time and supplied much of the industrial and consumer goods used throughout the island. When reading the State papers of the day, there is a haunting similarity to some of the false arguments which were recently proposed.

There has been much recrimination, over the years, about the historical role of the Dublin Government, which was perceived among Nationalists in the North, as having abandoned them to the new State of Northern Ireland[8], which was very hostile to their interests. The long history of discrimination in housing and employment against Catholics in the new Northern State; the abolition of proportional representation; the whole gerrymandering of electoral districts to the point where elections at local Government were largely uncontested; as well as the partisan nature of policing, represents a dark stain on the political history of the United Kingdom[9]. It was also a time when the authorities in Dublin did not distinguish themselves, when there was a crying need for an effective reaction to the occurrences, north of the Border.

During this era, the Irish Government was largely ineffective, apart from pointless propaganda campaigns. It was only with the outbreak of the "Troubles" in the late 1960s in Northern Ireland, that the Irish Government, in reality, took an active and hands on approach to the interests of its own citizens in the North.

The Good Friday Agreement transforms the situation

After 30 years of violence and circa 3,500 deaths, countless injuries, both physical and psychological[10], as well as tens of thousands of people passing through the prison system, the GFA brought the "Troubles" to an end and ushered in a period of unprecedented stability. It was overwhelmingly endorsed in referenda, in the North (71%) and the Republic (95%). It can be safely assumed that the GFA would still command a strong majority in both parts of Ireland today.

The beauty of the Agreement is that it allows for huge ambiguity in a conflict which was essentially about identity. Under the terms of the Agreement, Nationalists in Northern Ireland could mentally ignore the border; get their Irish passports in the local Royal Mail Post Office, play in any sport for an Irish team, engage in all Ireland cultural organisations, travel to work across the border daily, etc., and feel part of what has been described as "the Irish Nation". This was psychologically important and greatly ameliorated their sense of alienation from the Northern Ireland State, and to some extent, the State institutions in the Republic.

Unionists in Northern Ireland saw the GFA from a different perspective. They welcomed the end to a violent campaign to remove their home from the United Kingdom and a recognition that Constitutional change could only come through the consent of a majority. They greatly welcomed the stability that the GFA brought. There was also the hope that if Northern Ireland became less of a cold house for Nationalists, then the impetus for a United Ireland among their Catholic neighbours would lessen. It would become a more long-term project, and in the meantime, the communities could live in peace.

The DUP opposed the Agreement in 1998 but accepted it, with some very minor and largely cosmetic changes in the St Andrews Pact 2006[11]. The initial DUP opposition centred on early prisoner releases and also the lack of a firm commitment to paramilitary decommissioning in the GFA. Subsequent events removed these issues. Essentially, the only opposition to the Agreement today lies among fringe groups on the Republican and Unionist extremes.

Because of demographic changes in Northern Ireland, most Nationalists believed that it was only a matter of time until their "side" would achieve the majority position. Their long-term case for reuniting Ireland was further bolstered by the growing prosperity of the Republic and the fact that the Southern State has economically strongly outpaced the North in recent years.[12].

In many regards, both communities in Northern Ireland were content to park the sovereignty issue for the time being. In the meantime, Northern Ireland would be governed in a way outlined in the GFA which gave "parity of esteem" to both aspirations and identities. This would be underpinned by what was reputed to be the toughest anti-discrimination laws in Europe[13].

In any case, the lines of national identity have always been blurred in Ireland, with many Irish people, who regard themselves as British, also proud of their Irishness, and with substantial numbers of Irish people not regarding the English, Welsh and Scots as foreigners since almost all of us have family relations in Britain[14]. The blurring of citizenship and identity in the GFA, which allows people in Northern Ireland to identify themselves as Irish, British or both, as well as the recognition of the close and special relationship between Britain and Ireland, in effect, reflected the reality of the complex situation. The arrival of Brexit threatened to shatter some of these ambiguities.

The EU and the Good Friday Agreement

The Attorney General of Northern Ireland, John Larkin, proffered his opinion that leaving the EU in a Brexit would not have any domestic legal impact on the legislation giving effect to the GFA, namely the Northern Ireland Act (1998)[15]. The issue of whether the North is either inside or outside the EU will not substantially change the terms of the GFA. Despite that view, serious questions must arise about the durability of the Agreement in a new Anglo–Irish relationship, post Brexit. The GFA is more than a dry legal document, it must be viewed in its wider political context. With the UK outside the EU and Ireland inside, there is bound to be a growing divergence in the commonality of the two sovereign Governments' approach in a wide range of areas, relating to the North.

The creation of a new EU/third country boundary between the Republic and Northern Ireland will bring with it a whole series of new challenges, which, without doubt, will throw up unforeseen difficulties which may require some novel solutions. Whether the EU will be amenable to such creative thinking, is a moot point.

While ambiguity is a cornerstone of the GFA, the European Union's approach is in the opposite direction. In the guidelines to its negotiating position at the outset of the Brexit discussions, the EU boldly stated that any arrangements, post Brexit, agreed on the island of Ireland had to "respect the integrity of the Union's Legal Order"[16]. As I indicated earlier this restriction greatly limits the possible range of solutions to all new problems arising. I still find it difficult to understand why the Irish Government accepted this straitjacket at the opening of negotiations. At that time, on a number of occasions, I strongly criticised the Government's decision in the *Sunday Business Post*[17]. I believed then, and still hold the opinion today, that this Red Line inevitably led to much of the impasse in the talks, by restricting the range of possible solutions to the border question.

The EU, which has now been deemed by some as a guardian of the GFA[18], is not actually a party to the Agreement. The EU was not represented at the GFA Talks and essentially played no direct part at the time. It had a much lesser role than the USA, and indeed Canada. There was no EU equivalent to Senator George Mitchell (USA) or General John de Chastelain (Canada). John, along with his wife MaryAnn, subsequently became my family's neighbours and personal friends in Ottawa. The Canadian contribution to the Peace Process is often under reported. Apart from de Chastelain's vital work in the Talks themselves and later on decommissioning of paramilitary weapons, Judge Peter Cory (disputed killings), Judge William Hoyt (Saville Commission), Al Hutchinson (Implementation of the Patten Report and Police Ombudsman), Professor Clifford Sheering of Toronto University (member of the Patten Commission), etc. all played key roles. They had no equivalents from the EU, yet to listen to some Irish Government spokespersons, this is simply ignored. In the European Parliament, Guy Verhofstadt, on 3 October 2017, made the ludicrous claim that it was the EU that had brought peace to Northern Ireland[19].

However, it would be unfair not to record that the President of the EU Commission at the time, Jacques Delors, was genuinely sympathetic and wanted to underline support for the GFA with EU financial assistance, once the two Governments had secured the Agreement[20].

There are scant references to the EU in the GFA and also very little about the border. At one of the final drafting sessions of the GFA in a meeting between Irish and British Government officials at Castle Buildings in Belfast, where I was present, it was suggested in passing that a reference to the EU should be included in the final text. There was no opposition and the following words were inserted in the bilateral relations section, in relation to the two Governments, "Wishing to develop still further the unique relationship between their peoples and the close cooperation between their countries as friendly neighbours and as partners in the European Union."[21]

The Agreement also contains a direct reference to the European Union in the Strand Two section on North/South structures. It identifies relevant EU programmes such as Leader, Interreg, and the Peace Programme, as possible areas for a North/South cross border implementation body[22]. Post Brexit, this section needs to be re-formulated, while maintaining these programmes, possibly on a bilateral basis between Ireland and the UK, with EU assistance.

However, the absence of direct references to the EU in the GFA should be viewed against the context in which the Agreement was concluded. The common membership of the EU was an understood underpinning, and both administrations were working on the basis that our common membership, including membership of the Single Market and the Customs Union, would continue indefinitely. This helped both Governments to offer one of the biggest incentives for Nationalists/ Republicans, namely physical changes on the border. However, in recent times there has been a retrospective attempt to magnify the EU input into the creation of the Agreement. Any reading of the actual text, or contemporary accounts, will show that to be manifestly false.

Disappearance of the physical border

During the discussions in Castle Buildings in 1998 and, especially over the last fortnight of the talks, strenuous efforts were made by the two Governments to get all the parties on board. One of the major attractions of the Agreement to the Nationalist/Republican side was the promise, given in exchanges by the two Governments to the parties, that once the peace was secured and the threat level diminished, there would be no need for any fixed and/or permanent installations along the border. These physical structures, some of which dated back near to the partition of Ireland under the Government of Ireland Act of 1920, were to be dismantled.

The ugly security installations at places such as Cloghogue, Aughnacloy, Rosslea, the Camel's Hump in Strabane, etc., would be removed from the landscape[23]. It was a huge prize for the communities on both sides of the border. For the first time since the early twentieth century, people and goods could transverse that line without any fear of official blockages. This was psychologically very important. It reinforced the Nationalist feeling of being part of the "Irish Nation", while greatly strengthening the peace process. It showed that positive engagement and dialogue worked. It was also welcomed by the vast bulk of Unionists, especially those who lived in border areas, as a sign of the growing stability the Peace Process had brought. The new era, post GFA, of open and frictionless travel was hugely welcomed. The old forts, with their military hardware on display, had a chilling effect on many who travelled between the two jurisdictions in Ireland. Nobody mourned their passing.

Therefore, any idea of going back to the "bad old days" of border checks caused an immediate adverse reaction. This is the main reason why both the British and Irish Governments have been very determined, since the outset, to avoid any return. Therefore, huge efforts were made throughout the Brexit negotiations to ensure that the historic achievement of the GFA in eradicating the physical border was maintained. This was a shared objective of all parties and the Withdrawal Agreement (Mark 2) ensured this by the highly controversial mechanism of treating Northern Ireland as different to the rest of the UK. However, these arrangements would hopefully never come into operation and would be superseded by the future trade pact.

This was one of the many differences between the GFA and the earlier Sunningdale Agreement which of course, among other things, did not deliver an end to border restrictions. For communities, all along the border, it was a boom. The Governments had quickly followed up on their promises and the forts were removed and many of the cross-border roads, which had been sealed off during the Troubles, reopened, including the iconic Aghalane Bridge, which was renamed in honour of the Chairman of the Good Friday Talks, ex-US Senator George Mitchell[24].

One of the most tedious arguments, which is occasionally aired, is that the GFA is only the old Sunningdale Agreement, Mark 2[25]. This is a clever political slogan but even the most cursory examination of the Sunningdale Accord (1973) and the later Anglo-Irish Agreement (1985), shows this line of approach to be bogus, as the GFA is a much more comprehensive and inclusive set of arrangements, compared to any of the earlier attempts at a settlement.

The GFA includes fundamental policing reform; changes to the administration of justice; a Constitutional route to the reunification of Ireland; changes to the Irish Constitution and the Government of Ireland Act; new fair employment commitments; a human rights section, supported by new human rights commissions; new all island broadcasting commitments; new Irish language supports including in the education area; a new sensitivity to national symbols and emblems, based on parity of esteem; new commitments to integrated education, shared housing and communal reconciliation; release of prisoners; etc. It would require a very long list to tabulate fully the differences with the earlier attempts at a settlement. It was also, of course, different in another more fundamental way, namely it was much more successful in bringing conflict to an end.

The GFA institutions on Life Support

While the mechanisms, established by the GFA, worked well in the initial years, when there was strong political commitment and direct engagement by the two Governments, this did not continue after changes of administration in both Dublin and London. Neglect set in and in recent years the GFA has not been in rude good health. While all and sundry regularly proclaimed their commitment to preserving the Agreement, the reality is that the actions of the two Governments pointed in the complete opposite direction.

The Irish Government, throughout much of the Brexit negotiations, temporarily jettisoned its responsibilities to the Agreement to prioritise its relations with Brussels. It has not always lived up to its commitments to accept the principle of consent; treat both communities with parity of esteem; and be a partner and mutually supportive of its neighbour and ally Britain. We also failed to live up to our commitment in the GFA to discuss all matters of bilateral interest by referring London to Brussels, when they first looked for formal discussions with us on the border arrangements, post Brexit[26]. The late conversion of Taoiseach Leo Varadkar to direct talks with the British Government in the Cheshire meeting, showed just how perverse the earlier policy of leaving everything to Brussels was. As in some other areas, the U-Turn by the Taoiseach was left unchallenged by the Irish media.

The British Government abandoned all semblance of neutrality and parity of esteem by entering into a political alliance with the Democratic Unionist Party. It directly violated the undertaking in the GFA that in relation to the North "the power of the sovereign Government with jurisdiction there shall be exercised with rigorous impartiality." Whatever it may have stated publicly about treating both communities and traditions in the North equally, its arrangements with the DUP in Westminster had, in essence, given that party a veto over British Government policy in the North for two years. It would be difficult to design a bigger breach of the spirit of the GFA. The rupture of relations between the Johnson administration and the DUP owed more to political expedience than a desire to return to the fundamentals of the GFA.

The present situation is the culmination of years of neglect by London and Dublin. During the period of Enda Kenny as Taoiseach, the Dublin political establishment, with a small number of honourable exceptions, ignored the North. The then Taoiseach's visits were extremely rare and confined to a few set pieces such as meeting the Confederation of British Industry (CBI), etc., occasions where there was almost no chance of meeting any ordinary members of the public. Gone were the days when former Taoisigh such as Albert Reynolds, Brian Cowen and Bertie Ahern travelled extensively in the North. They were personally known and had a wide range of contacts, among all shades of opinion, throughout the six counties. The Irish Government of Enda Kenny, in their very limited engagement in Northern Ireland, seemed obsessed in trying to build links to the DUP and ignore the Nationalist community, and especially the main Nationalist Party, Sinn Féin. This left Dublin in a very weak position when the Brexit storm hit. They had very little ability to influence events.

Even representatives of Loyalist organisations were quietly bemoaning the lack of any meaningful Dublin engagement. This view was widely shared across political opinion in the North. It would be only fair to acknowledge that both Taoiseach Leo Varadkar and his deputy, Simon Coveney, have tried to pull back the situation somewhat. The neglect of the North by the Irish Government was equalled by the London administration which gave Northern Ireland very little attention, taking the line that the GFA had "sorted" the problem. Meanwhile, the bilateral structures of the GFA were allowed to wither away[27]. Martin McGuinness once claimed he met US President Obama as often as he had met Prime Minister Cameron, despite being in effect co-leader of the Northern Ireland's administration.

At a recent conference to mark the twentieth anniversary of the signing of the GFA, organized by Yale academic Dr Bonnie Weir, which I attended, a former senior US official, who did outstanding work in the North, shook his head and said that "the GFA is dead." The conference was taking place in the hallowed halls of Yale University in Connecticut and featured several who were involved in the original negotiations in 1998[28]. He intimated that events such as that in Yale were essentially requiems for that historic achievement.

However, his claim has merit.

The Agreement at its core is a bilateral arrangement between the two sovereign States. Today the London–Dublin axis has been in tatters for a number of years and the trust that is so needed, especially at head of Government level, has been sadly lacking.

Another central element of the Agreement was the establishment of a local administration in Stormont, which would be representative of the whole community in the North and would allow the transference of as much power as possible to Belfast, thus ameliorating somewhat the sharp differences in national allegiances. The absence of partnership Government in the North lasted three years and undermined confidence in the political institutions. However, the local electoral setbacks for both the DUP and Sinn Féin undoubtably acted as a spur for both parties to get Stormont up and running and avoid a new Assembly election. Meanwhile, reconciliation in Northern Ireland has taken a big knock and all sides agree that there is greater communal division than for a considerable time[29].

The North South Ministerial Council was mothballed, with the Implementation Bodies, existing only on a care and maintenance basis for the three years of the impasse, thus adding to the general disillusionment with the political process. Even areas, such as policing, have deteriorated as the percentage of Catholics in the PSNI has fallen consistently in recent times. Reports indicate that in the latest recruitment intakes, only one in five new recruits have come from the Catholic side of the communal divide[30]. On the ground, there are no PSNI officers today living on the City Side in Derry or in the large Nationalist areas of West Belfast. A drive past Grosvenor Road or Woodburn police stations in Belfast is like a journey back in time, as they are as heavily fortified now as during the Troubles. We need to break the spiral downwards. Low level paramilitary violence has gradually crept back into trouble spots in both Republican and Loyalist communities.

Of course, the withering away of the GFA cannot be ascribed as being due to Brexit alone, but it has certainly made a bad situation much worse. It is difficult to see Dublin moving away from its alliance with Brussels in the short to medium term and giving the London/Dublin relationship the importance of previous years. There is not much confidence that the Johnson administration in London will seriously engage on Irish matters, unlike the Major and Blair Governments but hopefully we will be pleasantly surprised.

GFA used as a weapon

The Brexit discussions were characterised by a very aggressive approach by the EU, led by Michel Barnier of the Commission. They were a formidable opponent with considerable resources at their disposal. The EU approach was tough, professional and unbending. On the British side, the contrast was stark. The performance of former Prime Minister, Theresa May, and her team of civil servants was very poor. Mrs May was very tentative and tried to appease Brussels. The difference in approach of the two teams was sharpest in matters relating to the Irish border.

The issue of Ireland and the GFA had been rarely mentioned during the Brexit Referendum campaign. This was because both sides expected the vote to be a rejection of the Brexit proposal. There was also a huge lack of appreciation among Brexiteers of the implications of Brexit on the delicate political and security balance in Ireland that the GFA had brought about[31].

Once the result was known and the dreary steeples of south west Ulster emerged yet again from the Brexit fog, the divisions in Ireland were seized upon for political gain by elements in London and Brussels. Many in these two capitals, and indeed in Dublin also, were unwilling to accept the outcome of the referendum. This alliance soon realised that Ireland and the GFA could be used as a very effective weapon to frustrate the democratic outcome.

It is somewhat ironic that an Irish Government would work hand in glove with elements of the British establishment, including the House of Lords[32], to undermine a demand for greater independence for a Parliament in our neighbouring island. The betrayal of Parnell and later John Redmond and his Irish Parliamentary Party by a similar coalition of forces in London, evoked no reflection or sense of irony among Government figures in Dublin.

The question of a "frictionless" border was avidly seized upon by Brussels, as a way of putting pressure on the British Government and hopefully to make the exit process so difficult and messy that the British would be forced to hold a second referendum. If this was not possible, the Irish border issue would be extremely useful in putting the British on the back foot in the discussions, especially on the issue of a financial settlement. With former Remainers, under Theresa May, in charge of the British side of the discussions, and extremely anxious, perhaps almost desperate, to reach an accommodation with the EU on the terms of the divorce settlement and transitional arrangements, the UK agreed to the following in the December 2017 Agreement:

> In the absence of agreed solutions, the United Kingdom will maintain full alignment with those rules of the Internal Market and the Customs Union which, now or in the future, support North-South cooperation, the all island economy and the protection of the 1998 Agreement[33].

EU negotiators maintained that this meant that in the absence of any other agreed solution, Northern Ireland would remain in the Customs Union and Single Market when the rest of the UK departed the EU, described as the NI Backstop option by the Irish Government. This would have essentially passed over the economic management of the area to Brussels. While the EU and Irish Government's interpretation of the meaning of alignment almost certainly represented some overreach in World Trade Organisation (WTO) terms[34], the UK Government, possibly suffering from buyer's regret, heavily disputed this interpretation. Even more crucially, it was not acceptable to political parties in Westminster. As a compromise, the British extended the Backstop from the North to include the whole of the United Kingdom[35]. This was an ideal outcome for those, who never wanted Brexit, as it kept the UK within the economic orbit of Brussels, possibly indefinitely.

This concept, namely the Backstop, bedevilled the Brexit process for two years. Its inclusion in the Withdrawal Agreement of November 2018 ensured that the British Government suffered the biggest ever defeat recorded in its Parliamentary history. It went down by 230 votes on 15 January 2019[36] when seeking Parliamentary approval for that Agreement. It was rejected heavily on two further occasions by the House of Commons[37]. The fourth attempt to bring it back essentially killed off the ailing May administration.

In Dublin, the scale of the 230-vote defeat was a huge shock. It finally brought home to those charged with developing a Brexit Policy that their line of approach was in serious danger of failing. There was now a strong possibility, that the not-an-inch policy on the Backstop would not only not succeed but risked plunging the UK into No Deal territory. There was immediate confusion internally but a defiant and uncompromising public stance. It was described by an insider in Dublin to me as like a drenching in freezing water.

The EU, with the strong support of the Irish Government, had staked everything on forcing the British Government to back down and accept a wholly unsatisfactory withdrawal settlement. They may have been encouraged by the weakness and duplicity of the official British negotiators. Theresa May, a former opponent of Brexit, would have happily wrapped up a deal on the basis of the one-sided Withdrawal Agreement. However, it was not within Mrs May's power to deliver. The British Parliament was never going to agree to arrangements, which gave power to each of the 27 remaining EU countries individually, to veto indefinitely the British departure from the hated Backstop, unless the UK conceded to their demands.

The election of Boris Johnson as Prime Minister in London changed the calculations. Ireland then was faced with a situation where if it dug in and refused to compromise, it could have ended up suffering all the disadvantages associated with a messy Brexit, including a hard border on the island of Ireland, imposed by Brussels. Leo Varadkar did not want to go down in history as the man who rebuilt the border for the EU. In addition, there would be huge animosity against Ireland in Britain as the root cause of the failure of the Brexit discussions and this sentiment might also have arisen in some capitals in mainland Europe. Already the EU solidarity was beginning to crack[38].

The GFA, which the EU and Dublin decided to wield against

Britain in the Backstop, turned out to be a double-edged implement, potentially inflicting damage on both parties. I had constantly pointed out from the beginning that hitching our wagon to the Backstop was a major error strategically[39]. Fortunately, the Irish Government, late in the day, realised that their strategy would not work and undertook a radical U-turn.

Up to that point, the Irish Taoiseach Leo Varadkar had been a loyal son of Brussels throughout the Brexit negotiations. He was seen in Ireland and in the EU capitals as a valuable and effective ally of the Commission and in particular Jean-Claude Junker and Michel Barnier. In contrast among Brexiteers in Britain, Varadkar and his chief lieutenant Simon Coveney, have shouldered much of the blame for the intransigence and arrogance, which was associated with the EU. Polls in the UK consistently showed that Varadkar was blamed by many for the long and frustrating impasse[40].

Varadkar and Coveney were happy to go along with that role, coupling it with a hefty dose of old-fashioned Anglophobia and initially this was enthusiastically supported by the Irish electorate. Their tough stance and determined speeches sounded good and showed up remarkably well in comparison with the shambles and indecision of the Theresa May Government. There was widespread belief in Dublin at that time that Brexit was either going to be reversed or at worst, would result in a BRINO (Brexit in Name Only). After all, the EU had been successful in either ignoring or reversing so many referenda in the past, including in Ireland. The crushing defeats of Mrs May's Withdrawal Agreement in the House of Commons was the first wake up call.

Subsequently, the results of the local elections in England and later the European elections in summer 2019 brought a change of leadership in London and with it, the cold realisation in Dublin that the new Prime Minister Boris Johnson was prepared to leave the EU, with or without a deal. He was determined to deliver on the result of the referendum.

The prospect of a hard border on the island of Ireland, and huge trading difficulties with Ireland's most important economic and strategic partner, the UK, suddenly loomed large on the horizon. Ireland had done very little credible preparation for a Hard Brexit, viewing it as only a remote possibility. Several of the main ports in the Republic were years away from being ready for a No Deal. Events had taken a sudden turn for the worse.

The public mood began to change, and the opinion polls started to reflect that unease. Confidence in Varadkar's handling of Brexit slipped down to only 41%,[41] well below the level he had achieved a year before. His Fine Gael party, in turn, also saw its polling numbers beginning to reflect a slow and persistent slide. Heading a minority Government and with four tricky byelections on the horizon, there was an urgent need to change course. It was becoming clear that the Irish Government could be an early casualty of a No Deal Brexit, something that their previous actions had helped to make more likely.

Varadkar then reversed gear and went to Cheshire for direct and productive talks with the Prime Minister, something he and other EU leaders had persistently described as out of the question. Apart from tearing up the embargo on direct negotiations, the sacrosanct Withdrawal Agreement was suddenly open to change, and the Backstop was greatly modified. In addition, there is no doubt, but that Johnson's amiable personality and openness, in marked contrast to the rigidity of May, made the job much easier for Varadkar. After the Varadkar–Johnson meeting, there was a temporary surge in support for the Taoiseach and his Fine Gael Party. The achievement of a deal which avoided a hard border and allowed for a smooth withdrawal was hugely popular in the Republic, even if it had no real impact on the country's subsequent general election in February 2020, which Varadkar lost heavily.

Varadkar played a constructive and supportive role in helping Johnson secure a more acceptable withdrawal Deal. However, without the threat of a No Deal, neither Varadkar nor the EU would have moved an inch. They would have had no incentive to do so. However, in retrospect, it is clear that the use of the GFA as a weapon had retarded progress for two years.

Effect of the Brexit and the Backstop controversy in the North

The present debate in Ireland has become intertwined in the public mind with a spat with our old adversary, Britain. In such circumstances, it is inevitable that there is pressure to "don the green jersey." This was accentuated in the North where attitudes were increasingly split on traditional lines on Brexit. The horrific killing of journalist, Lyra McKee, made the search for a political settlement more urgent but the gap between the two main parties remained very wide[42]. The British Government's alliance with the DUP was hugely damaging to the notion of an unbiased guardianship of the process by London. It greatly fermented Nationalist discomfort with the present Constitutional arrangements and strengthened the case for a United Ireland, not only among the Catholic community but more widely[43].

The failure of any of the major British Parties to give any real consideration of the potential effect of Brexit on Northern Ireland during the referendum demonstrated to Nationalists again that there is very little regard for the interests of Ireland, North or South, in the British Parliament. Better to cut remaining ties.

On the Unionist side, the Brexit process has been particularly painful. There was dismay at the Irish Government's role as cheer leader for the intransigence of Brussels, even when it was self-evidently against the Irish national interest. Former DUP MP for South Belfast, Emma Little Pengelly, tweeted, "Sad that the behaviour of the Irish Government has so fundamentally fractured the carefully built relationships with unionists – the destruction of which will be so very hard to heal. I have never known a time where it has been so broken. A sad testimony to the last 21 years."[44]

While some pro-EU Unionists initially may have been considering a more tolerant view of a future in a new political union on the island of Ireland, the harshness of Dublin and Brussels represented a blow to those seeking a new beginning[45].

The Irish Government, through the Irish Constitution, is committed to the promotion of Irish Unity[46]. Yet any such political settlement would bring in hundreds of thousands of citizens who are very pro-British. They would expect their attachment to the neighbouring island to be reflected in any new Irish Governmental structures and approach. The failure of the Irish Government to act as a partner and friend of the UK, as promised in the GFA, would appear to be counter intuitive to aspirations of bringing about reconciliation and the peaceful unity of Ireland.

The Irish Government's championing of the Backstop and a possible customs border in the Irish Sea between Northern Ireland and Britain, while vigorously ruling it out on the land, smacked of double standards[47]. It showed scant regard for the concept of parity of esteem. Irish Foreign Minister Simon Coveney's enthusiasm for technology in policing a maritime boundary but rejecting outright its use on the land, again demonstrated an alarming level of hypocrisy[48]. How could Unionists trust their future and those of their children to a Government which was so overtly insensitive to their interests? As Hillaire Belloc's poem "Jim" outlined:

And always keep a hold of nurse

For fear of finding something worse

Hence, for Unionists it might be a lot safer to stick with London than to take on trust the untested promises of Dublin. In the circumstances, the Unionist community were very willing to place their confidence in the newly elected Boris Johnson as Prime Minister.

However, that trust was soon shown to be misplaced. The renegotiated Withdrawal Agreement of 17 October 2019 contained a bitter shock for the Unionist community and in particular the DUP. Johnson secured a large number of concessions from the EU on the Backstop but had to concede keeping Northern Ireland in a special relationship with the EU to maintain a free and frictionless border on land. Even though this was part of the Withdrawal Agreement and could be superseded by an eventual comprehensive free trade agreement, the DUP reacted with fury. They again felt betrayed by their erstwhile allies in London.

The level of the resultant alienation of that community was a dangerous and unwelcome by-product of Brexit. Their hostile reaction helped to give Varadkar cover for what was a major change in policy on the Backstop.

The British general election in December 2019 was a very poor outcome for Unionists with the loss of the North and South Belfast seats to Nationalist candidates. In almost every constituency there was a fall in the Unionist vote. This exasperated the feeling within the Loyalist community that events were taking a turn against their interests.

For the Nationalist Community in the North, the strong pro-EU stance of Leo Varadkar has been very popular, especially as many felt betrayed by Theresa May's alliance with the DUP. Hence, the Taoiseach's public assurance to Irish Nationalists in the North that "There will be no hard border on our island. You will never again be left behind by an Irish Government"[49] was hugely popular among that community.

However, the re-election of Boris Johnson as British Prime Minister, with a huge majority, has changed the equation. The achievement of Brexit has essentially ended the hopes of Irish Nationalists in the North of staying in the EU. Some form of border in Ireland now threatens the Peace, even if the EU is the likely party demanding it.

By their actions, neither Dublin nor London were contributing to reconciliation in Northern Ireland.

Any Irish Government seeking to bring about unity with the North will need the active support of the British Government. The UK has given that commitment in the context of the GFA, should the proposal be endorsed by referenda in both jurisdictions in Ireland[50]. This undertaking was given during a period of unprecedented good relations between Dublin and London. Each country was sure their partner was very favourably disposed to the other. That Dublin–London relationship is now in shreds and shows little sign of reviving. It was a very short-sighted policy by Dublin to jettison the new beginning envisaged in the GFA in order to curry favour with Brussels. Also, the British Government alliance with the DUP was hugely damaging for those who wanted to see the Constitutional position become less contentious.

The absence of a functioning Executive in Belfast during crucial periods of the Brexit negotiations has been cited as a major drawback for the area. However, this is not supported by the evidence. Neither the Scottish nor Welsh administrations would claim that they had any major influence on the direction and content of the Brexit policy of the UK. In addition, on 24 January 2017, the British Supreme Court unanimously rejected the claim that the UK central Government needed the consent of Belfast, Cardiff and Edinburgh to trigger Article 50. The President of the Court Lord Neuberger stated:

On devolution issues, the court unanimously rules that UK Ministers are not legally compelled to consult the devolved administrations before triggering Article 50. The devolution statutes were enacted on the assumption that the UK be a member of the European Union, but do not require it. Relations with the EU are a matter for the UK Government[51].

A much stronger argument could be made that the absence of the seven Sinn Féin MPs from Westminster, during the height of the Brexit controversy in the House of Commons, represented a much more important lost channel of influence. However, it has to be admitted that any abandonment of abstentionism by Sinn Féin would represent a huge about-turn, after its strong endorsement by the Nationalist electorate at the 2017 Westminster election. The return of a Conservative Government in the December 2019 election with a massive majority has made that argument much less relevant.

Brexit and the Dissidents

There has been much discussion of the effect of Brexit on the level of paramilitary activity on the island of Ireland but especially in the sensitive border areas. Any significant resumption of armed activities, by what has been generically termed Dissidents, clearly has the potential to destabilise the political and security situation, especially if the final outcome failed to preserve the frictionless frontier.

Therefore, it was no wonder that groups, closely associated with Dissident Republicans welcomed the Brexit vote[52], along with some hard-line Unionists who wished to see the changes made under the GFA reversed. The former Chief Constable of the PSNI, Sir Hugh Orde, said that re-imposition of border controls would "embolden" the Dissidents. He wrote in the *Irish Times*:

The vision of Border controls plays into the hands of those who have yet to realise the armed struggle is over. I remember just how important "demilitarization" was in terms of policing and the Agreement. The removal of the towers along the Border was a significant event. It represented a shift to civilian policing, and a recognition that significant political achievements had created the conditions that allowed it to happen. Any step backwards is a really bad idea[53].

The re-imposition of a border would, in the words of former British Prime Minister Tony Blair, be a "disaster"[54]. The former Irish Minister for Foreign Affairs, and also ex-Minister for Justice, Dermot Ahern, who lives close to the border, also described in hearings in the Irish Senate the likely prospect of border controls as "terrible for Ireland" and for the local people in county Louth on the southern side of the border[55].

Any difference in tariff rates on either side of the frontier will inevitably lead to smuggling. There is already a big problem with diesel. The main beneficiaries of any renewal of smuggling will be organised criminal elements. These elements often have strong links with paramilitary organisations.

Former Assistant Chief Constable of the PSNI and widely respected across both communities, Peter Sheridan, explained a probable scenario in the event of a hard border in the seminar at Yale University. Firstly, custom posts are erected, they will inevitably become targets for local paramilitaries. The police will have to investigate and provide some protection. However, heavily armed Republican groups would then attack the police. In order to provide the necessary back up for the police, the British Army would be needed and in no time, the situation could revert to conditions similar to the pre-GFA days.

Brexit is happening as the security situation in areas of the North appears to be entering a challenging phase, especially around Derry and Strabane. The activities, both political and paramilitary, of groups which have been associated with the Republican Dissidents, have become more prominent. Large-scale rioting, the killing of the journalist Lyra McKee and the election of councillor Gary Donnelly at the head of the poll in the Moor electoral area of Derry[56], are demonstrations of their increasing impact. It also shows that there is a growing body of opinion in some areas which has become disenchanted with the mainstream Republican leadership and possibly with the overall Peace Process.

The classic reaction of the Irish Government and the political establishment in both the Republic and the North is to dismiss these groups as wholly unrepresentative of the wider community and essentially outcasts who should be shunned and confined to the margins of any civilised society. That would be a mistake and would only repeat the errors of yesteryear when dealing with the gradual rise of Sinn Féin. The language used in demonising the Dissidents is hauntingly familiar with that which was used during previous times on Gerry Adams, Martin McGuinness, etc.

Any visit to Creggan or Shantallow shows that there are serious issues of social alienation which are simply not being addressed. Of course, these problems are by no means unique to these areas but there are specific elements present there which, if left unaddressed, will pose strong challenges to the body politic in Ireland. It is simply not good enough to state that democratically elected politicians from these areas are beyond the Pale.

While the Dissidents have the intent to cause mayhem, so far, they have lacked the military capacity but more importantly large-scale public support for an effective campaign. They wait for that to change.

The Army Council of the largest Dissident group, the New IRA, was reported in the Irish Edition of the *Sunday Times*, as meeting with journalist John Mooney. They outlined their position on Brexit.

> Brexit is an English construct devised by the Tory party. There is an awakening of issues concerning the presence of the border now. Brexit has forced the IRA to refocus and has underlined how Ireland remains partitioned. It's put the border on the agenda again. We would be foolish not to capitalize on the fallout when it happens[57].

The Loyalist paramilitaries are but a pale shadow of the big organizations which carried so much menace in the early parts of the Troubles. It is now very clear that the UVF, UDA, Red Hand Commandos, LVF, etc. were all greatly assisted by some elements in the British Security Services, through a process known as collusion. Their capacity to carry out independent action may be fairly limited but that does not mean that they will remain ineffective in the longer run. The sense of betrayal in the Unionist community in the wake of the Johnson/EU Withdrawal

Agreement means that there is fertile ground on which the Loyalist groups can re-emerge as a threat.

While the revival of paramilitarism is a danger, a much more serious problem long term would be the alienation of whole communities and the potential for civil disturbances, should the EU force the Irish Government into erecting a hard border, or the Unionist community felt that the British Government had totally abandoned them.

Way forward

It is clear that Brexit has inflicted severe damage to the cohesion of society in the North of Ireland. Both Governments now need to work closely together to ensure that the Peace Process itself is maintained and to reassure those, in both communities, who feel excluded from, and threatened by, the changes which Brexit will bring.

In addition, both Governments need to reach across the political divide in the North to those whom they have antagonised; namely the British Government need to initiate some confidence building measures with Nationalists, while the Irish Government need to accept that some of their actions and rhetoric in Brexit has been unwise and counterproductive. They need to be cognisant that they should respect the parity of esteem concept.

All parties on the island of Ireland will need a fresh start after the travails of Brexit.

In addition, there is probably a need for a new Agreement, which should dispense with some of the mechanisms in the GFA, relating to the Northern Ireland Assembly which has caused that body to be dysfunctional. This might include reforming the Petition of Concern, which has allowed one-third of the Assembly to block all progressive reforms, despite the majority wanting to modernise. It might also include the dispensing with the automatic entitlement to Ministerial positions, depending on party strength. It is probably time to allow for voluntary coalition formation, provided any new administration had significant cross community support. That might be a start in a reconciliation process.

It is also clear that the Brexit process has brought the issue of reunification much more to the fore in Ireland and raised the possibility of a unity referendum. In that context, there is an urgent need for all parties on the island of Ireland to begin to spell out what that would entail in practical matters. The example of Brexit, where major Constitutional changes resulted from a referendum outcome and where very little consideration or planning was done for such a consequence, is a seminal warning. Because the outcome may be uncomfortable for certain groups and vested interests, this is no excuse for failing to prepare for such a possible scenario.

References

1. Despite popular belief that the individual party leaders in Northern Ireland signed the GFA, this is untrue, only PM Blair and Taoiseach Ahern's signature are on the original. The many copies of the GFA signed by negotiators are simply personal souvenirs.

2. David Phinnemore and Dr Katy Hayward, Queen's University Belfast "*UK Withdrawal (Brexit) and the GFA*". Available to on the European Parliament website and from the Queen's Brexit Resource Guide.

3. Gerry Moriarty "*David Trimble formally begins legal challenge to the Backstop*". Irish Times, 12 February 2019. *https://www.irishtimes.com/news/ireland/irish-news/david-trimble-formally-begins-legal-challenge-to-backstop-1.3791713*. Retrieved 13 December 2019.

4. David McKittrick. "*After the deluge, dreary steeples still stand their disputed ground*". Irish Independent 25 September 2001. *https://www.independent.ie/irish-news/after-the-deluge-dreary-steeples-still-stand-their-disputed-ground-26075129.html*. Retrieved 13 December 2019

5. "*introduction to the Cahir Healy Papers*" Page 7 Public Records Office of Northern Ireland, Nov 2007. Retrieved 29 April 2019

6. Notice by the Commissioners of Customs and Excise, "*Traffic with the Irish Free State*" March 1923. Copy displayed in the Ulster Museum, Stranmillis Belfast

7. Documents on Irish Foreign Policy, Volume 2 Page 73

8. Eamonn Phoenix "*South abandoned North says ex Chaplain*". Irish News, Belfast, 4 November 2014, *http://www.irishnews.com/opinion/2014/11/04/news/south-abandoned-north-says-ex-chaplain-107040/*. Retrieved 30 April 2019

9. Frank Gallagher "*The Indivisible Island*" p 196–265

10. McKittrick David, Kelters Seamus, Feeney Brian, Chris Thornton and David McVea *Lost Lives: The Stories of the Men, Women and Children Who Died as a Result of the Northern Ireland Troubles 2001*, Mainstream Publishing

11. Agreement reached in multi-party negotiations held in St Andrews in Fife, Scotland, from 11 October to 13 October 2006, between the two Governments and all the major parties in Northern Ireland, including the Democratic Unionist Party (DUP) and Sinn Féin". Published 16 July 2006 by UK Government

12. Paul Gosling and Pat McArt "*The Economic Impact of an All Island Economy*" self-published March 2018

13. The Fair Employment and Treatment Order 1999.

14. *Through Irish Eyes*. Report on Irish attitudes towards the UK, commissioned by the British Council and British Embassy in Ireland, published 11 February 2004.

15. Joe Watts "*Brexit legal challenge dismissed: Northern Ireland case against EU withdrawal will not be heard*". *The London Independent*, 28 October 2016, https://www.independent.co.uk/news/uk/politics/brexit-legal-challenge-dismissed-northern-ireland-article-50-case-eu-withdrawal-not-heard-latest-a7384386.html Retrieved 1 May 2019.

16. European Council (Article 50) Guidelines for Brexit Negotiations, section 11. Published by the European Union 29/April 2017

17. Ray Bassett, "*Mind the gap between the Brexit 'backstop' and our national interest*", *Sunday Business Post*, 5 May 2018. *https://www.businesspost.ie/insight/mind-the-gap-between-the-brexit-backstop-and-our-national-interest-2f4cc9e7*. Retrieved 13 December 2019

18. Martina Anderson "*Anderson reminds Barnier of Mandate to protect GFA*" *Derry Daily* 16 November 2017. *https://www.derrydaily.net/2017/11/16/anderson-reminds-barnier-of-mandate-to-protect-good-friday-agreement/*. Retrieved 30 April 2019.

19. *https://www.bing.com/videos/search?q=%2c+guy+verhofstadt+on+3+october+2017+peace+northern+ireland&view=detail&mid=1A0048E6C54D7200B73C1A0048E6C54D7200B73C&FORM=VIRE*. Retrieved 14 December 2019

20. Paul Gosling "*Cementing Northern Ireland's Peace*" *www.paulgosling.net/2016/08/cementing-northern-irelands-peace. R*etrieved 1 May 2019

21. GFA, 1998, "*Agreement between the Government of Great Britain and Northern Ireland and the Government of Ireland*", 3rd paragraph. Published by the Irish Government

22. Strand 2 of the GFA, paragraph 17 and section 8 of the Annex of Strand 2.

23. Ray Bassett *After Brexit, will Ireland be next to Exit?* p 26. Policy Exchange London, 2017

24. Theresa Judge "*A bridge to close the gap and open up a town*" Irish Times, 12 February 1999, *https://www.irishtimes.com/news/a-bridge-to-close-the-gap-and-open-up-a-town-1.151821*. retrieved 1 May 2019.

25. Thomas Hennessey" *Slow learners'? Comparing the Sunningdale Agreement and the Belfast/GFA*" *oxfordindex.oup.com/view/10.7228/Manchester*. Retrieved 1 May 2019

26. Kevin Doyle "*Coveney rules out 'bilateral talks' with the UK on Border*" *Irish Independent* 5 March 2018, *https://www.independent.ie/business/brexit/coveney-rules-out-bilateral-talks-with-the-uk-on-border-36668993.html*. Retrieved 1 May 2019

27. Duncan Morrow "*Playing with Fire; Brexit and the Decay of the GFA.*" *https://blogs.lse.ac.uk/brexit/2018/08/01/playing-with-fire-brexit*. Retrieved 1 May 2019

28. *Twenty Years of Peace Conference*, MacMillan Centre, Yale University, 30 November 2018, *https://20yop.yale.edu/*. Retrieved 19 Nov 2019

29. Lisa O'Carroll *"Brexit threatens Northern Irish peace, academic study finds"* The Guardian 14 September 2018, *https://www.theguardian.com/uk-news/2018/sep/14/brexit-threatens-northern-irish-peace*. Retrieved 1 May 2019

30. Gerry Moriarty *"Four out of five PSNI recruits are from Protestant community"* Irish Times, 1 October 2018, *https://www.irishtimes.com/news/ireland/irish-news/four-out-of-five-psni-recruits-are-from-protestant-community-1.3647672*. Retrieved 1 May 2019

31. William Dunne "*Brexiteer Jacob Rees-Mogg told Bertie Ahern he'd 'no idea what Irish border was*" MSN News, 29 April 2019, *https://www.irishmirror.ie/news/irish-news/politics/bertie-ahern-brexit-jacob-reesmogg-14968080*. Retrieved 1 May 2019

32. Henry Mance and Jim Packard "*UK House of Lords faces backlash over Brexit bill*" Financial Times 9 February 2017, *https://www.ft.com/content/bfc0d1e2-eec1-11e6-930f-061b01e23655*. Retrieved 1 May 2019

33. Joint report from the negotiators of the European Union and the United Kingdom Government on progress during phase 1 of negotiations under Article 50 TEU on the United Kingdom's orderly withdrawal from the European Union, 8 December 2017

34. Anthony Costello *"The UK needs to clarify what 'full regulatory alignment' means before the next phase of the Brexit negotiations" https://blogs.lse.ac.uk/ brexit/ 8 February 2https://uk.reuters.com/article/uk-britain-eu-davis-alignment/britain-says-regulatory-alignment-for-northern-ireland-could-apply-to-whole-uk-after-brexit-idUKKBN1DZ1WR018.* Retrieved 1 May 2019

35. Reuters Report *"Britain says regulatory alignment for Northern Ireland could apply to whole UK after Brexit"* 5 December 2017. Retrieved 1 May 2019

36. Heather Stewart *"May suffers heaviest Parliamentary defeat of a British PM in the democratic era" Guardian* 16 January 2019. *https://www. theguardian.com/politics/2019/jan/15/theresa-may-loses-brexit-deal-vote-by-majority-of-230.* Retrieved 16 December 2019

37. Joe Murphy, Nicholas Cecil and Kate Proctor *"Brexit vote result: Theresa May's Withdrawal Agreement defeated for the Third Time" Evening Standard* 29 March 2019, *https://www.standard.co.uk/news/ politics/theresa-mays-withdrawal-agreement-defeated-for-the-third-time-a4104456.html.* Retrieved 1 May 2019

38. MSN Editorial *"The Brexit crisis is cracking the veneer of solidarity among European leaders"* 9 April 2019, *https://www.msn.com/en-gb/news/ columnists/the-brexit-crisis-is-cracking-the-veneer-of-solidarity-among-european-leaders/ar-BBVLTkn.* Retrieved 1 May 2019

39. Ray Bassett *"Mind the gap between the Brexit 'backstop' and our national interest" Sunday Business Post* 6 May 2018. *https://www.businesspost.ie/ insight/mind-the-gap-between-the-brexit-backstop-and-our-national-interest-2f4cc9e7.* Retrieved 15 December 2019.

40. Laura O'Callaghan *"Varadkar condemned for blocking Brexit in Express poll –'Rejected proposals at every step'* Express UK, 11 October 2019, *https:// www.express.co.uk/news/politics/1189193/brexit-news-boris-johnson-leo-varadkar-no-deal-brussels-poll-results-uk-politics.* Retrieved 30 October 2019.

41. Adam Higgins *"BREXUALLY UNSATISFIED Just 41% of Irish voters happy with Taoiseach Leo Varadkar over Brexit, Irish Sun/Red C poll reveals" Irish Sun* 29 August 2019. *https://www.thesun.ie/news/4454998/*

brexit-ireland-voters-happy-leo-varadkar-red-c-poll.
Retrieved 30 October 2019

42. Gerry Moriarty *"Lyra McKee killing is unlikely to lead to Stormont breakthrough"* Irish Times, 24 April 2019. *https://www.irishtimes.com/ news/ireland/irish-news/lyra-mckee-killing-is-unlikely-to-lead-to-stormont-breakthrough-1.3869714.* Retrieved 15 December 2019.

43. Joey Miller *"The Price of Brexit? Support for United Ireland Soars after Border Talks Chaos".* The Express website 29 December 2019, *https:// www.express.co.uk/news/politics/897526/brexit-irish-border-poll-united-ireland.* Retrieved 29 April 2019

44. Emma Pengelly, tweet on 10 April 2019, E Little Pengelly @ little_pengelly, retrieved on 29 April 2019.

45. Mike Nesbitt former leader of the Ulster Unionist Party, *"Some unionists are now weighing up Irish unity"*, story by Sam McBride, Belfast Newsletter, 26 February 2019. *https://www.newsletter.co.uk/news/mike-nesbitt-some-unionists-are-now-weighing-up-irish-unity-1-8824491.* Retrieved 15 December 2019

46. Attorney General of Ireland Rory Brady 2002-2007, quoted in Section 2 of the Oireachtas (Irish Parliament) Joint Committee on the Implementation of the GFA of the report Brexit & The Future of Ireland, Uniting Ireland and its People in Peace & Prosperity. The report was published August 2017. The rapporteur of the Committee was Senator Mark Daly.

47. Karl McDonald "If Britain insists on a hard border, Ireland wants it to be in the sea" inews 28 July 2017, https://inews.co.uk/news/politics/britain-insists-hard-border-ireland-wants-sea-522260. Retrieved 29 April 2019

48. Jennifer Bray, *"Simon Coveney says technology could help customs checks".* The *Times (Irish edition)*, 18 September 2018, *https://www.thetimes.co.uk/ article/technology-could-help-goods-checks-l2mq87c38.* Retrieved 29 April 2019

49. Statement by Leo Varadkar, 8 December 2017, Fine Gael Website, *https://merrionstreet.ie/en/NewsRoom/News/Statement_on_Brexit_ negotiations_by_the_Taoiseach_Leo_Varadkar_T_D_.html.* Retrieved 29 April 2019

50. GFA, Constitutional Section para (iv)

51. Will Podmore, *Brexit: The Road to Freedom* p 80

52. Claire McNeilly and Laura Larkin *"Violent Dissidents are jumping on the Brexit Bandwagon" Irish Independent* 29 April 2019, *https://www.independent.ie/business/brexit/violent-dissidents-are-jumping-on-brexit-bandwagon-37754721.html.* Retrieved 15 December 2019

53. Hugh Orde *"Return of Border controls after Brexit is inevitable." Irish Times* 31 May 2016. *https://www.irishtimes.com/opinion/hugh-orde-return-of-border-controls-after-brexit-is-inevitable-1.2666251.* Retrieved 15 December 2109.

54. Ajay Nair *"It really would be a disaster: Blair denounces hard Irish border and talks Brexit U-turn" Express*, 12 May 2017, *https://www.express.co.uk/news/uk/803819/Tony-Blair-says-hard-Irish-border-after-Brexit-disaster-radio-northern-ireland-republic.* Retrieved 29 April 2019.

55. Marie Louise McConville *"Dermot Ahern: 'Hard border' Brexit would be 'terrible' for Ireland" Irish News*, Belfast, 6 February 2017, *http://www.irishnews.com/paywall/tsb/irishnews/irishnews/irishnews//news/brexit/2017/02/06/news/dermot-ahern-hard-border-brexit-would-be-terrible-for-ireland-921068/content.html.* Retrieved 29 April 2019

56. Adam Forrest *"Northern Ireland elections: Dissident Republican wins in Derry ward where Lyra McKee was killed"* MSN News 4 May 2019. *https://www.msn.com/en-gb/news/uknews/northern-ireland-elections-dissident-republican-wins-in-derry-ward-where-lyra-mckee-was-killed/ar-AAATMEJ.* Retrieved 31 October 2019

57. John Mooney, *"New IRA says Brexit helps it to recruit" Sunday Times* (Irish Edition) 28 April 2019. *https://www.thetimes.co.uk/article/new-ira-says-brexit-helps-it-to-recruit-vwc6b6l97,* Retrieved on 29 April 2019

PART II

Chapter 5

History of the Irish State's Attitude to European Integration

"As you know, we have hitherto been on the side of voluntary co-operation in Europe rather than of Federation in supra-national authorities."

Michael Rynne, Assistant Secretary Department
of External Affairs, Sept 1953

Early Days

The Irish State's attitude to developments in Europe has been shaped by the country's experiences in history, and particularly by the events that totally changed Ireland between 1914 to 1926. The betrayal of John Redmond on the Home Rule issue, the triumph of Ulster Unionist secessionists, the 1916 Rebellion, the War of Independence, the Anglo-Irish Treaty, the Civil War and the outcome of the Boundary Commission, were monumental events, which deeply scarred the Irish national psyche. These episodes in our past, together, with the enduring legacy of the Great Famine in the nineteenth century, resulted in a deep and enduring suspicion, among the Irish population generally and its Diaspora in the United States, of the British State and, particularly, of politicians in London. Europe was often viewed as a counterweight to British domination of Ireland. This still permeates the background of some Irish attitudes to Brexit.

Ireland emerged from the Anglo-Irish war as a truncated State, which was no longer part of the United Kingdom, but certainly was not fully an independent sovereign entity[1]. Almost 30% of the Irish people were not included in the Free State and the powers that were handed over to the new administration in Dublin, were only those which the British authorities grudgingly agreed to give, all within the umbrella of the British Empire. The six north eastern counties, which formed the new Northern Ireland State, represented the industrial heartland of the country and is reported to have accounted for the bulk of the then Irish national industrial output[2]. The new Irish Free State (Saorstát Éireann) had little in the way of industry outside the capital city of Dublin. The new leaders, Arthur Griffith and Michael Collins, were handed a very difficult task. The Anglo-Irish Treaty was a very unbalanced document and largely forced on the Irish delegation in December 1921, at the threat of a resumption of the Anglo-Irish War[3]. In the end, Collins decided to settle for an unsatisfactory proposal on the basis that it was about the best that could be obtained and crucially, it paved the pathway to further developments. The thorny issue of the partition of Ireland would be greatly ameliorated by a Boundary Commission[4]. The Treaty provisions provoked a bitter civil war and consequent destruction in parts of the new State. Collins himself paid the ultimate price when he was killed by forces opposed to the Treaty.

The Free State was given the largely undefined status of a Dominion; its powers were proscribed as being the same as that of Canada[5]. Collins and Griffith would have been aware that Canada was by far the most independent of the Dominions and ambitious to develop further its independence. Hence the decision to couple the new Irish status with the Federation of Canada. The new Irish State may not have been free but as Collins so wisely observed, "In my opinion it gives us freedom, not the ultimate freedom that all nations desire and develop to, but the freedom to achieve it"[6].

De Valera may have been theoretically right about the limitations of the Irish Free State under the Treaty, de jure, including the imposition of a foreign head of State. However, the new State was lucky to find itself part of a process in the 1920s, when the Dominions began to use any flexibility they had, to push out the boundaries of independent action.

In the new British Commonwealth (it was still the British Commonwealth at that stage), Ireland rapidly found common cause with Canada and South Africa in seeking to establish an international identity for themselves, separate from London. The Canadians, regarded as the senior Dominion, had wrung a number of important concessions out of the British, including the right to join the new League of Nations as a separate voting entity (1920), the right to send a separate diplomatic representative to Washington and the right to sign, in its own name, a treaty with the USA (the Halibut Treaty 1923). These were all ground-breaking developments which were changing the nature of the Dominion status. Hence from the beginning, a separate Irish State was trying to distance itself from the UK, in order to create an international identity and role for itself.

Up to World War One, Dominions were mere extensions of the mother country. For the Great War, Canada had not even bothered to declare war on Germany, it was just taken for granted that Canada, Australia, Newfoundland, etc., would automatically be at war once London declared it. After the appalling losses of WWI, one of the priorities of the Government in Ottawa, under William Mackenzie King, was to establish a much greater independent international role for a Dominion, including the right to remain neutral during armed conflict involving Britain, if the Dominion so wished. In 1922, Canada made it clear that if the UK went to war with Turkey in the Chanak Crisis, it would not participate[7]. This was another major departure from the past.

The new Irish Free State enthusiastically used the Canadian precedents to strike out on its own, although as one can learn from reading the early dispatches of Irish representatives abroad, the host nations had no idea as to what the diplomatic status of these new missions were, and usually consulted the British Embassy to find out if they should provide any formal recognition to the new Irish representatives. The Free State was constantly trying to distance itself from the British overseas. To be fair to the British, they did assist in places like Paris and Washington, in getting these new Irish representatives some official access to the local administrations[8][9]. There was a surprisingly high level of cooperation and coordination between Dublin and Ottawa during the 1920s, as they both made common cause in limiting British control of their international relations.

The new Irish State tried everything in the 1920s, within the limits of the Treaty, to show that we were an independent State, even though the British Privy Council remained the highest court of appeal in

Southern Ireland. Britain retained three ports in the Free State for its own military use. In addition, Westminster still arguably had the right to legislate internally within the 26 counties on domestic matters, as with all Dominions. The British only formally renounced this power in the Statute of Westminster in 1931[10], which is probably the real date of full Irish Independence, coupled with the arrival of Fianna Fáil in power under the formerly untouchable "Irregular" Éamon de Valera. This new Irish Government never accepted the British right to legislate for Southern Ireland. Therefore, unlike the other Dominions, it did not feel the need to formally put the Statute into Irish law. The new Government set about systematically to "dismantle" the Anglo-Irish Treaty. Throughout that period, Ireland was constantly and consciously trying to establish a separate international identity and saw the UK as the main obstacle to achieving that. Early Irish State documents are full of evidence of an obsession with defining Ireland as non-British. However, there was still a very long road to travel.

Even Irish membership of the League of Nations was in a special category, labelled members of the British Empire. The fact that the North's first Premier, Sir James Craig, was keen on Northern Ireland joining the League, shows that membership did not signify Independence. Colonial India was a member also in the 1920s. The British Government, under Lloyd George, vetoed Northern Ireland's ambitions to join the League of Nations[11].

Naturally the desire to make ourselves different to the British, ensured that Ireland would look to Europe for support and recognition. The USA was always going to be closely allied to its Anglo-Saxon sister the UK, for strategic and economic reasons, even if Ireland could exert some influence at the political level in Washington. But many of the European countries had long standing rivalries with the British. As in the Proclamation of the 1916 Rising, Ireland then looked for inspiration to its gallant allies in Europe. It also wanted to emphasise that it was an old European nation. There was a certain naivety about this as the gallant allies, as in the case of the Kaiser, were often only interested in using Irish nationalism for their own ends.

It is also very striking when reading the early Irish State papers, how much the Catholic religion was intertwined with the concept of a separate, non-British, Irish identity at that time. Also, the Irish Government wanted to emphasise its devotion to Catholicism and its links with the Vatican as showing its European credentials.

The desire to interact with other nations in Europe, predated even the formal establishment of an Irish State. In the revolutionary days of 1920–21, Irish emissaries went around Europe seeking support for the new Republic, declared in 1916. Reports of these activities are outlined in the Royal Irish Academy series on Documents on Irish Foreign Policy. They make for very interesting reading and provide an invaluable insight into the attitudes of our early political leaders.

One such report outlines that in 1920, when travelling through Italy, the Sinn Féin representative, Sean T O'Kelly, went to Milan and met a certain Benito Mussolini. In his report of 16 September 1920, Sean T, who later became President of Ireland, wrote:

Mussolini, editor and proprietor of the "Popolo d'Italia" is a thoroughgoing friend and supporter of ours due to the influence of Mme. Vivanti, with whom I called upon him. I thanked him on behalf of the Republic for his support which seemed to please him greatly. He promised to give us the fullest support possible at all times provided we supplied him with the necessary material. Since I saw him, he has published about six different articles from stuff I have sent him, and on each occasion, he has printed his articles under big headlines similar to the samples enclosed[12].

This was just one of a long series of meetings and lobbying in Europe. While sound judgement in the Mussolini case was missing, Europe has always been regarded psychologically by Irish Nationalism as a counterpoint to British influence. This was important for a people who struggled under the rule of a much stronger neighbour for many centuries or subsequently, post 1922, struggled to escape the shadow of our larger neighbouring island. As with cosying up to the future Il Duce, it has sometimes been an unfortunate policy, where the obvious shortcomings and self-interest of our European neighbours are overlooked.

Post-War Period

However, in the immediate post-World War Two period, Ireland was obsessed with one issue, namely the ending of the partition of the country. Local political thought was well away from the European mainstream. The early moves to establish a Europe-wide political and economic arrangement, did not get much of a positive response, even in the agriculture area, from the then Irish Government. The members of the de Valera administration had been part of the struggle for independence and were not going to throw away that hard-won national sovereignty.

Ireland was very isolated in the immediate post-War period, as the victorious Allies had not been sympathetic to the country's neutral position in the War. The presence of hundreds of thousands of Southern Irish volunteers in the Allied armies helped ameliorate some of the wrath but not entirely. In addition, the withdrawal from the Commonwealth by the Fine Gael-led Government in 1949 had the effect of loosening and reducing the State's formerly close connections with the old Dominions, Canada, Australia, New Zealand and South Africa.

Even though it was keen to lessen its political isolation, Ireland was wary of moves to establish a political Federation in western Europe. Neutrality had proven very popular during the war years and there seems to have been little appetite in Government circles for major entanglements with the politics of post-war Europe.

Despite Ireland's lack of interest, the whole landscape of western Europe was undergoing change. Major developments were taking place with the Schuman Declaration 1950, the Treaty of Paris 1951, Messina Conference 1955, Treaty of Rome 1957, etc.

History is littered with examples of attempts to unify Europe under a single authority, stretching back to the Roman Empire. The most recent manifestation is traced back to the post World War Two period. The chief architect is usually recognised as the French diplomat, politician and business figure, Jean Monnet, although Monnet was actively pursuing his ideas well before the Second World War[13]. His Action Committee for a United States of Europe (ACUS) essentially wrote the blueprint of the present Project[14]. Its main features are a supranational authority, not answerable to national Governments or changeable through national elections; the subordination of the traditional Nation States; and the end result of a single Superstate with its own army, diplomatic missions, and the elimination of national differences within the Superstate. That would not be an easy sale to de Valera and his lieutenants.

It is striking that at the meeting in Paris between the Irish and French Foreign Ministers, Frank Aiken and Robert Schuman, on 13 July 1951, the developments which were to shape the future direction of Europe were not even mentioned in the official notes of the meeting[15]. This was shortly after the Treaty of Paris (formally the Treaty establishing the European Coal and Steel Community), was signed on 18 April 1951 between France, West Germany, Italy and the three Benelux countries (Belgium, Luxembourg and the Netherlands). Ireland wanted to discuss the evils of Partition with Schuman, not the Treaty of Paris.

The State papers do show, however, that interest was starting to pick up soon afterwards. Yet while Ireland's representatives began to compile reports on the developments in Europe, the policy remained that the eventual goal of European unification was inconsistent with Ireland's desire for self-determination. However, we did not adopt the dismissive attitude, which has been attributed to the United Kingdom at the time. The British representative on the Spaak Committee (which was tasked with following up on measures agreed at the Messina Conference), Russell Bretherton, an Under-Secretary in the Board of Trade, was reported to have said:

> The future Treaty which you are discussing has no chance of being agreed; if it was agreed, it would have no chance of being ratified, and if it were ratified, it would have no chance of being applied. And if it was applied, it would be totally unacceptable to Britain. You speak of agriculture, which we don't like, of power over customs, which we take exception to, and institutions which frighten us. Monsieur le president, messieurs, au revoir et bonne chance[16].

After giving his short speech, Bretherton is reported to have walked out and there ending Britain's immediate interest in these developments.

Ireland, unlike Britain, was not antagonistic to the developments of closer European integration, just not involved. However, given the overwhelming role that agriculture played in the Irish economy at the time, the country had no option but to be interested in the French proposal for a "Green Pool", which was an embryonic Common Agricultural Policy. The French were moving in the direction of a Monnet style authority to oversee agriculture in western Europe. Again, caution dominated the Irish response.

Later that year, on 16 November 1951 the Irish Cabinet considered the French Government's proposal and recommended that cooperation should be within the existing inter-governmental structures, rather than creating a new supranational body[17]. They were concerned about giving up national sovereignty to an unaccountable agency.

When the issue of the proposed ill-fated European Defence Community (later scuppered by France over concerns over national sovereignty) came up, Ireland used the continuation of partition on the island of Ireland to exclude itself from the proposal. The then Minister for Finance, Seán MacEntee, speaking at the Council of Europe, Ministerial meeting, stated in November 1951:

> We, the members of the Irish delegation, could not associate ourselves with that Resolution nor participate in the discussion of it. The reason which debarred us was stated at the time. I neither desire nor intend to state it again, though it is necessary for me to say that it still remains and that so long as it does remain, our people will not be disposed to range themselves voluntarily or whole-heartedly behind any project for the formation of a European Army, any more that it has permitted us to associate ourselves with the North Atlantic Treaty Organisation[18].

Here again, there was no evidence of a pressing desire from the then Irish Government to become associated with the Defence Community. Unlike today, they had no wish to be at the centre of European developments, particularly if these involved handing over the hard-won powers of self-government to an international quango.

In a memorandum for Government, prepared by the Department of Agriculture on 4 March 1953, that Department puts it plainly: "The Government feel that no Supra-national Authority could give to farming communities the assurance and confidence which they could hope to obtain from national Governments."[19]

At its meeting on 13 March 1953, the Irish Cabinet endorsed the Department's approach and instructed that the Irish Ambassador to Paris, Con Cremin, who was to lead the Irish delegation to a conference to discuss the French proposals, to indicate that Ireland was unable to support the plan[20].

Those seeking to establish a Monnet-style arrangement in Europe were viewed with suspicion in official circles in Dublin. The Assistant Secretary in the Department of External Affairs, Michael Rynne, writing on 25 September 1953, to Ireland's first female ambassador, Josephine McNeill, in the Hague, stated:

> With reference to your letter of 21st September 1953, and enclosure, we feel that it might be on the whole wiser if you found yourself unable, because of other engagements, to accept an invitation to the European Movement Congress to be held from 8th to the 10th October. The body is very "vocal" and publicity conscious, and would certainly advertise the fact of your presence, thus suggesting an interest on the part of the Irish Government in the aims of the Congress, viz., the arousing of public opinion in favour of the creation of a European Political Community. As you know, we have hitherto been on the side of voluntary co-operation in Europe rather than of Federation in supra-national authorities[21].

The Irish authorities were also watching developments in the alternative proposal, mainly pushed by the British, of the establishment of a European Free Trade Area (EFTA), based on intergovernmental cooperation, rather than surrendering powers to a supranational authority. In instructions from the Taoiseach's Department to External Affairs on 26 November 1956, the following was the line to follow, as indicated by the then Taoiseach Eamon de Valera:

> Generally, we should maintain the attitude of reserve, and need not take any very active part in the proceedings of the Working Party. At the same time, we may let it be seen that, in principle, we are favourably rather than unfavourably, disposed towards the idea of a European Free Trade Area. We may also lend support to the devising of escape clauses for countries whose economies

are not fully developed and, particularly, for countries in which an unusually low proportion of productive resources is devoted to manufacturing industry[22].

However, this relatively liberal view was not universally shared within the Government system. At an interdepartmental meeting, 2 January 1957, chaired by the then Secretary of the Department of Finance, T K Whitaker, the issue was discussed as to whether Ireland wanted to be associated with the move towards free trade in Europe, involving a free trade zone, which would also have some association with the Customs and Excise Union of the original six (France, West Germany, Italy, Belgium, Luxembourg and the Netherlands). While External Affairs were in favour, possibly with a long transition period, the Secretary General of Industry and Commerce, J.C.B. MacCarthy opposed the move towards freer trade, stating that:

It would be industrial suicide to tinker with five to ten-year plans if there was anything binding about them…it was unrealistic to talk about revamping our economy if by that was implied the abandonment of industrial production or limitation of production to lines which could subsist without protection[23].

These exchanges are in direct contradiction of the prevailing wisdom in Ireland, namely that the then Taoiseach Éamon de Valera was in favour of protectionism and that his successor, Seán Lemass, the political boss of MacCarthy, was the person who espoused free trade.

When the Cabinet considered the issue on 8 February 1957, the more liberal view prevailed. The Government decision was recorded as follows:

Ireland welcomes the proposal to form a European Free Trade Area. While her attitude to the question of participating in the Area will, as in the case of other countries, be determined in the light of considerations of her own national interests, Ireland views with sympathy this latest movement towards closer association among European countries and wishes the proposal every success[24].

Hence, the official Irish attitude in the 1950s was to favour a gradual move toward greater free trade between European countries, but not at the price of losing sovereignty. Therefore, the EFTA concept was much more attractive than the Monnet-style supranational authority model. However, it should be noted that despite this sympathetic view, Ireland never actually joined EFTA, when it was formally established in 1960. Ireland had wanted a series of derogations for its protected industries and did not get enough assurances to pursue the EFTA route. However, the internal and external environments were about to change radically. The decision on Ireland's future direction was about to be taken out of its hands.

Change of Heart on Europe

Firstly, after dominating the political scene for many decades, the towering figure and long-time Taoiseach Éamon de Valera, decided to step down from leadership of his party Fianna Fáil and also the Irish Government in 1959. At that time, he stood for the largely ceremonial role of President and was duly elected. His replacement as Taoiseach and leader of the party, the former Industry Minister, Seán Lemass, began to make changes in the economic area, greatly influenced by the Secretary of the Finance Department Whitaker. Ireland's interest in what was taking place on the European mainland increased hugely.

The external environment also underwent a sudden alteration. British Prime Minister Harold Macmillan, having been scornful of efforts to bring about closer integration in Europe, began a fundamental re-examination of Britain's position in a number of areas. His landmark speech on the future of the British Empire in Africa, describing "the wind of change" which he made in Capetown, South Africa, on 3 February 1960, was soon followed by a change of heart on Europe[25]. Given Ireland's economic dependence, where the UK went, Ireland would have to follow. Macmillan's "change of heart" on the Common Market was the decisive element in pushing Ireland towards Brussels. There has been a certain amount of rewriting of history recently, which claims that Ireland made a conscious decision alone to opt for Europe. This does not chime with the facts at the time.

The new Taoiseach in Dublin quickly aligned Ireland with the United Kingdom's application for EEC membership in 1961, but when the French President de Gaulle vetoed the UK application in 1963, Ireland's attempt at membership simply fell away. This was repeated in 1967, when de Gaulle again felt that UK membership was incompatible with the Common Market.

With the resignation of de Gaulle in 1968 and his replacement by Georges Pompidou, new applications by Ireland, Denmark, Norway and the United Kingdom for membership of the EEC were submitted. Fresh negotiations began and in 1972 the Treaty of Accession was signed. A referendum held in May 1972 confirmed Ireland's entry into the European community, with 83% of voters supporting membership.

The main political parties, Fianna Fáil and Fine Gael, as well as farming organisations and business groups supported Ireland's entry, while the Labour Party, Republican Groups and the Union movement were the main opponents. It was a classic right/left split. The earlier Euro-scepticism of Fianna Fáil, under de Valera, was forgotten. At the time, Ireland was the poorest of the applicants, and poorer than the existing members[26]. The country suffered from poverty, mass unemployment and emigration, and was heavily dependent on agriculture and trade with the United Kingdom. However, things were changing well before membership of the EEC. The 1960s had seen a remarkable economic revival, and, vitally, educational reforms, which made second and third level education much more accessible to many families. The State's population had begun to rise again after well over a hundred years of decline[27]. However, the country, even with new vigour and record growth rates, had a lot of catching up to do.

Irish membership of the EEC

On 1 January 1973, three of the applicant countries became members of the (then) European Economic Community (EEC). Norway, which had been included in the accession negotiations, rejected membership in a referendum, despite overwhelming Parliamentary support in Oslo, an early demonstration of the gulf between a pro-European elite and a more sceptical general population.

The admission of Ireland to the then EEC required a Constitutional amendment in 1972. Having been so suspicious of European integration in the 1950s, Ireland had moved to being amongst the most ardent supporters. This is reflected in the change to the Irish Constitution.

The Third Amendment to the Constitution states that:

3° The State may become a member of the European Coal and Steel Community (established by Treaty signed at Paris on the 18th day of April 1951), the European Economic Community (established by Treaty signed at Rome on the 25th day of March, 1957) and the European Atomic Energy Community (established by Treaty signed at Rome on the 25th day of March, 1957). No provision of this Constitution invalidates laws enacted, acts done or measures adopted by the State necessitated by the obligations of membership of the Communities or prevents laws enacted, acts done or measures adopted by the Communities, or institutions thereof, from having the force of law in the State[28].

The new article has extraordinary wide scope, even relative to similar Constitutional provisions in other Member States.

In a court case, *Commissioner for Environmental Information v An Taoiseach*[29], after a request to examine documents relating to what had been discussed at Cabinet and after having pointed to the Constitutional provision relating to Cabinet confidentiality, the EU legislation, a directive (secondary source) in this instance was held to have supremacy over the Irish Constitution. Justice O'Neill had misapplied the law in that case and when confronted with the fact the Irish Constitution couldn't stand up to any EU law passed, very appropriately described the situation as "violence done to the judicial architecture of the State."

It was an example of the Irish trying to demonstrate their European credentials or being more European than the Europeans. It was a sign of a country that lacked self-confidence. Ireland was determined to be part of the European Club after several decades in the wilderness and would go to the strongest degree to prove its euro credentials. It had a new role.

However, this has not always penetrated through to the general population. While the Irish electorate have, in the main, been happy to support the Government's pro-European line, there have been some serious hiccups along the way.

The Irish were very comfortable with the old concept of the European Economic Community (EEC), where interactions were essentially intergovernmental and economic/social. The desire to push this model into "an ever-closer union" does not sit well with the Irish population. In two referenda on European Treaties, Nice and Lisbon, the Irish electorate rejected the centralising tendencies of the EU. In both cases, the Irish people were required to vote again, to get the "right" result.

On 7 June 2001, a referendum was held in Ireland to seek approval for the Treaty of Nice, which had been concluded the previous December. The electorate voted by 53.9% to 46.1% against ratification of the Treaty, which proposed to implement a range of institutional and other reforms to facilitate the expansion of the EU up to 27 members. After securing a number of national opt-outs, Ireland voted to accept the Treaty by a wide margin 18 months later[30]. However, it was clear that Brussels never had any intention of allowing Ireland's initial referendum to thwart the adoption of the Nice Treaty. In 2008, in another referendum, the Irish electorate rejected the Lisbon Treaty. Turnout on this occasion was 53.1%; with 53.4% voting No and 46.6% voting Yes. Then the recession hit and Ireland's voters in 2009 were threatened with Armageddon, if they did not accept the Treaty. A frightened electorate did so[31].

Looking back on the two referenda, it might have been better for Brussels to have heeded these "canaries in the mine", as warning signs not to push further with the European project, without strong popular backing. If they had done so, they probably would not now be facing the unpleasant consequences of Brexit.

Before the Brexit crisis, the Irish population was showing signs of a more critical approach to the EU's plan for further consolidation of powers in Brussels. However, the dispute between Dublin and London on the Backstop changed things in the short term.

Effect of Brexit on Irish attitudes to the EU

Ireland is today a much-changed country from 1973. It has a much more diversified economy and its relationship with the rest of the world has greatly changed. It has grown much richer, more liberal and more self-confident. It has greatly benefited from EU membership, both financially and socially. There are, in consequence, very few who would disagree, in retrospect, with the original decision to join the EEC in 1973.

One of those major changes includes its relations with the United Kingdom. Much of the old Anglophobia in Ireland, especially in the Republic, had been dissipating. The desire in Ireland to define ourselves essentially as non-British, had been replaced by a more positive outlook. As bilateral relations between Britain and Ireland blossomed, the old prejudices in Britain against the Irish had also lessened considerably. There is no doubt but that common membership of the European Union, as well as the Peace Process in Northern Ireland, was very helpful in bringing about this rapprochement.

However, the decision of the British electorate to leave the EU has greatly challenged these positive developments. As the arguments heated up on the terms of Brexit, certain Irish politicians adopted an aggressive and anti-British attitude and harped back to past wrongs. The Irish Government, under Taoiseach Leo Varadkar, is widely perceived in Britain, on all sides, as having been antagonistic to the UK during Brexit. This has caused a reaction in Britain where antagonism to Ireland and our political leaders has resurfaced, occasionally in a nasty form. Hopefully, this will be a temporary phenomenon, brought on by the intensity of the controversies surrounding Brexit. The disgraceful comments of Home Secretary, Priti Patel, in December 2018, as a backbencher, advocating the UK cause food shortages in Ireland to induce a more pro-British response, reached a new low in such developments[32]. Ms Patel seemed to have developed amnesia about her country's role in the Irish Famine.

The growing maturity of the Irish population in relation to British–Irish links has been challenged by Brexit. This thrust the age-old problem of an unpopular border into the mix. At least for the present, it has trumped all other considerations. In these circumstances, official Ireland has reached out for our old allies in continental Europe, despite the latter's consistent historical inability to assist Ireland in its times of need.

Some 58% of those polled in 2019 in Ireland stated that the Brexit process has improved their opinion of the EU[33]. Even though this poll was commissioned by the European Movement, who regularly sponsor fairly meaningless polls, asking questions likely to give an answer to bolster their pro-EU view, there is no reason but to accept that this poll reflects popular opinion. The establishment media in Ireland has swung completely behind the anti-Brexit sentiment. Whether this is a high watermark for europhilia, underpinned by a strong economy and the Brexit crisis as the backdrop, is the key question. Once the Irish population see that Brexit has occurred and the sky did not fall in; and the Irish economy comes off the boil; it will be extremely interesting whether this level of pro-EU sentiment can be maintained.

The growing disenchantment with a centralising EU has been temporarily reversed by the passions that Brexit has unleashed[34]. The worries that a hard border in Ireland and the prospect that Ireland would somehow be thrown back to the bad old days of British domination has struck a chord with the Irish population and generated a robust, and I believe a temporary, reprieve for the EU's appeal in Ireland.

The generally inept handling of Brexit by the Theresa May Government in London has added to that feeling, as has the continuing uncertainty with the Johnson administration's intentions, post the Transition period. However, it would be a major mistake if Ireland allowed our historic feelings of antagonism towards the British establishment to cloud our judgement. At times of heightened Anglo-Irish tension, there is a natural tendency for Irish people to rally to the flag. However, the Irish people should realise that the Backstop provision in the Withdrawal Agreement was promoted by the EU primarily to punish Britain and to protect its own sacred Single Market. That has become increasingly clear over time. The EU emphasis switched from protecting the GFA to maintaining the integrity of the Single Market. The Irish/EU common approach is bound to come under heavy pressure as the interests of Brussels and Dublin diverge in the talks on the future trade arrangements.

Brexit is a passing period in history. Eventually after much bungling and hesitancy, the UK has managed to depart the EU, and soon will also leave the Customs Union and Single Market. It will be successful and, while not a glorious resurrection of the great days of the British Empire, Brexit will not be the disaster that the resolute Remainers have forecast (and devoutly wished for) come to pass.

The former President of the European Council, Donald Tusk, speaking after the Council meeting in Brussels on 28 May 2019, claimed that Brexit was a "vaccine" against euroscepticism[35]. In Ireland's case there is no doubting, but that Brexit has clouded Ireland's view of Brussels. However, many vaccines only offer temporary protection and the immunity they provide degrades over time.

Meanwhile, our geographical position as its nearest neighbour and our ethnic connections with our neighbouring island, will remain permanent. It is vital that we do no long-term damage to our country in the present period, by short term decisions. The relative advantage of remaining in the EU after Britain's departure and by the changing nature of the EU and our relationship with it, calls for a more reflective decision on the way forward and not one based on short term and emotive considerations.

It is only a matter of time before Ireland, in a post-Brexit situation, will have to give serious consideration as to whether it should continue with EU membership or seek its own exit from the EU, namely an Irexit. Ireland probably needed the period of EU membership and support to allow it to mature its relationship with the UK. That EU shelter is no longer needed. We should not let the shadows thrown from our turbulent history distort our judgement of the way forward.

References

1. Nicholas Mansergh *The Irish Free State, its Government and Politics* 1934. Published by George Allan and Unwin;

2. Eoin O Malley "*The Decline of Irish Industry in the Nineteenth Century*" *The Economic and Social Review*, Vol. 13, No. 1; October 1981, pp. 21-42

3. *Documents on Irish Foreign Policy*, Volume 1, p 354-55

4. Ibid. p 350

5. Final Text of the Articles of Agreement for a Treaty between Great Britain and Ireland as signed London 6 December 1921, Documents on Irish Foreign Policy Volume 1 p 356–361

6. Debate in Dáil Éireann on the Anglo-Irish Treaty (Dáil Éireann – Volume T – 19 December 1921)

7. Levine, Allen *William Lyon Mackenzie King: A Life Guided by the Hand of Destiny* Toronto: Douglas & McIntyre, 2011 page 131.

8. Report from Irish Representative I Paris Sean Murphy, 14 March 1923, Documents on Irish Foreign Policy Volume 2, p70

9. Message from Desmond Fitzgerald to Timothy Smiddy, Irish representative in Washington, 25 June 1924, Documents on Irish Foreign Policy, Volume 2, p 309.

10. Statute of Westminster 1931, legislation.gov.uk. Retrieved 14 May 2019

11. Documents on Irish Foreign Policy Volume 2, p 75

12. Extract from a letter from Sean T O Ceallaigh to Diarmuid Hegarty, 20 September 1920, Documents on Irish Foreign Policy Volume 1, p 89

13. Christopher Brooker and Richard North *The Great Deception* p 20

14. Ibid. p 87

15. Documents on Irish Foreign Policy Volume 10, p 19

16. Roy Denham *Missed Chances* p 199

17. Documents on Irish Foreign Policy Volume 10, p 72

18. Ibid. p 124

19. Ibid. p 224

20. Ibid. p 226

21. Ibid. p 277

22. Ibid. p 682

23. Ibid. p 716

24. Ibid. p 755

25. Christopher Brooker and Richard North *The Great Deception* p 118

26. Countryeconomy.com. GDP Country by Country 1973 – *https://countryeconomy.com/gdp?year=1973*. Retrieved 15 May 2019

27. Census 1971 – Volume 1- Population, Central Statistics Office, Ireland

28. Bunreacht na hÉireann (Constitution of Ireland), Article 29.

29. Judgment of O'Neill J. in An Taoiseach v. Commissioner for Environmental Information [2010] IEHC 241,

30. Thomas Harding *"Ireland says yes to Nice Treaty" The Daily Telegraph*, 21 October 2002. *https://www.telegraph.co.uk/news/worldnews/europe/ireland/1410856/Ireland-says-yes-to-Nice-treaty.html*. Retrieved 15 May 2019

31. *"Lisbon Treaty passed with decisive 67% in favour". Irish Times*, 3 October 2009. *https://www.irishtimes.com/news/lisbon-treaty-passed-with-decisive-67-in-favour-1.847182*. Retrieved 15 May 2019.

32. James Gant *"Patel accused of 'famine threats' as she says risk of food shortages could be used against Republic"* Belfast Telegraph 8 December 2018, *https://www.belfasttelegraph.co.uk/news/brexit/patel-accused-of-famine-threats-as-she-says-risk-of-food-shortages-could-be-used-against-republic-37605632.html.* Retrieved 15 May 2019

33. Simon Carswell, *"Increased number believe Brexit makes United Ireland more possible – poll"* Irish Times 2 May 2019. *https://www.irishtimes.com/news/politics/increased-number-believe-brexit-makes-united-ireland-more-likely-poll-1.3877678.* Retrieved 10 Dec 2019

34. Jon Stone *"Brexit: Support for Ireland staying in the EU hits a record high of 92%, latest poll shows"* London Independent 8 May 2018. *https://www.independent.co.uk/news/uk/politics/brexit-ireland-population-majority-remain-eu-poll-border-solution-theresa-may-latest-a8340941.html* Retrieved 15 May 2019

35. *"Tusk says Brexit served as 'vaccine' against eurosceptic EU vote"* Reuters. *https://www.reuters.com/article/us-britain-eu-tusk-idUSKCN1SY2DJ.* Retrieved 29 May 2019

Chapter 6

Ireland's Changing Position in the EU

"You are not even aligned to the non-aligned movement."
Andrei Gromyko, Soviet Foreign Minister to Irish Foreign
Minister, Garret FitzGerald.

It could be argued, with some conviction, that the EU has been beneficial in transforming and modernising the Irish State, although it is not clear whether the modernisation of Ireland would have occurred anyway, once the effects of the educational reforms of the 1960s took effect. Ireland's ascent from being a rural backwater was well underway before 1973, greatly helped by the Anglo-Irish Free Trade Agreement of 1965[1]. That is a discussion, however, which can never produce a definitive outcome.

But, as the banking fraternity regularly warn us, past performance is no guarantee of future returns. Even if it is conceded that Ireland did very well out of the EU and its earlier manifestations, we are clearly in a different situation now and are about to experience further changes on the Brussels front. None of these changes are to our liking.

With the UK departing the EU, Ireland is at an historic fork on the road. For centuries, Ireland was linked closely in some institutional format with its neighbouring island, Britain. Even after Ireland became a Republic in 1949, and left the Commonwealth, the links persisted and there remains a huge web of interconnections, at all levels of society, between our two islands. It is hard to find any two countries with such close associations, even to the extent that neither State treats the other's citizens as foreigners[2].

However, the desire of the British to again become an independent sovereign State and the Irish Government's grim determination to cling onto Brussels, essentially means that all the old cosy arrangements may be in jeopardy. Brexit runs directly counter to the road map being followed by Brussels and to which the present Irish Government has pledged its undying allegiance.

The Irish Government had no hesitation when facing the challenges of Brexit in throwing its lot immediately in with Team EU. The years of reliance on the EU has had its psychological effect and it is clear that Dublin never even gave a second thought to any alternative. There was also the added complication in that the Remainers in the establishment in Britain actively encouraged the Irish along these lines.

Ireland's political elite want to be at the centre of Europe. It seems to be the most defining element in the political philosophy of Taoiseach Leo Varadkar[3]. But what does that actually mean, beyond the slogan and posturing? The choices the country will make now may have profound consequences. Yet they seem to have been made with no national debate. The Dáil in recent years appears to have been reduced to a caricature of a national debating chamber. The standard of discourse is extremely poor, with the bulk of contributions on the Government side involving the monotone reading out of scripts prepared by the civil servants. The whole operation is so stage-managed that there is little or no spontaneity or real interplay of ideas. It stands poor comparison with national Parliaments in London, Ottawa, Canberra, Washington, Copenhagen, etc. The only worthwhile debate that occurs in our national Parliament takes place in the relatively powerless Upper House, the Seanad (Senate). The present situation is not good for the health of our democracy.

In the post-Brexit world, we would be greatly served by a vigorous and far reaching debate, centred on our national Parliament, but that is distinctly lacking. We are committing ourselves to a very divisive policy, with ramifications on relationships on the island of Ireland, between Ireland and Britain and with huge economic implications. It is placing immense strain on the continuation of the GFA, as well as conjuring up the possibility of a hard border between North and South.

It behoves us to carefully look at what we are buying into, namely the current, and more importantly the future policies, of the EU. In many ways, Brexit will help define the future of the Irish State. We need to look carefully at what we are committing ourselves to.

As I mentioned earlier, the Ireland which entered the then EEC in 1973 is very different than the Ireland of today. The same observation could be made on the current EU, as the European Project continues on its long journey towards ever closer union. Hence, the Irish relationship with the EU has changed drastically over the course of those decades and is changing all the time. In addition, there is scarcely any new EU policy direction which suits Ireland.

If we let the current Brexit process and the consequent spat with the UK dominate our thinking, we may wake up embedded in an EU, that is not very much to our liking. I outline some of the negative developments, from an Irish point of view, below. This is not to make the claim that everything relating to the EU is bad for Ireland. It has been very beneficial in areas like the environment. However, Brussels and the Irish establishment have an army of propagandists and huge resources devoted to the task of praising the European Project. I outline the list below in the interest of balance. It is not an exhaustive list and I am sure some others will have their own areas to point to.

The EU Budget and Ireland's net Contribution

There is still a widespread perception in Ireland and the UK that the EU continues to pay over large sums of money to the Irish exchequer and that the country's standard of living is dependent on receiving Brussels' largesse. This image is bolstered by the mainstream media. Few people know the true picture and the Irish Government is strangely coy about revealing figures, in case it dents the popularity of the EU in Ireland, particularly with the ongoing Brexit process. The myth of the euro fairy godmother is out of date.

The position of Ireland in relation to the EU budget has undergone a radical change. When we joined the EEC, we were the poorest and least developed State in the club. We have made massive progress since. This has produced some envy. There was, for a long period, a slightly carping view among UK commentators that our improving economic performance was solely due to EU subsidies. The underlying prejudice was that we could not have achieved this on our own efforts. While there was some element of truth in the importance of EU assistance at that time, it was essentially Ireland's major upskilling of its own population, coupled with our ability to attract Foreign Direct Investment, which was the major driving force in our transformation. Other countries had the same access to EU funds as Ireland but did not achieve anything like the same progress.

Since the Irish State joined the EEC, it has been the beneficiary of financial transfers from Brussels. The Department of Finance estimate that from accession in 1973 up to 2015, Ireland received €74.3bn in receipts from Europe, while contributing €32bn, a net gain of €42.3bn[4]. However, this figure is massively reduced (or even eliminated) when the costs of the EU enforced Bailout and the catastrophic collapse of exchequer receipts which it caused, are also factored in.

However, the direction of the financial flows was reversed in 2013. This was when Ireland, for the first time, moved from being a small net recipient of EU funds to a small contributor. In 2018, this changed greatly and the country's net budget contributions to Brussels began to escalate significantly, as indicated by the Department of Finance figures below. When I initially published figures in January 2018 in the *Sunday Business Post*[5], it caused unease in some Government circles. Unlike most net contributors, at that stage there was a reluctance to publicly acknowledge our position, lest it might lessen local support for the EU in the Brexit negotiations.

The Department of Finance in Dublin are regularly revising recent figures so that they may change slightly in different publications, but the table below is taken from the Budgetary Statistics 2018 which was published in November 2019[6].

Year	Receipts from EU Budget	Payment to EU Budget	Net Receipts (€m)
2009	1,813	1,486	327
2010	1,885	1,352	533
2011	1,950	1,350	601
2012	1,838	1,393	445
2013	1,673	1,726	-53
2014	1,423	1,685	-262
2015	1,774	1,952	-178

Year	Receipts from EU Budget	Payment to EU Budget	Net Receipts (€m)
2016	1,635	2,023	-388
2017	1,586	2,016	-430
2018	1,799	2,519	-720
2019	1,700	2,835.	> 1bn

The 2019 figures are estimates of the Department and are based on the level of receipts remaining stable at around €1.7bn per annum, with the payments rising to €2.8 bn, meaning a deficit of over €1bn for that year. These figures show that Ireland is currently subsidising the EU, at the same level as the UK, given that the UK's economy is 10 times that of Ireland.

It is also worth noting that the EU Commission publish a different set of figures which claim a much lower net contribution. The Commission is engaged in a slight of hand, by reallocating some of the Member States' payments as "EU own resources." This is based on a percentage of a country's VAT income and on custom duties. However, it is the Member States' citizens who are paying this notional amount which in reality forms part of a national contribution to Brussels.

The situation outlined above places us in a much different position than we were in the past when Ireland, as a net recipient, almost automatically supported greater resources for Brussels. While our contributions to the EU budget have continued to rise, the Department of Finance expects our receipts, which have been static for some time, to go in the opposite direction. Ireland gets the bulk of those receipts from the CAP[7], hence the proposed cuts in this area, under the reforms proposed by former Agriculture Commissioner Phil Hogan[8], and the more recent EU budget proposals, would widen the gap further.

The departure of the UK from the EU now further complicates the picture. The British were the second largest net contributors to the EU budget after Germany. Therefore, there are serious consequences for the level of net contributions for a number of countries, including Ireland, post-Brexit.

The present Multiannual Financial Framework (MFF), a seven-year programme for regulating the budget, will finish at the end of 2020, the same time as Britain is scheduled to stop its very large contributions. Former Budget Commissioner Günther Oettinger and his team initially outlined the dimensions of the problem for the next MFF. They have estimated on the revenue side that the EU budget faces a shortfall of around €10bn, per annum[(9)], a little more than some earlier estimates. This means in terms of resources, available to Brussels, in the next MFF period, Brexit will result in a shortfall of circa €75bn, a massive sum. This is only half the picture because Brussels has expensive new plans for a major escalation on the expenditure side in a number of areas. Oettinger outlined these areas where Brussels would like to take over more responsibility from the Member States including "fighting terrorism, internal and external security, border control, investing in defence and defence research in the interest of our taxpayers and citizens as well as major research projects to improve our competitiveness in the digital age. All that has to be funded."

Oettinger has also indicated his preferred method of meeting these challenges, a combination of spending cuts and increased contributions from countries such as Ireland, Germany, Austria, France, etc. It is also noteworthy that the former Commissioner particularly singled out the CAP, which accounts for nearly 40% of total expenditure, for cuts, as well as the Cohesion Funds. None of the new areas of operation would bring in any major receipts into Ireland but the cuts would disproportionately affect us because of our reliance on the CAP. The net effect of these proposals would be to impoverish farming families and cut attempts to assist countries in southern and eastern Europe. The beneficiaries would be the armaments industry and the well healed economies of western Europe. No wonder alienation is increasing in the EU. It is unlikely that new EU Budget and administration Commissioner, Austrian Johannes Hahn, will try to alter the current direction.

The Department of Finance's chief economist, John McCarthy, was quoted in the *Irish Times* in May 2018[(10)] as saying that Ireland's contribution could rise by as much as an additional €400 million a year as a result of the Brexit hole left in the block's budget, albeit this was still subject to negotiation. You can also take it for granted that the Department's estimates are on the conservative side, given the pro-EU outlook of their political bosses. This suspicion was confirmed by reports in November 2019 that the EU Commission estimated that the British departure and new expenditure would add an annual bill of €760m to Ireland. The Taoiseach accepted that the annual bill would rise "very significantly."[11]

With these bleak figures being talked about, one would expect Ireland to look at reducing the overall EU budget as the EU itself will be smaller, post-Brexit. Other small/medium States which are net contributors, such as the Netherlands, Austria, Sweden, Denmark, etc. have expressed their determination not to allow the rapacious demands of the Commission in Brussels to prise more funding from their own national budgets. A Dutch Government spokesperson was quoted as stating, "A smaller EU means a smaller EU budget. In addition, new priorities need to be funded from the savings of existing programmes."[12]

These net contributors have expressed opposition to the Commission proposal to increase contributions from 1% of Gross National Income (GNI) to 1.11%. This represented a blatant move at empire building by the Commission. It is worrying that the extra demands for finance are coming at a time when the citizenry in Member States are baulking at the prospect of increased centralisation in Brussels.

However, Ireland initially took the opposite view from States in a similar position to this country. Taoiseach Leo Varadkar indicated a willingness to increase national contributions[13]. The suspicion was that the Taoiseach was trying to curry favour with the EU Commission during the Brexit process, by taking a stance that appears at odds with our national interest. If this was the case, and as history has amply demonstrated, then it would be remarkably short sighted, as it is impossible to claw back concessions, given by the individual countries, to Brussels.

However, even the ardent europhile Varadkar was forced to retreat as the details of the new MFF proposals were tabled by EU Council President Charles Michel in early 2020. On 21 February, the Taoiseach described the proposal as "one that we can't accept".

"Essentially it means that Ireland will contribute much more to the EU budget, but we will actually receive less back in terms of payments to Irish farmers and also funds for regional development and social development,"[14], a belated but nevertheless welcome, dose of realism and a show of independence.

The future economic outlook for Ireland looks challenging, as the international business cycle seems destined to enter a low period, interest rates may start to rise and our economic model of attracting FDI through low corporate tax rates comes under pressure. It is not a time to throw away some of our hard-earned resources to a European Army, grandiose projects of creating a euro border defence force, etc. Any increased financial contribution to Brussels will inevitably mean less resources for other areas such as housing, health, rural support and is likely to become much more controversial in the future with increasing demands of an ageing population and pressure to reduce our share of corporate taxes.

There is very little public awareness in Ireland that our State is making very large contributions to Brussels. Unlike similar EU Member States in the same situation, our local politicians either do not know or prefer to keep silent on this transfer of resources. In the post-Brexit situation, the position is likely to deteriorate significantly. It is naïve of some of our political figures to call on the EU Commission to provide major resources to Ireland to meet the challenges of a post-Brexit world. In reality, we are much more likely to be asked to provide Brussels with more net financial support, as they struggle with the loss of the British contribution and push on with their grandiose schemes.

The Irish love affair with Brussels was primarily based on the belief that membership of the club brought direct financial benefits to the country. It created a mindset which looked to Brussels as a milch cow, which effortlessly supplied an extra boost to the Irish economy. Today the cow has run dry and is eating a lot of our grass and resources. This is one area where the terms of our membership have certainly altered for the worse.

Fisheries and Marine Resources

One of the most striking statistics to emerge from the Brexit referendum was a survey by the University of Aberdeen, which showed that 92% of those who worked in the fishing industry in Britain, intended to vote for Brexit[15]. No other group gave such unequivocal support for quitting the

EU. For those who have studied this industry over the years, this was not surprising. The Fishing to Leave campaign played a significant part in the Brexit debate.

The issue of fishing rights is one of the most contentious in the history of the EU. It was the primary reason why Norway refused membership and was instrumental in keeping the Faroe Islands and Iceland out of the European project. It was also the main cause for the departure of Greenland from the EEC in 1985. It certainly played a part in securing a pro-Brexit majority in the UK and looks like it will remain a major issue in any future EU–UK Brexit trade negotiations. The UK is determined to recover sovereignty of its waters and become an independent coastal State again. Brussels seems determined to resist a loss of control. There are serious economic interests at stake.

The UK, under current arrangements, only takes around 40% of the total fish catches in its waters, a disappointing figure from a British point of view but it is still well above Ireland's share in our own waters. Writing for the Politico.eu website, the then British Environment Secretary, Michael Gove, pointed out that the Common Fisheries Policy (CFP) worked heavily against the UK, stating:

> As for fishing, I grew up in a coastal community in northeast Scotland where my father was a fish merchant. I know first-hand how the CFP has led to over-fishing and undermines local economies. In the Atlantic, North Sea and Baltic Sea, many stocks are still being fished at unsustainable levels. And while our fleet catches on average around 120,000 tons of fish from other Member States' waters, EU vessels catch more than 850,000 tons of fish in U.K. waters[16].

There are conflicting estimates of the percentage of total fish catch taken by Irish boats, in Irish waters. When I requested this information from the Irish Department of Agriculture, Food and the Marine, under the Freedom of Information (FOI) procedure they were unable, or unwilling, to come up with a similar figure. However, while it varies from year to year, all agree that it is below 30% and may be as low as 16% of the total.

This is an area where there is universal agreement in Ireland that the country has gotten very poor treatment from the EU down the years.

The Irish State territory represents four-fifths of the land area of the island of Ireland, together with its exclusive economic maritime zone. In essence, this means that 90% of the geographical area, where the Irish State can claim exclusive economic rights, is maritime[17].

Ireland did very well out of the United Nations Convention on the Law of Sea Agreement 1982 (UNCLOS)[18], where my former boss, the late Ambassador Mahon Hayes, a very decent and honourable man, played an influential role as the Irish delegate. Ireland, as a much more sovereign country at that time, was prominent in relation to the adoption of a new legal regime on the issue of the continental shelf and the rules of maritime boundaries. In consequence, Ireland gained considerably from these new rules, adopted under the Convention. I am not sure that Ireland would be able to play such a key role today as the EU has taken over much of the former international commitments of the Member States.

This huge maritime area for which Ireland now has legal entitlement is rich in marine life. Hence, it should follow that Ireland has a large fishing industry. This unfortunately is not the case.

Ireland's weakness in this area long predates our membership of the EU. While the country had a thriving fishing industry in the 1600s[19], over the next three centuries it declined into almost insignificance. Very few in Ireland realised the potential of the country's sea resources. Arthur Griffith, the first leader of an independent Ireland, as Head of the Provisional Government in 1922, had remarked earlier in 1911, "We dare say the number of public men in Ireland who realise that the sea fisheries of this country could be an industry second only to agriculture might be counted on one hand."[20]

By 1938, only 8,700 tons of fish were recorded as having landed in Irish ports. The quantity of sea fish landed increased from 25,000 tonnes in 1963 to 87,000 tonnes in 1972[21]. Ireland had come very late to reviving the local fishing industry in the years leading up to entry into the EEC. However, the industry was on a decidedly upward curve.

Unfortunately, the lure of entry into the EEC and the greedy eyes of some of our European neighbours on our fish resources, meant that this growing industry was in jeopardy. In the discussions on entry, securing a good deal for agriculture was given priority. With Ireland constantly promoting the cause of our farmers, the Government's main concern is always to keep Brussels on side. Fisheries and our fishermen could be easily sacrificed and the fleets from other EU States allowed plunder our maritime resources as a quid pro quo, as long as our farmers' interests were looked after.

The betrayal of our maritime industry began at our accession. In a wholly opportunistic move, and in anticipation of Ireland, the UK, Norway and Denmark signing up to join the then EEC, the pre-existing six members, France, West Germany, Italy, the Netherlands, Belgium and Luxembourg created a new Fisheries Regulation 2140/70, which allowed access for all members to Irish/UK/Danish/Norwegian rich fishing grounds[22].

There was essentially no legal basis for this grab of the marine resources of the accession States. These candidate countries had one thing in common, they were endowed with some of the richest fishery grounds anywhere on the planet. While fish products had been mooted in the Treaty of Rome, there was little or no discussion on the matter until the prospect of access to the rich fishing grounds of Ireland, Norway, the UK and Denmark came into view.

Sir Con O'Neill, the British diplomat who led the official team at the British Accession negotiations, related this sudden change: "When our negotiations opened on 30 June 1970, the problem of fisheries did not exist. It came later in the same day. From then on Fisheries was a major problem."[23]

O'Neill, the son of an Ulster Unionist MP, was an uncle of Terence O'Neill, who served as Premier of Northern Ireland.

It is now clear from documentation later released, that during the Accession discussions, the French authorities woke up to the potential of using the desperation of then British Prime Minister, Ted Heath, to join the EEC at almost any cost, to suddenly push for a common fisheries policy, with the right of access for all community vessels up to the shoreline. O'Neill summed up the British approach in his official report. "We had to get in."[24] It is also clear that the then British Government, Heath and Geoffrey Rippon, the Minister in charge of the negotiations, deliberately lied to the British Parliament over the terms of the final deal on fisheries[25].

This was taking place against a background, where international norms were changing and fishery limits, which had been 3 to 12 miles, were being increased to 50 miles or more ambitiously to 200-mile exclusive national zones, or even to the edge of the continental shelf. It has been reported that some of the original six Member States of the EEC were privately embarrassed by the rapacious behaviour of the French. It was against that background that our own potentially rich fish industry was sold out, along with our fishermen. It is a moot point as to whether the Irish Government could have made much difference, given that the accession negotiations were essentially about British entry, and Denmark and Ireland were coming in to preserve their valuable food export markets in Britain. However, there is no real evidence of any Irish resistance. The betrayal of Irish fish interests, which traditionally is blamed on the Irish Foreign Minister at the time of the accession negotiations, Paddy Hillary, is probably a little unfair. The real power lay with Heath and Rippon and it was the British Government that decided fishing interests were expendable. It was simply a take it or leave it choice for the other three States. Of course, in the end Norway decided to leave it and rejected membership.

The Irish Government got a number of sweeteners at the time to allow our tiny fishing fleet to expand, but nothing like what was required. This was under what was known as the Hague Preferences[26]. The neglect of the interests of Irish fisheries and fishermen continued well after accession.

The new European fisheries regime worked on the basis that fish was a common resource and available to all nations in the EEC, unlike other natural resources such as oil, gas and mineral wealth. Even countries, which had no coastline, were theoretically entitled to a fishing quota.

In Ireland, there was never any serious attempt to reverse the betrayal of the industry. In a past Irish administration, Foreign Affairs Minister, Dr Garrett FitzGerald, refused to hold out for a 50-mile limit, saying that it would be "extremely disruptive of Community solidarity, offensive to our partners and would have caused great irritation."[27] This was at a time when Irish and British fishermen were campaigning strongly for national 50-mile limits. Fitzgerald's dismissive attitude to our fisheries has a long history.

My good friend, Tim Pat Coogan, who has written many books with a historical theme and was the last editor of the *Irish Press*, in 2009 recounted a conversation that he had with the then Fisheries Minister in the 1960s:

"A more fundamental cause goes back to that conversation I had with Brian Lenihan [the future Finance Minister's father] back in the 60s when Ireland was planning to enter the European Economic Community (EEC) as it was then known. The conversation occurred during an interview I was conducting with the junior Minister — that status should have given me a clue — on the prospects for developing the vast untapped fisheries potential of the Irish coastline. Brian, a pleasant man, interrupted me suddenly to ask "Tim Pat! Do you know how many whole time and part time farmers there are in this country?" I did not know exactly but he rattled off the answer correct to a decimal point (around a quarter million, as I remember). Then he asked me did I know how many whole time and part time fishermen there were in the country. "including lobster men, currachmen, and the teacher who goes out in the summer night with a net after a few salmon?" Again, I could not reply with certainty, but Brian could again answer with pinpoint accuracy, something just over 9,000 as I recall. "That," he continued, "would hardly elect one Fianna Fáil TD on the first count in a five-seater. Now do you get me?" Realpolitik meant that we had to give up our rich fishing grounds".[28]

The Common Fisheries Policy has been argued by certain commentators to have had disastrous consequences for the environment. This view may be correct but there is also historical evidence revealing that fishing stocks have been in chronic decline over the last century, as a result of intensive trawl fishing techniques. The EU Commission in 2009 estimated that 88% of monitored marine stocks were overfished, using data that stretched back 20-40 years. According to scientific research published by the University of Exeter in Britain in 2010, the depletion of fishing stocks is a consequence of mismanagement long before the Common Fisheries Policy came into being and in particular the destruction of sea-beds by trawling. The research found

Annual demersal fish landings from bottom trawl catches landing in England and Wales dating back to 1889, using previously neglected UK Government data. We then corrected the figures for increases in fishing power over time and a recent shift in the proportion of fish landed abroad to estimate the change in landings per unit of fishing power (LPUP), a measure of the commercial productivity of fisheries. LPUP reduced by 94% – 17-fold – over the past 118 years. This implies an extraordinary decline in the availability of bottom-living fish and a profound reorganization of seabed ecosystems since the nineteenth century industrialization of fishing[29].

Nonetheless, the Common Fisheries Policy has continued the trend of ineffective fisheries management in European waters. Indeed, the Common Fisheries Policy has done little if anything to reverse the decline of European fish stocks. There are simply too many fishing vessels, especially from foreign countries, fishing the depleted stocks around these islands.

The extent by which the other EU countries have benefitted from access to Irish waters is a contentious issue. Any adverse comment on the EU pillage of Irish marine resources immediately raises the hackles of the EU funded industry in Ireland. The respected Dublin City University lecturer, Dr Karen Devine, who is one of the very few academics to critically examine Ireland's changing position within the European Union, was the subject of severe criticism, when she described the EU exploitation of Ireland's seas as "rape" at a conference in Dublin in February 2018. Devine estimated that the total loss to Ireland from 1975 to 2010 from EU exploitation of our fisheries was in the region of €200bn at 2018 prices. This estimate was based on fish landings valued at €67bn and approximately twice that amount from subsequent processing[30]. While it is always possible to dispute figures, no one, even those in receipt of EU and Irish Government funding, can dispute that the EU common fisheries policy has adversely impacted on Ireland's ability to grow its marine industries. No wonder that euroscepticism enjoys strong support among ordinary Irish fishermen.

The situation is in total contrast to the experience of another North Atlantic country, Norway. Over the last 40 years, the Norwegian fish industry has grown in strength, bolstered by a careful policy of conservation of stocks. The country is now the second largest exporter of seafood in the world, with exports in 2016 totalling $10.5bn[31]. It is the country's second biggest export industry after oil and gas. While there are obvious differences in the potential of the seafood industry between Ireland and Norway, the contrast in the fortunes of these two North Atlantic countries could not be starker; Ireland's seafood exports for 2017 was estimated at €331m[32]. Iceland is another example of a country, which has managed its marine resources well. It had an unemployment rate of below 2% in December 2018. As an independent coastal State, it too can keep the Common Fisheries Policy well away from its shores.

The UK and Ireland have extensive fishing grounds, making up a sizeable proportion of the total EU waters. The withdrawal of the UK from the Common Fisheries Policy may mean that Irish fishermen could no longer fish off the west coast of Scotland, nor in British waters in the Irish Sea where they have traditionally gone at certain times in the year. Some Irish fishermen have serious concerns that fishermen from Britain and Northern Ireland will not be curtailed by EU quotas and will take a much bigger share of what is often common stock.

Probably more threatening is that fishermen from other EU countries, who may be excluded from UK waters, will almost certainly seek new and alternative fishing quotas off Ireland. Already Irish fishermen regularly have to sit in port, after their meagre quota allocations have been filled, and gaze out at foreign fishing craft, often quite substantial, as they continue to take large quantities of fish out of our waters. Now there will inevitably be a large displacement of foreign trawlers post-Brexit from the UK fishing grounds, the richest in the EU.

In this context Patrick Murphy, the head of the Irish South and West Fish Producers Organisation, has called for a renegotiation of the entire Common Fisheries Policy to ensure Ireland isn't flooded with hundreds of additional fishing boats post-Brexit[33].

Once Britain takes back control of its seas and starts a policy to favour its own fishermen, as an independent coastal State, these huge foreign fleets will be looking for new waters to catch fish. It is almost inevitable that the bureaucrats in Brussels will propose some compensation in Irish waters, to the further detriment of our own people and the long-term health of Irish fish stocks. However, it will be interesting to see if the British, with their own control, can revive their fishing industry, which has the potential to make a major comeback and follow the Norwegian course.

The Chief Executive of the Killybegs Fishermen's Organisation (KFO), Sean O Donoghue has stated on the KFO website (15 December 2018) "Ireland's two biggest fisheries, mackerel (60%) and nephrons/prawns (40%), are hugely dependent on access to UK waters, with an overall dependency for all stocks of 30%."[34]. The changes in access to UK waters will undoubtably affect our fishermen who will need a better deal in their home area.

However, on the post-Brexit possibilities, the Dublin authorities appear to be giving politics and their desire to be good Europeans, priority over history and the requirements of geography. Marine resources in our part of the North Atlantic would be best managed in a bilateral cooperative arrangement with our nearest neighbour. The British Government post-Brexit are very willing to entertain such cooperation. However, Ireland needs to take its own fishing interests much more seriously.

Independent county councillor Danny Collins from Cork took up this call for much greater Irish Government commitment to our fishing industry and the need to safeguard it post-Brexit. Collins was quoted in the *Southern Star* newspaper, in December 2018 as saying, "Also others have highlighted that foreign vessels who are in UK waters at present will have to exit those waters and it is widely believed there is only one place they are going and this is into Irish seas, which are flooded with foreign vessels already."[35]

Collins further claimed that Spanish trucks are coming to the Cork fishing port of Castletownbere and "daily taking thousands of tonnes of fish from Irish seas from foreign vessels back to their country." Collins and a number of his fellow county councillors called for a separate Minister for Fisheries and a separate Department, taking it away from the Agriculture portfolio, where it will always be the junior partner.

The importance of access to waters around Ireland and Britain to other EU States was again emphasised when French President Macron in November 2018 declared that he would not agree to any British exit from any transition arrangements with the EU and the Irish Backstop, unless the UK agreed to French fishermen having access to its waters. Macron stated this was a Red Line for him[36]. It seems that our continental neighbours are much more conscious of the valuable resource that our rich fishing grounds represent, than many of our own leaders. Macron's remarks also contributed to stiffening British Parliamentary resistance to Mrs May's Withdrawal Agreement.

At the inaugural meeting in Dublin in 2018 of the Irish Freedom Party, which supports Irexit, where I spoke as an independent guest, it was noticeable that several people present came from fishing ports. However, unlike the position in Britain, some of the leaders of the Irish fishing industry seem pleased with the crumbs that fall from the EU table and are delighted to personally participate at the Brussels meetings where Irish fishing interests have been so neglected in the past.

I believe that even the most ardent europhile in Ireland would have great difficulty in claiming that Ireland's fishing interests are best served by our continued membership of the CFP. Most people in that camp simply regard the betrayal of the long-term potential of our marine resources, as a price worth paying for our EU membership. However, it is obvious that our marine industry would greatly benefit from the Irish State exiting the Common Fisheries Policy and agreeing with the UK for a joint management of fish stocks around the islands of Ireland and Britain.

Foreign Policy

One of the most enduring aspirations of those seeking a separate sovereign Irish State was, in the words of the Irish patriot Robert Emmet, that "Ireland would take its place among the Nations of the Earth." Even before the Anglo-Irish Treaty in 1922, the Irish revolutionaries established missions in places like France and the United States. Their primary aim was to gain international recognition for the newly declared Irish Republic, and secondly to seek financial assistance from the Irish Diaspora, through raising an external loan[37].

Their first initiative involved sending a deputation from the first Dáil, (a rebel Parliament set up by Irish MPs, who boycotted Westminster and established their own Assembly in Dublin) to the Paris Peace

Conference in 1919. The delegation, under future President Sean T O'Kelly, tried unsuccessfully to secure separate Irish representation at the Conference[38].

Shortly afterwards, Éamon de Valera, Harry Boland and Seán Nunan went to the USA to seek recognition from the Wilson administration in Washington for the Republic and also to raise funds. While official recognition was unsurprisingly not forthcoming, the Diaspora rallied to the cause and raised significant sums in support of the rebel Dáil.

In the period after the Treaty, Ireland tried, with the assistance of other British Dominions, especially Canada, to push out the boundaries of the limited status that the Treaty allowed the new Irish Free State in international affairs. As part of this process, Ireland joined the League of Nations (albeit as part of the British Empire) and worked through the Imperial Conferences in London in the 1920s and 30s, to further expand our ability to have a separate international profile, including making treaties with other countries, having an independent foreign policy and establishing our own diplomatic missions.

It was however, with Ireland's entry into the United Nations in 1955, after enduring ten years of a veto on Irish membership by the Soviet Union, that the Irish State's role in foreign affairs blossomed[39]. The Soviet action was particularly unfair, as Ireland had supported its application to join the old League of Nations in the 1930s, despite strong pressure from some other European countries[40]. The 1955 deal, which allowed 22 new entries into the UN was engineered by Irish Canadian, Paul Martin Snr. His son, also Paul Martin, later became Prime Minister of Canada. While serving as Irish Ambassador to Ottawa, I occasionally met with the former Prime Minister, we both were Trustees of the Irish Studies Department of Concordia University in Montreal. Paul was very proud that his father had assisted the land of his ancestors gain admittance to the UN. The younger Paul Martin was actually present in the UN in New York when Ireland was finally accepted. Once in the door of the UN and under the leadership of able Foreign Ministers, like Liam Cosgrave and Frank Aiken, Ireland developed a profile in areas such as peacekeeping, decolonisation, self-determination and the struggle against apartheid; on nuclear disarmament and non-proliferation; on protecting and promoting human rights; and on advancing human development. It was the golden age of an independent foreign policy. Ireland even risked the wrath of the United States and indeed the Catholic Church in America to support the entry of "Red China" into the UN[41], a brave move in the climate of those times.

There was also great pride in the country when the Irish army became involved in UN peacekeeping missions. Countless thousands of Irish men had travelled to far-flung parts of the British Empire, under the Union Jack to defend the colonial power; many had served as Wild Geese in the armies of continental Europe; others in the American, Canadian, Australian and New Zealand armies; but now for the first time, our people were going to places like the Belgian Congo, Cyprus, Middle East, etc., under the flag of peace. I, like many thousands of other schoolkids, came out for the funerals of Irish soldiers killed on peace keeping duties by rebel forces in the Congolese Province of Katanga (now Shaba)[42]. There was a huge outpouring of support for our troops at that time.

Giving up our ability to act independently in international matters, was not on the cards when Ireland joined the EEC in 1973. We were part of the western family of nations but not aligned to any military pact. In fact, as I heard frequently inside the Department of Foreign Affairs, Soviet Foreign Minister, Andrei Gromyko, once remarked to Irish Foreign Minister, Garret Fitzgerald, "You are not even aligned to the non-aligned movement." While we may have been unusual at the time, Ireland, and the people, were very much at ease with our independent international role.

When Ireland first joined the then EEC, this independent policy was not in danger. Cooperation with our fellow Member States was carried out in the European Political Cooperation (EPC) framework. This was essentially an informal method whereby intergovernmental cooperation and consultation was promoted through the foreign ministries, without any great central bureaucracy. The cooperation lay outside the Treaty framework. Meetings were chaired by the country holding the rotating EU Presidency and all meetings were held in the capital of the current chair of that Presidency. It was not centralised in Brussels. Communication between the capitals was through a secure system, known as COREU, an acronym based on the French Correspondence

Européene. At meetings, delegations could speak in English or French, without any translation. During my first three years in the Department of Foreign Affairs, I worked in the EPC area.

Cooperation between the capitals was good and although much of the work was pointless, decisions were non-binding and there was no effort made to railroad countries into supporting policies with which they did not agree. It was an excellent forum for information sharing and contact building. The EU Commission attended meetings as an observer.

However, those seeking "ever closer union" could not leave well enough alone. It was decided that EPC should be brought into the Treaty framework. The new Treaty entitled "The Single European Act" (SEA)[43] was adopted by Ireland in 1987 and this, inter alia, brought the informal EPC into the legal framework of the newly named European Community (EC). While the Government downplayed the change that the SEA represented, the courts took a different view.

In a landmark judicial decision, the Irish Supreme Court, in a case brought by the Trinity College lecturer, the late Raymond Crotty, decided that incorporation of EPC into EEC law represented a new surrender of Irish sovereignty, noting that the Irish Constitution in Article One states that the Irish Nation affirmed "it's inalienable, indefeasible and sovereign right to determine its relations with other nations." Therefore, it would require a referendum to surrender this right. This was the commencement of the requirement for any EU Treaty which represents a significant surrender of sovereignty to be put to a referendum (see Chapter 9).

The Single European Act was also the commencement of a series of new Treaties, all of which curtailed the scope for an independent foreign policy by individual Member States. Bit by bit, the Member States of the old EEC were ceding their powers to a Brussels bureaucracy and the Irish Government was enthusiastically cheering all the way. So much for the sacrifices of the men and women of 1916. However, things continued to move on.

The Maastricht Treaty created the new Common Foreign and Security Policy (CFSP) which introduced much greater coordination and restriction on the freedom of action of Member States. It also created the new European Union, discarding its former titles of the EEC and the EC. While the Maastricht Treaty still required that foreign policy decisions would need unanimity among Member States in the Council of the European Union, but once agreed, it also provided that certain aspects could be further decided by qualified majority voting.

Further changes occurred in subsequent Treaties such as Amsterdam and Lisbon, all in the same direction, to develop the European Union as a global player and to lessen the profile and relevance of the individual countries. The Amsterdam Treaty created a new position, the office of the High Representative for the Common Foreign and Security Policy, again lessening the role of the rotating Presidency in Foreign relations matters.

The 2009 Lisbon Treaty went much further than others and created the post of EU High Representative for Foreign Affairs and Security Policy. This, in effect, merged the post of EU Commissioner for External Affairs and the European Neighbourhood, with the High Representative. This new position is backed up by the European External Action Service (EEAS)[44] which is the EU's own diplomatic corps. It also carries the status as Vice President of the EU Commission. More and more of a State's apparatus was being put in place for the EU.

The EEAS sees itself as supplanting the individual national foreign services, similar to the role the State Department plays in the United States. While the EEAS has to be careful in dealing with the embassies and consulates of the larger EU Member States, it has no such restriction with the rest. I can readily testify that from my time as Irish Ambassador in Ottawa. There is a resentment and suspicion within the EEAS at the activities of individual embassies and a desire to control contacts with third countries.

Looking at how the Irish State acquiesced in this process, it seems that they are doing the precise opposite to what the founding fathers of the Irish State were attempting. Our early leaders wanted to enhance Ireland's role and profile internationally, while our new leaders seem to want to shrink it into being part of the new Empire of the EU. It seems a betrayal of all the heroic effort that went into nation building in the early part of the last century.

Now the British Government have declared that on Brexit, the country will take back full control from the EU of its foreign policy. This will include diplomatic relations, peacekeeping, defence and its overseas aid programme and will mean that the UK will not be subject to external restrictions in foreign affairs for the first time in 26 years.

The UK has signalled that it would like a cooperative arrangement in the area of security but no supervision or diktats from unelected officials in Brussels.

Given Ireland's history of no State involvement in colonialism, the strong antipathy to slavery in Ireland in the early nineteenth century, our rise from rags to riches, our disavowal of the arms industry and our strong commitment to humanitarian assistance, including generations of Irish missionaries, it is doubtful that we can be comfortably housed in foreign policy matters, with former colonial powers, such as Belgium, the Netherlands, France, etc.

If Ireland shook off the constraints of the CFSP, the country would be freer to pursue our own national policies. The Irish elite and our Government's excessive europhilia have tried to destroy Emmet's dream.

The level of EU coordination and attempted control of the foreign policies of the Member States is largely unknown among members of the general public. There was some surprise in Ireland when the Tánaiste and Minister for Foreign Affairs, Simon Coveney, raised doubts about Ireland's legal ability to impose a ban on imports of goods manufactured in the Occupied Territories of Palestine[45]. Coveney intimated that EU international commercial policy would not allow Ireland to engage in such an initiative, although this legal advice was strongly contested by the opposition parties.

It is depressing to listen to the Minister for Foreign Affairs and Trade answer Parliamentary questions in Dáil Éireann. Most replies seem to involve just explaining the EU position on the particular subject under discussion. There is very little national sentiment on display. It is a demonstration of how little independence Ireland exercises in the area of foreign policy. No wonder there is so little public interest in these question periods.

The onward march to extinguish the independence of the Member States continues. The former President of the EU Commission, Jean

Claude-Juncker, had proposed taking more decisions in the foreign policy areas by majority voting. In his State of the Union speech in September 2018, he proposed three new areas for this new procedure including; the launch and management of civilian security and defence missions; deploying sanctions; and collective response to human rights abuses[46]. He claimed that these amendments did not necessarily involve any Treaty changes. If adopted the days of a separate, independent Irish foreign policy would be ended and absorbed into a new Global EU.

Again, foreign policy is another area, which many people in Ireland feel uncomfortable with the changes that are taking place in the EU.

Summary of the Evolution of EU Common Foreign Policy

1970:   Introduction of the European Political Cooperation (EPC).

1986:   EPC Codified and brought into EEC structure by Single European Act (SEA).

1992:   Maastricht Treaty introduced the Common Foreign and Security Policy (CFSP). Decisions require unanimity in the European Council but once agreed further aspects can be decided by majority voting.

1997:   Amsterdam Treaty introduced the High Representative to be the face of EU. Increased EU role in Peacekeeping

2008:   Lisbon Treaty. High Representative gets place on EU Commission and chairs Foreign Affairs Council. EEAS set up and HR heads up European Defence Agency. EU Constitution actually used the title of EU Foreign Minister but dropped for Lisbon Treaty.

Irish Neutrality and the EU

One of the key elements in any decision on the best way forward for Ireland, post Brexit, relates to security policy. There are ongoing pressures within the EU to strengthen military cooperation between the Member States. Many of the EU Federalists make no hidden mystery about their strong desire for a European Army, under the control and direction of Brussels[47]. Some of these groups want the EU to become a global power, with the ability to project military might around the world.

This desire is linked to a growing detachment from the United States and resentment at the domination by that country of present military arrangements under NATO. President Macron of France went so far as to describe NATO as "brain dead"[48]. There is a fear among the more militaristic elements in Europe that the US is entering into one of its periodic bouts of isolationism[49]. This will have serious implications for those with a desire to engage militarily overseas. At present, the individual European countries have only a limited capacity to throw their weight around and rely on the US for logistical and other support systems to operate in conflict zones. As the US becomes more wary of foreign adventurism, some within the EU want to fill the vacuum left by Uncle Sam. To do that, they want a European Army, with a large European industrial-military complex in support.

There are many in Ireland who believe that claims of a future European Army are just scare stories. Former European Minister, Lucinda Creighton, even described reports about an EU Army as "pathetic", in the Irish edition of the *Sunday Times* on 7 May 2019. Yet, this is completely contrary to the evidence. In fact, the proposal to militarise the EU is receiving growing support among establishment figures in mainland Europe. The London Independent in November 2018 reported on the "delight" of the former EU Commission President Juncker at the support for a European Army from German Chancellor Angela Merkel and French President Emmanuel Macron[50]. On 13 November, Merkel, speaking to the European Parliament, had expressed unambiguously her support for "a real, true European Army." This echoed the strong commitment of Macron for a military wing to the EU. Macron had, somewhat farcically, earlier called for a European Army to protect the EU from Russia, China and the US[51], drawing a sharp rebuke from President Trump[52].

In January 2019, France and Germany signed a new friendship treaty in the German border city of Aachen, where Merkel again returned to the theme of an Army for the EU. She described the Treaty as another step forward towards the creation of a European Army[53]. The main opponent of a military arm for the EU, has always been the UK. Former Prime Minister David Cameron regularly denounced the idea[54]. Now with the Brits departing, the push for a European Army will be much more difficult to stop.

However, the European track record in this area is not good. The recent history of military interventions by the West, often initiated by European powers, in conflicts in the Middle East, and misadventures in places like the Ukraine, has been nothing short of disastrous and, in fact, shameful, bringing death and misery to countless innocent persons. It has helped create a tsunami of refugees heading for Europe. Speaking on Fox TV in April 2016, outgoing US President Barack Obama said that the intervention in Libya to oust President Gaddafi was the worst mistake of his Presidency[55]. He placed the blame squarely on the advice he took from his western European Allies, in particular France and the UK. In addition, some of the military hawks in Brussels have been building up the threat to western Europe of a resurgent Russia under President Putin as the pretext for greater security spending. This is essentially a nonsense and does not have any great evidential basis for these fears. If you are seeking to build up the military and extract large amounts of treasure from the State, it greatly helps to have an identifiable enemy, however unrealistic.

An obvious question must be raised as to why there has been so little in the mainstream media in Ireland on the issue of the militarisation of the EU. The establishment in Ireland know how unpopular this development is and want to either lessen the public impact by downplaying it as much as possible or ridiculing those who raise it as a serious concern. They hope that, as in some other areas, the public will learn to gradually accept that they will inevitably end up as part of an aggressive military alliance.

This type of militarist thinking at present finds no real resonance in Ireland, because of our history and political outlook. On the contrary, the Irish public have a long attachment to the concept of neutrality[56]. While the origin of that attachment lies deep in our history, it strengthened greatly in the second half of the twentieth century.

One of the early advocates of Irish neutrality was Dubliner Wolfe Tone, the Irish revolutionary figure and one of the founders of the United Irishmen movement. Tone is generally regarded as the father of Irish

Republicanism. In 1790, Tone published a pamphlet on the forthcoming British war with Spain where he advocated Irish neutrality[57]. He felt Ireland had no business getting involved in imperial wars, on behalf of the English Crown or any other overseas power. His United Irishmen movement followed Tone's approach on the issue. Irish Revolutionary leader James Connolly later captured the essence of this theme with his exhortation to Irishmen and women during the First World War, "We serve neither King nor Kaiser."

Over the course of centuries, Ireland or more accurately Irish people, have been heavily involved in every conflict where the British Empire became militarily engaged. The British administration in Ireland also had a heavy military element. This association with overseas conflicts and colonial pomp and glorification at home of all things military, ensured that the new administration in Dublin, post the Treaty, wanted to disengage with that element of our past. It wanted nothing to do with the tradition of helping to fight foreign wars, on behalf of others. As with many other countries, the horrors and futility of the First World War greatly added to this anti-imperialist sentiment in Ireland. But as with many other matters, the Irish Free State at its inception was not free to chart its own course but things were changing.

The British retained three ports in Southern Ireland post Treaty and declared their right to the use of any other Irish harbour facility at a time of conflict. It took to 1938 to finally get the three Treaty ports back. There were also other restrictions on the Free State in the military area, including restrictions on the size of any new Irish Army as well as limitations on an Irish Navy, including a bizarre prohibition on the Irish State building submarines, without the agreement of the British and other Commonwealth States[58].

The new Irish Free State, greatly assisted by independence impulses in Canada, gradually shook off the restrictions of the Treaty. (The Prime Minister of Canada, William Mackenzie King, was the grandson of William Lyon Mackenzie, a Scottish immigrant, who had been a leader of the Upper Canada (Ontario) rebellion in 1837 against British misrule.) The Canadian Prime Minister also had opposed conscription during World War One and was required to delicately balance French/English relations in Canada. The French speaking population of Canada and its political representatives were less than enthusiastic about participating in foreign wars on behalf of the English monarch.

As every schoolchild in Ireland knows, Irish neutrality came into its own during the Second World War, when Taoiseach Éamon de Valera doggedly pursued a public policy of neutrality, while covertly assisting the Allies. This maintained the peace internally, while hundreds of thousands of Irishmen and women volunteered for service with the Allies. The Irish policy of neutrality was roundly condemned by many on the Allied side and especially so by British Prime Minister, Winston Churchill. However, de Valera's policy was deeply popular with the domestic Irish public, who realized that any policy, other than neutrality would have opened up old wounds. It had the support of the main Opposition parties at the time. Only one Parliamentarian, James Dillon, who resigned from the Opposition party Fine Gael, was the sole Parliamentary voice calling for Ireland to join the Allies. Dillon later served as a Cabinet Minister and went on to be elected leader of Fine Gael[59].

The neutrality stance managed to save the Irish State from the mayhem of that global conflagration. The row with Winston Churchill only served to bolster support in Ireland for the policy. It is almost an iron rule of Irish politics that once a Dublin/London spat breaks out, the Irish population will rally to the home cause. Hence, neutrality entered into the theology of the young Irish State.

This was further consolidated in the post war period. Throughout the 1950s and 60s, Ireland regularly proclaimed itself proudly as a neutral State, while also maintaining a strong anti-communist position. Hence the issue of neutrality, and the strong Irish public support for it, was the subject of controversy when the decision to apply for membership of the EEC was taken. None of the six founding countries, nor either of the two other new entrants, Denmark or the United Kingdom, were neutral.

At that point in time, the Irish public cherished neutrality and regarded it as an expression of Irish identity and an element, which distinguished Ireland from Britain. This was of course in direct contradiction to the idea of an ever-closer union in Europe with a single State, with its own army, currency, diplomatic corps, etc. However, the then EEC did not have a defence element, leaving such matters to the larger organisation,

NATO. There was no real pressure on Ireland to abandon its traditional policy of neutrality during the early years as a member of the EEC.

As part of the campaign to have the Nice Treaty ratified in Ireland after the failed first referendum, Ireland secured the agreement of the other members of the EU to the Seville Declaration at the European Council meeting in that southern Spanish city[60]. This was a political declaration which recognised Ireland's triple lock before Ireland could participate in EU military operations. Such deployments must be approved by the UN Security Council; the Irish Parliament; and, also, the Irish Cabinet. While the declaration had no legal standing, it was an important political proclamation and helped win the second Nice referendum. It demonstrated the strength of feelings on the issue of neutrality in Ireland at the time.

Today, the situation is totally changed. There is less and less tolerance for neutrality inside the EU. Having worked with several Irish Foreign Ministers, I saw at close quarters that our politicians were genuinely worried about the erosion of neutrality. On the other hand, there were always officials who were anxious to push Ireland down the military alliance route but Ministers such as Dermot Ahern, David Andrews, etc. were very clear about their views and baulked at any hint of abandoning the policy. This reflected the Irish public's genuine attachment to the tradition of neutrality.

While there is external pressure to row in with the militarisation of the EU, there are now voices being raised by pro-EU elements inside the country calling for Ireland to abandon the neutrality policy. This is a relatively new development and reflects the growing assertiveness of the local EU lobby.

On 9 March 2018, the then four Fine Gael MEPs, together launched a policy document entitled "Ireland and the EU: Defending our Common European Home"[61]. This document marked a huge sea change with the previous Irish consensus, and indeed generations of Fine Gael politicians by calling, inter alia, for:

The dropping of the Triple Lock by allowing the Irish Defence Forces take part in overseas missions, not sanctioned by a UN Mandate

Supporting the emerging EU Defence Union

Redefining Neutrality

Much greater expenditure on the military

Developing an Irish Defence industry

Supporting the Irish Government's decision to join PESCO.

Speaking at the launch of the policy paper, Dublin MEP, Brian Hayes was quoted as saying that post-Brexit Ireland needed to demonstrate its commitment to the EU and hence moderate its former neutrality stance. This new initiative represents a threat to Ireland's traditional position, but there is no real evidence that it has any popular support, but will no doubt be backed by elements in the establishment, including europhiles in the diplomatic service and the media.

The desire to sacrifice our neutrality to appease Brussels was also demonstrated by the Irish Government decision to join PESCO. This acronym stands for Permanent Structured Cooperation and is the latest move towards a common defence policy. In all 25 members of the EU signed up, including Ireland. However, the UK, Malta and Denmark did not agree to take part[62]. The Bill to ratify the Irish membership of PESCO was rushed through the Dáil, with very little notice and a very short debate. The vote in favour was 75 to 42, with Fine Gael and Fianna Fáil providing the necessary votes. The Irish general election in 2020 changed the arithmetic in the Dáil and it would be more difficult to get such an authorisation through the new Parliament.

PESCO is a framework, established under the Lisbon Treaty to deepen defence cooperation among Member States, under a number of headings. Countries can decide which areas they wish to participate in. Membership of PESCO entails sustained financial commitments and for countries like Ireland, much greater military expenditure. There is an underlying commitment to strengthen the European arms industry, which post Brexit will be essentially French.

The suspicion must be that Ireland signed up for PESCO to ingratiate itself with Brussels during the Brexit discussions. There is very little appetite for militarism in Ireland, and the long-term ambitions of

PESCO certainly seem incompatible with Irish Neutrality and indeed with Article 29.9 of the Irish Constitution which states, "The State shall not adopt a decision taken by the European Council to establish a common Defence pursuant to Article 42 of the Treaty on the European Union where the common Defence includes the State."

This article is the last obstacle against an abandonment of our neutrality but no doubt the Irish people will be subject to a conditioning process and then be suddenly faced with a decision to ditch the article, or face huge negative consequences, at some point in the future. It will require a lot of softening up in advance to convince the Irish people along that line. Some of that softening up has already taken place and the initiative of the Fine Gael MEPs and their policy document should be seen as part of that process.

One other point to consider is that, with cross Atlantic rivalries increasing and the UK aligning itself with NATO and the Americans, and the Europeans going their own way in military terms, the Irish border may at some stage in the future be the frontier between two competing military alliances. That would be a very uncomfortable position for Ireland. The decision of Denmark to stay out of PESCO might be seen to be much wiser than Ireland's desire to curry favour with Brussels during Brexit. It should also be noted that de Valera was very careful to continually give reassurances that Ireland would never allow itself to be used as a base for a foreign power to attack Britain[63].

It is very difficult to reconcile Ireland's traditional policy of neutrality with our current Taoiseach Leo Varadkar's personal view as reported, namely that a "Europe that is worth building is a Europe worth defending."[64]

Again, defence and security are areas where many in Ireland would have concerns about the way the EU is developing.

Agriculture

For those who support the EU in Ireland, the Common Agriculture Policy (CAP) was the jewel in the crown. It was, probably, the main attraction for Ireland in joining the then EEC. At that stage, according to EU figures nearly 24% of the working Irish population was engaged in the food industry[65]. This totally dominated the Irish attitude to the EEC in the early years of membership. The bulk of our receipts from Brussels have always come via the CAP. Right from the outset, Ireland was among the staunchest defenders of the system, even when agricultural support took up the bulk of the EEC budget, 73% in 1985[66]. Today the CAP still supplies two-thirds of the Irish receipts from the EU or €1.2bn per annum.

Even those, including myself, who today believe that Ireland would be best served by looking seriously at Irexit should recognise the valuable contribution that the CAP made to rural Ireland, and by extension to the Irish economy in the early years of membership of the EEC. That membership, and consequently access to agricultural support, was a huge boom for Irish farmers and their families. In the 1960s, I spend most summers in rural county Laois helping on farms, owned by relatives, near the little village of Rosenallis, nestled at the base of the Slieve Bloom Mountains. They were hard-working, honest people who produced the most wonderful food. It was the best education I ever got. There was nothing like days of weeding beet, feeding pigs and thinning turnips to keep a person grounded. It left me with a life-long affection for rural Ireland.

However, my relatives, as with all farming families, had to contend with our next-door neighbour's policy of keeping the price of food stuffs as low as possible, the British cheap food policy. Ireland was very much a price taker in those days, and it had the effect of keeping farm incomes low. It was not all doom and gloom and changes were taking place in the 1960s in agriculture, just as in every other sector of the economy. Farm incomes had risen by 52% between 1960–68 and the number of holdings had fallen by 17% during the same time period[67]. Looking back on the 1960s, it is as if Ireland woke up from a Rip Van Winkle like sleep and started functioning again after decades of slumber.

The arrival of a system whereby there was a guaranteed price for products such as beef, milk, tillage crops, sheep meat, etc., brought a new and very welcome prosperity to the countryside in Ireland. It reinforced the upward trend in farm incomes.

Therefore, Ireland became a fierce defender of the CAP and the interests of the farming community. In our desire to preserve the CAP, Ireland relied heavily on France, another country with a large agricultural sector. After all, the establishment of a CAP was one of the conditions that France required before it agreed to the Treaty of Rome in 1957. France also insisted that EEC financing of the CAP was in place before the UK could join. As former British Prime Minister, Ted Heath, wrote in his autobiography, *The Course of My Life*, "The French did not wish the British to be at the table taking part in the formative discussions on the CAP, for fear we might disrupt the very favourable arrangements they otherwise had every reason to expect."[68]

There have been innumerable attempts at reforming the CAP over the years, some more successful than others. Throughout these negotiations, Ireland could always look to France as our bulwark against the more radical attempts at reform. Even so, the % of the EU budget that goes to agriculture had fallen to 37% in 2017[69].

The current French President, Emmanuel Macron, has issued conflicting signals on whether that traditional French support for the CAP is about to change. The new MFF (EU Budget) for 2021–2027 is under negotiation. This will determine the level of funding that the CAP will receive over that period. Since Irish farming is overwhelmingly reliant on the direct farm payments under CAP[70], there is, naturally enough, great anxiety among farming families about their future incomes.

This Hiberno-French alliance could come under strain, as the French have signalled a change in French policy. The authoritative website Politico.eu., reported that Macron wrote urging Brussels to prioritise defence and education, while undertaking a "deep reform of the oldest policies (the Common Agricultural Policy – CAP – and cohesion policy)" in order to "better meet the challenges to which these policies must respond, for the sake of looking for efficiency and to add value at the European level."[71]. In diplomatic speak, Macron was calling for deep cuts to the CAP.

The French President did not seem anxious at that time to take on a difficult battle, preserving the CAP, but with his support level plummeting in the opinion polls, Macron returned to the traditional supportive position once detailed proposals emerged from the EU on potential CAP savings in their initial MFF proposals[72]. Clearly any radical changes here are likely to disproportionately affect Ireland. Changes in the CAP would be vigorously resisted by the powerful farming community in Ireland. They would also lead to a further ballooning out of the large Irish net contribution to the EU budget. They would herald the ending of the love affair between Irish farmers and the EU.

As demonstrated in a number of other areas, France can articulate completely different viewpoints at the same time and is well capable of an effortless 180-degree about-turn in policy. President Macron's U-turn on national budget deficits, in the face of the yellow vest protests, is a very good example. Relying on French support is not a firm foundation for securing the future of Irish agriculture. It may be time to have a fundamental rethink of our attitude to the CAP.

The Commission proposals by Commissioner Hogan, on 1 June 2018, represented a complex and far reaching effort to balance the demands for reform and a curtailment of costs, with the very desirable objective of ensuring a viable and socially sustainable rural economy[73]. This is the start of another very difficult process of reform, with a particular emphasis on the further reduction in the cost of the CAP.

Ireland would be a lot better off in seeking to use new flexibility, contained within the Commission proposals, for more support at a national level for rural communities, rather than merely calling for more overall money for the CAP. Given Ireland's small proportion of overall CAP receipts, most of any extra money sent to Brussels from Ireland in the hope of supporting our farmers, will be swallowed up elsewhere in the EU.

The glory days of Irish Agriculture Ministers returning from Brussels with large increases in financial support to great acclaim from farming organizations are long gone. The role of Irish Agriculture Ministers, at the moment, seems to be about managing decline and explaining to Irish farmers why support levels are being cut.

It seems that with every new trade deal that the EU enters into, the difficulties for European, and particularly Irish agriculture, are increased, especially so for beef farmers. This was starkly illustrated by the agreement of the EU to a trade deal with Mercosur, an organisation of American States. The deal, which includes a new facility to import 99,000 tons of South American beef at preferential tariff rates, will impact adversely on Irish beef farmers. The President of the Irish Farmers Association, Joe

Healy, called the deal a sell-out of Irish agriculture: "This is a bad deal for Ireland and for Irish farmers, it's a bad deal for the environment and it's a bad deal for EU standards and consumers"[74].

Unfortunately, this trend is likely to continue in future trade deals. In an unprecedented move, the Irish Parliament (Dáil), supported a Sinn Féin motion to reject the Mercosur deal by 84 votes to 46[75]. This represents a sea change in Irish attitudes.

With the change from price support for products to direct farm payments, it means that the paymaster can much more readily be switched from Brussels to Dublin. Since there would be a large saving to the Exchequer in Dublin from Ireland exiting the EU, there should be no difficulty in providing the same, or even more support, to farming families, should Irexit occur in the future. In fact, support to farmers in Ireland would appear to be much more secure in the longer term by a renationalising of agriculture rather than in maintaining the CAP. The Irish State today is a wealthy northern European country where the latest census reveals that only 4.6% of total employment is in farming[76]. Ireland could reshape its rural development policy to give greater support to families in farming and secure an environmentally sound future for them, if we were outside the CAP.

It should be noted that non-EU countries in western Europe, including Switzerland, Norway and Iceland all provide strong financial support for their farming communities. Therefore, an Irish exit from the CAP may be more in the rural communities' longer-term interests. The situation is completely different from accession in 1973, when Ireland could not have afforded strong support for its farmers. Here again the changes in the EU are running against Ireland's national interest.

Social Policy and Human Rights

In many discussions in Ireland where I have been involved, the issue of social policy and the beneficial role of the EU comes up regularly. Many older people in Ireland still remember with gratitude, the part the EU played in the modernisation of social attitudes in Ireland. At accession in 1973, Ireland was the most socially conservative country of the nine members of the EEC.

Many of the restrictions on women, such as a marriage ban in public sector employment, which had been widespread in western societies until the mid-twentieth century[77], still were in force in Ireland by the time of accession[78]. The marriage ban In the United Kingdom, including Northern Ireland, which prohibited married women from joining the Civil Service and required those already in the service to resign when they married (unless granted a waiver) was abolished for the Home Civil Service in 1946 and for the Foreign Office in 1973. The recruitment of large numbers of women into the British Civil Service during the Second World War, hurried the change in Britain[79].

Ireland was indeed required by EEC membership to bring itself into line with European developments. This was a very progressive influence in the sense that it hastened change. There are some pro-EU supporters in Ireland who seem stuck in the 1970s. Again, this attitude is completely outdated and is actually insulting to Irish people, as if the population cannot be trusted and need an external big brother to ensure that it does the right thing.

Ireland has greatly changed and no longer needs an outside authority to push it into giving women and members of the LGBT community their civil and human rights. The Irish referendum in May 2015, which approved same sex marriages, showed just how much Irish society has changed. The referendum result was a 62% vote in favour of providing for same sex marriage, with an overall turnout of 60%[80]. It should be noted that another EU country, Slovenia, voted against a similar proposal in a referendum in December 2015[81]. Membership of the EU was not a relevant factor in either referendum. The election of Leo Varadkar, an openly gay man, as Taoiseach is a further illustration of these trends. There has been much more interest abroad in Varadkar's personal preferences in this regard than in Ireland.

While the EU has its own Charter of Fundamental Rights[82], many Irish people confuse the roles of the Council of Europe's Court of Human Rights in Strasbourg, with the EU's court of Justice in The Hague.

The Charter was instituted to enhance the concept of the EU as a State, with all the trappings of the traditional Nation State. As former Trinity College Dublin lecturer Dr Anthony Coughlan wrote:

A basic objection to the conferral of a human rights competence on the EU, whatever one's view as to the content of human rights, is that such a development is quite unnecessary as all the Member States are already bound by the provisions of the European Convention on Human Rights, which they acceded to well before the EU Charter of Fundamental Rights was thought of. Moreover, there are already human rights provisions in the national Constitutions of each Member State. The only reason for the EU arrogating to itself a human rights competence would seem to be a desire to build itself up further as a quasi-Federal State[83].

Any decision by Ireland to leave the EU should not affect the country's participation in the Strasbourg body, which is a Europe-wide institution and not just confined to EU members. This court has played an important role in the development of human rights in Ireland, e.g. the McGee contraception case, the Norris gay rights case and the case against the British Government over the use of inhuman and degrading treatment of some Internees in the 1970s in the North. Human Rights should be seen as universal and not the preserve of any institution or exclusively confined to any group of nations. Leaving the EU, an Irexit, would have little effect, good, bad or indifferent, on social and human rights policy in Ireland.

Overall

I believe it is fair to state that the Irish experience in the EU has been beneficial overall, especially in the early years but that balance is shifting significantly, as the country's internal and external situation changes. Now with the departure of the UK that net balance of advantage from full membership has disappeared and the negative side has grown considerably. It is very hard to find correspondingly positive developments which would rebalance the ledger back in favour of continued membership.

Therefore, I believe that it is time for those who advocate the continuation of Ireland's membership of the EU to articulate a new vision on why we should continue on with the present arrangements, as bit by bit the conditions change for the worse for Ireland. It is no good just relying on old fashioned Anglophobia. Post Brexit, the UK will be out of the equation.

This theme is further developed in the chapter on the ever-closer union.

References

1. Rachel Donnelly *"Trade pact improved Anglo Irish relations"* Irish Times, 2 January 1996 *https://www.irishtimes.com/news/trade-pact-improved-anglo-irish-relations-1.18236*. Retrieved 16 May 2019.

2. Terry McGuinness and Melanie Gower, *"The Common Travel Area, and the special status of Irish nationals in UK law"* Briefing Paper Number 7661, 9 June 2017, House of Commons Library. *https://researchbriefings.files.parliament.uk/documents/CBP-7661/CBP-7661.pdf*. Retrieved 16 May 2019

3. Tony Connolly *"Varadkar speech bolsters European credentials"* RTÉ website, 17 January 2018. *https://www.rte.ie/news/analysis-and-comment/2018/0117/933987-varadkar-europe-speech/*. Retrieved 16 May 2019

4. Department of Finance figures, https://www.gov.ie/en/organisation/department-of-finance/?referrer=/updates/budget-statistics-2016

5. Ray Bassett, *"We will be soon picking up the bill for Brexit"* Sunday Business Post 14 January 2018, *https://www.businesspost.ie/opinion/well-soon-picking-real-bill-brexit-406498*. Retrieved 17 May 2019.

6. Department of Finance Publication "Budgetary Statistics 2018", 14 November 2019. www.gov.ie/en/publica, retrieved 16 December 2019.

7. Conor Finnerty *"Who got the biggest CAP payments in Ireland last year?"* Agriland, 31 May 2017. *http://www.agriland.ie/farming-news/who-were-the-top-beneficiaries-of-cap-payments-in-ireland-last-year/*. Retrieved 17 May 2019

8. Conor Finnerty *"Hogan concedes that cuts to the CAP budget are 'realistic"*. Agriland 20 April 2018. *https://www.agriland.ie/farming-news/hogan-concedes-that-cuts-to-the-cap-budget-are-realistic/*. Retrieved 18 May 2019

9. European Commission Blog, Gunter Ottinger *"A budget matching our ambitions"* Speech, 8 January 2018. *https://ec.europa.eu/commission/commissioners/2014-2019/oettinger/blog/budget-matching-our-ambitions-speech-given-conference-shaping-our-future-812018_en*. Retrieved 17 May 2019

10. Eoin Burke-Kennedy *"Ireland's budget contribution may rise to over €3bn"* *Irish Times*, 6 May 2018. *https://www.irishtimes.com/business/economy/ireland-s-eu-budget-contribution-may-rise-to-over-3bn-1.3486204*. Retrieved 17 May 2019

11. Ronan McGreevy *"Taoiseach predicts steep rise in Ireland's contribution to the EU budget"* *Irish Times*, 15 November 2019, *https://www.irishtimes.com/news/ireland/irish-news/taoiseach-predicts-steep-rise-in-ireland-s-contribution-to-the-eu-budget-1.4084499*. Retrieved 16 December 2019

12. Rebecca *Perring "EU on the BRINK as Netherlands REFUSE to pay more to plug Brexit blackhole". Express.* 19.Feb 2018. *https://www.express.co.uk/news/world/920975/Brexit-news-netherlands-EU-latest-news-budget-contributions-Brexit-blackhole*. Retrieved 17 May 2019

13. Margaret Donnelly *"Ireland would consider increasing EU contributions, if CAP is protected – Varadkar". Irish Independent*, 21 February 2018. *https://www.independent.ie/business/farming/ireland-would-consider-increasing-eu-contributions-if-cap-is-protected-varadkar-36620227.htm*l. Retrieved 17 May 2019.

14. Juno McEnroe *"Leo Varadkar rules out supporting the EU Budget"* The Irish Examiner, 21 Feb 2020. *https://www.irishexaminer.com/breakingnews/business/leo-varadkar-rules-out-supporting-the-eus-proposed-budget-983222.html*. Retrieved 4 March 2020

15. Lindsay Razaq *"Study finds 92% of fishermen will vote for Brexit"* The Press and Journal,10 June 2016. *https://www.pressandjournal.co.uk/fp/news/uk/942753/skippers-want-out-of-eu-according-to-aberdeen-university-research/*. Retrieved on 17 May 2019

16. Michael Gove *"Brexit is a chance to take back control of our enviro*nment" Politico.eu, 25 January 2018. *https://www.politico.eu/article/michael-gove-opinion-brexit-is-a-chance-to-take-back-control-of-our-environment/*. Retrieved 17 May 2019

17. Ireland's Ocean environment. *http://www.askaboutireland.ie/reading-room/environment-geography/marine-environment/irelands-ocean-environmen/*. Retrieved 17 May 2019

18. United Nations Convention on the Law of the Sea. *https://www.un.org/Depts/los/convention_agreements/texts/unclos/unclos_e.pdf*. Retrieved 17 May 2019

19. John de Courcy Ireland "Ireland's Sea Fisheries, a History 1981" p 31-37

20. Michael Hennigan *"Irish fisheries industry and myth of EU stealing our fish"* 30 November 2015. *http://www.finfacts.ie/Irish_finance_news/*

articleDetail.php?Irish-fisheries-industry-and-myth-of-EU-stealing-our-fish-392. Retrieved 17 May 2019

21. The Economic and Social Research Institute *"Development of the Irish Fishing Industry and its regional implications"* July 1980 p2

22. Christopher Booker and Richard North *The Great Deception* p 180–184

23. Ibid. p 180

24. Daniel Johnston *"The Price of Entry". Daily Telegraph*, 9 September 2000 *https://www.telegraph.co.uk/comment/4254752/The-price-of-entry.html.* Retrieved 17 May 2019

25. Christopher Booker and Richard North *The Great Deception* p192

26. The Hague Preferences is a CFP mechanism designed to adjust national fish allocations to take account of the needs of certain fisheries dependent areas of Ireland and northern regions of Britain

27. Dáil Debate, 296 Cols 666 669

28. Tim Pat Coogan's Blog *"The disaster that is the Irish fishing industry"* 9 April 2009. *http://www.timpatcoogan.com/blog/2009/04/the-disaster-that-is-the-irish-fishing-industry/.* Retrieved 18 May 2019

29. *https://ore.exeter.ac.uk/repository/handle/10871/30201#5OPkAWwhJDMsp Eze.99.* Retrieved 18 May 2019

30. Remarks by Dr Karen Devin at the Irexit Conference 3 February 2018. *https://www.youtube.com/watch?v=L2r6Vqllnmw.* Retrieved 18 May 2019

31. Norwegian Seafood Council *"Norwegian seafood exports will exceed NOR 90bn in 2016".*23 February 2017. *https://en.seafood.no/news-and-media/news-archive/norwegian-seafood-exports-will-exceed-nok-90-billion-in-2016/.* Retrieved 18 May 2019.

32. Bord Iascaigh Mhara (BIM) Ireland's (Marine Fisheries' Board) *"The Business of Seafood 2017". http://www.bim.ie/media/bim/content/publications/corporate-other-publications/7097-BIM-Business-of-Seafood-2017.pdf.* Retrieved 18 May 2019

33. Killian Woods *"Why Irish fishers are right to be worried about the UK taking back control of its waters"* FOR A 16 July 2017. *https://fora.ie/irish-fishing-brexit-explainer-3495322-Jul2017/.* Retrieved 18 May 2019

34. KFO website 15 December 2018. *http://www.kfo.ie/* Retrieved 30 March 2019

35. Kieron O Mahony *"Irish fishermen are the 'poor relation' and should have separate ministry"* 13 December 2018. *https://www.southernstar.ie/news/*

farming/articles/2018/12/13/4166240-irish-fishermen-are-the-poor-relation-and-should-have-separate-ministry/. Retrieved 18 May 2019

36. Tim Sculthorpe "*Macron warns he will FORCE Britain into Irish border 'backstop' if it does not give the French access to UK fishing waters*". 25 November 2018. *https://www.dailymail.co.uk/news/article-6426739/Macron-warns-Britain-FORCED-backstop-fishing.html.* Retrieved 18 May 2018

37. Documents on Irish Foreign Policy, Volume 1, p xi

38. Ibid. p 5

39. *Ireland 60 years at the United Nations,* published by the Department of Foreign Affairs and Trade, 2015. *https://www.dfa.ie/media/dfa/alldfawebsitemedia/aboutus/globalhorizonsyouthinitiative/Ireland---60-Years-at-the-United-Nations.pdf.* Retrieved 18 May 2019

40. Documents on Irish Foreign Policy Volume IV p306-309

41. Joe Carroll "*Frank Aiken: Nationalist to Internationalist*". ed. by Bryce Evans and Stephen Kelly (Irish Academic Press)

42. David O Donoghue "*The Irish Army in the Congo, 1960-1964: The Far Battalions*" Irish academic press. *https://www.historyireland.com/20th-century-contemporary-history/the-irish-army-in-the-congo-1960-64-the-far-battalions/.* Retrieved 18 May 2019

43. *https://eur-lex.europa.eu/legal-content/EN/TXT/?uri=LEGISSUM%3Axy0027.* Retrieved 18 May 2018

44. European External Action Service website. *https://eeas.europa.eu/headquarters/headquarters-homepage/82/about-european-external-action-service-eeas_en.* Retrieved 18 May 201

45. Miriam Lord "*A daring U-turn on occupied territories, FF veteran goes from opposing to supporting Frances Black's Bill, but Coveney's not happy*" Irish Times, 14 July 2018. *https://www.irishtimes.com/news/politics/miriam-lord-a-daring-u-turn-on-occupied-territories-1.3564484.* Retrieved 18 May 2019

46. European Commission, 12 September 2018. *http://europa.eu/rapid/press-release_IP-18-5683_en.htm.* Retrieved 18 May 2019

47. BBC News "*We need a European Army, says Jean-Claude Juncker*" 9 March 2015 *https://www.bbc.com/news/world-europe-31796337.* Retrieved 19 May 2019

48. "*Nato alliance experiencing brain death, says Macron*" BBC News, 7 November 2019, *https://www.bbc.com/news/world-europe-50335257.* Retrieved 17 December 2019

49. Charles Krauthammer *"Trump's Foreign Policy Revolution"* 27 January 2017, National *Review. https://www.nationalreview.com/2017/01/ trump-foreign-policy-isolationsim-america-first-allies-nato-trans-pacific-partnership/.* Retrieved 19 May 2019.

50. Jon Stone *"EU Army: Brussels delighted that Angela Merkel and Macron want to create European military force"*, London Independent 14 November 2018. *https://www.independent.co.uk/news/world/europe/ eu-army-angela-merkel-macron-germany-france-military-european-commission-juncker-a8633196.html.* Retrieved 19 May 2019

51. Euractiv *"Macron calls for 'true European army' to defend against Russia, US, China"* 7 November 2018. *https://www.euractiv.com/section/defence-and-security/news/macron-calls-for-european-army-to-defend-against-russia-us-china/.* Retrieved 19 May 2019

52. Chris Stevenson and Jon Stone *"Trump attacks Macron's call for European Army to defend against USA as very insulting"* 9 November 2018. *https:// www.independent.co.uk/news/world/americas/us-politics/eu-army-trump-macron-france-europe-military-us-russia-china-defence-a8627176.html.* Retrieved 19 May 2019

53. Julian Robinson *"Merkel boasts Germany and France have taken the first steps towards 'a European ARMY' after signing friendship treaty with Macron"*. Mail on line 12 January 2019. *https://www.dailymail.co.uk/ news/article-6618789/Merkel-boasts-Germany-France-taken-steps-European-ARMY-signing-pact.html.* Retrieved 19 May 2019.

54. Bruno Waterfield *"David Cameron fights off EU Army plan"*, *Daily Telegraph* 19 December 2013. *https://www.telegraph.co.uk/news/ worldnews/europe/eu/10528852/David-Cameron-flies-to-Brussels-determined-to-fight-EU-drones-programme.html.* Retrieved 19 May 2019.

55. The Guardian, *'Barack Obama says Libya was 'worst mistake' of his presidency"*, 12 April 55 2016. *https://www.theguardian.com/us-news/2016/apr/12/barack-obama-says-libya-was-worst-mistake-of-his-presidency.* Retrieved 19 May 2019.

56. *"New Red C Poll Shows that Irish People Want Neutrality"* Shannonwatch publication, 17 *September 2013. http://www.shannonwatch.org/story/new-red-c-poll-shows-irish-people-want-neutrality.* Retrieved 19 May 2019.

57. Theobald Wolfe Tone *"The Spanish War 1790"*. Republished by PANA. *https://www.pana.ie/download/spanishwar.pdf.* Retrieved 19 May 2019

58. Defence section of the Anglo-Irish Treaty(7-10). Documents on Irish Foreign Policy, Volume 1, p368.

59. Maurice Manning *James Dillon, A biography*, 2000 Wolfhound Press.

60. Text of Saville Declaration 21. June 2006 RTÉ News website.
https://www.rte.ie/news/2002/0621/26908-declarations/.
Retrieved 19 May 2019

61. Peter Murtagh *"Ireland should consider joining EU Defence Union,
say MEPs" Irish Times*, 9 March 2018. *https://www.irishtimes.com/
news/politics/ireland-should-consider-joining-eu-defence-union-say-
meps-1.3421127*. Retrieved 19 May 2019

62. Evan Short *"Objection voiced as Ireland signs up to EU defense pact"* Irish
Central, 12 December 2017. *https://www.irishcentral.com/news/politics/
ireland-neutrality-eu-defense-pact*. Retrieved 19 May 2019.

63. Documents on Irish Foreign Policy Volume V p106

64. Speech by Taoiseach, Leo Varadkar, to the European Parliament,
17 January 2019. *https://merrionstreet.ie/en/NewsRoom/Speeches/Speech_
by_An_Taoiseach_Leo_Varadkar_to_the_European_Parliament.html*.
Retrieved 19 May 2019

65. European Union Representation in Ireland Website. *"Impact of EU
membership on Ireland"*. *https://ec.europa.eu/ireland/about-us/impact-of-
EU-membership-on-Ireland_e*n. Retrieved 20 May 2019

66. *"CAP expenditure in the Total EU expenditure"*. *https://ec.europa.eu/
agriculture/sites/agriculture/files/cap-post-2013/graphs/graph1_en.pdf*.
Retrieved 20 May 2019

67. *"The Lead up to Joining the EEC" Irish Country Life History*.
6 August 2018 *http://countrylifehistory.ie/index.php/2018/08/the-lead-up-
to-joining-the-eec/*. Retrieved 20 May 2019

68. Edward Heath *The Course of My Life* p 222

69. European Commission "How the Budget is spent" https://europa.eu/
european-union/about-eu/eu-budget/expenditure_en.
Retrieved 30 May 2019

70. Gillian Dufficy *"Direct payments keeping the average Irish drystock farm
afloat"*. Agriland 1 June 2017. *https://www.agriland.ie/farming-news/
direct-payments-keeping-the-average-irish-drystock-farm-afloat/*.
Retrieved 20 May 2019

71. Emmet Livingstone, Maia de la Baume and David M Herszenhorn
"Macron breaks French Taboo on Farm Subsidies" 20 April 2018. *https://
www.politico.eu/article/emmanuel-macron-breaks-french-taboo-on-farm-
subsidies-cap-policy-eu-budget/*. Retrieved 20 May 2019

72. *"Macron vows to support French farmers amid threats of CAP cuts"* Farming Independent 23 Feb 2020, *https://www.independent.ie/business/farming/news/world-news/macron-vows-to-support-french-farmers-amid-threats-of-cap-cuts-38982372.html.* Retrieved 6 March 2020

73. European Union Website *"Future of the Common Agricultural Policy". https://ec.europa.eu/info/food-farming-fisheries/key-policies/common-agricultural-policy/future-cap_en.* Retrieved 20 May 2019

74. *'A bad deal for Irish farmers': EU signs massive trade agreement with South American countries".* The Journal.ie 28 June 2019. *https://www.thejournal.ie/beef-farmer-trade-deal-4702670-Jun2019/.* Retrieved 30 June 2019

75. Mícheál Lehane, *"Govt defeated as Dáil votes to reject EU-Mercosur trade deal"* RTÉ News, 11 July 2019. *https://www.rte.ie/news/politics/2019/0711/1061588-mercosur-dail-vote.* Retrieved 18 July 2019

76. Ciaran Moran *"Proportion of farmers in the workforce down 85% in last 50 years – CSO"*, 15 June 2017. h*ttps://www.independent.ie/business/farming/rural-life/proportion-of-farmers-in-the-workforce-down-85-in-last-50-years-cso-35829292.htm*l. Retrieved 20 May 2019

77. Marriage Bar, *Revolvy https://www.revolvy.com/topic/Marriage%20bar&item_type=topic.* Retrieved 20 May 2019.

78. Civil Service (Employment of Married Women) Act, 1973. *http://www.irishstatutebook.ie/eli/1973/act/17/enacted/en/html.* Retrieved 20 May 2019

79. Women in the Civil Service – History. *https://civilservant.org.uk/women-history.htm*l. Retrieved 20 May 2019

80. Éanna O Caollaí and Mark Hilliard *"Ireland becomes first country to approve same-sex marriage by popular vote". Irish Times* 23 May 2015, *https://www.irishtimes.com/news/politics/ireland-becomes-first-country-to-approve-same-sex-marriage-by-popular-vote-1.2223646.* Retrieved 20 May 2019

81. Eleanor Ross *"Slovenia rejects same-sex marriage proposal in referendum"* The London Independent 21 December 2015. *https://www.independent.co.uk/news/world/europe/slovenia-rejects-same-sex-marriage-proposal-in-referendum-a6781586.ht*ml. Retrieved 20 May 2019

82. EU Charter of Fundamental Rights. *//ec.europa.eu/info/aid-development-cooperation-fundamental-rights/your-rights-eu/eu-charter-fundamental-rights_en.* Retrieved 20 May 2019

83. Anthony Coughlan *"Tackling the EU Empire, Basic critical facts on the EU/Eurozone. Better Off Out".* P 39

Chapter 7

Ireland's Business Model and Irexit

"The European Commission's recent conclusion that the Irish Government has given the US tech giant Apple unusually favourable tax treatment, along with the stepped-up international scrutiny of tax havens, will require Ireland to create a new growth model, one that does not rely so heavily on low corporate taxes."

Ashoka Mody, International Monetary Fund

Any questioning of Ireland's current membership of the EU immediately causes the pro-EU elements in the country to go into apoplexy. It is not something where it is easy to even have a rational conversation. If that can be managed, then they immediately point to our relative backwardness prior to joining the old Common Market, as their initial defence. It is almost as if everything that happened before 1 January 1973 was a failure and a new society was born at that date, a bit like Pol Pot's year zero in Cambodia but in this case for modern Irish society.

The achievements of the Irish State prior to EU membership were considerable, despite some obvious failures, and in the teeth of extremely adverse conditions, but these are totally to be disregarded. There is a mantra, pervasive in the liberal establishment in Irish society today, that it was only with accession to the EU that Ireland finally began to realise its potential, economically and socially. This line of reasoning is powered by many, including academics and politicians, who have personally benefited from EU largesse and whose status would be threatened by our departure.

In addition, these advocates claim that it is vital for our welfare that the EU connection is rigidly maintained, as venture any distance from the mothership EU and the country's prosperity and modernity will vanish. It is very reminiscent of the type of argument that was used against Irish Republicans, seeking to separate the country from the old British Empire. In this context, the issue of Ireland's present business model is inevitably rolled out as the main reason to still stick close to Brussels.

It is clear that for Ireland, free and unfettered access to the EU Single (internal) Market has been a cornerstone of the country's economic strategy. The cry goes up that there is no alternative. The country's prosperity is totally dependent on EU membership and essentially that our Government needs to continue kowtowing to the bureaucrats in Brussels. It is a powerful argument and one which has an initial attraction.

From the outset, it should be readily admitted the present Irish economic approach has been successful. The question has to be asked whether the recent success is solely due to EU membership and more importantly, can the present policy mix and conditions be maintained, within the framework of a future EU membership, when Brussels is so determined to change the rules of the game?

External environment

There is, no doubt, but the external environment is changing. There is not enough recognition that, in a post-Brexit situation with Ireland operating in a different customs union to the United Kingdom and physically isolated from the rest of the EU, the terms of trade will be altered radically. This coupled with possible public and official attitude changes to the acceptability of aggressive corporate tax avoidance by multinational companies, means that our business model is increasingly under scrutiny. In fact, even the practise of multinational companies moving offshore to lower their tax liabilities is being questioned as never before in the United States[1], by far the biggest investor in Ireland. Ireland can no longer be sure that the rules of the game are not about to change for the worse.

Ireland developed strongly in economic terms over the last forty years. It is now among the countries in Europe with the highest per capita income[2], even if some of the official figures are suspect. It has been transformed. While some would ascribe this change in fortune solely to the EU, others would plot the commencement of that transformation to an earlier era and one of the most effective reforms ever undertaken in the Irish State. This was the decision of the Irish Government in the mid-1960s, through its then Education Minister Donogh O'Malley, to provide free education for students at second level, supported also by a means tested grant scheme for third level students. He also introduced new regional Technical colleges throughout the State. This helped greatly to change Irish society. It mirrored the educational reforms, which had taken place in the United Kingdom under the post-War Labour Government of Clement Attlee. I was personally a beneficiary of this new enlightened approach in Ireland.

Traditionally Ireland had exported much of its labour force as unskilled and semi-skilled workers, especially as factory operatives and in construction. The overwhelming destination of this flood of migrants was England[3]. The radical upgrade of the educational and technological skill levels of the Irish population, which followed in the wake of the O'Malley reforms, had a profound effect on the country. Within one generation, there was a quantum jump in the skills level. Today, Ireland has one of the highest percentages of its population with 3rd level qualifications in the OECD[4].

Having a highly educated workforce, allowed the Republic to successfully exploit access to the EU Single Market. As world trade liberalisation gathered pace and tariffs generally fell to low levels[5], the opportunities for external trade, both inside the EEC and wider afield, rose exponentially. Having a skilled workforce was only part of the equation.

The second element was having the industries to use these new graduates. It was the country's ability to attract a disproportionate level of Foreign Direct Investment (FDI), especially from the United States, which was the other vital ingredient in our economic success[6]. The Government decided strategically on a policy of low corporate tax to attract in new industries. This tax friendly environment, together with an educated English-speaking workforce, made Ireland very attractive to potential US investors.

In addition, the liberal use of "special" concessions to a limited number of large multinational companies was often the clincher in getting prestigious inward investments. These headline creating investments sent out a very positive message globally to those seeking locations for their expansion into Europe.

Although the national industrial promotion body, IDA Ireland, was very effective in securing FDI, it could not have done so, in some cases, without the active cooperation of the Revenue Commissioners. This resulted in some multinational companies paying only a small fraction of the headline 12.5% corporate tax[7]. The Irish Government has often publicly stated that the country's low corporation tax is under attack. However, it is the company specific arrangements and the very generous ability to write off payments for intellectual property rights, etc., which greatly lower the tax take from 12.5%, that are really under the microscope[8]. In a modern era, it is hard to justify ethically some of these arrangements. There is no statutory prohibition on former State officials of the Revenue Commissioners or IDA Ireland taking up employment with FDI companies in Ireland, something which needs to be seriously considered to ensure no perception of a conflict of interest.

Companies flocked to Ireland to use it as a European base to export, tariff free, to the rest of the EU; and also back to the US. World leaders in the pharma, medical devices, biotechnology, organic chemicals field, etc. made Ireland their European Headquarters. While the general principle was fine, the Irish authorities pushed the gambit to the limit, which caused an adverse reaction. As the international community became much less tolerant of aggressive tax avoidance by large multinationals, Ireland was forced to change some of its more brazen tax dodging schemes in the face of growing international pressure, especially from the OECD in Paris[9]. It has not been alone in this respect as the Netherlands and Luxembourg have faced similar pressures. In addition, there have been a number of special investigations by the European Commission, into the tax arrangements for specific companies in these countries, which included the Apple Corporation in Ireland. These audits indicate clearly that the days of murky tax deals in EU Member States may be numbered[10].

Dodgy practices

The Double Irish, with a Dutch sandwich[11], was a blatant tax avoidance technique whereby certain large corporations, mainly American, used a combination of Irish and Dutch subsidiary companies to shift profits to low or no tax jurisdictions. It involved sending profits first to an Irish company, then a Dutch one and finally a second Irish company. The second Irish company would normally be headquartered in a tax haven, such as the Bahamas. The net result reduced these companies tax liabilities dramatically. The Irish Government ended the scheme in the Finance Act 2015, but companies with established structures could continue with this dubious scam until 2020.

A variation of the Double Irish is known colloquially as the Single Malt[12]. It is again an aggressive tax avoidance scheme, which uses Malta instead of the Dutch leg. The Irish authorities agreed to close down the Single Malt in September 2019. The Irish Government used the base erosion and profit shifting programme (BEPS) mechanism under the OECD[13] to agree with the Government in Valetta to close off this blatant technique which was used to avoid paying a fair share of tax.

The cumulative effect on Ireland's reputation, as a responsible member of the international community, has been damaging. This has led in turn to calls for countries like Ireland to reign in their tax friendly regimes.

To a hard-pressed public, the practise of multinational companies avoiding paying their fair share of tax, by using locations such as Ireland, has become toxic. Oxfam in its report, "Tax Battles" claimed that Ireland was the sixth worst country examined for facilitating companies in tax avoidance, behind the Bahamas, Cayman Islands, The Netherlands, Switzerland and Singapore[14]. While the grounds on which Oxfam made this assessment can be challenged, the perception created by this report and others, is profoundly damaging. Here again Ireland needs to assess the situation or it risks being on the wrong side of a historic change in attitude.

CCCTB

The European Commission is determined to introduce some form of common consolidated corporation tax base (CCCTB) for companies inside the EU[15]. This would entail companies paying tax based in part on where their products are sold, rather than where they are headquartered. The CCCTB would involve a single set of rules to calculate companies' tax liabilities inside the EU. The CCCTB would ensure that companies which operate across borders would have to comply with a single EU system and not report to individual national authorities. It would strip Member States of their ability to act independently in this area and concentrate the power in Brussels. This is yet another example of the europhiles calling for "more Europe."

There are varying estimates of the cost to Ireland of a CCCTB, with the EU Commission claiming that it would only reduce revenue to Ireland by 0.2%[16], while the Irish Business and Employers Confederation (IBEC), the Irish equivalent of the CBI, believe, more realistically, that the cost would be around 7.7% of total tax revenue or €3.9bn[17].

While Ireland, in theory, could continue to resist granting the EU more powers in the tax area, without its key ally the United Kingdom, it is doubtful whether Ireland and the Netherlands will be successfully able to resist this pressure from France, Germany and the EU Commission in the longer run. This danger to Ireland was highlighted in a letter to then Finance Minister, Michael Noonan, from International Law Firm, Baker McKenzie. The *Irish Times* in April 2017 obtained correspondence through the Freedom of Information Act and reported: "The new tax regime will decrease the incentives for companies to locate in Ireland international legal firm Baker McKenzie has outlined, in a letter sent to the Minister for Finance on the 20th of January 2017."[18]

The advisory letter claims the CCCTB proposal advantages market over producer States by giving weight to the location of sales in the apportionment formula, which disadvantages States such as Ireland which may have a small market but are home to export-oriented enterprises.

The paper, in the same report, quoted Dr Aidan Regan, a politics and international relations lecturer at University College Dublin who stated: "The major veto against things like the Common Consolidated Corporate Tax Base is now gone. The European Commission have made this one of their core priorities, and it's no surprise this came back on the agenda after the Brexit vote."

Even if Ireland managed to stop EU-wide moves toward tax harmonisation, some countries may enact new domestic tax arrangements that would make Ireland less attractive from a tax efficient perspective.

Attack on globalisation

In addition, the election of Donald Trump, as President of the United States, has changed the atmosphere for US companies investing abroad. It was reported that a US company in Ireland, Eli Lilly, postponed a planned €200m expansion in Kinsale, County Cork, over fears that it might antagonise the Trump administration and also over uncertainty over future US tariffs on imported pharma[19]. The company commenced production at its Kinsale facility in 1981 and currently over 500 people are employed at the site. This would indicate that existing investments are probably not at risk, but that in future, Ireland cannot count automatically on the old business model of attracting US FDI, based on low local tax and an acquiescing US official attitude. Thankfully, after this initial hesitation, Eli Lilly, in this case, decided to go ahead with the investment. However, the change in official US attitude to overseas investment may be more detrimental to future company plans for FDI than ones currently in the pipeline.

The whole concept of globalisation is under sustained scrutiny as Governments weigh the benefits to ordinary citizens of the freeing up of trade arrangements that have mainly benefitted multinational companies. For the last twenty years, these companies have been big enough and have had enough clout to change policies and indeed Governments. In the process of globalisation, they have become inordinately wealthy. Their very success has now placed the process in danger and with the withdrawal of the US from the Trans-Pacific Partnership and the stalling of the proposed US/EU trade deal, their power may have indeed peaked. Also, the changes in the Investor Protection Mechanism in the Canadian/EU free trade deal (CETA) also signals a challenge to their untrammelled influence[20].

Digital tax

The primary focus of public resentment against an unfair tax system has centred on the huge digital companies that have been at the forefront of the new technological revolution. This has led to moves to introduce special tax arrangements to counter these companies' ability to shift profits into tax havens or low tax jurisdictions.

The present tax arrangements are clearly unable to properly reflect economic reality as the large tax take from these companies in some jurisdictions, including Ireland, is in no way representative of the substance of their economic activity in that State. In other States, the tax returns from these companies has been derisory, despite the huge economic activity they represent and is rapidly becoming a public scandal, particularly as public services come under increasing strain. These companies are exploiting current international tax arrangements to extreme levels and are using these tax advantages to unfairly undercut small companies that do not have the international connections or the leeway with Governments to ensure similar sweetheart deals to the multinationals. In this way, they are allowed to totally dominate important segments of the market, and in the end are actually anti-competitive.

The EU Commission in 2016 demanded that Ireland claim €13bn from the Apple Corporation, as the sweetheart deal it had arranged with Ireland's Revenue Commissioners amounted to State Aid[21]. This was the biggest fine ever imposed on a company in European history. The appeals against this fine are still ongoing with Ireland supporting the American multinational against the European Commission, despite the obvious benefits that a windfall of €13bn would bring to the country.

The respected economist Cormac Lucey wrote in the Irish edition of the *Sunday Times* on 18 February 2018:

> The EU Commission concluded that the Revenue Commissioners issued two tax rulings to Apple which "substantially and artificially" reduced its tax liability by €13bn. Ireland allowed Apple to avoid tax on sales generated throughout the EU. All profits were ascribed to two Apple companies, Apple Sales International and Apple Operations Europe, and not taxed by the Irish authorities. While the Irish authorities claimed that nothing was wrong with this, the scheme was wrapped up. Hence Apple just moved its corporate tax avoidance to Jersey. No democratic oversight, no review no barriers on revenue commissioner people getting jobs in multinationals[22].

In a later article in the same newspaper Lucey added that "the European Commission reported in 2016 that Apple Sales International had only paid an effective corporate tax rate in Ireland of 0.005% in 2014, down from 1% in 2003."[23]

Against this background, Governments in the larger States simply have to act and are starting to use the level of turnover in a market as a base for taxation, rather than declared profits. This is a clear danger to Ireland's disproportionate tax income from these companies.

The UK has introduced a special 2% tax from 2020, which will target revenues earned by online companies, including those providing search engines and social networks[24]. It will affect companies such as Apple, Google, Amazon, Facebook, etc. This tax will apply to companies with a global turnover of over £500m pa and is expected to generate around £400m pa to the British Exchequer.

The EU is also making proposals and envisages a 3% tax on turnover for companies with a global turnover of over €750m and have a taxable income inside the EU of over €50m[25].

The EU proposal has stalled somewhat as Ireland, Sweden, Finland and the Czech Republic have opposed the move. This has prompted France to announce that it will follow the UK and introduce its own national arrangements[26]. France unveiled its own 3% digital services tax in March 2019. This tax, which has been dubbed the GAFA tax, named after its intended targets, Google, Apple, Facebook and Amazon will apply to companies with a global turnover of over €750 m and French revenues of over €25m. This has led to tensions with the USA[27] and President Macron has agreed to a US request for a temporary postponement.

Impatience with the failure to implement a fair tax system for the digital companies has now affected a growing number of EU countries. Apart from France and Britain, tax authorities in Austria[28], Italy, Germany and Spain[29] are considering national action on the issue.

Ireland and the other net beneficiaries of the present arrangement are pleading that the issue of taxing the global digital companies should be left to the OECD in Paris[30]. The attraction for Ireland is that the United States is one of the 35-member group in this organisation and since the digital companies are essentially all US corporations, there is a much better prospect of favourable treatment of these companies under any proposals, which are likely to emerge from the OECD, than from the EU. Ireland along with a small number of other EU Member States believe that the OECD membership is also likely to be more sympathetic to American multinational companies than the State orientated bureaucrats in Brussels.

However even the OECD is coming around to the inevitability of change. The present system of taxation, based on a permanent physical presence, is outdated when dealing with the digitals.

In February 2019, the OECD produced a formal consultation document "Addressing the Tax Challenges of the Digitalisation of the Economy".[31] It claims that it represents a renewed appetite amongst OECD members for a fundamental review of the current international tax framework: the OECD aims to agree a solution by the end of 2020. However, the kernel of any new OECD proposals is likely to recommend concentrating the tax return from the digitals in the countries where their economic activity takes place, not where they are legally registered. This is not good news for the Irish Department of Finance where the corporation tax take in Ireland from these companies has represented an unsustainable windfall in recent years.

Overall

Any detailed examination of Ireland's overseas trading patterns shows that the country's economic links with mainland Europe are overwhelmingly concentrated in the multinational companies. Our indigenous businesses trade and invest mainly in the Anglophone world. This is not to say that these links with Germany, France, etc., are not extremely important for the State, however it does mean that Ireland is very vulnerable to international changes in the area of FDI. The country must be seen and indeed act as a responsible member of the international community, something it has failed to do in the past in a small number of areas, with such activities as the double Irish, etc. These dubious activities sullied our good name and for little real advantage to the State. However, they do reveal that in the past, our legislators and tax authorities were not cognisant enough of our good name internationally and were a little too keen to appease tax avoiding international firms. It was an attitude mired in a much poorer Ireland of the past and should have no place in a modern and successful economy.

Our membership of the EU seems based, in the public mind, in large measure on our ability to provide a tax efficient location for foreign, principally American, firms. These Irish located firms trade all over the world but primarily within Europe.

There is little understanding in Ireland that duty free access to the Single Market can be, and indeed has been, negotiated for a number of countries outside the EU, including Norway, Iceland, Lichtenstein and Switzerland. In addition, Canada through the CETA free trade Agreement will now enjoy tariff free access for 98% of its industrial exports to the EU. Therefore, it is very possible to act as a European base outside the EU, provided companies, based in Ireland, can still trade freely with the European continent.

It is a short-sighted policy to place our future on keeping a limited number of large multinational companies sweet, while our Government goes about antagonising our traditional and most important trading partner, namely Britain, in the Brexit negotiations. These multinational companies have brought huge benefits to Ireland, but their loyalty is to their shareholders and their ability to offer a good return on capital invested. If the international climate turns sour and more particularly if resistance grows inside the United States to FDI, coupled with new taxes on these companies in Europe, then Ireland could be in a difficult situation. These companies are very mobile and can leave our shores without any qualms. Our present business model may be incompatible with the changing international climate.

Ashoka Mody, visiting Professor in International Economic Policy at the Woodrow Wilson School in Princeton University, who led the IMF mission to Ireland during the financial crisis, stated in his book *EuroTragedy*: "The European Commission's recent conclusion that the Irish Government has given the US tech giant Apple unusually favourable tax treatment, along with the stepped-up international scrutiny of tax havens, will require Ireland to create a new growth model, one that does not rely so heavily on low corporate tax."[32]

There is no such thing as a free lunch and Ireland's love affair with the US multinationals may come to an end as our tax advantages are slowly stripped away. Mody very wisely advises Ireland to invest heavily in education and further upskilling of our workforce. They are echoes here of the 1960s policy of Donogh O'Malley.

Also if the climate inside the EU continues to become hostile to the type of tax arrangements, which Ireland offers to inward investment, it may be more advantageous for the country to free itself of the shackles of Brussels control so as to continue to be flexible on tax for FDI companies, provided that we can negotiate continued frictionless free access to the EU Single Market.

If the multinational companies decide to desert Ireland, it would leave us with very limited connections to mainland Europe. In such circumstances, the Irish Government's gamble in putting all its cards in the EU basket, while antagonising our nearest neighbour, could look very short-sighted indeed.

References

1. *"Trump attacks on outsourcing puts companies on guard"* Program Business 23 January 2017. *https://www.programbusiness.com/news/Trumps-Attacks-on-Outsourcing-Put-Companies-on-Guard.* Retrieved 21 May 2019

2. Statistics Times *"List of Countries by GDP (PPP) per capita"* 8 March 2019. *https://statisticstimes.com/economy/countries-by-gdp-capita-ppp.php.* Retrieved 21 May 2019

3. Catherine Dunne *An Unconsidered People. The Irish in London* New Island Books 2003.

4. OECD Data *"Adult Education Level"* 2017. *https://data.oecd.org/eduatt/adult-education-level.htm.* Retrieved 21 May 2019

5. Eurostat statistics Explained. *"International trade in goods – tariffs"* *https://ec.europa.eu/eurostat/statistics-explained/index.php/International_trade_in_goods_-_tariffs.* Retrieved 27 May 2019

6. American Chamber of Commerce Ireland *"Key Facts"*. *https://www.amcham.ie/About-Us/US-Companies-in-Ireland/Stats-Facts.aspx.* Retrieved 21 May 2019

7. Harriet Taylor *"How Apple managed to pay a 0.005 percent tax rate in 2014"* CNBC, 30 August 2016. *https://www.cnbc.com/2016/08/30/how-apples-irish-subsidiaries-paid-a-0005-percent-tax-rate-in-2014.html.* Retrieved 21 May 2019

8. Rochelle Toplensky *"Europe points finger at Ireland over tax avoidance Rules on royalties cited as example than can allow companies aggressively cut tax bills" Irish Times* 7 March 2018. *https://www.irishtimes.com/business/economy/europe-points-finger-at-ireland-over-tax-avoidance-1.3417948.* Retrieved 21 My 2019

9. Henry *McDonald 'Ireland to abolish controversial 'double Irish' tax arrangement", Guardian* 14 October 2014. *https://www.theguardian.com/world/2014/oct/14/ireland-abolish-double-irish-tax-scheme-apple.* Retrieved 21 May 2019

10. European Commission "*State aid: Commission investigates transfer pricing arrangements on corporate taxation of Apple (Ireland) Starbucks (Netherlands) and Fiat Finance and Trade (Luxembourg)"* 11 June 2014. *http://europa.eu/rapid/press-release_IP-14-663_en.htm.* Retrieved 21 May 2019

11. Julie Kagan and Chris B Murphy "*Double Irish With A Dutch Sandwich*" Investopedia, *https://www.investopedia.com/terms/d/double-irish-with-a-dutch-sandwich.asp.* Retrieved 21 May 2019

12. Dominic Coyle "*Multinationals turn from 'Double Irish' to 'Single Malt' to avoid tax in Ireland" Irish Times*, 14 November 2017. *https://www.irishtimes.com/business/economy/multinationals-turn-from-double-irish-to-single-malt-to-avoid-tax-in-ireland-1.3290649.* Retrieved 21 May 2019

13. OECD "*Base erosion and profit shifting*" http://www.oecd.org/tax/beps/. Retrieved 21 May 2019

14. Oxfam Policy Paper "*TAX BATTLES The dangerous global Race to the Bottom on Corporate Tax*", 12 December 2016. *https://www.oxfam.org/sites/www.oxfam.org/files/file_attachments/bp-race-to-bottom-corporate-tax-121216-en.pdf.* Retrieved 21 May 2019

15. Suzanne Lynch "*Moscovici resolute on common corporate tax base. EU commissioner urges member states to ensure fair share of tax is paid" Irish Times*, 12 September 2015. *https://www.irishtimes.com/business/work/moscovici-resolute-on-common-corporate-tax-base-1.2348986.* Retrieved 21 May 2019

16. European Commission "*Common Consolidated Corporate Tax Base (CCCTB)*" 25 October 2016. *http://europa.eu/rapid/press-release_IP-16-3471_en.htm.* Retrieved 27 May 2019

17. Eoin Burke-Kennedy "*Ireland could lose €4bn in revenue if EU tax plans go ahead, says Ibec*". Irish Times, 24 April 2017. *https://www.irishtimes.com/business/economy/ireland-could-lose-4bn-in-revenue-if-eu-tax-plans-go-ahead-says-ibec-1.3058505.* Retrieved 27 May 2019

18. Jack Power *"Brexit to make CCCTB reforms harder to block, UCD academic warns". Irish Times* 3 April 2017. *https://www.irishtimes.com/business/economy/brexit-to-make-ccctb-reforms-harderto-block-ucd-academic-warns-1.3034086*. Retrieved 27 May 2019.

19. Pádraig Hoare *"Eli Lilly decision on €200m plan under review" Irish Examiner*, 13 February 2017. *https://www.irishexaminer.com/business/eli-lilly-decision-on-200m-plan-under-review-442752.html*. Retrieved 27 May 2019

20. European Commission *"CETA: EU and Canada agree on new approach on investment in trade agreement"* Press Release 29 February 2016. *http://europa.eu/rapid/press-release_IP-16-399_en.htm*. Retrieved 27 May 2019

21. Sean Farrell and Henry McDonald *"Apple ordered to pay €13bn after EU rules Ireland broke state aid laws". Guardian* 30 August 2016. *https://www.theguardian.com/business/2016/aug/30/apple-pay-back-taxes-eu-ruling-ireland-state-aid*. Retrieved 27 May 2019

22. Cormac Lucey *"At least EU Commission's bite of the Apple has lifted the veil of Irish tax secrecy" Sunday Times* 2018, *https://www.thetimes.co.uk/edition/ireland/at-least-eu-commissions-bite-of-the-apple-has-lifted-the-veil-of-irish-tax-secrecy-mrwz2765z*. Retrieved 18 December 2019

23. Cormac Lucey *"As with rugby, Ireland must take its model of economic development to the next level" Sunday Times* 3 November 2019. *https://www.thetimes.co.uk/article/cormac-lucey-as-with-rugby-ireland-must-take-its-model-of-economic-development-to-the-next-level-2q6vhbq0f*. Retrieved 18 December 2019

24. Rupert Neath *"Hammond targets US tech giants with 'digital services tax'. Guardian*, 29 October 2019. *https://www.theguardian.com/uk-news/2018/oct/29/hammond-targets-us-tech-giants-with-digital-services-tax*. Retrieved 27 May 2019

25. Philip Blenkinsop "EU proposes online turnover tax for big tech firms" Reuters Report, 21 March 2018.https://www.reuters.com/article/us-eu-tax-digital/eu-to-unveil-plan-to-tax-turnover-of-big-u-s-tech-firms-idUSKBN1GX00J. Retrieved 27 May 2019.

26. BBC News *"France to introduce digital tax in New Year"* 17 December 2018. *https://www.bbc.com/news/business-46591576*. Retrieved 27 May 2019

27. Reuters Business News, *"U.S. sees unilateral taxes on web giants as 'discriminatory': Treasury official"* 12 March 2019. *https://www.reuters.com/article/us-usa-tax-harter/u-s-looking-at-responses-to-unilateral-digital-taxes-treasury-official-idUSKBN1QT1CT*. Retrieved 23 July 2019

28. *"Austria ramps up push for EU-wide digital tax on Big Tech"* Irish Times 16 July 2018. *https://www.irishtimes.com/business/technology/austria-ramps-up-push-for-eu-wide-digital-tax-on-big-tech-1.3566480.* Retrieved 27 May 2019

29. *"Germany, France, Italy, Spain seek new EU tax on digital firm revenue"* MNE tax.com 10 September 2017. *https://mnetax.com/germany-france-italy-spain-seek-new-tax-digital-firm-revenue-23398.* Retrieved 27 May 2019

30. Pat Leahy *"Ireland to fight proposed EU digital tax on internet giants."* Irish Times 2 December 2017. *https://www.irishtimes.com/business/economy/ireland-to-fight-proposed-eu-digital-tax-on-internet-giants-1.3312834.* Retrieved 27 May 2019

31. *"OECD seeing less corporate opposition to digital era tax revamp"* Reuters, 12 March 2019. *https://uk.reuters.com/article/uk-oecd-tax/oecd-seeing-less-corporate-opposition-to-digital-era-tax-revamp-idUKKBN1QT2L5.* Retrieved 16 June 2019

32. Ashoka Mody *EuroTragedy* p 432.

Chapter 8

Ireland and the Euro

"The euro was not a banker's decision nor a technical decision. It was a decision which completely changed the nature of the Nation States. The pillars of the Nation State are the sword and the currency, and we have changed that. The euro decision changed the concept of the Nation State, and we have to go beyond that."

EU Commission President Romano Prodi, April 1999

If Ireland ever decides post-Brexit it does not want to continue with full membership of the EU and hence the Eurozone, it faces a major obstacle. The country gave up its own independent currency, the Irish pound or in the Irish language, the punt. The euro banknotes and coins were introduced in Ireland on 1 January 2002, after a transitional period of three years when the euro was the official currency but only existed as "book money". The dual circulation period – when both the Irish pound and the euro had legal tender status – ended on 9 February 2002[1]. According to former senior Irish civil servant in the Department of Industry and Commerce, Michael Clarke, the changeover was achieved with remarkable efficiency and the smoothness of the operation may have induced a complacent attitude as to the enormity of the event. It was a huge step in the gradual absorption of Ireland into the process of creating a European Federal State. Only Denmark and the United Kingdom, wisely secured permanent optouts of the new common currency in the Maastricht Treaty. Ireland could have easily declined membership of the new Eurozone, along with our two fellow northern European countries. All new EU Member States are required to adopt the euro, although it is clear that some, including Sweden, Hungary and Poland, are very unenthusiastic, after witnessing the unfortunate fate of several that did.

Ireland's most important export markets, Britain and the United States, the first for our indigenous industries and the second for our large multinational sector, are outside the Eurozone. So why was Ireland so attracted to the new currency when the two other countries, which joined the EEC with us, declined the invitation. Since the economic arguments for joining were so weak, it can be safely assumed that the driving force was political, namely excessive europhilia as the Irish establishment sought to ingratiate itself with Brussels. It is just one more example of this group ignoring national interest when it conflicted with the European project.

That approach has left us with a difficult problem. As an integral part of the Eurozone, Ireland would no doubt face serious obstacles to exiting the system should it decide it needed to restore its national currency. Many believe that the lack of an independent currency could raise serious questions about the viability of an Irexit. This question inevitably is raised when discussing the various alternatives. It was an issue that the UK did not have to face when leaving the EU. It is a question that merits careful investigation.

While it could be theoretically possible to make some arrangements with the EU, and in particular the ECB, to continue using the euro in an Irexit situation, a formal break with the EU would inevitably cause the country to fundamentally reassess its continued usage of the multinational currency. This should be regarded as an opportunity rather than a negative. However, given the highly antagonistic and legally pedantic attitude of the EU Commission to the UK during the Brexit discussions, it would be unwise for Ireland in that situation to rely on a generous or accommodating approach from Brussels. Rather than assisting a post-Irexit Ireland, it is very likely for the EU to put as many obstacles as possible in our way. This should not deter Ireland. There is no doubt but returning to managing our own currency and a flexible exchange value, as well as setting appropriate interest rates, would be of huge long-term benefit to Ireland, particularly in a post-Brexit situation.

Therefore, I would reject the idea of unilaterally using the euro as Ireland's national currency, post Irexit, in the way which Kosovo and Montenegro currently do. It brings with it all the disadvantages of euro membership and also carries with it a vulnerability to vindictive action by the ECB. Better to take any short-term pain for the longer-term gain.

There is still a huge question mark over the future of the currency itself. It has been pointed out by a number of distinguished sources that multinational currencies do not survive indefinitely, without a political union, which has been the driving force behind the adoption of the euro[2]. The experience of the first ill-fated European Exchange Rate Mechanism (ERM) demonstrated this as does other historical experiences.

It is also noteworthy that one of the best economic periods in the Irish State's history was the short period when Ireland controlled its own independent currency and, in particular, the 1990s. The experience of the Irish State, when it was a minor part of the sterling area, should have forewarned the Government about entering a currency union, where it had no ability to influence the macro picture. The Irish pound had been created in the Irish Free State Currency Act of 1927, maintaining parity with the British pound until it finally broke with sterling on 30 March 1979[3], well after Australia, New Zealand and many other countries. I am unsure why it took so long, but the break with sterling is now accepted, without challenge, as a positive move. It was only when Ireland joined the European Monetary System (EMS) and the UK stayed out that the split finally occurred. By the end of 1978, Ireland was the only former sterling area country to have maintained an unchanged parity with the British pound since independence[4].

History of the common currency

The idea of a common currency for Europe had been around for many years but the euro got its first serious traction under French President Georges Pompidou in the 1960s, ably assisted by his Finance Minister Valerie Giscard d'Estaing. The French Government was nettled by successive devaluations of the Franc against the German Deutsche Mark[5]. Pompidou did not comprehend that it was not the Germans who were the problem but rather the inability of the French economy to keep pace with its eastern neighbour. It needed regular devaluations to maintain competitiveness.[6]. The subsequent French call on the EEC for a common currency, which would disguise their weakness, resulted in the Werner Report. This involved an examination of the proposal by a group under Luxembourg Prime Minister Pierre Werner. When published in 1970, it provided for the establishment of an economic and monetary union that would involve significant transfers of responsibility from States to the European institutions in the field of monetary policy[7]. It was not implemented as West Germany was not prepared to commit its resources to fund other States in economic difficulties.

There were a number of subsequent attempts at managing currency differences within the EEC, including the Snake and the European Monetary System, none of which were particularly successful. The Snake required participating currencies to stay within narrow ranges, relative to each other but the system itself could fluctuate against third country currencies. It was a blank cheque for speculators to make money. Sterling joined it in May 1972 but only managed to stay in it for one month. Italy left it in February 1973 and the whole operation gradually fell apart.

The common currency would have stayed as a pious, if unrealistic, proposal but for the conversion of German Chancellor Helmut Kohl to the idea in the immediate aftermath of the unification of Germany. Having been initially opposed to the idea on sound economic grounds[8], he was persuaded by French President Francois Mitterrand to back the idea for political reasons. Without Kohl, the euro would never have gotten off the ground. As with many converts, he soon became its strongest advocate stating in the German Parliament in a flush of hyperbole, "We need the joint European currency. It is a basic precondition for peace and freedom and building the European House."[9]

If a common currency prevented war, then we would have never had a civil war in any country.

The price of German participation in the common currency was a set of rules which gave guardianship to an undemocratic body, the European Central Bank, which was not accountable politically to any elected entity. It fitted neatly into the thrust of a supranational body, operating outside democratic control, along the lines that Jean Monnet had always advocated. Therefore, Article 107 of the Maastricht Treaty stated plainly in relation to the ECB, "Governments of the Member States undertake … not to seek to influence the members of the decision making bodies of the ECB or the national Central Banks in the performance of their tasks"[10]

It also involved a set of criteria, named after the Maastricht Treaty, which had no real empirical basis but sounded tough enough to convince the Germans that participating countries would keep good order. It also included the essentially idiotic idea that countries, which breached the 3% budget deficit criterion, would be subject to heavy fines. Of course, this power could never be used, other than to be vindictive and never against France or Germany. The biggest weakness of the system was that the participating countries have never been willing to make the structural changes to make a common currency work, especially large-scale transfers to weaker members so that devaluation would be unnecessary. When talking about a European bank rescue, then German Finance Minister Peer Steinbrück in October 2008, stated this clearly: "The Chancellor and I reject a European shield because we as Germans do not want to pay into a big pot where we do not have control and do not know where German money might be used."[11]

The system was made even more unstable with the wholescale fiddling of economic statistics by some countries, in order to qualify for membership. It was a disaster right from day one. Later Kohl would write in his memoirs that the euro cost him his Chancellorship[12].

The general background to the establishment of the euro was well known at the time but nevertheless, Ireland strongly lobbied to be part of this exercise, even though the two countries that joined the EEC with Ireland, declined the poisoned chalice. The adage of "fools rush in where angels fear to tread" springs immediately to mind. Ireland would pay a very heavy price for the rush of excessive europhilia later when the financial crash occurred.

It never made economic sense for Ireland to join up. The decision to participate was a purely political one and fully in keeping with Ireland's long-standing policy of showing blinkered solidarity with the European project. It was an earlier demonstration of the flawed Team EU concept. The debate on joining the euro which took place in the Dáil on 5 May 1992 shows virtually no understanding among the contributors of how the currency would work.

EU Commission President, Romano Prodi, said at the time that the euro was launched:

"The euro was not a banker's decision nor a technical decision. It was a decision which completely changed the nature of the Nation States. The pillars of the Nation State are the sword and the currency, and we have changed that. The euro decision changed the concept of the Nation State, and we have to go beyond that."[13]

Irish naivety

While working inside the Irish Civil Service, I well remember, in the build up to our joining, there was a steely determination in political circles to show the world that, in contrast to the British, we were good Europeans. We were determined to ignore the negative elements surrounding the creation of the euro. There was even a feeling of smugness at the time, that the UK, for internal political reasons was not joining but no doubt would be forced to sign up later. This complacent attitude was to wreak havoc on our economy during the crash. It would not be the last time, we totally misjudged political developments in Britain.

When we looked across at events in London, we did so through the prism of our own experiences with the main characters involved. The differences of opinion in London between then Prime Minister Tony Blair and his Chancellor Gordon Brown were put down to petty political turf wars. In Ireland, we had great admiration for Blair, who had helped deliver the GFA and in a manner which no other British Prime Minister would have been capable of doing. Blair was very pro-euro and this only re-enforced the Irish Government's view that the euro was a desirable place to be. The arguments that Brown articulated, which now look very sound, were given no real hearing[14]. Ireland, fortified with the assurances from Tony Blair that it was on the right course, with its enthusiastic commitment to the European project, sailed on and into disaster.

There was very little doubt in political circles but that joining the euro was right for Ireland. There was also very little deep analysis of the situation. As happens on many occasions, official Ireland was not even prepared to listen to the alternative. What we were going to do would have huge implications. It is a very serious step for any sovereign country to forsake some of the most valuable tools of economic policy, including influencing the value of your currency, ditching an independent Central

Bank, giving up printing your own money and your ability to decide on interest rates. Apart from a few academics, there was little or no debate. In the case of the euro, for Ireland, this was a step back into its past, as Frankfort took up the role, previously played by the Bank of England. From then on, our Central Bank would be a branch office of the ECB, dedicated to promoting the health of the euro, with Irish economic interests secondary. Yet some of our politicians saw giving up the Irish pound as a mark of our independence, rather than a major surrender of sovereignty, possibly because it showed us up as different from the UK, a very perverted logic. There was the promise of permanently low interest rates, as if interest rates were somehow totally detached from the real economy. Even the most basic understanding of how an economy works seemed to be lacking in Irish Government circles at the time. It was an Alice in Wonderland moment.

The fall

The initial omens were good. The changeover from the Irish pound to the euro was technically achieved in Ireland very smoothly. The project was well planned and there were little or no hiccups. Perhaps lessons might be relearned for an Irish Government wanting to change the currency again.

But the wider project was flawed from an Irish perspective from the onset. The ECB, like all EU wide institutions, must keep the bigger picture, namely Germany, primarily in mind. The euro is, de facto, a German-run currency and its operation is designed to assist the German economy. As Theo Waigel, German Finance Minister in 1996 stated, "The euro must speak German"[15]. Hence, during the period of the so-called Celtic Tiger, while Irish house prices were undergoing massive price inflation, the greatly diminished Irish Central Bank could not use the interest rate lever to slow the economy down as that power had been passed to the ECB. With the German economy very sluggish at that time, Ireland had to endure wholly inappropriately low interest rates. The net result was a calamity and thousands of young Irish people had to emigrate as the economy subsequently crashed. It was a terrible price to pay for earlier poor policy decisions. It was our young people who paid much of that price. The full horror of the financial crisis in Ireland and the subsequent Bailout have been well documented elsewhere. It was a direct result of the negligence and europhilia of our political class and their blind decision to join the euro.

The dangers of being boxed into a multinational currency was exposed again for Ireland in the immediate aftermath of the Brexit vote in the UK. Sterling fell heavily but Ireland's membership of the euro ensured that it could not adjust in a way that would reflect Ireland's close economic relations with the UK. There was no mechanism, available to Dublin, for rectifying the new currency misalignment between the two closely related economies. Hence there were industries, such as the mushroom growing sector, which were badly disadvantaged. The Republic of Ireland exports over 80% of its sizable production of mushrooms to the UK[16]. Thankfully sterling has recovered considerably since the immediate post-Brexit referendum days. The only option for a Eurozone country to regain competitiveness is through destructive internal austerity. In such circumstances, it is always the weaker sections of the community who pay the biggest price.

If Ireland had maintained its independent currency and operated on the international currency markets much as the Danish and Swedish authorities can do with their respective currencies, the value of the Irish pound, no doubt, would have fallen to reflect Ireland's links with the UK and the economic reality of Ireland's trading relations. This release mechanism was not available to the authorities. Ireland would not have had anything like the boom times of the Celtic Tiger without the euro, but it would equally not have had the severity of the economic crash. There is still a reluctance in Ireland to attribute the large imbalances that developed during the period of the Celtic Tiger to our membership of the euro, even though this seems self-evident. Today the country is still vulnerable to destructive currency swings, something it has no control over.

Other countries' experiences with the euro – the Eurozone

In the Netherlands, in February 2017, the Dutch Parliament voted unanimously to hold an enquiry into the country's future relationship with the euro. The investigation was to examine all eventualities, including whether it would be possible to withdraw from the euro and, if so, how?[17] The investigation was to be undertaken by the Council of State, the Dutch Government's legal advisor. The move reflected growing euro scepticism in the country, particularly after Dutch pensions lost much of their value by the quantitative easing policies of the ECB and the ultra-low interest rate regime. Again, the Dutch were having an inappropriate interest rate imposed on the country. It was also a ploy to counter the rising support for far-right leader Geert Wilders and his PVV party before a general election. This did not mean that the Netherlands was going to ditch the euro in the short term, but it does reflect the dissatisfaction with the common currency in that country.

The country that has probably suffered the greatest damage from its membership of the Eurozone has been the small Mediterranean Republic of Greece. The country should never have been included in the tranche of countries which joined in the early stages. By any reckoning Greece did not meet the Maastricht criteria[18]. By fudging the figures, with the reported active assistance of international bankers, Goldman Sachs, and the turning of a blind eye by the European authorities, the Greeks got in[19]. Again, it was an example of politics overcoming economics with terrible long-term results for the Greek people.

It all came crashing down on the Greeks, but the response of the EU was particularly unhelpful. As *Forbes* magazine described in August 2018, ten years after the financial crisis, the EU had managed to "drive the country into the worst peacetime depression experienced by any advanced economy in recorded history."[20] What happened to Greece and its people will be a blight and a stain on the history of the EU for generations to come. As mentioned earlier, Ireland did not distinguish itself in the situation. It is partly culpable, by aligning itself with the EU institutions in their destructive policies towards that unfortunate country.

While Greece was at the epicentre of the euro crisis in the past, the front line has moved to a much bigger economy, Italy. Like Greece and France, Italy has been plagued by its poor economic performance. The country's economy in 2018 was still 5% smaller than it was ten years before[21]. It was once one of the manufacturing powerhouses on the European continent but no longer, as the country has endured a woeful period economically for the last 12 years.

This has led to popular discontent and the electoral demise of the traditional left and right parties and their replacement with a radically different set of politicians, with very different views from the pro-EU parties of the past.

The Italian general election of March 2018 represented an electoral earthquake as the Italian political landscape was reshaped radically. The new Italian Government, under Prime Minister Giuseppe Conte was made up of a coalition arrangement between the Five Star Movement and the Lega (formerly Lega Nord), and its ascent to a position of authority sent shudders through the corridors of power in Brussels, Berlin and Paris.

Any decision by Italy to drop the euro, something which is probably necessary to revive its economic growth, would seriously endanger the future of the Eurozone. Italy had always relied on a depreciating Lira to maintain its position as a leading exporter. In 1982 alone, the Lira depreciated 25% against the German currency[22]. In regard to Italy, clearly the pressures for radical action on the currency situation are unlikely to ease.

Of the three Nordic countries in the EU, Finland alone decided to join the euro, in contrast to Sweden and Denmark. It is clear that the Finnish experience has been an unhappy one. When the country suffered from the demise of the Nokia corporation, Finland's membership of the euro deprived it of some of the economic tools to combat the collapse of its leading company.

Hence there are growing demands to ditch the euro. A study by Dr Peter Nyberg – a former Finnish senior civil servant who was chosen by the Irish Government to examine the Irish banking collapse – along with several colleagues took the example of Finland and examined how a country could successfully exit the euro. This study again indicated that history has clearly demonstrated that a multinational currency cannot survive unless there is a permanent political union[23]. There are several examples including the Scandinavian Monetary Union, Austro-Hungarian currency, etc. Since there is no real desire in Eurozone States for full political union, hence the longer-term prognosis for the euro is grim. The study shows:

Although there is a way out of the euro for Finland and other member countries, exit would not be easy, nor would its short-term costs be known beforehand with any clear margin. We find the lack of a domestic payments system and uncertainty concerning the redenomination costs to be the biggest risks associated with the cost of Finland's exit. Still, the costs of Finland's exit need not be very large, around 10 billion euros in the best-case scenario, but we also acknowledge a very costly scenario for the exit. Any member country considering exit from the euro should weigh the short-term costs of an exit against the possible long-run benefits of having a domestic currency.

As the Republic of Ireland and Finland are relatively similar in the size of their economies and in population terms, the study has obvious implications for Ireland.

Non-members of the Eurozone and the euro

Opposition to the euro is not confined to those countries which have adopted the currency and have had bad experiences. Among the Member States of the EU that are currently not a member of the Eurozone, there is only a short queue of impatient applicants waiting to get in.

As noted earlier, post Maastricht, all Member States and any new country that joined the EU are required to adopt the common currency. Two existing Member States at that time, Denmark and the United Kingdom, secured optouts from this compulsion because of local opposition. However, the europhiles in both these countries tried to overturn these optouts. In the UK, the Blair faction of the British Labour Party were thwarted by the then Chancellor of the Exchequer, Gordon Brown. This was a very lucky escape for Britain.

Denmark, a prosperous country in western Europe, not dissimilar to Ireland, decided to consult its people on the introduction of the euro. In 2000, the Danish Government held a referendum on introducing the common currency, which was defeated with 46.8% voting yes and 53.2% voting no, with a massive turnout of 87.6 % of the electorate. Again, the bulk of the establishment lined up to try to convince the Danish public to ditch its kroner and accept the euro. Fortunately, the electorate did not buy the proposition, another example of a gulf between the elite and the public.

As has been witnessed in many other cases, the Danish elite have not accepted the result of a people's vote when it went against them. Initially they hoped to run another referendum on euro membership, either as a separate poll, or together with the other Danish optouts in the Justice and Home Affairs area[24]. However, the euro question was dropped as public opinion polling showed strong and in addition growing resistance to the adoption of the euro. That opposition is consistently in the 65-70%. In December 2016, the Danish business publication Borsen surveyed public opinion on the issue and found that 65% opposed Danish membership of the Eurozone, 26% approved and 9% were unsure. With figures like that, there is no immediate prospect of the Danish establishment trying to get its electorate to come up with the "correct" answer to the question of euro membership.

Another small and prosperous northern European country, Sweden has also consulted its electorate on the issue. Unlike Denmark, Sweden, under the terms of its Accession Treaty in 1994, is actually required to drop the Swedish krona in favour of the euro. However, in September 2003, the Swedish population in a referendum voted to reject the euro with 56% opposed, with a turnout of 81.2%[25]. This opposition has hardened considerably with opinion polls consistently showing around 20% support for the common currency[26]. Hence there are no plans in Stockholm to change the situation in the short to medium term.

In Poland, an opinion poll in 2012 showed that 70% of those questioned opposed Polish entry into the Eurozone and the ruling Law and Justice Party supports this position[27]. Support for the euro in the Czech Republic was registered in 2017 at 21%[28]. In June 2015, Hungarian PM Viktor Orbán declared that his country would not be joining the Eurozone in 2020 as originally planned and that the Hungarian forint would remain "stable and strong for the next several decades"[29].

This litany is hardly a strong endorsement of the euro, yet the Irish and EU try and proclaim the single currency as a success. It is another example of political spin in the face of economic reality.

Future of the euro itself

The principal argument advanced by economists today against Ireland leaving the euro is the difficulties and cost of relaunching an Irish independent currency. I believe that there are very few economic experts who would now advocate euro entry for Ireland if we had maintained our independent currency. Hindsight allows for 20/20 vision.

There is no cost-free scenario for departing the euro but given the problems Ireland has in having any influence over its currency, it might be a price worth paying in the longer run. If South Sudan and Timor-Leste can launch their own currencies, surely one of western Europe's most advanced economies can do so. Hopefully, a relaunched Irish currency would hold its value, especially in the longer term, to ensure that the country's large foreign debt (a relic of the EU Bailout and its consequences), would not rise unduly because of adverse exchange rate movements. Given Ireland's good economic performance and the problems in the major Eurozone economies, Germany, France and Italy, this is not an unrealistic expectation. In fact, one potential danger, given Ireland's excellent economic performance, might be a strengthening of an Irish currency relative to the euro in the longer term.

While Ireland has had problems with the euro, the future of the currency itself is, of course, questionable[30]. As Nobel Prize winner in economics, Joseph Stiglitz, pointed out graphically in his publication, "The euro and its Threat to the Future of Europe", it is based on a flawed concept. Therefore, while we are going through a period of relative calm at the moment, that may be due more to the flooding of the financial system with large amounts of liquidity, through the ECB's quantitative easing programme, than any new-found inherent stability. There are reasonable fears that the euro crisis may be facing us anew before too long. The currency, by any objective judgement, has been a disaster for millions of Europeans. Philip Legrain, the former economic advisor to the President of the European Commission, Manuel Barroso, described the euro system as a "masochistic straight-jacket"[31] in his book *European Spring: Why Our Economies and Politics are in a Mess – and How to Put Them Right*. For many Europeans it has been an expensive misadventure. Even under its own terms, the euro has failed miserably.

On the other hand, it has been a triumph of political will over economic reality and necessity. It is simply amazing that the euro and Eurozone have survived the various crises. It has done so by a fierce determination of the political elite to ensure its survival. This commitment, for political reasons, to the survival of the euro was encapsulated in the famous remarks in 2012 by ECB President Mario Draghi that his organisation

"Within our mandate, the ECB is ready to do whatever it takes to preserve the euro. And believe me, it will be enough"[32].

His remarks helped to maintain the stability of the common currency but whether this was a temporary reprieve or something more permanent is a moot point. As the economic cycle in most advanced economies start to enter a more subdued phase, after a long period of strong economic growth in most of the world, though not in the Eurozone, further stresses are emerging to challenge the viability of the currency.

The question must arise as to how long can the political underpinning of the euro project continue in the face of such poor economic performance? At the heart of the euro project, its two principal backers, France and Germany, are at odds over how the system should work. For Germany, which agreed to give up the beloved Deutsche Mark in return for a major input into designing and policing the euro, it is all about a strict rules-based system, while for France it has been about exercising those rules with discretion. In addition, the Germans have ruled out major fiscal transfers between Member States, a basic requirement for a common currency area. It is no wonder that the project has staggered from crisis to crisis. The new President of the ECB, Christine Lagarde, will need all her famed political skills to keep the show on the road.

The French have constantly struggled economically in the currency union with Germany. Despite the numerous efforts at labour "reforms" and tax cutting, the French economy remains in the doldrums and its fiscal situation is regularly breaching euro criteria. Because of its privileged position within the EU, there is no real possibility of Brussels taking any punitive action, unlike the situation with Italy or the smaller countries. The remarks by former EU Commission President, Jean Claude Juncker, on the French Senate TV station, when asked about France's persistent breaching of the Maastricht criteria, admitted as much, with a shrug and indicated that no action would be taken, "Because it is France"[33]. This caused great annoyance in the smaller countries and encapsulated the uneven nature of how the Maastricht criteria are applied. It emphasized yet again that the euro is a political project which operates in an unfair way.

However, it is the euro which is at the heart of France's economic difficulties. The country cannot devalue against its German neighbour, as it would have done when it had the Franc. France may have devised the euro as a way of ending its periodic humiliation at having to devalue against the Mark, but it now has an even bigger problem on its hands.

While popular discontent with the economic situation boils over regularly, (even if it's under reported in Ireland and Britain), including the recent gilets jaunes, the French authorities remain reluctant to tackle the fundamental issue of using the euro. An exception to this was Marine Le Pen, Presidential election candidate for the Front National who consistently proposed the re-introduction of the Franc[34]. Her idea was to have the new Franc at parity with the euro, to ease the difficulty with public acceptance. After a period of time, the Franc would be allowed to float clear of the euro. She also proposed using this relaunched French currency domestically and a return of the old ECU (European Currency Unit) for transnational interactions. The ECU took its value from a basket of currencies of the old European Community. It was an electronic unit and not a full currency and had no notes or coins. It was essentially a book-keeping mechanism. Le Pen eventually softened her opposition to the euro as the Presidential election progressed. However, if the French economic weakness persists, questions will inevitably be raised about the country's continued use of the euro. The desire to ditch the currency will, almost certainly, become much more mainstream, rather than confined to the far Right. Otherwise, it may be that France will increasingly be seen as part of the Club Med group of nations, rather than a leading member of the northern European set.

France may be also hoping that the Lagarde Presidency of the ECB may result in a reorientation in the focus of that Bank in a more "French" direction and away from the German orientation which has heretofore been the dominant influence. However, it is very doubtful that Europe's central bankers, who have been schooled in the Berlin mentality of austerity, are likely to allow Lagarde exercise too much flexibility.

Sooner or later, we will have another crisis which will destroy the present arrangements. The fact that the euro crisis hit Ireland, Greece, Portugal, and Spain at the same time shows that the proposition that the fundamental causes of the crisis were home grown in these countries is ridiculous. There were all caused by the nature of the common currency itself[35]. The reality is that several of the countries which were so badly affected by the euro crisis, performed well before entry into the Eurozone. The system removed the tools of economic management to deal with a crisis from national Governments; it took control of interest rates; removed the option of printing of a national currency; restricted deficit budgets and a flexible exchange rate; and provided nothing in return. The electorates turned on the national Governments, without realising that those administrations were often powerless to react to a deteriorating situation. In turn, Frankfort and Brussels blamed the victims. Many well-educated young people who had studied hard and were well qualified, suddenly found that their job prospects had vanished and were forced to emigrate.

The situation may not survive another crisis. Therefore, it is preferable to have a planned escape route, put together in less troubled times, rather than be forced to leave in chaos, as with the ERM. It should also be remembered that it was the ECB and the EU Commission which insisted that the banking system should be regulated, independent of the national Governments and then blamed the local administrations entirely for the subsequent disaster[36].

Ireland departing the Eurozone

It would be the height of irresponsibility for any Irish administration not to have well developed plans to depart the euro, given its underlying weakness. There will of course be possible emergency measures, on file, ready in case of a sudden implosion but the Government needs, in addition, to look strategically at how it could escape this straight jacket, especially now that the UK has departed the EU.

Firstly, we need to look at our own historical precedent. The way Ireland cut the link with sterling was to have pegged the Irish pound to the British currency at an identical rate for many years. Ireland was a small part of the sterling area. Irish and British currency circulated freely in the Republic of Ireland and were interchangeable in shopping centres, etc.; notes and coins were issued in identical denominations to sterling.

When the Republic of Ireland was required to have an independent currency, the authorities in Dublin simply allowed the rate of exchange to drift depending on market sentiment. The British pound then appreciated against the Irish punt.

Today north of the Irish border, a similar situation to what pertained prior to the launch of a separate independent Irish pound still exists. Seven banks in Northern Ireland and Scotland are authorised by the Bank of England to issue banknotes.

The Bank of Ireland, Ulster Bank, Allied Irish Bank (trades as First Trust Bank in the North) and Northern Bank Ltd (which trades as Danske Bank) have all been authorised by legislation to issue banknotes. In Scotland, a similar situation pertains, with the Bank of Scotland, Clydesdale Bank and the Royal Bank of Scotland (RBC) the designated entities. This right to issue banknotes was originally established by the British Parliament as far back as 1845 and was reinforced more recently by Part 6 of the UK Banking Act, 2009[37].

The legislation authorised local banks in Belfast to provide the only Irish banknotes today, albeit in Northern Ireland. While these notes are theoretically legal tender throughout the United Kingdom, in practise they are not generally accepted in England and Wales.

In the case of the euro, Ireland could try to imitate the position in the North. Dublin could simply decide to issue Irish notes of equal value to the euro, or allow individual banks to do so, and allow both currencies to circulate internally within the Republic, with notes of similar face value. Ireland could continue to use only "real" euros for international trade. Government employees in Ireland would be paid in the new currency and the Government would honour these notes through the Central Bank. The Government would have regained its ability to issue banknotes and hence would not be as vulnerable as the Cowen/ Lenihan administration was at the time of the Bailout.

Once a decision to formally leave the Eurozone was made, the euro would cease to be legal tender in the Republic after a specified period but would be available through banks. The financial institutions would designate domestic savings and loans in the new Irish currency at the market rate relative to the euro. The relative exchange rate for the two currencies would then be allowed to drift apart on international money markets.

The co-circulation of the euro and the new Irish currency would last for a defined period. It would be a reverse process to the introduction of the common currency and hopefully would be achieved as smoothly.

This would cover domestic arrangements for a new Irish currency. At the same time, the Irish Central Bank would regain its independence and would be tasked with managing the external arrangements.

However, this type of escape scheme would clearly violate the rules of the ECB which has been given the sole right to issue banknotes within the Eurozone. Any scheme to have locally issued notes and euros operate in the Republic would require the active cooperation of the ECB, something which may be difficult to achieve, since leaving the euro threatens the ECB's monopoly and, in the long term, its very existence. However, given the challenges and dangers facing the euro and, in particular, the problems Ireland will continue to have with the bulk of its trade outside the Eurozone, we should actively lobby for permission to issue our own notes in a way similar to what happened when we were still part of the sterling area. For any administration, the dangers of the euro collapsing must be close to the top of any list of macroeconomic risk factors.

However, to be realistic, it would be an uphill task to convince the European Council, Commission and other EU institutions to agree to this scheme. While this method would be the preferred option, Ireland must be prepared to look at other approaches.

An alternative would be for the Government to designate any new notes as tax rebate certificates, something that would be currently permissible in the Eurozone. The rebate certs could then be used as currency inside the Irish State. The Government could also offer to issue Government bonds, again redeemable at the Irish Central Bank. However, tax rebate certs or Government bonds would have to be designated as Government debt, since they would be redeemable. It is likely that other countries will look in a similar direction.

In a thought provoking article on the prestigious Politico.eu website, Nobel Laurate and Economics Professor at Columbia University, Joseph Stiglitz,[38] discussed the possible ways Italy could leave the Eurozone, pointing out that while North America quickly recovered from the financial shock of 2008, the Eurozone failed to do so and he rightly ascribes that failure to the euro.

> "The result for the Eurozone has been slower growth, and especially for the weaker countries within it. The euro was supposed to usher in greater prosperity, which in turn would lead to renewed commitment to European integration. It has done just the opposite – increasing divisions within the EU, especially between creditor and debtor countries.

> The resulting schisms have also made it harder to solve other problems, most notably the migration crisis where European rules impose an unfair burden on the frontline countries receiving migrants, such as Greece and Italy. These also just so happen to be the debtor countries, already plagued with economic difficulties. No wonder there is a rebellion."

Stiglitz identifies the selfish economic policies of Germany as the central problem for the euro. Europe's largest economy dictated the modus operandi of the ECB and the rules surrounding the new currency but has failed to follow policies domestically, and in the Eurozone, which might have allowed the euro to thrive. The most effective remedial measure for the survival of the euro would be a German exit he argues, something which is very difficult to envisage.

He believes that for Italy, or indeed any country wanting to exit the Eurozone, debt restructuring has to be part of the equation. Without a restructuring, debt denominated in a foreign currency could greatly increase in value. Stiglitz argues plausibly that if an investor is getting a premium on yields on bonds, the investor has implicitly accepted that there is a greater risk of something going wrong.

Italy should start issuing a new Lira and simply redenominate all debts in this new currency and because of Italy's international obligations, including to the Eurozone, enact a super-Chapter 11 bankruptcy law to hold off predators. In this case, Italy may not even have to leave the Eurozone and state that the new currency is Government bonds.

Stiglitz claims that it is unlikely that the Eurozone would take decisive action against Italy, should it choose to start issuing Lira, either as a formal new currency or as Government bonds. However, as tensions grow between Brussels and Rome over budget deficit levels, the likelihood is that if a country exits the Eurozone, Italy is the strongest possibility, at this point, especially should Le Lega return to power.

An alternative approach was the one advocated by former Greek Finance Minister Yanis Varoufakis who, with colleagues in the Greek Finance Ministry, formatted an electronic payment system, based on a new Greek Drachma[39]. With advances in technology and with the growth of cryptocurrencies, especially Bitcoin, bypassing the euro electronically has become much more feasible.

Another study, this time by Professor Andrew Rose of Berkeley University looked at the experience of countries exiting a currency union from 1946-2005. These were mainly ex-colonies and Rose concluded that there was remarkably little macroeconomic volatility around the time of the currency dissolutions[40]. So maybe it is not as disruptive as we had imagined.

The inherent instability of the euro represents a danger to the future economic health of Ireland. The concept of a single currency covering such a diverse area in economic terms was always a difficult proposition and likely to be susceptible to a sudden collapse. However, another possibility is equally problematic. It is not that there is just a danger in its collapse but there may be greater danger if it continues to stagger on. Lord King, former Governor of the Bank of England, concluded

> "the tragedy of monetary union in Europe is not that it might collapse but that, given the degree of political commitment among the leaders of Europe, it might continue, bringing economic stagnation to the largest currency block in the world and holding back recovery of the wider world economy. It is at the heart of the disequilibrium in the world today."[41]

While there is a growing acceptance among economists in Ireland that entry into the euro was a mistake, the division is on whether it would be worth the risk of leaving. One is tempted to think of the old Laurel and Hardy routine, "This is another fine mess you got me into Ollie", when addressing the europhiles in Dublin.

In a recent intervention the Governor of the Hungarian Central Bank, György Matolcsy, gave a very candid assessment of the single currency, stating[42] that

> ""two decades after the euro's launch, most of the necessary pillars of a successful global currency – a common State, a budget covering at least 15-20 per cent of the Eurozone's total gross domestic product, a Eurozone finance minister and a ministry to go with the post – are still missing."

He added that it was originally a French scheme to curtail the economic power of Germany which has badly misfired. It was time, he said, for EU States both in and outside the Eurozone to admit that the euro had been a "strategic error".

He concluded: "We need to work out how to free ourselves from this trap. Europeans must give up their risky fantasies of creating a power that rivals the US.

> "Members of the Eurozone should be allowed to leave the currency zone in the coming decades, and those remaining should build a more sustainable global currency."

Matolcsy called for a mechanism to be devised to allow countries to exit the euro, something which of course did not get an enthusiastic response from his European colleagues. Nevertheless, Ireland should look at the issue again and consider seriously how to escape the euro's clutches.

Given the problems with the euro, it is almost certainly a risk worth taking. There is no doubt, but the euro greatly eased the situation for the average citizen travelling within the countries that use the currency. This was probably the only demonstrable gain. However, the negatives are much more powerful and the "debtors' prison" it has created for many of the countries of southern Europe represents a huge risk both politically and economically, apart from its dubious morality. Countries which stayed out of the Eurozone, UK, Sweden, Denmark, Poland, Czech Republic, etc., have done well relative to the Eurozone[43].

The saddest part of the euro episode is that after all the sacrifices made, there is no evidence that adoption of the common currency actually achieved any economic purpose. The euro did not increase trade between EU countries. Trade between members of the Eurozone actually fell after its introduction[44]. It certainly did not promote economic convergence among the Member States[45]. However, to think along these lines is to totally miss the point of the exercise. The former Irish Attorney-General and later EU Commissioner, Peter Sutherland, stated

> "that the ultimate rational of monetary union lies in its contribution to the larger political strategy of European integration. This is a profoundly political act".[46]

In the final analysis, it was a profoundly political act to take Ireland into the euro and it will take a profound political decision, with courage, to take us out.

References

1. Website of the European Commission
2. *"The euro May Already be Lost"* by Tuomas Malinen, CEO of GnS Economics, postdoctoral researcher at the University of Helsinki, co-written with Dr. Heikki Koskenkylä and Dr. Peter Nyberg. February 2017. *http://www.minyanville.com/business-news/markets/articles/2524EUR-2523euro-2523eurozone-2523GDP-2523trump-2523merkel/2/14/2017/id/59403*. Retrieved 18 December 2019
3. *"The Irish Pound, from Origins to EMU"* by John Kelly, Quarterly Bulletin Spring 2003, *https://www.centralbank.ie/docs/default-source/consumer-hub-library/the-irish-pound-from-origins-to-emu.pdf?sfvrsn=2*. Retrieved 18 December 2019
4. Patrick Honohan and Gavin Murphy " *BREAKING THE STERLING LINK: RELAND'S DECISION TO ENTER THE EMS*" Prepared for the session: "The Choice of Exchange Rate Regime in Historical Perspective" at the XVth World Economic History Congress, Utrecht,

August 2009. *http://homepage.eircom.net/~phonohan/Weighingshort.pdf.* Retrieved 18 December 2019

5. Mody, *EuroTragedy* p 36

6. Ibid. p 37

7. Report to the Council and the Commission on the realisation by stages of ECONOMIC AND MONETARY UNION in the Community (Werner Report)), 1970. *http://aei.pitt.edu/1002/1/monetary_werner_final.pdf.* Retrieved 18 December 2019

8. Mody *EuroTragedy* p 93

9. Ibid. p 112

10. Cormac Lucey *Plan B* p 14

11. Mody *EuroTragedy* p 217

12. Ibid. p 122

13. Campaign against Euro Federalism quoting the *Financial Times* 9 April 1999. *http://www.caef.org.uk/whatsaid.html.* Retrieved 18 December 2019

14. Larry Elliot *"Brown can't be ousted from driving seat" Guardian* 8 Oct 2001. *https://www.theguardian.com/politics/2001/oct/08/uk.euro.* Retrieved 18 December 2019.

15. Anthony Coughlan. *The EU, Brexit and Irexit – A handbook for Irish and European Diplomats, Whether Politically Centre, Left of Right* p 15

16. Henry McDonald *"Weak sterling puts Irish mushroom farmers in the shade" Guardian* 12 Nov 2016. *https://www.theguardian.com/business/2016/nov/12/plunging-pound-puts-irish-mushroom-farmers-in-the-shade.* Retrieved 18 December 2019

17. Toby Sterling *"Dutch relations with euro up for debate after lawmakers commission probe"* Reuters 24 February 2017, *https://www.reuters.com/article/netherlands-election-euro-idUSL8N1G95BX.* Retrieved 18 December 2019

18. Mody *EuroTragedy* p 130

19. *"Greece's reforms Just in time? Can Greece's Prime Minister, Costas Simitis, hold on to power?"* Economist Magasine 18 September 2003. *https://www.economist.com/europe/2003/09/18/just-in-time.* Retrieved 18 December 2019

20. Frances Coppola *"Lessons For The Eurozone From The Greek Debt Crisis" Forbes*, 20 August 2018, *https://www.forbes.com/sites/*

francescoppola/2018/08/20/lessons-for-the-eurozone-from-the-greek-debt-crisis/#683bdbdb55dd. Retrieved 18 December 2019

21. Convergence Report May 2012" (PDF). European Central Bank. *May 2012. https://ec.europa.eu/economy_finance/publications/european_economy/2012/pdf/ee-2012-3_en.pdf.* Retrieved 18 December 2019

22. Mody *EuroTragedy* p 65

23. Malinen, Tuomas and Nyberg, Peter and Koskenkylä, Heikki and Berghäll, Elina and Mellin, Ilkka and Miettinen, Sami and Ala-Peijari, Jukka and Törnqvist, Stefan, *"How to Leave the Eurozone: The Case of Finland"* (August 23, 2017). Available at SSRN: *https://ssrn.com/abstract=3024551 or.* Retrieved 21 May 2018.

24. ANDREAS MARCKMANN ANDREASSEN *"Danish Government wants second referendum on euro" EU Observer*, 22 November 2007, *https://euobserver.com/institutional/25202.* Retrieved 18 December

25. *"Swedes say No to Euro"*, BBC News, 15 September 2003, *http://news.bbc.co.uk/2/hi/europe/3108292.stm.* Retrieved 18 December 2019

26. 2017 Eurobarometer Report Overview. *https://ec.europa.eu/commfrontoffice/publicopinion/index.cfm/Chart/getChart/chartType/lineChart//themeKy/29/groupKy/183/savFile/118.* Retrieved 19 December 2019

27. *http://pieniadze.gazeta.pl/Gospodarka/1,123718,12207129,CBOS__Wprowadzenie_euro_popiera_25__badanych_Polakow_.html,*

28. roslav Bukovský. Vstoupit do eurozóny? Až bude euro za dvacet korun, shodli se Babiš s Rusnokem. Published on 5 December 2017 and retrieved 19 December 2019

29. *"Orban: Hungary will not adopt the Euro for many decades to come"* Hungarian Free Press 3 June 2015. *http://hungarianfreepress.com/2015/06/03/orban-hungary-will-not-adopt-the-euro-for-many-decades-to-come/.* Retrieved 19 December 2019

30. Joseph E Stiglitz, *"The euro could be nearing a crisis – can it be saved?"* *Guardian* 13 June 2018. *https://www.theguardian.com/business/2018/jun/13/euro-growth-eurozone-joseph-stiglitz.* Retrieved 23 December 2019.

31. Phillipe Legrain, *Why are economies and politics are in such a mess and how to put them right* published April 2014

32. Verbatim of the remarks made by Mario Draghi President of the European Central Bank at the Global Investment Conference in

London 26 July 2012, published on the website of the ECB. *https://www.ecb.europa.eu/press/key/date/2012/html/sp120726.en.html*. Retrieved on 23 December 2019

33. Francesco Guarascio *"EU gives budget leeway to France 'because it is France' – Juncker"* Reuters report, 31 May 2016. *https://uk.reuters.com/article/uk-eu-deficit-france-idUKKCN0YM1N0*. Retrieved 23 December 2019

34. Laura Mowat *"Euro is dead, Marine Le Pen Brands Euro currency a burden and vows to reinstate the Franc"* Express 30 April 2017. *https://www.express.co.uk/news/world/798383/Marine-Le-Pen-Euro-is-dead-reinstate-Franc*. Retrieved 23 December 2019

35. Cormac Lucey, *Plan B* p 78

36. Ibid. p 79

37. Banking Act 2009. http://www.legislation.gov.uk/ukpga/2009/1/contents. Retrieved 23 December 2019.

38. Joseph Stiglitz, "How to exit the Eurozone" Politico.eu 26 June 2018. https://www.politico.eu/article/opinion-italy-germany-how-to-exit-the-eurozone-euro-reform/.

39. Mehreen Khan *"Greece news live: explosive Varoufakis parallel currency plot prompts official investigation"* Daily Telegraph, 27 July 2015 *https://www.telegraph.co.uk/finance/economics/11764792/Greece-news-live-explosive-Varoufakis-parallel-currency-plot-prompts-official-investigation.html*. Retrieved 23 December 2019.

40. Cormac Lucey *Plan B* p 129

41. Melvyn King, *The End of Alchemy: Money, Banking and The Future of the Global Economy*, Little, Brown 2016 p 248.

42. Ciaran McGrath *"Eurozone on the brink: 'The euro is a trap – ALL countries were better off before joining"* Express, 4 November 2019. *https://www.express.co.uk/news/world/1199577/eurozone-euro-brussels-hungary-eu-finance-brexit-news*. Retrieved 22 November 2019.

43. Stiglitz *The Euro: And its Threat to the Future of Europe* p67

44. Mody *EuroTragedy* p 424

45. Stiglitz *The Euro: And its Threat to the Future of Europe* p 92–94

46. Mody *EuroTragedy* p 116

Chapter 9

The Democratic Deficit

"Elections cannot be allowed to change Economic Policy"
German Finance Minister Wolfgang Schäuble

The reaction to the Brexit referendum, and the subsequent frantic efforts to overturn the result by Remainers in the UK, elements of the EU Commission and some Member States, particularly Ireland, brought the whole issue of democracy in Europe into sharp focus. The feeling among the pro-EU groups was that the good guys had lost and that the bad guys had triumphed. Hence, everything had to be done to overturn this perverse verdict. The end was to justify the means. Those who voted for Brexit must have been less intelligent and sophisticated, than the Remainers and Britain had to be saved from that lot. There was also the danger that if Britain successfully exited the EU, then it would set a very bad example to others. Therefore, the EU was morally right to overcome a temporary democratic outcome.

However, to fully understand this phenomenon, the reaction to the Brexit result should not be seen in isolation. It is part of a long history of disrespecting democratic outcomes, if they run counter to the onward march towards ever closer union.

"Elections cannot be allowed to change Economic Policy"

Former German Finance Minister Wolfgang Schäuble made this astonishing statement on 11 February 2015, at the Eurogroup Finance Ministers' meeting[1]. At that moment, he had probably, unwittingly, encapsulated the undemocratic and elitist philosophy of many at the centre of the EU. The scene is described in the book "Adults in the Room" by former Greek Finance Minister, Yanis Varoufakis, in the following terms.

'Elections cannot be allowed to change economic policy,' he began. Greece had obligations that could not be reconsidered until the Greek programme had been completed, as per the agreements between my predecessors and the Troika. The fact that the Greek programme could not be completed was apparently of no concern to him. What startled me more than Wolfgang Schäuble's belief that elections are irrelevant was his total lack of compunction in admitting to this view. His reasoning was simple: if every time one of the nineteen Member States changed Government the Eurogroup was forced to go back to the drawing board, then its overall economic policies would be derailed. Of course, he had a point: democracy had indeed died the moment the Eurogroup acquired the authority to dictate economic policy to Member States without anything resembling Federal democratic sovereignty.

Schäuble later added, in a warning to Greece, that "New Elections change nothing".[2]

The EU over the years has managed to break the direct link between the people and their Government. It has consistently enforced bankers' rule, mass unemployment, privatization, etc. over much of Europe, including post-crash Ireland. It always blames the victims of its policies, never the perpetrators. The corporate world is to be appeased and the interests of the Franco-German core must trump all other interests. Those who stand in the way are Neanderthals and do not really understand how the modern world works.

We have come a very long way from the idea that the countries of Europe had come together to preserve peace and promote the democratic system.

The initial decision by six western European countries to establish close institutional links in the 1950s was, in part, a reaction to the cataclysm of the Second World War. The memory of dictatorships throughout most of Europe and inter-State conflict was to be relegated to the pages of history. The new relationships would be based on mutual economic dependence and respect for democracy.

According to the EU Commission website, "The European Union, as a global actor and the world's biggest donor, is founded on the principles of liberty, democracy, respect for human rights, fundamental freedoms and the rule of law. The Treaty on European Union commits the EU to act on the global scene 'guided by the principles which have inspired its own creation.'[3]

Yet to many, there is a perception that the EU has strayed well away from these noble sentiments in its treatment of democracy within its own boundaries. This is particularly true of its record in relation to referenda in the individual countries.

There have been a large number of such referenda, as national Governments have consulted their citizenry about transference of sovereignty to Brussels. Most have been carried successfully by the Governments but a number have been rejected. However, the EU side have never accepted defeat with any grace. This undemocratic tendency inside the EU should give those in Ireland some reason to pause and reconsider their unquestioning devotion to this new Empire.

Referenda in Member States

The experience of Greenland, the first country to vote itself out of the European project, was illustrative of the attitudes in the EU towards withdrawal, even in the 1980s. The country, which is part of the Kingdom of Denmark, had voted against Danish entry into the EEC in the accession referendum in 1972, with 70% opposing membership[4]. The EEC decision to establish a Common Fisheries Policy was the determining factor in deciding Greenlanders' adverse reaction to accession. With Home Rule established in 1979, the new administration in Nuuk, the island's capital, organised a fresh referendum in 1982 on membership, which resulted in a 53% vote in favour of withdrawal. The indigenous Innuit part of the population was particularly opposed to EEC membership. Greenland eventually left the EEC in 1985.[5]

I was posted in Copenhagen as a junior Irish diplomat at the time and well remember the hostility of other foreign diplomats at the effrontery of these "backward" people voting against the onward march of progress. This was reflected in the discussions in Brussels.

One of the Greenland negotiators, Lars Vesterbirk, was quoted on the Slow Journalism Company website on 23 June 2016, as saying that he had great difficulty getting Member States to accept the legitimacy of the democratic result. He stated

"It was intense. The atmosphere between us and the Member States wasn't good," he reported. "We spent a lot of time convincing the EU (EEC) that of course you can leave – the EU is not a prison." Vesterbirk was also quoted as follows

"The negotiations were a surprisingly unpleasant job. The EU Member States would not take us seriously because they were not willing to accept that you should or could leave." He mentioned that Germany was the most antagonistic[6].

At that period, 1982-85, the European Project was still at a fairly flexible stage and even then, it was not easy to withdraw. This hostile reaction to electoral setbacks, and a lack of respect for those who hold contrary views, has become a common feature of ardent Federalists over the years. Democracy only works when the loser in any contest accepts the result and the legitimacy of the decision. This fundamental tenet of a democratic society is distinctly lacking among the group of officials who run the EU and their allies in the Member States.

The first reaction of Brussels is to ignore an adverse referendum result and if that is not possible to seek a rerun until the right result is obtained. This is accompanied by a demonization of those who will not row in with the drive for ever closer union.

One of the earliest shocks to Brussels and a serious setback to the Commission's plans for a Federal Europe came again from the Kingdom of Denmark. It was the result of the Danish referendum on the Maastricht Treaty on 2 June 1992[7]. This new Treaty renamed the European Economic Community (EEC) to the simpler title of the European Community (EC) to reflect a massive transference of power from the Member States to Brussels. It laid the foundations for the ill-fated euro and also moved the new EC well beyond its traditional economic area, to include competences in Foreign Affairs, as well as Justice and Home Affairs[8]. It set the European Project on a course which has led today to much discontent and to Brexit. The Danes voted by a whisker to reject the new arrangements, 50.71% to 49.3%[9].

There was incredulity among the elites in the various European capitals at the Danish result. The Danish Prime Minister at the time, the Conservative Poul Schluter, was embarrassed and was quoted as saying

"Can anyone seriously believe that our small nation with five million people can stop the great European Express of 300 million"[10].

There was condescension and attacks from other Member States. Any idea that Denmark was an equal member of this new European Community was dispelled. Denmark would have to rethink or be subject to penal action. There was no question of accepting the democratic result. Of course, the Danes backed down after such threats and after securing a number of optouts from the Treaty provisions. However, they proved much more resolute in subsequent referenda reversals for the EU. The second Danish referendum on the Maastricht Treaty took place on 18 May 1993 and the EU pushback, against the initial rejection, was successful on this occasion.

It is worth noting that Jean Claude Trichet, then a senior civil servant in the French Treasury, reacted to Denmark's rejection of Maastricht by stating at the European Monetary Committee that other European countries must proceed despite the referendum outcome and that Denmark should be punished for its foolishness[11]. It was a foretaste of Trichet's attitude later as President of the ECB and his lack of respect for smaller countries, including Ireland.

The French Government also asked its electorate for their view on the Maastricht Treaty in a referendum on 20 September 1992. The result was remarkably similar to the Danish outcome, but in this case the Treaty was endorsed by a whisker, 51.0% to 49.0%[12]. There was no call for a rerun, showing that the rules of the game are different for those seeking to stop the European project from those wanting to railroad through pro-Federalist policies. It should be noted that in a poll in France in 2012 almost two-thirds of those questioned would have rejected Maastricht at that stage[13].

The French "petit oui", the Danish rejection and the chaotic scenes in the British House of Commons as the Government of John Major struggled to get Maastricht ratified, through a Parliamentary procedure, marked a watershed in the evolution of the European project. It awakened national sentiment in the Member States and euroscepticism entered the mainstream seriously for the first time. The era of passive acceptance of plans for further European integration was over. Post Maastricht proposals would be subject to much greater scrutiny and the gulf between the soaring rhetoric of EU leaders about democracy and the reality on the ground of national sentiment in the Member States became much more apparent.

Ireland, along with Denmark and France, had a referendum on the Maastricht Treaty. It was held on 18 June 1992. The result was a resounding approval for the new Treaty with 69.1% voting in favour[14]. I was posted at the Irish Embassy in Australia at the time and remember being warmly congratulated by other European diplomats over the result. The warmest congratulations came from those working in the EEC Delegation in Canberra. I was told that Ireland had put the European bus back on the road. We were congratulated by all our EU colleagues.

However, that period of Ireland being regarded as the "best boy in the classroom", did not last. It received a rude awakening a few years later when the Nice Treaty referendum came around. This was a Treaty which proposed institutional changes within the EU to cater for the forthcoming enlargement of membership of the EU by ten new Member States.

At that stage, I was a more senior official, based back in the Department of Foreign Affairs in Ireland. I could see at first hand the complacency in official Ireland about the EU. Those opposed to the Nice Treaty were regarded as a ragbag of malcontents and there was no real engagement to persuade the Irish public of the benefits of the Treaty. There was arrogance and hubris in Government circles and a distain for the intelligence of the average voter. The pro-Treaty campaign itself was a shambles, but the possibility of defeat never really entered into the equation. Ireland had been among the most enthusiastic supporters of EU Treaties in a number of referenda but the percentage of those in favour had been slowly dropping. When the result came in, it was a political bombshell. It showed that the Irish electorate had rejected Nice by a margin of 53.9% to 46.1%, on a very low poll[15].

The initial reaction in Government circles was shock and disappointment. Irish politicians delight in their role in Brussels and, in particular, in currying favour with the EU Commission. Since the country is not an active participant of many other international gatherings, many politicians have been totally sucked into the conformist atmosphere in the Council of Ministers. Suddenly their mental world had been turned upside down. The condescending pats on the head had gone and a new less benign attitude was discernible in the corridors of Brussels.

After the Nice referendum I saw myself the derision of our European partners at our affront to the European project, coupled with the fear in Dublin of alienating our masters in Brussels. It was a long way from the spirit of 1916.

However, the Irish rejection was not to be taken seriously. At a meeting of the European Council in Goteborg in Sweden on 15–16 June 2001[16], it was decided that the national ratification processes would continue in the Member States, despite the Irish result. Just like with Denmark, Ireland would not be allowed to stop the integration process.

Ireland was offered a number of clarifications on the Treaty, inter alia, in the area of neutrality (Seville Declaration June 2002)[17] and required to hold a second vote. The second referendum on the Nice Treaty on 19 October 2002 was successful in getting the electorate's agreement[18]. Internally, the Irish Government had decided that fear was to be the dominant theme of their campaign and a Project Fear-type strategy was pursued. It worked. The result was 62.9% in favour.

The Irish and Danish experiences were by no means unique. The history of unsuccessful referenda, which were either ignored or overturned, include the following;

Ireland:
Referendum on the Nice Treaty June 2001.
Referendum on the Lisbon Treaty June 2008.

Denmark:
Referendum on the Maastricht Treaty June 1992.

Netherlands:
Referendum on the proposed EU Constitution June 2005.
Referendum on Ukraine EU Association Agreement April 2016.

France:

Referendum on the proposed EU Constitution May 2005.

Greece

Referendum on the terms of the second Greek Bailout July 2015.

This is only part of the equation. The Danes very wisely rejected the proposal to replace the local kroner with the euro in another referendum in September 2000[19]. Subsequently, serious consideration was given, by the pro-EU elements in Copenhagen, supported by Brussels, to try to overturn that decision in another poll. However, the poor performance of the euro and the financial crisis in the Eurozone put paid to that. As a consequence, joining the euro was, reluctantly, not included in a new Danish referendum to drop some of the optouts in the Justice and Home Affairs area, which had been included to help pass the second Danish Maastricht Treaty referendum. However, even without the controversial euro element, the attempt failed. Despite starting the referendum campaign with a 12% lead, the popular tide turned against the pro-integrationist forces and that lead dissipated in the campaign. On 3 December 2015, Denmark voted to reject the advice of its Government. The No side won with 53% of the vote[20]. Who would bet that this will be the end of the story for the Danes? They may be made to vote yet once again or until they get the result right.

The EU have also directly intervened to change Governments in two Member States, Greece and Italy. At the height of the Eurozone crisis in 2011, the EU Commission, the European Central Bank and the German Government acted in collusion to help unseat George Papandreou in Athens and Silvio Berlusconi in Rome[21]. Both Prime Ministers had shown a reluctance to follow dictates from the trio of Berlin, Frankfort and Brussels. They were replaced by two technocrats, favourable to European Federalism. It was an extraordinary period when democracy was dispensed with to safeguard the beloved euro.

Actually, the pro-EU forces have a poor record in popular referenda. In addition to the cases mentioned above, Norway twice rejected EU membership (September 1972 and November 1994), Sweden rejected the euro in September 2003, Greenland voted itself out of the EEC in February 1982 and Hungary rejected EU control of immigration quotas in October 2016. The UK voted in favour of Brexit in summer 2016. In December 1992, the Swiss electorate rejected membership of the European Economic Area, which was seen as a precursor to EU membership[22]. On 20 October 2013, the citizens of the tiny republic of San Marino rejected a proposal to commence membership talks with the EU because of a low poll[23]. With a track record like that, it is no wonder the europhiles are very antagonistic about popular votes. Democracy is fine but it has its limits. As EU President Jean Claude Juncker can say, without a trace of irony, "There can be no democratic choice against the European Treaties."[24]

In their world, there can only be a limited democracy, which cannot be allowed to upset the "Project". It is somewhat similar to the discredited Leonid Brezhnev doctrine of limited sovereignty for socialist countries[25], which was practiced by the Soviet Union with regard to its satellite neighbours in eastern and central Europe.

The popular rejection of centralising more power in Brussels has not dampened the enthusiasm of the europhiles but rather spurred them to call for more Europe. As French Statesman Talleyrand said of the restored Bourbon dynasty after the abdication of Napoleon, "They have learned nothing and forgotten nothing." Another example of doing the same thing over and over again and expecting a different outcome.

The former Chancellor of the Exchequer in London, Norman Lamont, pointed out in a debate in the House of Lords on 25 October 2018, that since its foundation the European Union, and its predecessors, have witnessed forty-eight different referenda on matters relating to integration. On no occasion has a referendum ever been rerun if the result favoured the cause of ever closer union, even when the initial outcome was extremely close.

EU Constitution

The desire to press on with establishing a European Superstate has been relentless. It spawned the idea that the EU should have its own written Constitution. In pursuit of this ideal, the proposed European Constitution was drawn up by a nominated group of europhiles under the Chairmanship of former French President, the aristocratic Valéry

Giscard d'Estaing. It included former Irish Taoiseach John Bruton. The new Constitution proposed greatly expanding majority voting in the Council of Ministers and provided a Constitution for the embryonic EU State. The final text was settled during the Irish Presidency of the EU in June 2004[26]. There was no popular demand for a Constitution, but the Federalists believed that any self-respecting State had to have a Constitution. The proposal also included a formal "national" anthem and the official adoption of a "national" flag. Only sovereign States have such trappings, yet the Irish establishment, along with Bruton, were enthusiastic supporters. It even proposed that the EU would have its own Foreign Minister.

Given the fundamental nature of the Constitution, a large number of States decided to consult their electorates. Ten Member States decided to follow this course, including the United Kingdom and Ireland.

It was planned to be a triumphal demonstration of the popularity of the EU. However, the elites in the capitals were out of touch with their electorates and things did not go according to plan.

While there were two successful referenda in Luxembourg and Spain[27], the Constitution soon ran into trouble. On 29 May 2005, the French people voted by 55% to 45% to reject the Treaty, with a turnout close to 70%. The same pattern of the pro-EU forces losing popular support, and a winning position, as the campaign progressed, was soon observed[28].

On 1 June, in the first referendum in the Netherlands for 200 years, the Dutch public showed a similar lack of enthusiasm for the grandiose schemes of Brussels, with 61% voting against ratification[29], despite the overwhelming support of the Dutch political establishment.

These two rejections were not well received. Neil Kinnock, the former leader of the British Labour Party called it "a triumph of ignorance"[30]. So much for respecting your opponent.

The remaining Member States, the Czech Republic, Denmark, Ireland, Poland, Portugal and the United Kingdom, where further referenda were planned, simply cancelled the vote. It was accepted that the popular will was clearly against this new development. In contrast, in those States, which ratified the Constitution, through a Parliamentary process, huge majorities were recorded in its favour. In Malta, not even one negative vote was registered in Parliament against the proposed Constitution[31]. This demonstrated the huge disconnect between the political pro-EU elite and the general populations throughout the Union.

The EU was not going to take this defeat lying down. Most other administrations would have taken the Dutch and French rejections as a signal to rethink the whole operation. Not so in Brussels, as the Commission does not have the inconvenience of having to face an electorate.

Brussels simply repackaged the contents as the Lisbon Treaty and it was decided that the new version (almost identical to the Constitution but shorn of the title, anthem and flag, as well as dropping the title of Foreign Minister) did not need to be put to the people of France or the Netherlands, or indeed anywhere else. Giscard d'Estaing stated bluntly that the Lisbon Treaty was the same as the EU Constitution, rejected by the Dutch and French[32]. Unfortunately for the EU, the Irish Constitution demands a referendum in any major transference of sovereignty.

The Irish electorate followed the French and Dutch lead and also rejected the proto-Constitution, under its new title of the Lisbon Treaty, by a margin of 53.4% to 46.6% on 12 June 2008[33]. This was another severe embarrassment to the Irish Government. They were worried about the reaction in Brussels, in the midst of an economic meltdown in Ireland. They were right to be worried.

The reaction in Brussels was well summed up in an article in the newspaper, the *Guardian*, in December 2008 by British journalist, Brendan O'Neill:

> The Irish were subjected to a tirade of slanderous abuse when they dared to reject officials' carefully crafted and profound (in truth, overlong and turgid) document on the future of the EU. One Brussels official described them as "ungrateful bastards", on the basis that Ireland has received lots of handouts from the EU and thus should be more obedient to its paymaster. Pro-EU commentators blamed "populist demagogues" for cajoling the Irish into voting no, and said the EU's plans should not be "derailed by lies and disinformation.

It was widely claimed that the Irish simply didn't understand the treaty, and may have been confused by its "technocratic, near incomprehensible language" (well, they are ignorant Paddies, after all). Some claimed that the Irish mistakenly, possibly even illegitimately, had used the referendum to register disgruntlement with their own ruling parties. Margot Wallström, vice-president of the European Commission, said officials should try to "work out what the Irish people had really been voting against." I would have thought that was obvious: they were handed the Lisbon treaty; they said no to it[34].

The mentality in Brussels is that the electorate is wrong and have been deceived. There is no element of self-reflection or doubt or even worse that the EU proposal is simply wrong.

I was at the Department of Foreign Affairs at the time and it was soon obvious that the Irish authorities had absolutely no intention of allowing the result to interfere with their plans, despite the Government claiming publicly they would respect the outcome and reflect on it. The only reflection undertaken in Iveagh House and Government buildings in Dublin was how to overturn the vote.

Project Fear was brought out again and in such troubled times, it worked. The Treaty was passed on 2 October 2009 in a new Irish referendum.

Irish Supreme Court and EU democracy

A lack of respect for real democracy is not confined to the corridors of power in Brussels. It can also be found within Government circles in Dublin on the issue of referenda relating to the EU. There have been attempts internally in Ireland to limit the local democratic process in relation to the transference of power from our national institutions to Brussels. As stated previously, the Irish authorities tried to fireproof their freedom of action in the extraordinarily wide amendment to the Irish Constitution when the country joined the then EEC in 1973. This essentially stopped the Constitution, the fundamental law of the Irish State, from invalidating any actions to support our new membership. It stated that "No provision of this Constitution invalidates laws enacted, acts done, or measures adopted by the State necessitated by the obligations of membership of the Communities."[35]

Crotty case

The limitations of this manoeuvre were exposed by the famous Crotty case in 1986–87[36]. In this instance, Raymond Crotty, an agricultural scientist and lecturer in Trinity College Dublin, challenged the constitutionality of the Single European Act. This was the first major revision of the original Treaty of Rome(1957). The Act was fundamental in the achievement of the Single Market and the codification of the European Political Cooperation (EPC). This foreshadowed the creation of the Common Foreign and Security Policy. The Single European Act was to have taken effect on 1 January 1987[37].

The then Irish Government under Taoiseach Garret FitzGerald sought to portray the Act as simply an administrative tiding up exercise and that the Houses of the Oireachtas (Parliament) could give approval. The changes proposed, he argued, did not require taking the decision to the people. Crotty and his legal team believed that the changes were so fundamental that it required an amendment to the Constitution, something that can only be done through a referendum.

Crotty's arguments attracted support from a number of eminent lawyers and jurists including Nobel Peace Prize winner, Seán MacBride, future President Mary McAleese, Rory Brady (later Attorney-General), Aindrias Ó Caoimh and Michael White (later High Court judges) who called for a referendum to be held[38]. This was rejected by the Taoiseach, FitzGerald, who had suffered two recent referenda defeats and did not wish to ask for a popular vote. The case ended up in the law courts in the late evening of Christmas Eve 1986. The Government, after a successful appeal in a lower court had rushed the Bill to the then Irish President, Paddy Hillary, a former EU Commissioner, who signed it into law, despite the impending appeal to the Supreme Court[39].

The Irish Government was so intent on showing its European credentials that it had the Irish Air Corps on standby at the military airport at Baldonnel, county Dublin, to fly the instrument of ratification to Rome, so that we would not inconvenience our partners. Italy was the designated country for ratification. However, just in time, Justice Donal

Barrington, as the duty judge in the High Court, granted an injunction preventing the Government from completing ratification before the Supreme Court could consider the matter. It was high drama[40]. It was a shock to the Government.

Subsequently, the Supreme Court ruled in a seminal judgement on 9 April 1987, in a split decision, that the Single European Act required a Constitutional amendment to be ratified. The Court decided that the amendment to the Constitution in 1972, which allowed for EU membership, only related to the powers that were mentioned in the Treaty of Rome. Any new powers, which in the case of the Single European Act went far beyond what the people had originally mandated in the area of foreign policy cooperation, must be approved by them[41]. It was a remarkable demonstration of judicial activism and also of the independence of the judges, who would be aware that their decision would be received very badly by the Government. The Court had essentially stated that the State cannot give away powers which it had been given by the Constitution. The State is a custodian of these powers, not the absolute owners. The EU proposals in the Single European Act went far beyond the exercise of powers that the people permitted when they voted in 1972 to join the EEC. The Supreme Court, on this occasion, had struck a very effective blow to secure the democratic rights of the people of Ireland, against the wishes of the establishment[42].

As President Hillary had signed the legislation into law, while the case was under consideration, this made Crotty's standing legally stronger, as he was now challenging legislation which had become an Act of the Oireachtas, as distinct from attacking a Bill which had yet to be signed into force. The most compelling argument advanced by Crotty's legal team was that provisions in the Single European Act committed Ireland to formulating a common European foreign policy, which would be repugnant to the Constitution, which asserts Ireland as a sovereign, independent, democratic State and affirms Ireland's neutrality.

The people of Ireland owe Raymond Crotty a huge debt of gratitude for his courageous stand, often in the face of official ridicule and derision. It also showed how invaluable the Constitution provision is which allows all citizens direct access to the courts. It was one of the finest moments in the history of the Supreme Court, which stands as the other guardian of our Constitution, apart from the President.

According to distinguished University College Dublin Law Professor, Gavin Barrett, the effect of the Crotty judgement resulted in the "deployment in Ireland of direct democracy to an extent unparalleled in the European Union"[43] or as he put it more colourfully, "The building of a Swiss Chalet in an Irish Legal Landscape."

The former Supreme Court Judge, Brian Walsh, in correspondence with his friend William Brennan of the US Supreme Court, explained his reasoning in the Crotty case, "I went out of my way to state the complete freedom of the Government to pursue any foreign policy it liked, but what I said was unconstitutional was giving away that freedom."[44]

Walsh also mentioned in an interview with the *Irish Times* on 4 March 1989 that the Department of Foreign Affairs had submitted a memo to the Court stating that the other EU States would be "very cross" with Ireland, if the Treaty was delayed. The memo cut no ice with the Court and may have been counterproductive. Official Ireland had not lost the colonial cringe, when it came to Brussels.[45] It seemed a direct transference from the days Dublin Castle shuddered at any disapproval from London.

Interestingly enough, the reasoning of the Irish Supreme Court found resonance in a decision by the German Constitutional Court in June 2009, which issued a warning to its Parliament. It stated that the German Constitution "does not grant the bodies, acting on behalf of Germany, powers to abandon the right of self-determination of the German people, in the form of German sovereignty under international law, by joining a Federal State," in a ruling in response to challenges. The court added that the German Constitution excludes the possibility "of depleting the content of the legitimization of State authority, and the influence on the exercise of that authority provided by an election, by transferring the responsibilities and competences of the Bundestag to the European level to such an extent that the principle of democracy is violated"[46]. This is an outstanding criterion by which all our actions in relation to the EU should be judged.

McKenna case

The Irish courts have also been instrumental in advances in other areas relating to local democracy and the EU. The courts have had a huge

229

beneficial effect on how referenda in Ireland are conducted. This is very important in a country, like Ireland, when referenda are undertaken under Articles 46 and 47 of the Constitution[47]. In these cases, the citizens are operating a direct legislative function on our most basic law, Bunreacht na hÉireann, the Irish Constitution. In our Republican system, the citizenry is sovereign and all power flows from them. This is different to the UK which operates on the principle of Parliamentary sovereignty and referenda can be overturned by Parliament. In the case of Ireland, the British Liberal Democrat plan to simply revoke Article 50 and cancel Brexit without a further referendum would be unconstitutional and therefore illegal. Hence, it is vital that referenda in Ireland are conducted in a fair and unbiased manner.

This was not a problem during the years 1937–87, where the eleven referenda were conducted in a fair manner and where the Government of the day made no attempt to draw on the public purse to push for the changes they wanted[48]. It is obvious that it would be manifestly wrong for the official side to use the unlimited resources of the State to campaign for something like the abolition of elections, establish new ways of enriching themselves, destroying an independent judiciary, etc. These are of course farfetched ideas, but they illustrate a point; if political parties in power want to change the Constitution, they should use their own finances to campaign for it.

However, for the first time in 1987, a new Government led by Fianna Fáil's Charles Haughey decided to ignore precedent and, in its anxiety, to get Ireland's signature onto the Single European Act, spent public money on a one sided "information" campaign. It again demonstrated the lengths that the pro-EU faction in Ireland would go not to antagonise Brussels. (It should be noted, that Haughey had actually encouraged resistance to the SEA, while he was leader of the Opposition.)

He then proceeded to use public funds to help get the subsequent referendum passed. That example of the misuse of public funds was soon followed by Albert Reynolds, who as Taoiseach, also committed taxpayers' money to assist in the passing of the Maastricht referendum[49].

This type of disgraceful disregard for fairness was finally ended by the Irish Supreme Court in the McKenna judgement in 1995[50], which held that Green Party politician, and former member of the European

Parliament, Patricia McKenna, was correct to object to the one-sided expenditure of public money in order to achieve a particular result in Irish referenda. Such practices were unconstitutional, undemocratic and inherently unfair to the citizens of Ireland. Along with the Crotty judgement, this was a landmark decision and one where the judiciary stood up for the rights of the average man and woman against the powerful forces of the Irish establishment.

Coughlan case

This was by no means the end of the story. In a subsequent case, veteran anti-EU campaigner Anthony Coughlan, who had been a supporter of Raymond Crotty and Patricia McKenna, brought a case before the courts in relation to party political broadcasts during referenda. Coughlan argued that giving extensive free time to political parties, usually on the same side of a referendum debate, does not constitute the obligation on public service broadcasters to be "fair to all interests concerned." In the 1995 Divorce referendum, 42 minutes were allocated to the pro-divorce side in free party-political broadcasts, while ten minutes were allocated to the No side. Coughlan was not involved in the actual referendum but wanted to establish a fair basis on which referenda could be carried out. The High Court found in his favour[51].

The decision related to the State broadcaster RTÉ but clearly had wider implications. The management of RTÉ, no lover of party-political broadcasts, wanted to accept the High Court ruling by the eminent judge, the late Paul Carney, but the politicians were outraged. Former Taoiseach and a founder member of the European Movement in Ireland, Dr Garret FitzGerald, who was a member of the board of RTÉ at the time, together with some other EU supporters at board level, managed to overrule the professional management in the station and to insist on an appeal to the Supreme Court. The appeal failed.

The collective result of these actions by Crotty, McKenna and Coughlan has been to ensure that a more level playing field is there for future referenda. However, the price of liberty is eternal vigilance and I have no doubt but there are people in powerful positions examining how to subvert the intent of these decisions. In this area, it took three public-spirited and principled citizens to ensure that the power of the executive was curtailed. They will all have an honourable place in the history of civil rights in Ireland, especially so for Anthony Coughlan who was the driving force behind all three cases. Coughlan and his wife Muriel are among the most civic-minded citizens, yet it is clear from the State archives that his movements were being monitored by the authorities. Others who were involved in questioning the Government had their details noted in police files[52]. This was taking place in a country which claimed to be in favour of free speech. It showed just how determined the pro-EU establishment in Ireland was to monitor any threat to the status quo.

There are ongoing arguments in legal and political circles about the applicability of the three judgements and how much leeway they allow a Government. The Pringle judgement in 2012 appeared to narrow the application of the three seminal decisions[53]. However, in one respect, this is largely irrelevant as they have changed the public discourse. In the wake of these judgements, the expectation among the citizenry has changed. Irish people expect their Government to put any Treaty change to a vote[54].

Ireland is not the only EU country where Governments try to avoid a fair democratic contest. On 14 March 2018, the Prime Minister of Slovenia, Miro Cerar, announced his resignation after the country's Supreme Court annulled the result of a referendum on a rail project. The project was estimated at costing in the region of €1bn and was an initiative that the Government favoured. The Supreme Court in that country found that the Government as an institution had not acted fairly and had spent public money on promoting a Yes vote[55]. No doubt but the judicial authorities there were well aware of the McKenna judgement in Ireland.

The UK Government, under David Cameron, spent £9.3m of public funds on a leaflet in the run up to the Brexit referendum, largely outlining the dangers of leaving the EU[56], essentially supporting the Remain side. This would not have been possible in Ireland, where the public purse cannot be used unfairly to promote one side of a referendum proposal.

Events in Italy

Reluctance to any democratic brake on EU integration is not confined to the island of Ireland, it is, of course, widespread throughout the EU.

Apart from the Brexit referendum and the UK leaving the EU, changes in attitudes in Italy must be very unsettling for ardent europhiles. Italy, traditionally a rich western European Nation and the cradle of much of our civilisation, has been encumbered with an unworkable currency, the euro, which has caused huge misery. A whole generation of young Italians have seen their futures blighted by the actions of enthusiastic pro-EU politicians, who appeared more interested in ingratiating themselves with Brussels and Germany, than with looking after the economic well-being of their own citizens. Many of these politicians subsequently went on to land lucrative posts in EU institutions.

In any normal functioning democracy, there is always the option of voting out the failed politicians and reversing their policies. However, this is not always how the game is played inside the EU. The result of the last Italian general election was clear cut in one respect. The Italian people were fed up with the old way of doing things and wanted radical and effective change. This propelled two parties, opposed to European Federalism, the Five Star Movement and the Lega, into a position where they formed a majority Government[57].

No matter how people may have viewed these parties, and there is certainly an unsavoury element to the Lega, there is absolutely no doubt but that they essentially won a fair, free and democratic election. However, their euroscepticism raised hackles in Brussels and more importantly in Berlin. The subsequent events showed the authoritarian and antidemocratic element present in the pro-EU establishment.

It was speculated that at the behest of the German Government and the Brussels establishment, the Italian President Sergio Mattarella (who was appointed by the pre-election failed Government) vetoed a proposed key appointment in the new administration[58]. The proposed new Finance Minister, Paolo Savona, consistently held for many years that Italy made an historic mistake by joining the euro. It was a statement of the blindingly obvious. However, this was a step too far for the europhile elements. In another time period, Galileo was once forced to recant his belief that the Earth revolved around the sun because it was at variance with the prevailing theology of the time. Now in the twenty-first century, the Italian President and Brussels wanted the new Government to recant its criticism of the effects of the euro on

Italy. Again, the established power wanted the empirical evidence to be ignored in favour of dogma.

The President added insult to injury, by asking Carlo Cottarelli, a former IMF senior official known as "Mr. Scissors" for making cuts to public spending, to lead a technocratic Government[59]. This was an overt signal that, despite the view of the Italian population, there would be strong resistance to any change to the Federalist course. If this happened in a third world country, liberals in the West would have been up in arms. However, clearly there is a double set of standards operating when the interests of the Brussels establishment are at stake. It was an attempted coup against the democratic outcome.

In a very prescient intervention, the leader of the 5 Star Movement, Luigi di Maio, was quoted as saying, "In this country, you can be a condemned criminal, a tax fraud convict, under investigation for corruption and be a minister … but if you criticise Europe, you cannot be an economy minister."[60]

Clearly Ireland is not the only country where the EU, and more particularly the euro, is regarded by some as a sacred cow, held in the guardianship of the elite.

Italy, a founder member of the EEC and an ardent europhile country in the past, has had a difficult time in the last decade and badly needs to escape the shackles of Berlin imposed austerity and membership of the euro. The statistics regarding loss of manufacturing capacity, unemployment – especially among young people – economic growth, demographic trends, sovereign indebtedness, etc. over the last two decades, all make grim reading. It needs to devise a completely new set of policies.

However, Cottarelli could get very little support and promptly stepped down.

Democracy can throw up Governments like the post-election Italian one, which was showing far too much independence. However, as clearly indicated by the results of the European elections in May 2019, the independent position of the Lega in that Rome administration commended widespread support.

The subsequent break-up of the Five Star/Lega administration in Rome, in no way justified retrospectively the blatant and undemocratic attempts by pro-EU forces to thwart that Government's electoral mandate.

European institutions and issues of democracy

The elitist distain for the will of the ordinary voter is also seen in the vocabulary of Brussels, which pours such scorn on phrases like populism, nationalism, etc. Looking after the interests of your fellow citizens with policies that reflect their desires, is akin to a crime, along with taking pride in one's own national identity. Hence the most powerful body is the unelected and independent European Commission which operates as the Executive in supranational fashion. It alone can be trusted with real power.

The attitude of the unelected Brussels establishment can be characterised, not so much as undemocratic, as in fact actively antidemocratic. While this is not surprising, given the level of self-interest involved for the Commission and other groups in Brussels, what is surprising is the craven attitude of the Governments of Member States that roll over in the face of Brussels' bullying. There must be a suspicion that this lack of backbone may be motivated more by self-interest, than a total deficit of moral fibre. Many in Government in the Member States aspire to a well-paid position with the EU, with low tax and enviable pension rights. For many diplomats and politicians, especially those from eastern Europe, a position in an EU institution will result in receiving multiples of the salaries they could earn at home. Hardly a recipe to encourage officials to protect the national interest or indeed for promoting objective judgement and analysis.

The lack of respect for democracy is further accentuated by the monopoly conferred on the European Commission to propose legislation. This means that this europhile body is essentially not going to propose anything which will reduce their own role. I am not aware of any other administration, where elected officials are expressly excluded from the initiation of legislative measures.

The EU Commission is undoubtedly the most powerful body inside the EU. New Commissioners take the following Oath of Office:

Having been appointed as a Member of the European Commission by the European Council, following the vote of consent by the

European Parliament I solemnly undertake: to respect the Treaties and the Charter of Fundamental Rights of the European Union in the fulfilment of all my duties; to be completely independent in carrying out my responsibilities, in the general interest of the Union; in the performance of my tasks, neither to seek nor to take instructions from any Government or from any other institution, body, office or entity; to refrain from any action incompatible with my duties or the performance of my tasks.

I formally note the undertaking of each Member State to respect this principle and not to seek to influence Members of the Commission in the performance of their tasks. I further undertake to respect, both during and after my term of office, the obligation arising therefrom, and in particular the duty to behave with integrity and discretion as regards the acceptance, after I have ceased to hold office, of certain appointments or benefits.[61]

This oath provides the legal shield against any back tracking on the moves towards ever closer union. The reality is that EU Commissioners are not delegates or representatives, their loyalty and their allegiance is to the EU, not their own countries. They are not there to represent the interests of their nominating State.

The counterargument to accusations about the lack of democracy is that the European Parliament and the Council of Ministers fulfil the democratic requirement. This has no credibility.

The Council of Ministers meetings are not open to the public (other than for window dressing) and there is very little general knowledge or information about what is taking place behind closed doors. This is hardly a shining example of the openness and public consultation which would normally be expected of any democratic process.

The Parliament has even more shortcomings. It can, in reality, only seek to amend Commission proposals. It cannot amend existing legislation or alter in any way the Treaties of the EU. The Parliament can "request the Commission to submit any appropriate proposal on matters on which it considers that a Union act is required for the purpose of implementing the Treaties. If the Commission does not submit a proposal, it shall inform the European Parliament of the reasons."[62]. I doubt if this threat keeps many in the Commission awake at night from worry. I could just imagine the howls of protest at any real attempt at reform or stripping away from the unelected Commission the monopoly for initiating new legislation. There are far too many vested interests in the present arrangements to countenance any move towards real democracy. That would endanger the whole thrust of the European Project.

The word democracy, derived from the Greek "demos", means rule by the people. Since there is no single people or demos in Europe, who identify with other fellow citizens in solidarity, the basic foundation for democracy is simply not there.

The European Parliament was originally and rightly designed as a consultative Assembly, made up of representatives from the National Parliaments. Ireland's most prominent member during that period was Senator Michael Yeats, a son of the Nobel Prize winner for Literature, William Butler Yeats. However, direct elections were introduced in 1979. The only reason for doing this is as a precursor to a fully functioning European State. It was to be a process that would engage the national electorates with the European Parliament. Unfortunately, it has simply not worked. In Ireland, very few people could name their MEP and once the European elections are finished, the vast bulk of winners and losers sink into almost total obscurity, as far as the average citizen is concerned.

Ireland previously sent eleven members to the 751-seat European Parliament (which was increased to thirteen after Brexit, in a smaller house of 705) and hence in Parliamentary terms the country is a complete nonentity as Ireland has under 2% of the seats. Why Ireland was such an enthusiastic supporter of the European Parliament is no mystery. Many politicians in Ireland aspire to the wealth and pension rights that a spell in the European Parliament entails. I remember a politician saying to me that if he served two terms in the Parliament, he was essentially set up for life. He could live comfortably on his pension rights after that. Another described the salary and allowances as a tap which was turned on and every time, a MEP looked at his/her bank balance, it had skyrocketed. Some badly needed reforms have been introduced since but there is still a very well-paid gravy train for some of our politicians there.

It would be very much in Ireland's interests if the European Parliament was abolished or it reverted to its original role as a consultative body, made up of representatives from the National Parliaments. However, the chances of getting Irish politicians to even look at those proposals would be challenging, to say the least. I once made that suggestion, as a possible concession to British Prime Minister David Cameron during his renegotiations with the EU, to a number of EU Ambassadors in Ottawa and was afraid that several were about to faint after hearing such heresy. The power of privilege and potential largesse which the EU has at its disposal has a major distorting influence on our establishment.

In January 2019, the main Opposition Party in the German Parliament, the far Right AfD called for the effective scrapping of the European Parliament and its 700+ MEPs and its replacement by a European Assembly made up of just 100 delegates. These delegates would be nominated by the National Parliaments[63]. The party felt that unless fundamental reforms were undertaken to row back on the European Superstate concept, it would be better for Germany to withdraw from membership.

In Ireland, the Courts, and very honourably, our Supreme Court, have been a strong defender of democratic values and the rights of citizens[64]. They have constantly curbed the tendency of the executive to overreach. However, there is no real point in looking for judicial structures in EU to play a similar role of curbing executive power at European level.

There is little likelihood of sympathy for those, who wish to restrict the exercise of untrammelled power by the Commission, from the Court of Justice of the European Union (CJEU), formerly known as the European Court of Justice (ECJ), in Luxembourg. The ECJ was originally established to adjudicate on matters of community law, in particular where it conflicted with the laws of Member States. It has massively increased its role by insisting on a Federalist approach.

As the leading German lawyer, Gunnar Beck, pointed out in his booklet "The Court of Justice of the EU, Imperial not Impartial" , the CJEU adopts an ultra-flexible approach to issues such as methodology, following its own previous decisions, etc., except for the thrust of its conclusions, which are invariably towards more integration. This ultra-flexible approach allows it to:

choose between various interpretative criteria and give weight to whatever best promotes a pro-EU outcome. Even where there is neither obscurity nor ambiguity, the same approach is used to depart from the text of its own treaties or law to reach a particular goal … Moreover, CJEU indifference to its own treaty law has been matched by a similar refusal to respect the principles and practice governing the working of international treaty law.[65]

The dice is loaded against those seeking to stop the onward march of ever closer union, who come before the court.

Hence, those who would look to the EU institutions to uphold democratic principles and fairness, are people who believe more in hope than experience.

Brexit and democracy

The most egregious recent example of the antidemocratic impulse of the pro-Federalists in the EU, of course, has been the reaction to Brexit, both inside the UK, the EU institutions and, also, by its fellow Member States of the Union. The outcome of the referendum unleashed a determined and vicious campaign against the implementation of that historic result.

Throughout the Brexit referendum campaign in Britain, leading pro-EU politicians, such as Prime Minister David Cameron, described the referendum as a once in a generation choice. Cameron, on British TV, made a direct appeal in the campaign to the electorate in words that were straight and unambiguous. "You will have to judge what is best for you and your family, for your children and grandchildren, for our country … Your decision. Nobody else's … At that moment, you will hold this country's destiny in your hands."[66].

Leading Liberal Democrat, Paddy Ashdown, was unambiguous. He stated: "I will forgive no one who does not respect the sovereign voice of the British people once it has spoken, whether it is a majority of one per cent or 20 per cent. When the British people have spoken you do what they command. Either you believe in democracy or you don't."[67]

This is difficult to reconcile with his party's steadfast opposition to the implementation of the referendum result.

Other leading figures on the anti-Brexit side promised faithfully to respect the outcome. The then Chancellor of the Exchequer, George Osborne, added that there would be no second vote and the referendum would settle the issue for at least a generation[68].

However, that is not how the EU operates. It had expressed its support for the Remain campaign, but generally kept its distance, realising rightly that too overt an intervention would be counterproductive.

The EU reacted with a complete lack of generosity to the outcome and was determined to make it as difficult as possible to exit. It also offered terms in the Withdrawal Agreement to Theresa May which were hugely unfair and designed to humiliate the UK. It was simply a vindictive exercise. In the words of veteran Brexit campaigner in the European Parliament, Nigel Farage, the terms offered in the Withdrawal Treaty were the type a defeated nation in war would be forced to sign. The Withdrawal Treaty even included reparations of £39bn[69]. The history of unequal treaties is that they are counterproductive and rarely achieve their purpose in the longer run. They lead to internal dissention and political instability in the "loser" country. They also rarely achieve anything lasting for the "victors".

There were a small number of people in Brussels who evidently had some qualms about the policy of forcing the British into a second referendum on Brexit. EU Commissioner for Economic and Financial affairs, Pierre Moscovici, stated that Britain should not be treated like Ireland on the issue of a referendum going wrong, as in the case of the first Irish referenda on Nice and Lisbon. "What a mistake is when the EU almost imposed a second referendum. This happened for example a few years ago in Ireland and this was really criticised."[70] There were no such qualms about forcing Ireland into a second poll on Nice and Lisbon. Clearly there are different standards for larger countries.

Ireland, which had signed as a partner and friend of the UK in the GFA, not only acquiesced in this injustice but actively participated in it, an approach totally at odds with our history and our national interest. Ireland had been forced to accept a very unequal Treaty after the War of Independence (1919-21), which directly caused a civil war and Ireland eventually broke the terms of the Anglo-Irish Treaty. We usually call the latter by a much more acceptable term, namely that we "dismantled" the 1921 Treaty. We were absolutely right to do so. Even if the original Withdrawal Treaty had managed to pass the House of Commons unaltered, it would have been a temporary arrangement and merely would have stored up trouble for later on. It would no doubt have been reopened by a later British Government.

All the malevolent manoeuvres of Brussels would have been much less successful, unless there were political figures in London prepared to play the EU's game. In the 2017 general election, both main parties, Conservative and Labour, stood on a platform of respecting the referendum result. Both parties saw their share of the poll increase strongly. The Conservatives gained 5.5% to 42.4%, its highest share since the Thatcher landslide in the post Falklands election of 1983. Labour had an even more dramatic rise by 9.6% to 40.0%, its highest since the Tony Blair landslide of 1997.

The election took place after the triggering of Article 50 in March that year. This was the second and most emphatic democratic endorsement of Brexit.

However, rather than accept this double defeat, some of the anti-Brexiteers claimed that the referendum had only been advisory and because the EU had offered such ungenerous terms, the whole operation should be abandoned or that the UK should settle for an intermediary status of half in, half out of the EU. This was completely in line with the pro-EU elements in previous referenda in other Member States. They demanded that the Brexit referendum be rerun, after making the process so difficult that enough supporters of Brexit would simply give up the ghost through exhaustion.

Of course, if the Remain side had won, however narrowly, there would be no question of a rerun of the referendum. Just imagine the establishment reaction if the Remain side won, and the Brexiteers in Parliament had decided to plough on with withdrawal, regardless of the referendum result. The level of hypocrisy on the Remain side was exemplified by former British Prime Minister, Gordon Brown, categorically ruling out any consideration of another referendum on Scottish independence, while calling for the rerun of the Brexit one[71]. It was an example of the old maxim on tossing a coin, "Heads I win and tails you lose".

However, the UK first past the post electoral system had given the Labour party an increase of 30 seats in the general election of 2017, which was enough to deprive the Conservatives of a working majority.

Pro-Remain members of Parliament, including most destructively those within the Conservative Party, used the hung Parliament to sabotage and discredit, as much as possible, the Brexit process. Despite their election platform undertakings, these MPs acted in an antidemocratic manner and created a massive mess in the Parliamentary process. Their plan was to make Brexit so difficult and unsatisfactory that the population would lose heart and accept a continuation of Brussels rule. Of course, the Irish authorities' insistence on the Backstop played heavily into that approach. Fortunately, they did not succeed but the whole episode has left a sour taste and exposed clearly the antidemocratic tendencies of Brussels and its supporters. Thankfully the outcome of the December 2019 British general election finally put these manoeuvres to bed.

There are winds of change blowing throughout Europe. Those who foisted Treaty after Treaty on an unwilling population have a lot to answer for. They have been a much bigger long-term danger to constructive cooperation and friendship among the peoples of Europe than those who urged a different approach, based on respect for national sovereignty. In fact, it has been the europhiles who have risked the future of European cooperation and have divided nations. They are ultimately responsible for Brexit and have shown no real respect for democracy. The tactics of the pro-EU side have always been the end justifies the means.

This was encapsulated by Jean-Claude Juncker's statement, as quoted in the *Wall Street Journal* on 9 June 2011 in their story "Luxembourg lies on secret meetings": "When things get serious, you have to lie"[72]. Democracy and the Brussels establishment are just not natural allies.

References

1. Yanis Varoufakis *Adults in the Room* p 237

2. Ashoka Mody *EuroTragedy* p 414

3. EU Website *https://ec.europa.eu/europeaid/sectors/human–rights–and–democratic.* Retrieved 2 May 2019

4. Folketingets EU-Oplysning, "Svar på spm. om Nicetraktaten, folkeafstemning, til udenrigsministeren", 27 July 2001. Retrieved 5 May 2019

5. Henry Bodkin *"Greenland showed how to leave Europe as far back as 1984" Daily Telegraph* 24 June 2016, *https://www.telegraph.co.uk/news/2016/06/24/greenland-showed-how-to-leave-europe-as-far-back-as-1984/*. Retrieved 2 May 2019

6. Maia de la Baume *"Greenland's exit warning to Britain"* Politico.eu *https://www.politico.eu/article/greenland-exit-warning-to-britain*, 22 June 2016. Retrieved 2 May 2019

7. *"Danish Maastricht Referendum 1992" enacademic.com/dic.nsf/enwiki/6640595.* Retrieved 2 May 2019

8. *European Central Bank, "Five things you need to know about the Maastricht Treaty"* https://www.ecb.europa.eu *15 February 2017.* Retrieved 2 May 2019

9. *Booker and North, The Great Deception p 341*

10. *Time International*, 15 June 1992 p 10.

11. Cormac Lucey *Plan B* p 124

12. Booker and North, *The Great Deception* p 347

13. Henry Samuel, *"French Majority now reject Maastricht Treaty" Daily Telegraph* 17 September 2012, *https://www.telegraph.co.uk/news/worldnews/europe/france/9548466/French-majority-now-rejects-Maastricht-treaty.html*. Retrieved 2 May

14. Booker and North *The Great Deception* p 343

15. Ibid. p 475

16. The Irish Referendum on the Nice Treaty, House of Commons Research Paper 01/57, 21 June 2001, *https://researchbriefings.files.parliament.uk/documents/RP01-57/RP*. Retrieved 2 May 2019

17. Declaration of the European Council, 21-22 June 2002

18. Booker and North *The Great Deception* P 496

19. T R Reid, *"Denmark rejects Common EU currency"* Washington Post 29 September 2000, *https://www.washingtonpost.com/archive/politics/2000/09/29/denmark-voters-reject-common-eu-currency/231c35d6-ef32-4526-91de-d2a6e24fa7de/* Retrieved 2 May 2019

20. Suzanne Lynch *"Danish voters reject referendum on EU justice legislation." Irish Times*, 4 December 2015, *https://www.irishtimes.com/news/world/*

europe/danish-voters-reject-referendum-on-eu-justice-legislation-1.2453614.
Retrieved 2 May 2019

21. Ashoka Mody *EuroTragedy* p 330–331

22. Alan Riding, *"Swiss reject tie to Wider Europe"* 7 December 1992, https://
www.nytimes.com/1992/12/07/world/swiss-reject-tie-to-wider-europe.
html. Retrieved 2 May 2019

23. Dave *Keating* "San Marino rejects EU Accession" Politico.eu 23
November 2013, *https://www.politico.eu/article/san-marino-rejects-eu-
accession/*. Retrieved 1 June 2019

24. Will Podmore Brexit: *The Road to Freedom* p 188

25. Brezhnev Doctrine, *https://ussr.fandom.com/wiki/Brezhnev_Doctrine*

26. Treaty establishing a Constitution for Europe, published in the
Official Journal of the European Union on 16 December 2004
(C series, No 310). *https://eur-lex.europa.eu/legal-content/EN/
ALL/?uri=OJ:C:2004:310:TOC.* Retrieved 2 May 2019

27. Helena Spongenberg, "Spain and Luxembourg call for 'pride' in EU
constitution" *EU Observer* 9 January 2007 https://euobserver.com/
institutional/23213

28. BBC News 30 March *2005, http://news.bbc.co.uk/2/hi/europe/4592243.
stm.* Retrieved 2 May 2019

29. *"Dutch say 'devastating no' to EU constitution" Guardian, 2 June 2005,
https://www.theguardian.com/world/2005/jun/02/eu.politics.*
Retrieved 2 May 2019

30. BBC News BBC News *http://news.bbc.co.uk/nolavconsole/ukfs_news/hi/
newsid_4600000/newsid_4602300/nb_wm_4602369.*

31. Paul Cachia *"Malta ratifies unanimously EU constitution"* di-ve news,
https://archive.fo/tJ2v8. Retrieved 3 May 2019

32. Giscard d'Estaing, *"The EU Treaty is the same as the Constitution"* Article
written by the former French President in the *London Independent,*
30 October 2007, *https://www.independent.co.uk/voices/commentators/
valeacutery-giscard-destaing-the-eu-treaty-is-the-same-as-the-
constitution-398286.htm*l. Retrieved 3 May 2019

33. Tom Peterkin, "EU referendum: Ireland rejects Lisbon Treaty" *Daily
Telegraph* 13 June 2008, *https://www.telegraph.co.uk/news/worldnews/
europe/2122654/EU-referendum-Ireland-rejects-Lisbon-Treaty.html.*
Retrieved 3 May 2019

34. Brendan O'Neill, *"What part of Ireland's no does the EU not understand"* 13 December 2008, the Guardian, *https://www.theguardian.com/commentisfree/2008/dec/13/eu-ireland-lisbon-treaty* Retrieved 3 May 2019

35. Article 29 of the Irish Constitution

36. Crotty v An Taoiseach [1987} IR 713, [1987] ILRM 400

37. Single European Act (SEA), Official Journal of the European Communities No L169/1, 29 of June 1987. Retrieved 3 May 2019

38. Vincent Martin *"A quarter century of voter power"*, *Irish Times*, 21 May 2012, *https://www.irishtimes.com/news/crime-and-law/a-quarter-of-a-century-of-voter-power-1.522779*. Retrieved 3 May 2019

39. Ruadhán MacCormaic *The Supreme Court* p 252.

40. Ibid. p 256

41. Crotty v An Taoiseach [1987] ILRM 713

42. Ruadhán MacCormaic *The Supreme Court* p 268–272

43. Gavin Barrett *A Road Less Travelled"* p 10

44. Letter to Brennan 11 May 1987, William Brennan papers box !!:103 quoted in MacCormaic p267

45. *Irish Times* 4 March 1987, quoted in MacCormaic p 268

46. Cormac Lucey *Plan B* p 95

47. Irish Constitution Articles 46 and 47.

48. Patricia McKenna *"Government use of Tax-payers' money to fund one-sided propaganda campaigns in Referenda"* p 25-31, published in *A Festschrift for Tony Coughlan* 2018

49. Ibid.

50. McKenna v An Taoiseach No 2 [1995] 2 IR

51. Maol Muire Tynan *"RTE considers move on Coughlan judgement"* Irish Times 26 May 1998, *https://www.irishtimes.com/news/rte-considers-move-on-coughlan-judgement-1.156713* Retrieved 3 May 2019

52. Deaglán de Bréadún *"An alternative voice in our democracy"* p 5-7, published in *A Festschrift for Anthony Coughlan* 2018 p 5-7

53. Thomas Pringle *"My challenge to an EU act of subterfuge, the ESM Treaty"* p 37-41 *A Festschrift for Anthony Coughlan* 2018

54. Ruadhán MacCormaic *The Supreme Court* p 388

55. Associated Press *"Slovenia's premier resigns over court ruling on referendum"* 14 March 2018, *https://www.foxnews.com/world/slovenias-premier-resigns-over-court-ruling-on-referendum.* Retrieved 3 May 2109

56. Peter Dominiczak *"EU referendum: £9m cost of taxpayer-funded leaflet warning about the 'damage' of Brexit angers Eurosceptics"* Daily Telegraph, 6 April 2016. *https://www.telegraph.co.uk/news/2016/04/06/eu-referendum-taxpayers-to-fund9m-leaflet-to-every-home-warning/.* Retrieved 1 June 2019

57. Patrick Smyth *"Italy faces political gridlock as voters back populist Five Star Movement"* Irish Times 5 March 2018, *https://www.irishtimes.com/news/world/europe/italy-faces-political-gridlock-as-voters-back-populist-five-star-movement-1.3415134.* Retrieved 3 May 2019

58. BBC News, *"Italy crisis: Call to impeach president after candidate vetoed"* 28 May 2018, *https://www.bbc.com/news/world-europe-44275781.* Retrieved 3 May 2019

59. BBC News *"Carlo Cottarelli: Italy president names stop-gap PM"* 28 May 2018, *https://www.bbc.com/news/world-europe-44280046.* Retrieved 3 May 2019

60. Oli Smith *"Do Italians decide or do the Germans decide?' Salvini's SCATHING attack on EU 'democracy"*, Daily Express, 29 May 2018, *https://www.express.co.uk/news/world/965984/Italian-political-crisis-Matteo-Salvini-League-Five-Star-EU.* Retrieved 3 May 2019

61. Article 245 of the Treaty on the Functioning of the European Union.

62. Article 225 of the Treaty on the Functioning of the European Union.

63. Justin Huggler *"Germany's AfD backs away from Dexit call as France's Le Pen pledges to reform EU from within"* Daily Telegraph 14 January 2019, *https://www.telegraph.co.uk/news/2019/01/14/germanys-afd-backs-away-dexit-call-frances-le-pen-pledges-reform/.* Retrieved 3 May 2019

64. Ruadhán MacCormaic *The Supreme Court* p 251–272

65. Gunnar Beck *"The Court of Justice of the ERU, Imperial not Impartial."* Politeia 2018

66. Darren Hunt, *"We will LEAVE!' Archive Cameron clip shows why Remoaners' anti-Brexit plot is LAUGHABLE"* Daily Express 5 January 2018, *https://www.express.co.uk/news/uk/900462/Brexit-news-UK-David-Cameron-Tony-Blair-European-Union-referendum-latest.* Retrieved 3 May 2019

67. Brexit central website 19 November 2019

68. Emilo Casilicchio *"George Osborne: EU referendum is once in a lifetime"* PoliticsHome 15 January 2016, *https://www.politicshome.com/news/uk/foreign-affairs/news/59324/george-osborne-eu-referendum-once-lifetime.* Retrieved 16 June 2019.

69. RT *"Nigel Farage compares May's 'betrayal' Brexit deal to treaty that helped bring Hitler to power"* 27 March 2019, *https://rt.com/uk/454886-farage-compares-brexit-hitler.* Retrieved 3 May 2019

70. Gavin McLoughlin *"Britain should not be treated like Ireland was on Nice and Lisbon referendums – Pierre Moscovici"* 23 January 2019 *Irish Independent, https://www.independent.ie/business/brexit/britain-should-not-be-treated-like-ireland-was-on-nice-and-lisbon-referendums-pierre-moscovici-37743258.html.* Retrieved 3 May 2019

71. John Ashmore *"Gordon Brown: Second independence referendum 'an unlikely prospect'* PoliticsHome, 12 June 2016. *https://www.politicshome.com/news/uk/constitution/scottish-parliament/news/76078/gordon-brown-second-independence-referendum.* Retrieved 3 June 2019

72. Liam Halligan and Gerard Lyons *Clean Brexit* p 103.

Chapter 10

Ireland and Ever-Closer Union

"I am the first and last President of an independent Irish Republic."

Éamon de Valera

The tensions between an intergovernmental approach to the European project and the proponents of a Union, dominated by an unelected Commission, have been there from the inception of the whole idea of closer European economic cooperation. Initially, Ireland shunned the developments, which led to the Treaty of Rome in 1957. It simply could not accept entering into a process which had as its final destination, however theoretical at that point, the extinction of the Irish State, as a separate sovereign nation (Chapter 5). The generation, which had won Irish independence, after a long and desperate struggle, was still in power in the early/mid 1950s. It is ironic to think that at that stage, the governing party Fianna Fáil, could be accurately labelled as eurosceptical. It is claimed that the politician who can justifiably be described as the most influential post-independence Irish figure, and founder of Ireland's largest and most successful political party Fianna Fáil, Éamon de Valera, was no admirer of ending the sovereignty of the countries of western Europe. There is fairly widespread belief that he voted against Ireland joining the Common Market in the 1972 accession referendum.

Anti-EU campaigner Anthony Coughlan broached the issue in *Village* magazine. He mentioned challenging members of the de Valera family on the rumour of a negative vote by the former President. Coughlan wrote

"One of Eamon de Valera's sons, Major Vivian de Valera, told the author of this document that 'He almost certainly did so,' when they met following the 1972 referendum, 'but he would not tell us definitely how he cast his vote on anything, as he considered that improper for the President.'" Decades later when Coughlan told this story to de Valera's grandson, Éamon Ó Cuív TD, the latter said that it chimed with a statement the then President made to his family when they gathered in Áras an Uachtaráin on New Year's Eve 1972, the day before Ireland joined the EEC: "I am the first and last President of an independent Irish Republic."[1]

This would be completely consistent with his position on national sovereignty. Earlier Dev spoke to the Dáil on 12 June 1955 after a trip to Strasbourg where he outlined his views on the Federalist concept of Europe. As detailed in the *Irish Independent* by journalist Bruce Arnold, Dev warned that Ireland would "end up losing its freedom and independence if it joined any European Federation." He also warned about the dangers of "a European Constitution and of getting entangled in European-led military adventures over which, ultimately, we would have no control."

Arnold further quoted the former Taoiseach, "It would have been most unwise for our people to enter into a political Federation which would mean that you had a European Parliament," pointing out the futility of having a tiny representation in a huge Parliament[2].

However, the attitude of the Irish State and Fianna Fail, has certainly changed in the meantime. Because of economic weakness, the country was ready to throw its lot in with Europe from the early 1960s. While there was certainly a change in attitude in official Ireland, this was not the main determining factor. Given the country's economic dependence on the United Kingdom it had no real choice once its larger neighbour, under Prime Minister Harold Macmillan, changed its attitude and decided to apply for membership of the then EEC in 1961.

However, over the years the rhetoric and tactics may have changed but the objective of the European project has essentially remained the same. The blueprint on which the current EU operates was designed by French politician and bureaucrat, Jean Monnet. The most fundamental principle is that there needs to be a supranational authority (the EU Commission) which is not subject to democratic vagaries and essentially is a developing European Government. It is a classic example of a technocratic State, with the outward trappings of democracy[3].

Irreversible transfer of power

Once the national Governments have ceded a competence to the supranational authority, it is irreversible. It is a one-way process. Power can only be transferred to Brussels and not the reverse. Once the Brussels Commission has acquired a competence, either through a Treaty change or by any other method, the new power becomes part of the acquis communautaire. This represents the body of laws which have been accumulated over the years and over which the Commission has property rights. These rights are guarded jealously.

All the talk about subsidiarity and returning power to the individual Member States, is a lot of hot air. It simply does not happen and there are serious structural impediments to any such reversal. During the Brexit referendum, British comedian John Cleese said he would have voted against Brexit, if he could honestly believe that there was any realistic prospect of reforming the undemocratic nature of the EU. He decided, rightly in my view, that reform of Brussels, is a forlorn hope. I know there are many well-meaning Irish people who cling to the hope of reform, but they are unable to actually articulate how this could be achieved.

John Cleese was quoted in the *Daily Mail* in Britain on 12 June 2016 as stating that "Britain had been 'swimming against the tide' in its bid to bring about change in Brussels, where bureaucrats had taken away 'any trace of democratic accountability.'"

Cleese, a prominent Liberal Democrat supporter, said it was a 'sad' situation and appeared to address his message to party grandee, the late Lord [Paddy] Ashdown, who was campaigning for Remain in the Brexit referendum campaign. "If I thought there was any chance of major reform in the EU, I'd vote to stay in. But there isn't. Sad. Sorry, Paddy," he tweeted[(4)].

Some of the pro-EU lobby argue that the Member States have the right, secured by Ireland after its rejection of the Lisbon Treaty, to nominate a Commissioner and hence can look to "our man/woman in Brussels" when the going gets rough. As ex-Agriculture Commissioner Phil Hogan (nominated by Ireland) rightly pointed out during the EU dispute with Dublin over the taxation of the Apple Corporation, when he was asked if the adverse finding on Ireland caused him embarrassment, answered unambiguously in the *Irish Times*:

I took an oath I would not be an Irish Commissioner but would be a European Commissioner. I have no difficulty at all – this is a decision what was proposed by the competition Commissioner after a long three-year investigation and of course the appeal system is there for all States and companies to have it tested to see is it the right decision or the wrong decision … If you don't accept Cabinet responsibility, normally you have to resign in this country and it's the same in Europe – if you don't accept the oath you took in the European Court of Justice, you should resign – but I am fully supportive of the 28-member Commission in terms of the decision they made.[5]

Hogan was absolutely correct. If he had done anything else, he would have been in breach of the oath he took when joining the Commission. When EU Commissioners take up their post in Brussels, they swear to forsake allegiance to their national Government (Chapter 9) and not to be answerable in any way to their home country.

Therefore, the democratically elected Governments are to be kept away from the governing of Europe, as far as possible. The unelected supranational body, the EU Commission, has an effective monopoly on initiating new legislation. While the Council of Ministers and the Parliament can seek to amend and veto new legislation, the Commission will, in reality, never propose any important measure which will limit their jurisdiction. Therefore, the scope for reforming the present set up in the EU to make it more democratic and accountable to the national Parliaments, and indeed the citizens of the individual countries, would seem to be very limited at best, and probably does not exist in reality. In fact, it was this block on reform which contributed to the Brexit vote in the United Kingdom.

The EU Commission is psychologically unable to think outside the centralising mandate it has given itself and its own self-interest. Its response to every problem could be summarised as an inevitable call for "more Europe", regardless of the question.

As former British Minister for Europe, David Heathcoat-Amory, stated on the Brexit Central website in October 2018 about his experience:

In 2001 I was elected to represent the House of Commons at the Convention on the Future of Europe. This two-year Convention, chaired by the ex-President of France, Valery Giscard d'Estaing, was instructed to create a Europe 'closer to its citizens', because it was admitted that the EU was 'behaving too bureaucratically'. It was even proposed that some powers should be returned to Member States. The European Commission was represented by delegates of its own and provided the secretariat. They immediately took control of the agenda and the proceedings. Nothing more was heard of reform, still less of any return of powers. Instead they produced a draft Constitution for Europe, with more powers handed to the centre.[6]

The unreformability of the EU was amply demonstrated when the then British Prime Minister, David Cameron, went to Brussels to seek to alter the terms of British membership. The derisory concessions[7] that Cameron was offered by the EU, actually had a major negative influence. The treatment of Cameron in those discussions strengthened the pro-Brexit campaign by demonstrating that the EU did not take into account local sensitivities and, in fact, is fairly contemptuous of national Governments and their legitimate concerns. I remember being personally astonished by the negativity of the EU at the time. It was very counterproductive from an Irish national standpoint. Unfortunately, our Government fully backed the stupidity of Brussels on this occasion. The Cameron renegotiation, in retrospect, represents not just a failure of the Irish Government to assist its neighbour and partner, the UK, but also for the EU to use the opportunity to bring about real reform on an EU wide basis. I also recall being surprised by the determination within the Irish Civil Service to resist any real concessions being given to London.

Lack of understanding of the EU

If the EU is so resistant to change and its course is towards ever-closer union (in reality code for a European Superstate and I believe that there is little appetite in Ireland for that outside a tiny coterie of self-interested groups in Dublin), why should we in Ireland hitch our future so strongly with Brussels. In addition, with so many negatives attached to disrupting the centuries old connections within our islands, again why is official Ireland so wedded to staying inside the EU? There must be very powerful reasons for staying in.

Is the EU option attractive enough to overcome these disincentives? Any decision making must also examine where the EU is heading and if Ireland wants to be part of these potential developments. It may well be that there is currently a lack of understanding and discussion within the country as to what Ireland is really signing up to. In fact, there are very few Irish politicians who have any real understanding of the EU, apart from being able to regurgitate a few meaningless platitudes, drafted by Government officials.

I believe that the case for departing is getting stronger by the day, while the case for remaining inside is progressively weakening. The EEC, which Ireland joined, was a very different animal to the current manifestation, whatever the long-term aspirations of some Federalists were at the time. It was a very benign institution, primarily concerned with the elimination of trade barriers and promoting cooperation among its Member States. It consisted of nine members, including West Germany. Although preunification Germany was the biggest economic power in the EEC, it was not predominant, and it behaved in a very collegial manner. France had not fallen heavily behind Germany in economic terms. The UK was a constructive, if occasionally restless, member of this exclusive club.

The nine consisted of like-minded countries, all fairly well developed economically, with strong democratic traditions. Ireland soon found itself very much at home in those surroundings. The rotating Presidency ensured that every country felt part of the club. There was no permanent official who acted as President of the European Council and chaired the Heads of Government meetings; nor any EU official as High Representative for Foreign Affairs and Security, with a role to "speak for Europe". Those positions fell to the Head of Government of the rotating Presidency. Irish Taoisigh, and indeed all other Heads of Government, revelled in their role as Chair of the European Council. It all worked remarkably well and there was very little public antipathy to the concept.

During my early years in the Department of Foreign Affairs, the EU Commission generally acted as a support for the Member States. It was a pleasure working with their officials. There was no attempt to become the "boss" and treat Member States as an inconvenient obstacle to Brussels domination, no attempt at "uno duce, una voce". In fact, the Commission was traditionally regarded as the guardian of the rights of the smaller nations[8].

However, Federalists within Europe could not leave well enough alone and proceeded to make ambitious plans for a greater concentration of powers in Brussels. New Treaty after new Treaty all pushed in one direction, namely the transference of power from the National Governments and Parliaments to a central EU authority. A whole raft of new areas became subject to majority voting in the Council. This has coincided with a growing alienation of sections of the European population with Brussels. As this concentration of power grew in the centre, and with the Enlargement process bringing in a host of new members, Ireland's ability to influence decision-making in Brussels waned considerably.

An analogy is sometimes made to Ireland's history in the Eurovision Song Contest. Here Ireland, prior to the admission of many eastern European countries, regularly won the contest. In recent years, Ireland's contribution to the Eurovision operation has been reduced to insignificance.

The loss of influence has been seen in the expanded European Parliament. The concept of a directly elected European Parliament makes no sense unless the aim is a United States of Europe. The democratic element in the EU is provided for by the individual Governments and their Parliaments. For a country like Ireland to agree to transfer powers to an institution like the European Parliament, where it has little or no say, given the relative sizes of the Member States, is bizarre to say the least. However, Ireland has been enthusiastic about giving up its powers to this unwieldly body. It is true that individual Irish people have attained powerful positions within the EU, but it was the same within the British Empire[9].

Throughout the gradual erosion of power of the Nation States, there has been remarkably little public dissension or controversy in Ireland. The loss of the Nice referendum caused the Irish establishment to create the National Forum for Europe in Dublin Castle, which operated from 2001 until 2009. The Forum's mandate was to examine, in a very public way, issues relating to the European Union. While the Forum did good work under its able Secretary General, Wally Kirwan, and its Chair, the late Senator Maurice Hayes, it never really caught the public attention and while well intentioned, did not result in the type of fundamental debate that was needed about the future direction of Europe. It was overwhelmingly pro-EU and the loss of the Lisbon referendum in 2008 showed that its deliberations had not impinged on the public consciousness. It was wound up shortly after the Lisbon defeat[10]. In short, it was not successful in bridging the gap between official Ireland and the electorate.

This lack of real debate has continued. Recent Irish Governments has also been remarkably quiet about the future development of the EU. It has never publicly spelled out what its concept of the EU actually entails. This gives the impression that it has put virtually no thought into how it sees Europe developing in the future, beyond the immediate issue of Brexit. The traditional Irish policy in Europe has been very short-sighted and gives the impression that it is solely about extracting the maximum short-term monetary value from membership.

The President of the European Commission, Jean Claude Juncker, on 1 March 2017, in a White Paper, listed five possible scenarios for the EU in the wake of Brexit (Table 2). As far as can be ascertained, the Irish Government has made no comment on the five possible approaches, though it is clear the Irish public would prefer the looser free trade area arrangement over the more grandiose schemes, favoured by France and Germany. While opinions throughout Europe were split on the way forward, there seemed to be unanimity that the White Paper was a poor document and an inadequate response to the growing crises in the EU.

The outgoing President of the European Commission Jean Claude Juncker has been a major problem for the image of the EU. When Juncker, a noted European Federalist, was proposed for the Presidency position, the British, under Prime Minister David Cameron, bitterly opposed the appointment. He argued, rightly, that the proposed appointment would do little to assuage British apprehensions about the future of the EU. In fact, the appointment, he opined, would make it more difficult for the then British Government to persuade the UK to stay in the EU as Juncker has long been associated with weakening the role of the Member States[11]. This warning went unheeded and no doubt but made the British withdrawal more likely.

Ireland, despite our obvious national interest in maintaining the UK inside the EU, sided with Juncker[12]. The then Taoiseach, Enda Kenny, supported the long-serving Luxembourg Prime Minister Juncker for the Presidency. It was just another decision by the pro-EU establishment in Leinster House which was contrary to our national interest and made Brexit more likely. Only Hungarian Prime Minister Viktor Orbán, backed the British opposition.

Presumably Kenny decided to ignore Ireland's strategic objective so as to support a candidate from the Christian Democrat party group (the European People's Party, EPP). Kenny's Fine Gael Party is a constituent member of the EPP. In retrospect, I imagine not even the most ardent pro-EU supporter would call Juncker's time in office as a success. He also appears unaware of his negative image in the UK. Juncker's self-delusion, and sense of self-importance, was typified by his claim as reported in the *Guardian* newspaper that if the British Government had agreed to him campaigning in the Brexit referendum, the result might have been different. It certainly would have been but not in the way he believed. It would have been a boost for the Brexiteers. I could not think of a more negative impact on the anti-Brexit campaign than Juncker appearing on TV to attack the concept of Brexit.

It should be also noted that Juncker in the *Guardian* interview appeared to be suggesting curbs on the freedom of the press in the UK[13], something which did not endear him to the more liberal minded members of the Remainers coalition in Britain, although increasingly in line with the intolerance displayed by some "liberal" pro-EU elements. In addition, the perception that the former President of the Commission was overly fond of booze, and pictures of him having difficulty in remaining standing at official ceremonies did not help his image. However, in all fairness Juncker identified his problems with sciatica as a primary cause of his physical instability[14].

The image issue with Juncker is one of a myriad difficulties which Brussels has faced. While Brexit is the immediate and most urgent issue, there are plenty of others. While the EEC, and later the EU, have faced problems in the past, the scale and depth of the current crop seem by far the most serious since the 1960s.

EU's problems multiply

There have been or are scheduled elections in a number of countries, all of which represent problems from an EU prospective. In the Netherlands, Italy, Sweden and Austria, there is a general shift towards a more eurosceptical position, even in the mainstream parties. In Germany, the dismal performance of the Christian Democratic Union (CDU), under Angela Merkel in the 2017 general election and the 2019 European elections essentially signalled the end of the Chancellor's unchallenged dominance of German politics. Mrs Merkel was for long the most powerful political figure in the EU. Today we are nearing the end of her long reign as leader of the CDU, which commenced in 2000. Her party's general election result in 2017 was the worst since 1949[15].

However, Merkel was not the biggest loser in that election. Her immediate opponent in the 2017 contest was the leader of the Social Democrats (SPD), Martin Shultz, who had been President of the European Parliament from 2012–17. Schultz, as with much of the Left in Europe had become synonymous with the cause of European further integration and a single EU State. His party was trounced and recorded its worst-ever performance. Unsurprisingly, Shultz was soon the party's ex-leader.

The main beneficiaries of the loss by the two main parties was the far right AfD, which came from nowhere to win 94 seats in the Bundestag. With the cry that that Germans "want their country back", this new party capitalised on the Chancellor's migration policy. While inevitably the German election had unique features, it was part of a continent-wide reaction against the demise of the old Nation States. It would have been impossible, just a few short years ago, to imagine that the main opposition party in Germany was flirting with the concept of a German withdrawal from the EU, unless more powers were returned to the Member States.[16] The deterioration in the position of the two main parties in Germany was confirmed by their poor showing in the 2019 European Parliament elections where they lost over 18% compared to 2014. In this case the anti-establishment Greens and the AfD benefitted from their losses.

The same dismal performance of mainstream pro-EU parties, especially of those on the Left, in national elections could be seen in the Netherlands, Austria and Italy.

In the Dutch general election, also in 2017, the ruling party, the People's Party for Freedom and Democracy (VVD) under Mark Rutte suffered losses but it was its coalition partner, the Labour Party (PvdA) which was almost wiped out[17]. This party included former Finance Minister, Joroen Dijsselbloem, who became so associated with austerity in southern Europe.

The election in Austria in September 2019 returned conservative leader Sebastian Kurz to power with further losses for the pro-EU Social Democrats. Kurz has been actively seeking reform of the EU freedom of labour principle and ways to lessen Brussels' domination[18]. He has been a persistent and vocal critic of Brussel's overreach. "Nobody needs EU regulations, for example for the preparation of schnitzel and fries," adding that "regulatory madness" and "paternalism" by "Brussels" was counterproductive and suggested that "instead of demanding more and more money, the EU should stop telling people more and more how to live."[19]

Hungary, and some of the Visegárd countries, are restless about migration. Poland feels completely alienated to the point of planning obstructionist tactics, while in Italy, the eurosceptic La Lega party is growing in popularity and demanding radical changes to EU policies on migration, while raising questions about the euro. France has major social unrest, Greece lies economically destroyed by austerity, Portugal and Cyprus are slowly recovering from financial crises, etc. There is a lot going on and very little of it is comforting for Brussels. Despite all the clamour for change, the nature of the EU, with the EU Commission operating the control levers, is simply not designed to react to popular sentiment. Something will have to give in the near future.

Meanwhile the long-term macroeconomic situation in Europe has worsened, as the Eurozone constantly fails to show any strong economic vigour and makes very sorry comparison with the longer-term economic performance of North America and Asia[20]. The Single Market has not delivered anything like the economic boost it promised. It is estimated that over 90% of economic growth in the next decade will be in markets outside the EU[21]. The failings of the EU as an economic proposition is feeding into popular discontent.

A danger is that the Federalists will decide post-Brexit that the problems in the EU are such that we need "more Europe"[22]. It echoes the old Maoist slogan that China needed a purer form of Communism at the start of the Cultural Revolution. This call for more Europe will grow stronger if the present divide between the EU and the USA grows more pronounced. Many in the European External Action Service (EEAS), the EU's own diplomatic corps, bemoan their lack of access to military resources and would dearly wish for the creation of an EU army, under the control of Brussels. They regard NATO as too dominated by the Americans. In the wake of Brexit, will Ireland and some like-minded countries be able to prevent the creation of an EU military force? If not, will Ireland willingly see its sons and daughters go to the Middle East to fight in a future EU sponsored military conflict in places like Iran, Yemen, etc.? Such conflicts would have very little popular support in Ireland. The furtive endorsement of the PESCO initiative, where the Dáil was given little or no notice of the Fine Gael-led Government's decision to ram through the required legislation, does not auger well in this area[23].

The Federalists will also push to remove from the Member States the autonomy they presently enjoy in fiscal matters. Is Ireland again ready to cede even more budgetary powers to Brussels in a post-Brexit era? Already the EU's attempt to dictate how Ireland funds its domestic water supply has encountered serious problems[24]. Does the country want future rows with Europe over purely domestic Irish issues?

The election of Emmanuel Macron as French President initially emboldened the Federalists in Brussels and their allies in the capitals of the Member States. His rhetoric and enthusiastic commitment seemed for a moment like a rescuer coming to the aid of the Eurocrats. Macron has talked about a relaunch of the EU, with further Treaty change, something that even France opposed in the past. He has spoken of reviving the Paris–Berlin axis as a driving force for further integration. However, it was a mirage. His election was due to his opponent being Marine Le Pen from the National Front. The French public are among the most eurosceptical in the EU[25]. This is in marked contrast with their political elite. Macron's popularity proved very transient, and in the face of poor economic growth, soon slumped. The spectre of a Parisian saviour coming over the horizon to protect the legacy of Monnet disappeared in the smoke of rioting on the Champs d'Élysées, as les gilets jaunes protesters on the streets of France strongly challenged his imperial style and haughty rule. As a consequence, support for Macron plummeted[26]. His party En Marche was outpolled by Le Pen's group in the European Parliament elections in 2019, a humiliation for the French leader, who had heavily campaigned in the contest.

In such an uncertain scenario and as Ireland ponders its future post Brexit, Ireland needs to clarify how it sees the EU evolving and also what role, if any, it seeks to play in that development. It also needs to have a Plan B, apart from just holding on tight to the European Commission for salvation. Ireland needs to be prepared for further discord and disharmony in Europe. This is hardly the time to irrevocably cast our lot in with Team EU.

Meanwhile, the EU continues its policy of weakening the authority and relevance of the Member States. It does this in a number of policy areas.

Immigration matters

Apart from Brexit, the immigration issue is the main topic which has dominated the agenda of the EU in recent years. One of the four fundamental freedoms of the Union is freedom of labour to access employment or establish businesses in any Member State. It is vital to the achievement of ever-closer union but is an issue which sharply divides the liberal establishment from the general population. Those who are in the business of employing people are, naturally, delighted to have a vast pool of potential employees to choose from and this undoubtedly keeps wages low and therefore improves national competitiveness. For that reason, immigration has a positive macroeconomic effect[27] but often the opposite at a micro level.

The effects of immigration for employees, especially those with relatively low skill qualifications, is entirely different from the more privileged elements in society. The added competition from immigrants has a direct and detrimental effect on the life prospects of this group. Large-scale immigration also puts huge pressure on public services. In addition, those in sheltered professions and senior bureaucrats have shielded themselves against such competition and hence are, in the main, very pro-immigration. They enjoy the benefits of large-scale immigration, without suffering any of the adverse consequences. This is a phenomenon which can be observed throughout the affluent world and has greatly contributed to the rise of populist resentment against established politicians and to negative perceptions among sections of the population to immigration[28].

It is an insult to the intelligence of the average citizen to state that immigration levels are not contributing negatively to the housing crisis in Dublin city. In 2018, the Central Statistics Office (CSO) estimated that 90,300 immigrated in the previous year into the Republic, a net gain of 34,000[29]. Many of these new immigrants were young and arrived in the capital city needing accommodation. It has greatly pushed up demand. Because of the freedom of movement for labour within the EU, Ireland cannot place restrictions on new immigrants from the EU arriving in areas with huge pressures on accommodation.

Added to these underlying fault lines is the simple fact that official projections of migrant trends in the recent past have proved hopelessly wrong inside the EU. At the time of the great Enlargement in 2004, Governments in western Europe dismissed the warnings of the eurosceptics, at that time, as being alarmist. If anything, the eurosceptics greatly underestimated the impending level of the mass migration of citizens from the old communist East to the more affluent West. The official projections were hopelessly wrong[30]. This has only accelerated the loss of trust in officialdom throughout the EU, when literally millions moved westwards and northwards.

The UK, in particular, has become the host for very large numbers of migrants. Undoubtedly this large influx contributed to the success of the Brexit vote, as British citizens witnessed huge pressure on their public services, from the new arrivals. There was a fear among some local authorities there about raising their concerns, for fear of being tagged with the label of being racists. At the end of 2017, it was estimated that 3.8m EU Nationals were residing in Britain, of whom 2.3m were working legally there[31], huge numbers for a relatively small island.

This strong public desire to regain national control of borders, and the composition of incoming migrants, is completely anathema to Brussels. It goes directly against the concept of a single European Superstate. There needs to be no internal borders inside the EU, if the national boundaries, along with the national authorities' ability to police these boundaries, are to be eliminated. Hence the higher the immigration levels, the better.

Therefore, the resolute resistance to the reasonable demands of Prime Minister David Cameron for British national control of immigration during his abortive attempt at renegotiation. Those seeking to regain some control of borders have been the recipient of insults. It is far too easy to label all those who want to see a sensible and sustainable immigration regime as racists or Neanderthals. It is perfectly reasonable for a national population to decide who, and in what numbers, can immigrate into their society. There are legitimate fears that wholescale immigration can quickly change the nature of the host society, in a way which the original population are uncomfortable with[32]. In addition, high profile crimes by a small number of migrants can rapidly sour the public attitude and contribute to a feeling that a society has lost control of its borders.

The attitude of official Ireland to immigration matters can be described as contradictory at times. Taoiseach Leo Varadkar complained bitterly about the number of bogus asylum seekers from Albania entering the Irish State[33], while supporting the opening of EU accession talks with the same country. The end result of those talks would undoubtedly be free movement between Ireland and Albania, namely no barriers to wholescale migration from that country. It seemed the Taoiseach wanted to have it both ways.

While legal migration has proven to be controversial, the issue of unofficial or uncontrolled mass movement of people into Europe's southern extremities has proven explosive. The horrific scenes of desperate migrants scrambling onto makeshift craft to try and cross the Mediterranean have been heart wrenching. This followed the catastrophic intervention by NATO countries in the Middle East and especially the illegal invasions and whole scale bombings of Middle Eastern countries, which were the fundamental catalysts for this mass migration. It is surely a lesson on why it would be so dangerous for "Europe" to develop a strong military arm, with the ability to start regional conflicts.

These refugees from war zones have now been joined by many from the African continent, who are essentially economic migrants.

The situation spiralled out of control when German chancellor Angela Merkel made the extraordinary decision to allow an uncontrolled number of migrants into her country, ignoring the Dublin Convention[34] which stipulates that would-be asylum seekers should make their application in the first EU country where they arrived. Over a million refugees streamed north from the Mediterranean, all anxious to reach Germany. It caused chaos all along the way. Of course, it was only a matter of time before the policy exploded in the face of Merkel, as some of these migrants engaged in serious crimes, including terrorism and sexual assault[35]. Germany moved to stop the tide, but Mrs. Merkel was fatally weakened.

These migrants arrived in a Europe, which had decided to abolish frontier controls. It was a deadly mixture and the subsequent crisis had the potential to tear the EU apart, as resident populations reacted unfavourably to this influx of new people, who do not share their values and in some cases represent a major security threat. The EU has proved completely incapable of managing the crisis. It's only answer, as it is to every question, is to fall back on the mantra "more Europe", namely give Brussels more power and especially more money rather than the more obvious one of scrapping freedom of movement[36]. The immediate crisis has abated somewhat but there is every possibility of a recurrence, after another crisis in either Africa or the Middle East.

In Ireland's case, there is a certain smugness among the elite about the issue of migration. It is indeed true that we start from a very sympathetic position. After all we are one of the great wandering nations of the Earth. We have been an emigrant country for centuries and the huge Irish Diaspora populations overseas are a testament to that phenomenon. While there are Irish ethnic links with many countries throughout the world, these groups are overwhelmingly concentrated in the Anglophone area, in places such as Canada, Australia, USA, England, Scotland, etc. It is still striking that the Irish, just like the British, seem to have no great desire to settle in mainland Europe.

For much of our period of membership of the EEC and the EU, the traditional net outflows of people predominated. However, since the turn of the century, Ireland has regularly recorded strong net immigration. The 2016 census showed that 11.6% of the Republic's population were not born in the Irish State[37]. While this figure overstates the level of the "foreign" element, since many Irish families had children while temporarily living abroad, including myself. In addition, most of Ireland's immigrants are from European countries such as Poland, England, Latvia, Lithuania, etc. and hence are not part of the identifiable minorities. They also share a broadly similar cultural and religious background to the native population.

The relative success of the integration process in Ireland should be viewed against the relative lack of migrants from Islamic and African locations but it is welcome, nonetheless. However, past success is no guarantee to future developments. Once the UK exits the EU, the policy of free movement of labour into Britain will cease. This will mean an inevitable diversion of many of the migrant groups, which traditionally went to Britain coming instead to Ireland. The reason for this is our open and successful economy and the fact that many would be migrants have English language skills and hence are attracted to an Anglophone country. Any sustained increase in immigration to Ireland, especially from countries with very dissimilar cultures, will undoubtedly put pressure on our previously relatively liberal and tolerant attitudes.

An obvious question has to be asked; why does the EU cling on so tightly to the free movement of labour when there is so much opposition? It should be realised that the four fundamental freedoms of the EU are not defended with huge vigour because of their own intrinsic value but rather because they are seen as means to an end, the march towards ever closer union and the Federal Superstate.

The present immigration process in Ireland is heavily weighed against the Irish Diaspora. It gives countries in the EU, which have little or no historic and cultural links with Ireland, priority over our traditional friends. It is hugely discriminatory. People who advocate Ireland regaining control over its borders are not against all immigration but want to ensure that the people of Ireland are able to control it and make it benefit the average citizen, not just those well insulated in secure positions. We should certainly be in the forefront of demands to end the unfettered freedom of movement and oppose any further moves in this area towards the holy grail of ever closer union.

Danish experience

This is not just a theoretical point. One country where I have personally witnessed a deterioration in attitudes to migrants is a country with

264

roughly the same population as the Republic of Ireland and likewise a long history of being a homogeneous society, namely Denmark. It is a country for which I have great affection, as is said in Danish, "Jeg elsker Danmark". I love Denmark.

When I was posted, as a raw and inexperienced Third Secretary, to the Irish Embassy in Copenhagen in the early 1980s, it was a very liberal and tolerant society. Then it was the only Nordic country in the EEC and to my Irish eyes, it had an extraordinarily generous welfare system, well-educated population and a welcoming regime for migrants. I remember also being impressed by the tolerance of the Danes and by the affluence of the city. My friends were all open and generous to the relatively small number of new Danes. While one occasionally came across a racist remark, referring to all immigrants as Turks, but this was much more the exception than the rule.

I returned thirty years later to attend a reunion dinner for the Copenhagen Exiles Rugby Club. This was the club that I played for, but more importantly socialized with, during the four years of my posting. Then as now it was a vibrant mixture of Danes and foreign residents. During my time with the club, I developed strong and enduring friendships with many of the players and officials from all round the globe. Hence the dinner was a celebratory event for those of us who had survived the intervening three decades. It was a hugely joyous experience to see so many old friends in that beautiful city.

However, it was somewhat shocking to see how attitudes had changed. Also, the economic gap that had existed between this city and my own Dublin in the past has long gone. Also gone were the old liberal attitudes to immigration and especially asylum seekers. My Danish friends had become much less starry-eyed about multiculturalism and immigration. The attitude was that those who come to Denmark are expected to conform and not to be a burden on the State. The old welfare State had, to some extent, been dismantled, partly because of a perception that it was being abused, especially by refugees. The whole immigration debate has been poisoned and the sharp end has been in the refugee area.

Taxi drivers in Copenhagen of a minority ethnic background, on the other hand, were also very vocal to me as a visitor about the hostility they encounter in their daily lives. Their views mirrored the conversations with Danish friends which all confirmed that the old liberal consensus of the 1980s was long dead, destroyed by the perception that the EU had permitted wholesale migration of people to their homeland who were refusing to adapt to a northern European society. While I fully accept that this perception is out of proportion to the actual situation, nevertheless it is real and driving Danish Government policy.

I was briefed about the harshness of the new asylum policy. The Danish Aliens Act[38] has been amended many times to make Denmark a less attractive destination for would-be asylum seekers. Among the measures is a three year waiting time for any family reunions, a requirement to live in special asylum centres and probably the most controversial of all, authority for the immigration service to seize the personal assets of asylum applicants over kr1,450, such as jewellery, except items of sentimental value such as wedding rings[39]. Some have harshly condemned this policy as reminiscent of the Nazi expropriation of the personal property of Jews. This criticism is of course over the top, but there is something uncomfortable about the policy, with echoes of more sinister times in the past.

The Danish authorities have even gone to the lengths of placing paid advertisements in Arabic newspapers in Lebanon advising against seeking refugee status. There is a large Lebanese connection with Denmark. It has had a dramatic effect on asylum applications with the number falling from a total of 20,825 in 2015 to 6,055 in 2016. In the first five months of 2017, only 1,268 applied[40].

The Danish Government has even announced that it will no longer automatically accept 500 refugees per year under the UNHCR scheme[41].

This new tough policy approach is not just the preserve of the Right in Danish politics[42] and is now shared across the political spectrum, something that would have been inconceivable in the past. The Social Democrats have supported the harsh new measures, and this greatly assisted them in their bid to regain power in the 2019 election. The perception that the country can no longer control its immigration programme because of the EU has been a prime cause of this alienation. If Denmark can undergo such a radical transformation in attitudes, Ireland should be very careful about alienating our own population.

Immigration issues in other EU countries

And Denmark is not alone in its attitude to asylum seekers. Throughout the EU, in places such as Italy, Hungary, Austria, the Netherlands, Germany, etc. the EU policy on free movement is increasingly under pressure.

The election of a new Italian Government in 2018, comprising the Five Star Movement and La Lega, represented a new and serious challenge to the EU authority in the immigration area. The country's new deputy Prime Minister, Matteo Salvini, leader of La Lega and Interior Minister deliberately confronted the EU over what he claimed, with justification, was Italy's unfair burden in the migration crisis.

Salvini introduced a series of new legislations to aid mass deportations, strip Italian citizenship from naturalized migrants if they have engaged in crime and close Roma camps[43]. Salvini also refused to allow ships, run by NGOs, land rescued migrants in Italian ports, arguing that the practice was only encouraging would be migrants to risk life and limb in a desperate bid to get onboard these ships to Italy. Salvini accused the NGOs of acting as a taxi service across the Mediterranean for the migrants.

Whatever the legal niceties of Salvini's actions, they were hugely popular with the Italian electorate who are tired of being directed by an unsympathetic elite in Brussels. He was hugely critical of France, as the country has lectured Italy about its obligations while taking on only a small proportion of the number of asylum seekers it promised to accommodate[44]. The Lega party had a storming election victory in the European Parliament election of 2019, built heavily on Salvini's immigration stance. While Salvini was ousted from power in 2019, he remains extremely popular in Italy and looks likely to play a major role in future Italian Governments.

In October 2018, the following countries had introduced "temporary" border restrictions, France, Austria, Germany, Denmark, Sweden and Norway (non-EU but a member of the Schengen arrangements). Hungary has built a border fence with Croatia and an anti-immigration party emerged as the largest party in the Slovenian general election in June 2018. Croatia is demanding the sovereign right to erect border controls and decide who can enter its territory. The immigration issue is tearing the EU apart.

In reality, the concept of free and unregulated movement of labour is not some holy scripture which cannot be challenged. Countries such as Canada, USA, New Zealand, Australia, Singapore, etc. all have high levels of controlled immigration and nowhere else in the world have countries totally abdicated responsibility for immigration. Controlling the numbers and the composition of migrants is a basic element in the apparatus of any State and not the preserve of racists. It should not be regarded as shameful to press for the return of these powers to the Nation States. The continuation of mass immigration of labour, especially in the low skill areas, is in nobody's interest, other than those who would seek to benefit from lowering the wage levels. It hurts the poorest and most vulnerable in society.

The argument against the present immigration arrangements has moved beyond the fringes of right-wing politics to encompass some who regard themselves as Liberal. The former Leader of the Lib Dems in Britain, Vince Cable, wrote in the *New Statesman*:

> I have serious doubts that EU free movement is tenable or even desirable. It does not apply to Indians, Jamaicans, Americans or Australians. They face complex and often harsh visa restrictions. One uncomfortable feature of the referendum was the large Brexit vote among British Asians, many of whom resented the contrast between the restrictions they face and the welcome mat laid out for Poles and Romanians...

> The economics are ambiguous.... But the benefits accrue mainly to the migrants themselves (and business owners). For the receiving country, the benefits are less obvious: a bigger economy but not necessarily a richer one[45].

While the arguments have raged in western Europe over the issue of free movement of labour, some countries on the eastern side of the EU have suffered greatly from a loss of their most talented citizens. The demographics in the area make grim reading. An estimated 3.4m Romanians left that country in the first decade after accession to the EU and almost 50% of the population have considered emigration[46].

Latvia, Lithuania, and Estonia have had significant losses of population. Bulgaria has shrunk from nine to seven million while Spain, Italy, Greece, Poland and Hungary are either flatlining or seeing a decline.

Moreover, there is real damage being done to the health care systems in many countries. The number of doctors in Romania fell from 21,400 to 14,400 over the period 2011 to 2013. Thousands of Greek doctors emigrated. In addition, the General Medical Council in Britain recorded 2,140 doctors who had qualified in Romania[47] as operating in the UK. Thus, some of the poorer countries are investing heavily in education, only to lose the benefits of their skills to the more affluent countries in the north-west.

The freedom of movement of labour dogma is causing huge social problems right across the EU and it is being done to satisfy ideology and a desire to diminish the sovereignty of the Member States. It is part of the drive for an ever-closer union.

European Committee of the Regions and Regional Authorities

The EU's war on the Nation States is also carried out by a policy known as European Committee of the Regions (CoR). Apart from co-opting the national bureaucracy into working with Brussels, the EU seeks to strengthen "sub-national" level structures, with which it can have a direct relationship, thus bypassing the national Government.

The Maastricht Treaty created the new entity, CoR.[48] This is a 350 strong consultative body, which advises the Council of Ministers and the Commission on matters relating to health, education, employment, social policy, economic and social cohesion, transport, energy and climate change. These are areas where the national Parliament and Government should have the responsibility of speaking to Brussels. The CoR is notorious for the lavish expenses, claimed by its members, and there have been a number of scandals in this regard. It strongly encourages domestic lobby groups to appeal to Brussels rather than the national capital. In the same category is the Economic and Social Committee, another expensive quango with 350 members, comprising representatives from farming, industry, consumers, professions, etc., which encourages these groups to engage in direct contact with Brussels.

While some countries have a tradition of strong regional administrative structures, such as the United Kingdom (Northern Ireland, Scotland, Wales, London, etc.), Germany with its Länder, France with Corsica, Spain's autonomous regions, Italy's regions, etc. In such cases, strong regional Government makes sense, while preserving their reporting function to the national capitals.

In Ireland, there is no tradition of strong regional political units, outside the special case of Northern Ireland. In fact, local Government representatives are given very little power in the Republic. There is also a well-deserved reluctance to give local authority councils any more responsibility, as the limited ones they currently hold have been characterised by a history, where these powers have been abused and corrupted, especially in the planning area[49].

In order to comply with the EU desire for sub-national Government structures, the Republic was at one stage divided into a number of unnatural regional areas, including the Border, Midland and Western (BMW) Region. It comprised 13 of the State's 26 counties and was created specifically to cater for obtaining EU funds, a bribe to bypass the national authorities. It even held Regional Assembly meetings, drawn from its local authorities, which served no useful purpose other than increasing the local councillors' ability to extract extra money through the generous mileage allowance. It even had a "HQ" in the tiny Roscommon town of Ballaghaderreen. The vast bulk of those living in the BMW region never gave this fantasy body a second thought.

Hence as the Irish State prospered, the region's GDP passed the qualifying mark for certain funds and lost its reason d'etre. It simply disappeared. The State was then divided into new artificial regions. Nobody, other than the local county councillors, even noticed the demise of the former bodies. They existed because the EU wanted a partner at the local level to bypass Dublin. It is very hard to understand how the Irish national authorities agreed to this attack on the sovereign Parliament in Dublin. Local councillors of course had no qualms about being enlisted by Brussels to undermine Ireland's national Government.

Ireland and the Council of Ministers

Politicians, who extol the virtues of the EU, seem unaware or want it to remain hidden that there has been an enormous transfer of power from the elected institutions in the Member States, not only to the supranational EU Commission, but also to officials in those Member States. The vast bulk of decisions, which are formally taken by the Council of Ministers are listed as "A" items on Ministerial meetings and are not open to debate. An A item means that agreement has been reached at official level, meaning at the Committee of Permanent Representatives in the European Union (COREPER) group. This is the meeting of Member States' Permanent Representatives, in reality, the Member States Ambassadors to the EU. Discussion at the Ministerial meetings are confined to a very limited number of issues and are usually about mitigating the worst effects of some EU proposal, rarely about fundamentals.

Former British Minister Alan Clark described his experiences in his *Diaries*[50]. Clark stated that before every Ministerial meeting he was coached by the officials in the UK's Permanent Representation about what "line to take". They even rewrote his speaking points for the meetings. When he raised questions about some items on the agenda, he was told he could not intervene as these items had been agreed at the weekly meeting of COREPOR. The whole operation in Brussels is so vast that individual Ministers, faced with europhilic officials and the whole Brussels apparatus, are normally overpowered and realise that they have very little ability to influence events. Most are content to sit quietly and let the relentless machine take its course. Most are simply unable to comprehend that the whole point of the exercise is to bring about a Federal European Superstate.

The EU Commission itself makes no secret of its desire for a Federal State. In 1990, the then EU Commission President Jacques Delors was unambiguous, "My objective is that before the end of the millennium Europe should have a true Federation. The Commission should become a political executive which can define essential common interests."[51]

Irish politicians have adopted a low profile on the issue of the ending of the Nation States. They have hoped that the end destination is so far in the future that they can safely ignore it during their political lifetimes and hence are prepared to barter away our independence piecemeal for some temporary monetary gain. The philosophy has been that it will be alright at the end of the day. It is the whistling past the graveyard phenomenon.

The British have rightly taken the Commission at their word. Therefore, a lot of the unmasking of the European project has come from London, in contrast to the silence of Ireland's own politicians. The then British Prime Minster, Margaret Thatcher, answered Delors in the following manner:

> The President of the Commission, Mr. Delors, said at a press conference the other day that he wanted the European Parliament to be the democratic body of the Community. He wanted the Commission to be the Executive and he wanted the Council of Ministers to be the Senate. No, No, No.[52]

Many have come to the defence of the Commission, stating that with a staff of "only 32,000"[53], it could not control the lives of 500 million citizens. This is to overlook how the Commission operates. It is at the centre of a network, which has co-opted the national Civil Services to the cause of European integration. It has no need to abolish the apparatus that it is seeking to control. It is the essence of the operation to get the national institutions to implement the decisions of the supranational body, hence to all outward observations, the old Parliaments, judiciary and public services continue but they are now often just branch offices of the Brussels operation. In their seminal publication, *The Great Deception: Can the European Union Survive?* Christopher Booker and Richard North made the following observation:

> It was central to the nature of the project that the Parliaments, officials and judiciaries of each of the Member States should be left in place. But behind them it erected a new supranational power structure which worked through these national institutions, controlling them and enlisting their active collaboration in a way that remained largely out of view.[54]

The system works through myriad working groups meeting in Brussels honing proposals for further harmonization and Brussels control.

These groups and preparation for Ministerial Councils are overseen by the country's Permanent Representation to the EU (Perm Rep) which ensures that officials and Ministers take the correct pro-EU line. Everything is arranged beforehand even communiques and the Ministers' job is to provide a fig-leaf of democratic accountability.

National institutions continue to function outwardly as if nothing has changed but they are now operating under Brussels agreed instructions. Hence the Irish Central Bank is really the local office of the ECB, the Environmental Protection Agency implements Brussels law, etc. In reality, the local Irish control is largely gone. They have been hollowed out and are now simply implementation bodies. It has been compared to a virus taking over the control centres of a healthy cell while using the cell's own apparatus to do so. Maintaining the local institutional façade reduces opposition.

Thus, the Brussels Empire is constructed, hidden in plain sight.

As a former EU Commission President Jose Manuel Barroso put it "Sometimes I like to compare the EU as a creation to the organisation of empire. We have the dimension of empire."[55]

He went on to clarify that instead of Superstate empires of old, the EU empire is built on voluntary pooling of power and not on military conquest – "What we have is the first non-imperial empire." Ireland's experience of Empire was far from satisfactory in the past, but the remark did not receive the attention it deserved in Ireland.

It is hard to understand why such sentiments cause outrage in the Royalist UK, which is often accused of nostalgia for Empire, but pass totally unchallenged in Republican Dublin, where generations were raised, including myself, to believe, as James Connolly, the Revolutionary leader stated, "We serve neither King nor Kaiser." We have seen a reversal of national roles.

This wilful denial of the obvious is also prevalent in relation to other aspects of the EU. A British official with a very Irish name, Bernard Connolly (no relation to the Revolutionary figure James), conducted a one-man war on corruption while holding a senior position in the Commission. He wrote a book, entitled *The Rotten Heart of Europe: The Dirty War for Europe's Money.* He was, unsurprisingly, subsequently relieved of his position. He stated that the purpose of the EU's activity was the creation of a European Superstate. The economic and social interests of the ordinary citizen are secondary. I am reminded of his quote when discussing European Union matters with officials in Ireland and their myopic attitude:

> What needs to be revealed is not the "facts" but their manipulation and distortion. The more blatantly obvious the falsehood, the more insistently its perpetrators will repeat it. My own decision to write this book… was born first of incredulity at the hundreds of "black is white" statements about the ERM, and then of anger at the treatment of anyone who tries to point out the lies.[56]

The bullying is not confined to officials. The former British Prime Minister, John Major, a good friend of Ireland, decided to make a complete change in UK attitudes to the EU after the Thatcher years. He wanted the UK to be at the heart of Europe but gradually got disillusioned at the manipulation of the EU by the Franco-German axis. Major learned to his cost that the UK would never be treated as an equal by the other two countries. This chimed with what Charles de Gaulle had once stated "Europe is France and Germany. The rest is just the trimmings."[57]

However, Major was shocked much more by the treatment of the smaller countries. In his memoirs, Major wrote of the European Council:

> Most decisions were proposed by the Commission, after negotiation with France, Germany, and the country holding the Union Presidency. The smaller Nation States, all of whom were net beneficiaries of the communal budget, often complained bitterly about this in private. Whenever I witnessed this phenomenon, Aneurin Bevin's famous explanation of how he persuaded reluctant doctors to join the NHS came unbidden to my mind: "I stuffed their mouths with gold". The glow of precious metal beamed out from the Franco- German consensus, and for Britain, highly irritating.
>
> The Commission was rarely challenged; and when it was, there was often a cowardice to the criticism: any counter proposal was preceded by a paean, together with a timid suggestion that, perhaps

for the best of reasons, the Commission was wrong. Jacques Delors, confident in his position, brushed aside such half-hearted complaints easily, often with German or, more likely, French support. Others rather smugly joined the consensus. Isolated, and made to feel they had behaved improperly, the critics conceded. It was cruel, and an absurd way to operate.[58]

It is a pity we have to rely on British sources for these insights. Irish public servants, politicians and officials alike, seem strangely reluctant to reveal the innards of the operation in Brussels.

In his book, *Adults in the Room*, the former Greek Finance Minister Yanis Varoufakis also describes a very unequal scene at a meeting of Finance Ministers in the Eurogroup.

At the same corner of the table as Draghi, but on the longer side and at right angles to him, sat Wolfgang Schäuble. Their proximity would on occasions give rise to intense heat, though never any actual light. Along the same side as Schäuble were what I came to see as his cheerleaders: the Finnish, Slovakian, Austrian, Portuguese, Slovenian, Latvian, Lithuanian and Maltese Finance Ministers. My seat was almost diagonally opposite Schäuble's, alongside the other profligates, nicely lined up together: to my left was Ireland's Michael Noonan, to my right Spain's Luis de Guindos, and next to de Guindos was Italy's Pier Carla Padoan. France's Michel Sapin also sat on our side, next to Padoan.[59]

Varoufakis also outlined how the Eurogroup operated:

In normal Eurogroup meetings a fascinating ritual illustrated the manner in which the Troika and its processes had taken over the governance of continental Europe – one reason why Greece's appalling drama, which gave rise to the Troika, is so significant. Every time an item was tabled for discussion – for example, the French national budget or developments in Cyprus's banks – Dijsselbloem (Dutch chair of the group) would announce the topic and then invite the representatives of the institutions to present their views in turn … Only after these unelected officials had given their assessment and set the tone and terms of the debate did elected ministers get a chance to speak. Moreover, for almost all the meetings at which I was present the ministers received no substantial briefing on any of the topics under discussion. A reasonable and impartial spectator might easily conclude that the purpose of the Eurogroup is for ministers to approve and legitimize decisions that had already been taken by the three institutions.

This type of operation has been severely damaging to the whole concept of European cooperation. The dispensing with democratic safeguards has eventually resulted in Brexit and the rise of far-right nationalist parties in many Member States. Those in Ireland who unthinkingly supported the Maastricht and Lisbon Treaties, as well as the ill-judged common currency, are now seeing the outcome of that rush to centralise. The lack of democratic input into EU decision-making was summed up by British Politician, Douglas Hurd, when discussing the infamous Maastricht Treaty, stated candidly "Now we have signed it – we had better read it."[60]

The lack of serious political reflection was also the immediate EU reaction after the Brexit referendum. When the obvious response to this huge setback would have been a reappraisal of policy and a deep rethink, the response was to attack the electorate and denigrate the process of referenda itself. The threat of dis-integration that Brexit represented caused an immediate, and almost certainly temporary, surge in support for the EU in the remaining 27 countries. The Brussels establishment and their allies in the Member State capitals have tried to cash in on this feeling to promote their desire for ever closer union. However, the outcome of subsequent elections put paid to some of the more grandiose notions.

One of the most interesting contributions on the future of Europe came from former British Prime Minister Tony Blair[61]. He was probably the most pro-EU leader of Britain since Ted Heath. Blair had the good sense to recognise that the drive for conformity and rigid Red Lines by Brussels was destroying any possibility of keeping the UK within the EU fold or ever returning to membership. The former Prime Minister has argued that if "comprehensive" immigration and other reforms are offered, British voters might realise their "genuine underlying grievances" can be addressed.

However, neither Blair nor many others who wish to see the EU reformed can point to how this could be achieved. Unfortunately, the drive for ever-closer union is part of the DNA of the European project.

Table 2

EU White Paper on the Future Direction post Brexit

Scenario 1. Carrying on as now

This involves leaving the institutional Architecture as it is now and muddling through.

Scenario 2. The EU concentrating on completion of the Single Market and drop all the drive for political union

Become simply a free trade area

Scenario 3. Allowing those who want to do more, to do so

This would preserve the EU's overall unity but allow those who wish to forge ahead with enhanced military, tax cooperation, etc. It would create a Multi Speed Europe

Scenario 4: Doing less but doing it more efficiently

This would mean limiting the areas that the EU is involved in, allowing the institutions to concentrate on a smaller number of areas but allowing for deeper integration in these chosen areas

Scenario 5: Doing much more together

This is really the creation of a Federal Europe with the EU alone representing all Member States in places like the UN

References

1. *Village Magazine* 27 February 2016. *https://villagemagazine.ie/*

2. Bruce Arnold, "*History warns us about the risks of ceding power to EU*" Irish Independent 11 July 2009. *https://www.independent.ie/ opinion/analysis/history-warns-us-about-the-risks-of-ceding-power-to-eu-26549913.html.* Retrieved 4 May 2019.

3. John R Gillingham *The EU, An Obituary* p 9–31

4. Matt Duthan, "*John Cleese backs Brexit and suggests the only way of reforming the EU is to kill EU President Jean Claude Juncker*" Mail on

Sunday, 12 June 2016, *https://www.dailymail.co.uk/news/article-3637610/ John-Cleese-backs-Brexit-suggests-way-reforming-EU-KILL-European-Commission-President-Jean-Claude-Juncker.html.* Retrieved 4 May 2019

5.   Barry Roche *"Phil Hogan: Apple ruling not bid to force corporation tax change"* Irish Times 5 September 2016, *https://www.irishtimes.com/ news/politics/phil-hogan-apple-ruling-not-bid-to-force-corporation-tax-change-1.2780368.* Retrieved 4 May 2019

6.   David Heathcoat-Amory, Brexit Central website, 10 October 2018 *https://brexitcentral.com/tag/no-deal/page/*

7.   European Council meeting(18/19 February 2016) Conclusions, EUCO 1/16

8.   Garrett Fitzgerald *"EU institutional structures favour the smaller states such as Ireland"* Irish Times, 30 October 1999, *https://www.irishtimes. com/opinion/eu-institutional-structures-favour-the-smaller-states-such-as-ireland-1.244648* retrieved 4 May 2019

9.   Stephen Howe *Ireland and Empire: Colonial Legacies in Irish History and Culture* Oxford University Press 2000

10. *"Government to scrap National Forum on Europe"* Irish Independent, 9 April 2009, *https://www.independent.ie/breaking-news/irish-news/ government-to-scrap-national-forum-on-europe-26527479.html.* Retrieved 4 May 2019

11. Nicholas Watt *"Cameron tells EU it may live to regret Jean-Claude Juncker appointment"* Guardian 27 June 2016, *https://www.theguardian.com/ world/2014/jun/27/david-cameron-eu-jean-claude-juncker.* Retrieved 4 May 2019

12. Daniel McConnell *"Juncker best candidate for EU role, says Kenny"*. Irish Independent 26 June 2014, *https://www.independent.ie/irish-news/politics/ juncker-best-candidate-for-eu-role-says-kenny-30385692.html.* Retrieved 4 May 2019

13. Daniel Boffey *"Juncker: British media disrespect human rights of politicians"* Guardian 6 October 2018, *https://www.theguardian.com/world/2018/ oct/06/juncker-criticises-british-media-and-urges-limits-to-press-freedom.* Retrieved 4 May 2019

14. Peter Dominiczac *"Fears over Jean-Claude Juncker's drinking -Concerns about the lifestyle of European Commission's president in waiting raised by EU leaders ahead of key summit"* Daily Telegraph, 26 June 2014, *https:// www.telegraph.co.uk/news/worldnews/europe/eu/10929427/Fears-over-Jean-Claude-Junckers-drinking.html.* Retrieved 4 May 2109

15. Seán Clarke *"German Election, Full Results"*, *Guardian* 25 September, *https://www.theguardian.com/world/ng-interactive/2017/sep/24/german-elections-2017-latest-results-live-merkel-bundestag-afd.* Retrieved 5 May 2019

16. Agence-France-Presse report in the Guardian *"AfD party votes to campaign for German exit from EU"* *Guardian* 13 January 2019, *https://www.theguardian.com/world/2019/jan/13/afd-party-to-campaign-for-german-exit-from-european-union.* Retrieved 5 May 2019

17. Mathew Weaver, Clare Philips, Alexandra Topping and Hanna Yusuf *"Dutch elections: Rutte starts coalition talks after beating Wilders into second – as it happened"* *Guardian* 26 March 2017, *https://www.theguardian.com/world/live/2017/mar/15/dutch-election-voters-go-to-the-polls-in-the-netherlands-live.* Retrieved 5 May 2019

18. Greg Heffer *"Austria calls for overhaul of EU free movement"* Sky News website, 30 May 2018, *https://news.sky.com/story/austria-calls-for-overhaul-of-eu-free-movement-11389831.* Retrieved 5 May 2019

19. Florain Edar *Politico Playbook* 13 May 2019

20. Ashoka Mody *EuroTragedy* p 200.

21. Liam Fox *"90% of growth will be outside the EU, and Brexit means Britain can benefit"* *Sunday Times*, 24 January 2018, *https://www.thetimes.co.uk/article/90-of-growth-will-be-outside-the-eu-and-brexit-will-give-britain-chance-to-benefit-htp2dm2bh.* Retrieved 5 May 2019

22. *"As demand for EU global engagement rises, 140 Delegations have responsibility and opportunity"* Website of the European External Action Service. 28 August 2017 *https://eeas.europa.eu/headquarters/headquarters-homepage_en/31426/As%20demand%20for%20EU%20global%20engagement%20rises,%20140%20Delegations%20have%20responsibility%20and%20opportunity.* Retrieved 23 Nov 2019

23. Kieran Allen *"Pesco makes us choose defence spending over housing homeless. EU army requires fivefold hike in Irish military spending on machines of death"* *Irish Times*, 15 December 2017, *https://www.irishtimes.com/opinion/pesco-makes-us-choose-defence-spending-over-housing-homeless-1.332760.* Retrieved 5 May 2019.

24. Arthur Beesley *"Water charges irreversible in EU law, say lawyers"* *Irish Times*, 29 March 2016, *https://theliberal.ie/water-charges-are-irreversible-in-eu-law-according-to-lawyers/.* Retrieved 5 May 2019

25. Christian Oliver *"Enthusiasm for EU in sharp decline throughout Europe, not just UK. Only 38% of French people and 47% of Spaniards are now*

favourable to European project, study shows" *Financial Times*, 7 June 2016, *https://www.ft.com/content/1740f3a6-2cc2-11e6-bf8d-26294ad519fc*. Retrieved 5 May 2019

26. Maxime Schlee *"Macron's approval ratings hit record low: poll. Voters think French president is launching 'too many reforms,' according to new survey"*. Politico.eu 23 March 2018, https://www.politico.eu/article/emmanuel-macron-france-approval-ratings-hit-record-low-poll/. Retrieved on 5 May 2019

27. Jim Power and Péter Szlovak, *"Migrants and the Irish Economy"* October 2012, *atlanticphilanthropies.org*. Retrieved 6 May 2019

28. Frances McGinnity, Raffaele Grotti, Helen Russell and Éamonn Fahey *"Attitudes to Diversity in Ireland"* March 2018, published by the Irish Human Rights and Equality Commission and the Economic and Social Research Institute. *https://www.ihrec.ie/app/uploads/2018/03/Attitudes-to-diversity-in-Ireland.pdf*. Retrieved 6 May 2019

29. The Central Statistics Office Cork, Population and Migration Estimates April 2018.

30. David Barrett *"Immigration from eastern Europe was massively underestimated, says official report"* *Daily Telegraph*, 10 April 2014, *https://www.telegraph.co.uk/news/uknews/immigration/10757336/Immigration-from-eastern-Europe-was-massively-underestimated-says-official-report.html*. Retrieved 6 May 2019

31. *"Number of EU nationals working in Britain reaches record level, official statistics show" Daily Telegraph* 15 November 2017. *https://www.telegraph.co.uk/news/2017/11/15/number-eu-nationals-working-britain-reaches-record-level-official/*. Retrieved 6 May 2019

32. "Cultural Effects of Migration, Globalisation 101. The European Immigration Debate" *www.globalization101.org. Levin Institute, 2017*

33. Arthur Velker *"DANGEROUS' Leo Varadkar warned about 'gas-lighting' comments aimed at Georgian and Albanian asylum seekers" Irish Sun*, 4 Nov 2019. *https://www.thesun.ie/news/4735049/leo-varadkar-gas-lighting-asylum-seekers-georgia-albania*. Retrieved 5 Nov 2019

34. Council Regulation (EC) No. 343/2013, Official Journal of the European Union L(50/1), 25 February 3003

35. Justine Huggler *"Migrant crime in Germany rises by 50 per cent, new figures show" Daily Telegraph*, 25 April 2017, *https://www.telegraph.co.uk/news/2017/04/25/migrant-crime-germany-rises-50-per-cent-new-figures-show/*. Retrieved 6 May 201

36. Ian Traynor "*Refugee crisis: Juncker calls for radical overhaul of EU immigration policies*" *Guardian*, 9 September 2015, *https://www.theguardian.com/world/2015/sep/09/refugee-crisis-eu-executive-plans-overhaul-of-european-asylum-policies.* Retrieved 6 May 2019

37. Census 2016 Published by the Central Statistics Office of Ireland

38. Consolidation Act No. 608 of 17 July 2002 of the Danish Ministry of Refugee, Immigration and Integration Affairs

39. Edward Delman, "*How Not to Welcome Refugees. With its new immigration law, Denmark is once again sending a blunt message to migrants.*" *The Atlantic*, 27 January 2016, *https://www.theatlantic.com/international/archive/2016/01/denmark-refugees-immigration-law/431520/.* Retrieved 7 May 2109

40. Mara Bierbach, "*Denmark's asylum policy: explained*" INFOMIGRANTS, 11 July 2017 *https://www.infomigrants.net/en/post/4109/denmark-s-asylum-policy.* Retrieved 7 May 2019

41. "*Denmark suspends quota refugee programme*" *The Local* 22 November 2016, *https://www.thelocal.dk/20190130/denmarks-government-change*s. Retrieved 7 May 2019

42. Peter Nedergaard "*The Immigration Policy Turn: The Danish Social Democratic Case*" 25 May 2017, Social Europe; *https://www.socialeurope.eu/immigration-policy-turn-danish-social.* Retrieved 7 May 2019

43. Angela Giuffrida *"Italian Government approves Salvini bill targeting migrants*" *Guardian*, 24 September 2018, *https://www.theguardian.com/world/2018/sep/24/italian-government-approves-bill-anti-migrant-measures-matteo-salvini.* Retrieved 7 May 2019

44. "*Italy demands apology for France's 'hypocritical' criticism on migrants*" The Local 13 June 2018, *https://www.thelocal.fr/.../aquarius-migrant-ship-italy-france-europ*e. Retrieved 7 May 2019

45. Vince Cable, "*Why it's time to end free movement*" *New Statesman*"4, January 2017 *https://www.newstatesman.com/politics/uk/2017/01/why-its-time-end-eu-free-movement.* Retrieved 7 May 2019

46. Shaun Walker "*Romanian hospitals in crisis as emigration takes its tol*l" *Guardian*, 21 April 2019, *https://www.theguardian.com/world/2019/apr/21/romanian-hospitals-in-crisis-as-emigration-take-its-toll.* Retrieved 7 May 2019

47. Will Podmore *Brexit: The Road to Freedom* p231

48. Website of the EU "European Committee of the Regions (COR)" *https://europa.eu/.../european-committee-regions*

49. Transparency International *"Transparency International Ireland launches 'Integrity Index' of Irish Local Authorities"*, 16 May 2018, *https://www.transparency.ie/news_events/transparency-international.* Retrieved 7 May 2019

50. Alan Clarke(1993) *Diaries* (London Weidenfeld and Nicholson) p 139

51. Charles Grant *Delors: Inside the House that Jacques Built* p 135

52. Hansard 1990, 30 October, col. 873.

53. European Commission website, *"European Civil Service" https://ec.europa.eu/.../organisational-structure/commission-staff.* Retrieved 7 May 2019

54. Christopher Booker and Richard North *The Great Deception* p 358.

55. Bruno Waterfield *"Barroso hails the European 'empire'"* Daily Telegraph 11 July 2007. *https://www.telegraph.co.uk/news/worldnews/1557143/Barroso-hails-the-European-empire.html.* Retrieved 7 May 2019

56. Anthony Coughlan *A Handbook for Irish and European Diplomats, whether politically Centre, Left of Right*, p 15

57. Christopher Booker and Richard North *The Great Deception* p 358

58. John Major *The Autobiography of John Major* p 583

59. Yanis Varoufakis *Adults in the Room* p 232.

60. Cormac Lucey *Plan B* p 25

61. BBC News *"Tony Blair: EU reform can change UK minds on Brexit"* 1 March 2018, *https://www.bbc.com/news/uk-politics-43241776.* Retrieved 7 May 2019

PART III

Chapter 11

The EU Propaganda Machine in Ireland

Ample Opportunities to misspend

Marian Harkin MEP

There are considerable difficulties for any person or organisation in Ireland today trying to initiate a fundamental debate on the country's future relationship with the EU. They are faced with powerful vested interests. These interests feel threatened by any suggestion that the country's destiny may lie outside the framework of the ever-closer union. While the Irish establishment may smugly disprove of the vigorous British media scrutiny of Brussels, admittedly including some fairly ridiculous examples of misinformation, they shriek at any hint of criticism, however rational, of the EU closer to home. While calling for a balanced debate in Britain, they never seem to recognise that no such thing exists in Ireland.

It is indeed paradoxical that those who most loudly proclaim their liberal credentials seem to be super neuralgic in this regard. When I began writing for the *Sunday Business Post*, an approach was made to the then owner of the newspaper by some so-called pillars of society, including a former senior Irish Government Minister, politely requesting that I and a number of others whom they regarded as contrarians, be dropped as columnists, because of our critical views of the EU. These people regard themselves as among the elite of society and regularly rant against censorship in other countries but fail to connect their own intolerance, with what they criticise in others. It is always very striking that at any meeting involving pro-EU groups, the audience is extremely well-heeled. There is scant presence of the average citizen. This mirrors the position in England where the affluent were mainly pro-EU, while working class areas were predominantly pro-Brexit.

Within the establishment in Ireland, the pro-EU sentiment is greatly bolstered by the movement of officials, both elected and from the permanent public service, in and out of European institutions. There is a veritable revolving door, with flows in both directions. These people often feel that their identity and indeed Ireland's place in the world is defined solely by our membership of the EU. It is a reassuring blanket that Brussels, and its institutions, stand as a bulwark against the great unwashed and their stubborn adherence to national identity and culture. It mirrors the Irish officials who worked diligently for the British colonial administration throughout the old Empire, placing their talents and allegiance at the disposal of the Imperial administrations.

Throughout the Irish people's long struggle for self-rule, the counterargument from the colonial administration and its camp followers was that the Irish were incapable of governing themselves. These sentiments are often put forward today by those seeking to maintain Brussels hegemony over Ireland. A series of local public scandals has often reinforced this type of negativity.

Hence in Ireland, there has been, over the years, a virtual avalanche of material and publications all extolling the virtues of the country's membership of the European Union. The bulk of this material is financially supported by the EU, either directly or through sources, which are themselves the beneficiaries of EU largesse in some form. It would be a brave recipient of such support to criticise or in any way undermine the "Brussels is good for you" official line. Outside of totalitarian countries, I know of no example of a State which unashamedly engages in such egregious self-promotion as the EU. Generous funds for initiatives, such as Europe for Citizens Programme, are designed to try and create an artificial EU identity. Of course, many groups are only too happy to accept the cash, which in reality is a crude attempt to buy influence at the taxpayers' expense. They quickly sign up to being part of the EU propaganda machine in Ireland.

The use of TV and other outlets to promote the EU project
Even RTÉ, the Irish National Broadcaster, receives a subsidy from the European Parliament to cover their activities. Eimear Cusack, Director of Human Resources, confirmed the subsidy in a letter to former senior Irish civil servant Michael Clarke. Ms Cusack states:

However, in common with many other European broadcasters, RTÉ News is reimbursed by the EU Parliament for some expenses incurred in sending a journalist from our Political Unit, based in Leinster House, to Strasbourg for Plenary Sessions of the European Parliament, usually once a month. The journalist covers the Parliament for RTÉ News and also produces the European Parliament Report Programme which is broadcast on RTÉ One television.[1]

The ethics of this arrangement are dubious since the European Parliament is using Irish taxpayers' money for propaganda purposes. It would be interesting to find out what other bodies are paying a subsidy to RTÉ to promote its events.

RTÉ is also involved in another propaganda drive to create an EU identity and that is through its close relationship with the news channel Euronews. As any regular viewer of this station will readily testify, it has a pro-EU outlook. The channel is often available on RTÉ News channel as well as having its own slot on the spectrum of stations. Its pro-EU bias is hardly surprising, since about one-third of its funding is provided directly by the EU itself, despite it being privately owned[2]. In a written question in the European Parliament, the Maltese Socialist MEP Alfred Sant pointed out that Euronews was getting between €26m and €29.5m annually[3] directly from the Commission. From 2014 to 2018, the EU gave the station €122m[4]. That type of money, which originates from the Member States' taxpayers, buys a lot of loyalty. Euronews HQ is in spanking new high-tech offices in the French city of Lyon.

I approached RTÉ about its relationship with Euronews. I spoke with Jon Williams, Managing Director, News and Current Affairs. He was very helpful, indicating that RTÉ has a 1% share in Euronews, as do many other European Broadcasters. He strongly rejected any insinuation that the large subsidy from the EU Commission had any effect on editorial content in Euronews. I have absolutely no reason to doubt Jon's sincerity but the fact that Euronews is required by its contract with the EU Commission to have a "European dimension" is, in itself, a political requirement.

However, it is also difficult to reconcile Jon's assertion with the report that any Commission Directorate-General can buy a short or long magazine contribution, which will be aired fifteen times on the station.[5] There is a budget of €6.5m for this purpose. I believe that this arrangement definitely blurs the line between journalism and PR content. It stands in huge contrast to the lengths CNN go to avoid any appearance of a conflict of interest. However, the proposal of an EU wide licence fee to pay for Euronews[6] or that part of national licence fees should be given to Euronews, is likely to go down badly with cash strapped national broadcasters in the Member States.

With a whole machine engaged in trying to popularise the EU in Ireland, the production of this propaganda has created the false impression that Ireland is one of the most pro-EU countries in the Union. The pro-EU image is often bolstered by the results of totally meaningless and expensive polling by self-interested groups, asking if a respondent thought that membership of the EU had been good for Ireland, not about the future intentions of Brussels and new initiatives for concentrating power in that city. I would concede that, in the past, EU membership has been beneficial in the overall context for Ireland, but I also believe that continued membership is not in Ireland's interest now. Hence, many of these "surveys" are meaningless about our future intentions.

Irish public buildings, including Dublin Castle, Iveagh House, Farmleigh, etc. are regularly given out, gratis, to pro-EU campaigning groups. The EU Commission directly dispenses research grants, separate from the National Governments, even though these grants are paid for by the taxpayers in the individual Member States and often require matching funds from the Irish Exchequer[7]. In 2016, the EU Commission directly spent €156m in Ireland, all designed to create the impression that this largesse has somehow magically arrived from Brussels[8]. That amount of money can buy you serious influence and popularity. However, many in Ireland do not realise that this is their own money coming back, with suitable deductions to pay for the expensive officials in Brussels. How often do we hear on Irish television, local county councillors expressing gratitude for support from Brussels, not realising that they should be thanking their fellow citizens for providing the funding?

There are many who haunt the Irish media, giving their views on subjects like Brexit, who fail to also own up to having personally benefited from some EU support. Self-interest is a strong motivation. As former Australian Prime Minister Paul Keating regularly pointed out "Put your money on self-interest in any horse race because you know they are trying."

Many public officials are very interested in getting themselves onto the EU gravy train.

European Parliament's gravy train

Irish politicians and indeed their colleagues throughout the EU often aspire to membership of the European Parliament, which is very much part of a lucrative gravy train. Membership of this exclusive club certainly has its privileges, with a minimum of oversight.

The lack of accountability was illustrated by the recent controversy over "the general expenditure allowance" or GEA. This is a special allocation of €4,416 paid to each MEP every month. This is on top of their normal gross salary of €8,611.31pm. Unlike virtually all other personal payments for expenses in the public service, there is actually no requirement to account for this cash.

In the very diplomatic language of former Irish MEP Marian Harkin (and now a member of the Dáil), there is "ample opportunity to misspend", in other words, to simply trouser the cash that the GEA provides. Another ex-MEP, who like Harkin had his GEA audited and published, Matt Carthy of Sinn Féin, described the lack of accountability as scandalous[9].

Attempts to get some scrutiny of this expenditure, which amounts to some €40m per annum, were shot down by the Parliament's Bureau, a group made up of the then President of the European Parliament, Italian Antonio Tajani, and the fourteen Vice Presidents, including Ireland's Mairead McGuinness. She was the first Vice President of the Parliament and acted as Tajani's deputy. The decision of the Bureau was taken behind closed doors at a late-night meeting in Strasbourg[10]. Many MEPs, who wanted to make the Parliament more accountable, were dismayed by the decision.

The Bureau also rejected proposals which would have required MEPs to return any unspent funds, rather than keeping them for themselves and also to keep accurate accounts, including receipts, etc.[11].

Subsequently, a group of twenty-nine journalists, from all twenty-eight Member States at the time, tried through other mechanisms to uncover more information on the GEA. Firstly, freedom of information requests were refused. These were appealed to the courts. After three years of deliberations, the General Court of the European Union in Luxembourg ruled against the journalists. The Court found in favour of the Parliament's desire for secrecy, on the basis that the protection of personal data was more important than the public interest in this case. This ruling was given despite the statement by the EU Data Protection Chief that politicians had to accept strong limitations on their rights in this area in the name of transparency[12].

The Court also refused to sanction the publication of material, with names redacted, on the basis that it would put too heavy a burden on the administrative capacity of the Parliament. In the context of any national administration, such reasoning would have been savaged. There would have been rushed legislation to overturn the perverse decision, as politicians feared a democratic backlash, but nothing happened. However, the suspicion must arise that the Court was trying to shield the Parliament from the type of reactions which accompanied the publication of expenses in several national Parliaments, including in Ireland, the UK, etc. This was understandable from an EU point of view, given the poor standing that the Parliament already enjoys with the public.

The judicial action in sparing the blushes of the Parliamentarians was described in the *Telegraph* on 25 September 2018, by Transparency International's Nick Aiossa, in the following terms:

> The European Court of Justice has dealt a severe blow to transparency today by allowing the European Parliament to keep MEP's allowance spending completely secret from the public. At a time when trust in the EU institutions is so low, this is a ridiculous message ahead of next year's European Elections.

It was yet another example of the CJEU acting as a guardian of the EU establishment, something it has done repeatedly over the years. It was no wonder that the UK authorities were so anxious to remove it and its perceived bias from adjudications on EU/UK matters post-Brexit. As indicated in Chapter 9, leading barrister Gunnar Beck, in his publication "Imperial, not Impartial" has catalogued the court's great ability and "flexibility" in arriving at decisions which invariably are favourable to Brussels[13].

Subsidised NGOs and EU Institutions in Ireland

The gravy train is not confined to elected officials.

The first organisation in Ireland which actively promoted membership of the EEC, back in the 1950s, was the European Movement. Despite the Irish State's initial suspicion of this organisation (see Chapter 5), it has been treated very well since.

According to its own website, the International European Movement is the largest pan-European network of pro-European organisations. It is present in 39 countries and encompasses 36 International Associations, bringing together European civil society, business, trade unions, NGOs, political parties, local authorities and academia. Founded 70 years ago, it has continuously advocated in favour of European co-operation and integration.

In other words, this is a campaigning group for European Federalism.

On the local Irish branch of the European Movement's website, it openly states that it is involved in advocacy campaigns. It states that "EM Ireland can be proud of its contribution to the relationship between Ireland and the EU. For nearly sixty years, European Movement Ireland has made the case for Europe."

The Irish branch was founded in 1954 by a number of local prominent figures, including the former Taoiseach Garret FitzGerald. The current President of the EM in Ireland is our Head of Government, Leo Varadkar. The Tánaiste (Deputy Prime Minister) and Minister for Foreign Affairs and Trade, Simon Coveney, is among the Vice Presidents; as is the leader of the Opposition, Fianna Fail's Micheál Martin; and also, former President of the European Parliament Pat Cox, etc.[14]. The full list of office holders is a line-up of the great and good of Irish political life.

While this is laudable, and everyone is entitled to his/her political views, I have to question whether people such as Simon Coveney,

Ireland's Foreign Minister, should funnel public money into an organisation which is overtly political and where he has held office.

In 2018, the Department of Foreign Affairs and Trade paid, on behalf of their Minister and the EM Vice President, Mr Coveney, €425,000 of Irish taxpayers' money to this organisation. This consisted of core funding of €180,000 and a special grant of €245,000[15]. I am unable to find any similar grant to an organisation which holds contrary views on Europe. The generous patronage of the State is apparently available only to those supporting the Government agenda. Again, there are ethical questions about being a Vice President of an organisation and then adjudicating on their grant application.

The European Movement enjoys unrivalled free access to Irish State buildings, including the HQ of the Department of Foreign Affairs and Trade, the former sumptuous town residence of the Guinness brewing family, Iveagh House, on St Stephen's Green; as well as the Permanent Representation offices in central Brussels. I have my doubts that a eurosceptical organisation would be as successful in seeking free use of these public buildings. There is no attempt at fair play when it comes to Europe.

Another body in the field is the Institute for International and European Affairs (IIEA). The IIEA purports to be an independent Think Tank on International and European matters. It has always portrayed itself to be independent of Government[16] but in the past it has received direct funding from the Department of Foreign Affairs and Trade. Moreover, it still receives a large part of its funding through the corporate membership of Government Departments and Agencies. This does not encourage the IIEA to engage in any radical thought or indeed actions which might run counter to Government policy.

It has often been described as a retirement home for former Irish diplomats, as many ex-officials of the Foreign Affairs Department are today associated with the IIEA.

Although to be fair to the IIEA, under its former Director General and ex-Irish Government Minister, Barry Andrews, and its Chief Economist, Dan O'Brien, it has asked people who are critical of the EU to address meetings, even if the bulk of its activities is directed at further popularising the EU. Again, its Board of Directors is a compilation of the usual suspects in Irish elite society, many of whom have been overtly associated with promoting the EU.

Given the paucity of Think Tanks in Ireland, the IIEA does have an important role in providing a platform for speakers on EU-related topics. I hope that in future, it will widen its programme to give greater balance to the various policy options.

There are also specific projects which are aimed at popularising the European Union and creating an artificial "European Identity" so beloved by Brussels. The Jean Monnet Programme fits neatly into this category. It is an initiative to encourage "teaching, research and reflection in the field of European integration studies in higher education institutions"[(17)].

According to its own promotional material, the programme includes the network of Jean Monnet European Centres of Excellence, university-level institutions recognised by the European Commission for high quality research into, and teaching of, topics relating to European Integration. The Commission also funds Jean Monnet chairs and Jean Monnet teaching modules. In Ireland, Jean Monnet Chairs have been established, inter alia, in Belfast (Queen's), Maynooth and in Dublin (University College Dublin).

The programme was originally launched in 1989 and helped to set up 162 Jean Monnet European Centres of Excellence, 875 Jean Monnet Chairs and 1001 Jean Monnet Teaching Modules worldwide in 72 countries in five continents. These projects bring together 1,500 professors and reach approximately 500,000 students every year. According to the EU, Jean Monnet Projects are selected on the basis of their academic merits and following a process of rigorous and independent peer review. The projects are implemented in strict compliance with the principle of academic autonomy and freedom, (provided you support EU integration).

This has created a vast number of institutions and academics who have a vested interest in promoting the EU, all paid for by the taxpayers, regardless of those taxpayers' views on European integration. It is a propaganda exercise on a vast scale, almost matching the type of similar exercises in Stalinist States.

According to the EU Commission:

A Jean Monnet Chair is a teaching post with a specialisation in European Union studies for university professors. It can only be held by one professor, who must provide the minimum of 90 teaching hours per academic year over a period of three consecutive years. In addition, the Chair must carry out at least one additional activity per academic year.

The Commission provide a maximum grant of €50,000 per chair and the position must be maintained for three years. Naturally enough, there is a huge demand for this grant aid.

Look at the website of any Irish university and you will see Jean Monnet lectures, seminars, etc., a virtual army of EU programmes all designed to create this artificial identification with the European Union. The programmes are targeted specifically at young people. Why is there a need for such high levels of propaganda and self-promotion if there is really an organic and self-sustaining pro-EU feeling about?

On several occasions, I have been invited to address European student societies in Irish universities. It always causes a large curiosity element. There is open amazement that anybody could have contrary views on the EU to the prevailing official narrative. It is shocking that many of these students are unaware of the counterarguments. It is never raised in their classes or tutorials, a huge indictment of our higher-level colleges. To be fair to the students, they are always very open to discussion and reasoned debate, but many have confessed that they have never been exposed to anything but pro-EU propaganda.

The propaganda push is not only at third level institutions. As the "European Project" shows signs of failing throughout the Member States, the EU Federalists seek new ways of trying to win back popularity through the educational system. The Blue Schools Programme according to the European Movement in Ireland website:

is a primary school initiative that aims to foster better knowledge and understanding of the European Union and how it affects our lives among Irish primary pupils through classroom projects and activities. The Programme introduces participants (pupils, teachers, parents and the wider community) to the EU, what it means and how it works. The goal of the Programme is to foster a strong sense of citizenship (European) among participants that goes far beyond the school walls and into the wider community. The objective of the Programme is to encourage primary schools to undertake a module of tasks and projects related to the EU.

The Blue Star Programme is a venture of the 'Communicating Europe Initiative', supported by the office of the Minister of State for European Affairs, Helen McEntee TD; the Department of Foreign Affairs and Trade; the European Commission Representation in Ireland; the European Parliament Information Office in Ireland; and the Department of Education and Skills. European Movement Ireland is the "National Implementation Body for the Programme.[18]

It is again supported financially by the Irish Government and involves the supply of resource kits, arranging VIP visits to the schools, etc. Again, there have to be ethical questions about subjecting primary school children to this form of propaganda exercise. It seems more like a programme from a dictatorship than a healthy democracy.

The European Commission had two representation offices in Ireland, one in Dublin and another in Belfast. In addition, the European Parliament maintains a separate office in Dublin. These offices of European institutions are all well-staffed throughout the EU and have large resources to promote pro-EU groups and initiatives. With Brexit however, the office in Belfast, ironically enough located on the Dublin Road, was closed, although the EU has asked for it to be reopened.

Everywhere one travels in Ireland there are reminders that certain projects have attracted EU funding, although it is essentially Irish taxpayers' money originally. However, despite all the propaganda and official support, the Irish electorate have twice rejected EU Treaties, Nice 2002 and Lisbon 2008. The media, especially the influential *Irish Times*, all the main political parties and much of the academic and intellectual sources in the country are unashamedly pro-EU. Yet Irish Governments are extremely nervous about putting any Treaty change to the popular vote. Why is there this paradox at the heart of the Irish attitude to the European project and how has it arisen?

One of the main reasons is that Irish politicians and business regularly speak about the EU as if it is an economic project. This is to totally miss the whole raison d'etre for the EU. The project is essentially political in nature. The creation of a protectionist multinational market with common external tariffs is a mechanism to assist in the building of the real objective, namely a single Federal European State. The EU propaganda machine avoids mentioning the end objective but speaks in ambiguous terms.

Brexit and the Irish media

Any review of the Irish media coverage of Brexit from 2015 onwards would show that the local commentators got the bulk of their analysis hopelessly wrong. As with other elements of the establishment, the Irish media was unprepared for Brexit and has essentially, with a small number of honourable exceptions, rowed in with the suffocating conformity of the general anti-Brexit line. While huge amounts of TV and radio time and newspaper space have been devoted to the issue, much of the debate has been characterised by a lack of depth and a temerity in the face of official spokespersons. The Taoiseach and Government Ministers can be evasive and indeed contradict their earlier pronouncements, without any serious challenge from an interviewer. The treatment of the failure of the Irish Government to give a straight answer for a long period on the issue of border arrangements, in the event of a No Deal outcome, was particularly egregious. Ignoring the Irish Government's role in making the Brexit process in Britain a holy mess, and the consequent disruption, was widespread, as if the self-defeating Backstop emerged from outer space. There has been no serious analysis of the long-term damage to British-Irish connections; and to relations between the pro Union part of the community in the North with the rest of the island. Ireland could badly do with our own Jeremy Paxman, Emily Maitlis, etc.

There has been a serious lack of balance in the coverage of EU matters, often with full panels vying with each other in intensity, all trying to explain that the British are insane and making the outlandish claim that the British desire for full independence is a longing for the British Empire, without being able to point to any evidence. Every piece of bad news in the British economy is seized upon and magnified, while ignoring any good news. It is almost a classic example of groupthink in action. It sometimes seems that the Irish idea of diversity is to have a panel of "experts", made up of equal numbers of men and women, all of whom are of the one pro-EU opinion.

While being interviewed by journalists, I have been told privately that their newspaper has an "editorial policy" in favour of the EU and that the journalist is not at liberty to show any sympathy for my Irexit views. In one case, I was told that an interview would be pulled as it did not suit the paper's pro-EU policy.

The tone of questioning on radio and TV of pro-EU contributors can be totally different to the hostility that those critical of the EU have encountered, although in my own case, I have never had reason to complain. I have, however, witnessed it on occasions to others.

There has been a tendency to concentrate on interviews in Britain with people who hate Brexit, which gives Irish audiences a very skewed perspective on the state of public opinion in our nearest neighbour. Asking well known anti-Brexiteers like Peter Mandelson, Alistair Campbell, Kevin Maguire of the *Daily Mirror*, etc. to comment on political developments in London, without a corresponding pro-Brexiteer spokesperson, does not serve to create informed opinion in Ireland. The tone of the reporting from Irish media outlets based in the UK has been overwhelmingly anti-Brexit. There is not even the pretence of impartiality.

The poor performance of the mainstream Irish media on the Brexit issue is not an isolated case. The Southern Irish media was largely irrelevant throughout the Troubles in the North. Despite the mayhem and the huge implications for the future of our island, the Dublin-based media was notable by its risk averse approach. As an Irish Government official, along with my colleagues in Dublin, we watched, read and listened out for the Belfast or British-based media for any worthwhile investigative journalism.

The failure of the Republic's media was in part due to censorship by the Irish Government and also reflected a much wider fear in the South about contagion of unrest and radical Republicanism from the North. Those few who challenged the cosy consensus, such as Tim Pat Coogan, were marked out as potential enemies of the State. One Government

Minister, Conor Cruise O'Brien, even wanted Coogan arrested for his role as editor of the *Irish Press*[19]. That newspaper regularly reported disturbing activities by State agencies in the North, including widespread collusion by the security services with Loyalist paramilitaries. Coogan also bravely tried to expose gross abuses of human rights of Irish citizens in the region. His efforts at balancing the unequal activities of the bulk of the rest of the Southern media stands as a huge contribution to maintaining press freedom in the Republic. Perhaps it is time for the Irish State to positively acknowledge Tim Pat's role at that time.

The North was different and produced journalists of the quality of Eamonn Mallie, Barney Rowen, David McKittrick, Lena Ferguson, Ken Reid, Deric Henderson, Martina Purdy, etc. all of whom were serious commentators. Governments listened and took heed when these reporters uncovered stories and provided valuable insights into controversial issues. They were regularly sounded out privately on sensitive topics on an "off-the-record" basis.

Yet all the efforts of the pro-EU elements in Europe constantly come up against the reality that national identity remains strong and enduring. Former Irish Taoiseach, John Bruton, bemoaned the "lack of European Patriotism" in an interview with the publication *The Irish Catholic*. In launching his book *Faith in Politics*, Bruton stated that the "lack of emotional and spiritual support for the European Union could ultimately lead to its break-up"[20]. However, it is very difficult to create an artificial EU identity. Even the powerful EU propaganda machine in the Irish media has its limitations.

It should be acknowledged, in contrast, that social media in Ireland has promoted a vigorous debate over Brexit and the longer-term implications of continued EU membership for Ireland.

References

1. Letter from Eimer Cusack, Director of Human resources to Michael Clarke, 1 November 2018

2. Alex Spence and James Panichi "*Tycoon takeover puts Euronews funding in focus*". https://www.politico.eu/article/tycoon-takeover-euronews-funding-meps-commission-egypt-naguib-sawiris/. Retrieved 7 June 2019

3. Question for written answer P-001066/2017 to the Commission Rule 130 Alfred Sant (S&D)

4. Lili Bayer *"EU auditors raise concerns about Euronews funding"*, Politico. eu, 15 May 2019. https://www.politico.eu/article/eu-auditors-raise-concerns-about-euronews-funding/. Retrieved 7 June 2019

5. Ronny Patz *"Euronews becomes EU Commission propaganda channel" https://polscieu.ideasoneurope.eu/2012/04/11/euronews-becomes-eu-commission-propaganda-channel/.* Retrieved 7 June 2019

6. *"EU licence fee would maintain quality TV, says Euronews boss"*, euactive. com, 18 July 2011. *https://www.euractiv.com/section/languages-culture/ news/eu-licence-fee-would-maintain-quality-tv-says-euronews-boss/.* Retrieved 26 November 2019.

7. Website of the EU Representation Office Dublin, *https://ec.europa.eu/ ireland/home_en*

8. Material supplied to the author by the Department of Finance Dublin 2018

9. Patrick Smyth *Irish Times*, *"The opaque world of MEPs' expenses is cause for concern"*, 27 September 2018. *https://www.irishtimes.com/news/world/ europe/the-opaque-world-of-meps-expenses-is-cause-for-concern-1.3642493.* Retrieved 12 May 2019

10. Maia de la Baume *"MEPs reject scrutiny of their expenses"*, Politico.eu 7/ March/18. *https://www.politico.eu/article/strasbourg-european-parliament-meps-reject-scrutiny-of-expenses/.* Retrieved 12 May 2019

11. Ibid

12. Nikolaj Nielsen *"EU Court delivers transparency blow on MEP expenses"*, EU Observer, 25 September *2018 https://euobserver.com/eu-election/142946.* Retrieved 12 May 2019

13. Gunnar Beck –*"The Court of Justice of the EU, Imperial, not Impartial "*2018. Published by Politeia, London

14. European Movement Ireland Website 3 November 2018. *https://www.europeanmovement.ie/*

15. DFA website on funding allocation *https://www.dfa.ie/*

16. Website of the IIEA, *https://www.iiea.com/*

17. Website of the European Commission *https://eacea.ec.europa.eu/erasmus-plus/actions/jean-monnet_en*

18. *https://www.bluestarprogramme.ie*

19. Father Sean McManus "TCD's symposium on Conor Cruise O'Brien was sycophantic; and underplayed his misogyny, sectarianism and zealous censorship." Irish National Caucus, 27 November 2017.

http://www.irishnationalcaucus.org/tcds-symposium-on-conor-cruise-obrien-was-sycophantic-and-underplayed-his-misogyny-sectarianism-and-zealous-censorship/. Retrieved 26 November 2019

20. Susan Gately *"Lack of European patriotism is threat to EU"* 29 January 2016. *https://www.catholicireland.net/lack-european-patriotism-threat-eu/*

Chapter 12

The Anglophone World and Ireland's Diaspora

"All Politics is Local"

Thomas P "Tip" O Neill,
Speaker of the US House of Representatives

There are important fundamental relationships which should always be taken into account in formulating Ireland's interactions with the international community. Ireland is geographically in Europe and clearly needs close and friendly relations with all its immediate neighbours. However, there is also a global aspect to Ireland's profile. To any outside observer, the striking characteristic feature of Ireland is its huge Diaspora. The number of Irish born people living abroad is per capita one of the highest in the world (see Table 3). In addition, there is a much larger group who identify themselves as having an Irish ethnic connection, through descent. This group is regularly quoted as 70m strong[1], (although the basis of this calculation is somewhat murky). It is a huge resource and strength for Ireland. This is extremely large relative to the population of the island of Ireland which in 2018 was estimated at 6.7m[2]. However, until relatively recently there was no real attempt by successive Irish Governments to establish a coherent official strategy, with the necessary policies and resources, in relation to the Diaspora.

This changed after the GFA and was driven by Taoiseach Bertie Ahern and more directly by the then Foreign Minister Brian Cowen. The GFA resulted in the first substantive reference to the Diaspora in the Irish Constitution[3]. A more inclusive approach to Irishness, both on the island of Ireland and overseas, underpinned this new initiative. A special Task Force, under former SDLP politician and leading barrister, the late Paddy O'Hanlon from Armagh, drew up a blueprint for a new formalised relationship between the authorities in Dublin and the Diaspora[4]. As part of these new arrangements, a dedicated unit inside the Department of Foreign Affairs, the Irish Abroad unit, was to be established. However, our Department of Finance, which will never be accused of innovative new thinking, and its then Minister Charlie McCreevy, were not sympathetic and put up a rear-guard action against any serious effort to commit State funds to the initiative. The fact that McCreevy was under heavy media attack, with calls for his replacement in Finance with Brian Cowen, probably played a part in his lack of enthusiasm for Cowen's Diaspora initiative. However, things took a very advantageous turn for the better with the Government reshuffle in 2004 and my former boss Cowen moved to the Finance Department[5]. With Brian Cowen installed in Merrion Street as Minister, he ensured that adequate resources were made available to the new unit.

I had the privilege of having the unit within my area of responsibilities for five years 2005–10, during which the Irish Government's interaction with the Diaspora greatly developed. When I returned from Belfast to head up the Consular and Passport Division in the Department, I requested from our Secretary General Dermot Gallagher, that the brand-new unit be added to my areas of responsibility and Dermot readily acceded to my request. Dermot was also hugely interested in the area and a great support to myself and the new unit, as was Paddy O'Hanlon who was always available for an informal chat. The Government strongly expanded the resources it invested in our overseas communities and the unit also had responsibility for raising issues of concern to our Diaspora with all official agencies in Ireland. It was to be the Diaspora's ombudsman within Government. I believe that Brian Cowen never got proper recognition for his contribution to establishing strong institutional links with the Diaspora. He had huge empathy for issues relating to our overseas communities and demonstrated that in a very practical way in Government. As Minister for Finance and later as Taoiseach, he kept a close and sympathetic interest in the Irish Abroad unit. We always knew we had a supportive friend in Government when he was in power.

The Irish State's Diaspora strategy is now regarded as a world leader in this area. Many countries have sent delegations to study the Irish programme. However, we have a great advantage, a large and committed population overseas who are well organised. They are hugely self-supportive but welcome interaction with the Irish Government while not wishing to be centrally controlled by anyone or any institution. However, they are anxious and, in many cases, very able to assist the Irish authorities. There are very few books on the world-wide Irish Diaspora. The most prominent is Tim Pat Coogan's *Wherever Green is Worn*[6].

The largest and most active Irish Diaspora populations are in North America. In census returns, 10.6% of Americans[7] and 14% of Canadians[8] designate themselves as having Irish ethnic links. It always surprises people in Ireland that the Canadian figure is higher than the American one. In fact, the Canadian census produces the highest percentage of Irish of any overseas census. Much of the Irish settlement in Canada predated the Irish Famine.

In virtually every North American city, there are active and committed Irish-related organisations. This gives any Irish Government tremendous influence with politicians of all political persuasions. As Irish Ambassador in Canada, I had access to the highest level of Governments and their agencies. None of my colleagues in mainland European capitals had anything like the same political relevance to their hosts. I had a number of private discussions with Canadian Prime Minister Stephen Harper, usually about the Irish community in Canada, and the possibility of increasing working visas for Irish people. Harper's wife Laureen's family, had emigrated from Rathkeale in county Limerick to Alberta. When I related my experience in Ottawa at an Irish Heads of Mission conference, our man in Berlin said that he had never had a direct one to one conversation with the German Chancellor, Angela Merkel. It would simply never happen. To any politician in North America, Ireland has an importance and relevance that is lacking among our continental European partners. Whether we like it or admit it, we are an integral part of the Anglophone family.

Harper knew that many of his Ministers, party workers, officials, family, etc. had Irish links and hence was anxious to ensure that there were no thorny problems in our relationship. Our ties with the countries where our Diaspora resides are based on a very firm foundation, including an element of self-interest among local politicians. As the celebrated former Speaker of the US House of Representatives, Thomas

"Tip" O'Neill once stated, "All politics is local." Irish America and Irish Canada are very local to North American politicians.

Ireland has been for much of its history part of the English-speaking Anglophone world. Apart from Québec[9] and Argentina[10], the major Irish Diaspora populations are all in English speaking-countries, namely England, Scotland, Wales, the USA, English speaking Canada, Australia, New Zealand and South Africa. Our connections with the Diaspora are essentially links with the Anglophone world. These centuries old connections and cultural affinities form a strong and enduring bond, to which the present course of action by the Irish Government, with its eurocentric policy, is not giving enough prominence. In addition, all these English-speaking countries share much in terms of language, political institutions and common law which links the Anglophone world. The English-speaking countries of the Caribbean also form part of the cultural and linguistic linkages. I learned somewhat to my surprise, as Irish Ambassador to Jamaica about the strong Irish connections with that island and the numbers of Irish that settled there, even taking in some of our Famine migrants[11]. There is even an Irishtown, just outide Kingston. Like Jews, we were fated for most of our history to be a wandering people, seeking shelter and advancement throughout the world.

Because of EU freedom of labour policies, we now actively discriminate against our Diaspora in favour of countries of the EU. Hence those from traditional Irish areas such as South Boston, Newfoundland and the Western Districts of Victoria are put to the end of the queue for immigration purposes, while those from Latvia, Slovenia, etc. are given priority. Yet relatively few Irish want to move to mainland Europe, while our young people are clamouring for visas for the USA, Canada, New Zealand and Australia.

Ireland has benefitted hugely from being part of this world-wide grouping, referred to on occasions as the Anglosphere. There are deep Irish connections in all English-speaking countries. This has given Ireland and Irish people access to a major international stage and allowed our English language writers to be known and acclaimed worldwide. In comparison, traditional Irish cultural connections with mainland Europe are fairly slim pickings.

The North American Diaspora has also been a huge resource when it comes to attracting FDI to Ireland. The Irish connections have, in many cases, been the link that has allowed IDA Ireland access to senior management in many multinational firms, although the pro-business environment and tax incentives will be more important in the long run. However, that vital initial entry through the door has, in many cases, been facilitated by our extensive ethnic linkages.

Irish investors seeking opportunities abroad stay very close to the Anglosphere world. In a study by the respected London consultancy firm Primary Access[12], the figures for investment flows are stark. Primary reported that

> when it comes to direct inward and outward investment, Ireland is overwhelmingly tied to the US and the UK. Ireland has €93bn committed to the US, and €88bn to the UK in direct investment abroad; the comparable numbers for France and Germany are €4.4bn and €3.1bn respectively. The same pattern repeats in terms of inward direct investment. The US has €179bn, and the UK €58bn invested in Ireland; France has €15bn and Germany €5bn.

The Primary Access report, using figures from the Irish Central Statistics Office (CSO)[13] shows also that in terms of international trade in both goods and services, the USA and Britain are by far and away Ireland's most important trading partners. (Trade in goods with Belgium and the Netherlands is heavily distorted by the so-called Rotterdam/Antwerp effect, namely that these countries operate as the warehouses of Europe. The level of "real" trade with them is difficult to estimate but significantly lower than the official figure.)

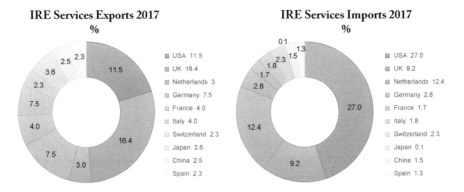

IRE Services Exports 2017 %

USA 11.5
UK 16.4
Netherlands 3
Germany 7.5
France 4.0
Italy 4.0
Switzerland 2.3
Japan 3.6
China 2.5
Spain 2.3

IRE Services Imports 2017 %

USA 27.0
UK 9.2
Netherlands 12.4
Germany 2.8
France 1.7
Italy 1.8
Switzerland 2.3
Japan 0.1
China 1.5
Spain 1.3

IRE Goods Exports 2017
%

- USA 27
- UK 12
- Belgium 11
- Germany 8
- Switzerland 5
- Netherlands 5
- France 4
- China 4
- Italy 2
- Japan 2

IRE Goods Imports 2017
%

- USA 24
- UK 21
- Belgium 13
- Germany 9
- Switzerland 6
- Netherlands 3
- France 2
- China 2
- Italy 2
- Japan 2

The departure of the United Kingdom from the European Union will see a realignment in the English-speaking world, as well as changes within the EU. The importance of the EU to the Anglosphere will diminish greatly after Brexit but in other areas of the world, there will be a revival of the old connections with the UK.

North American relations post Brexit

The UK, which had essentially run down its old role with the Anglosphere and the Commonwealth, wants to begin building up its capacity to undertake international trade negotiations and is urgently seeking new trade agreements. Its primary target is the largest consumer market in the world, the United States and its neighbour Canada.

Despite the short-term quixotic behaviour of the Trump administration, there is every possibility of the emergence of an Anglophone North Atlantic free trade area, encompassing the USA, Canada and Britain[14]. This would form part of an alternative trade strategy for the UK, post Brexit. There is a strong sense of kinship in these countries with Britain. The aim of these arrangements, with Canada and the United States, would be the creation of an Anglophone North Atlantic Free Trade and Investment Area, involving both North American countries and the UK. This combined market would have a GDP of $25tr, comfortably larger than the present combined EU GDP of over $19tr., which falls by circa $3tr when the UK element is removed[15].

During his visit to the UK in June 2019, President Trump was enthusiastic about a bilateral deal with the UK, stating that the US is committed to a "phenomenal trade deal" with the UK as soon as it leaves the EU[16]. When Ireland's two biggest trading partners start moving towards a mutually beneficial new agreement, it is time to take serious note.

The more radical possibility would be actual UK membership of the North American Free Trade Area (NAFTA). While many in the UK would see this as a very desirable outcome, there are considerable difficulties on the regulatory side, even if tariffs are already extremely low between the NAFTA countries and the EU, including the UK[17]. However, the traditionally close relationship between London and Ottawa/Washington should ensure that any potential obstacles could be overcome. In any event, if membership of NAFTA was to be off the agenda, the UK could confidently expect to conclude early separate trade agreements with the US and Canada, once circumstances allow the UK to enter into trade agreements post-Brexit. In addition, the threat from US Speaker Nancy Pelosi to scupper any US–UK trade deal, if the post-Brexit arrangements on the island of Ireland pose a danger to the GFA, is a potential hazard further down the road[18]. Whether this is a serious issue or merely rhetoric remains to be seen but it would be a foolhardy Irish Government that would place huge reliance on it.

The Irish economic model has been built on American investment and easy trade arrangements between the EU and the USA. Anything which threatens that environment is a major risk to Ireland. Also, any extra advantages given to the UK over Ireland would obviously be detrimental to Ireland's interests. Therefore, the likely developments in the next few years need careful watching, from a Dublin point of view.

While US relations with the UK are likely to warm considerably in the next few years, the same cannot be said for EU–US relations, which have been under strain since President Trump was elected in the USA in 2016.

The immediate risk of an Atlantic trade war was averted by an agreement struck during the visit of EU Commission President Jean Claude Juncker to Washington in July 2018, which included bilateral commitments to have a fundamental look at future arrangements over a wide range of areas. This may be a temporary truce as there are potential disputes in areas such as intellectual property rights; taxing the digital giants; food standards, including the use of genetically modified organisms (GMOs); data protection issues, etc.[19]

It would appear that Germany is the main target of the US's unhappiness with the EU. This stems from the view in Washington that Germany is unduly benefitting from the low currency rate of the euro. The German trade surplus of 8% of its GDP provides ample credibility to Trump's claim[20]. In addition, Trump's support for the Brexiteers in the UK has angered the Remainers in London and Brussels. A flavour of the President's view can be gauged from his personal tweet: "Too bad that the European Union is being so tough on the United Kingdom and Brexit. The E.U. is likewise a brutal trading partner with the United States, which will change. Sometimes in life you have to let people breathe before it all comes back to bite you!"[21]

Ireland has a huge interest in maintaining harmonious relations between Brussels and Washington. However, it is doubtful if Ireland's economic interest will be a major consideration for the EU Commission and its relations with Washington. It will be primarily concerned with bigger ticket items, like German car exports and that country's investment in the USA.

Unlike mainland Europe, the Irish have serious political clout in the US, with 33m Americans, declaring themselves to have Irish ethnic origins. In Canada, the number is 4.5m. This means that administrations in Washington and Ottawa are much more receptive to Irish concerns and that the access that Irish representatives have in those capitals, can be used to mitigate protectionist tendencies against our goods, provided we are not a small subcategory of the EU.

There has always been a desire in the US to assist Ireland. It goes back to the early days of the Irish Free State. On 27 March 1933, the newly elected US President Franklin D Roosevelt met with the new Irish State's diplomatic representative in Washington, Michael McWhite, and discussed the possibility of a bilateral trade agreement between Ireland and the US. In the official report of the meeting, the President is quoted as saying that something "ought to be done on the line of a reciprocal agreement between the United States and the Free State." He instanced "woollens, homespun, linens, lace, etc. in the manufacture of which you Irish excelled and for which there would be such a demand here."[22] That goodwill for Ireland is still strong in Washington. If

Ireland was outside the EU, it would be free to have its own free trade agreement with the Americans or be part of a North Atlantic free trade area with the UK, Canada and the US. Even if we had to go it alone, the strength of the Irish lobby in Congress is such that it is likely that we could obtain good terms and there would be no danger that we would become unintentional collateral damage in an EU–US trade spat.

In the case of Canada, as I experienced myself, there has always been an open door to Irish representatives and a sympathetic hearing. Canada was the country which gave refuge to so many of the Irish Famine migrants, assisted the new Irish Free State to get international recognition, etc. In the recent recession, following the financial crisis, Canada generously opened its immigration door to young Irish migrants, a practical demonstration of goodwill. In addition, the Canadian authorities assisted in several other ways during the Bailout. This was a reflection of our ethnic links with that country. Australia and New Zealand also provided employment opportunities during the great recession in Ireland.

Britain, Ireland and the Commonwealth

The UK is also looking to its traditional links with Australia and New Zealand, two countries which also have strong Irish connections, for early free trade agreements, which would be very attractive to these States. Although not large in economic terms, the two southern hemisphere countries clearly represent an early opportunity for the UK to conclude trade arrangements with like-minded advanced economies. Both countries have clearly stated their desire to conclude early deals with the UK.

The then New Zealand Prime Minister Bill English, said in Downing Street on 13 January 2017, "In the longer term, we agree on the potential for a bold, new UK–New Zealand free trade agreement and I look forward to starting early discussions on this in due course."

Both sides followed up and on a visit to London in January 2019, the New Zealand Prime Minister Jacinda Arden, confirmed that her country was "ready and willing" to sign a post-Brexit trade deal with the UK. Once the UK recovered its ability to enter its own trade arrangements, this deal will be signed, she insisted[23].

As early as the G20 summit in Hangzhou, in September 2016, the then Australian Prime Minister Malcolm Turnbull, said, "From our point of view, (we are) getting in to deal with the British early, to ensure that we are able to negotiate a very strong, very open free-trade agreement with Britain."

Australian Trade and Investment Minister, Steven Ciobo, told Bloomberg News after meeting the then UK Secretary of State for International Trade, Liam Fox, in March 2018 that a UK–Australian trade deal could come into force the day after the transition period, post-Brexit, ended[24].

These developments could have implications for Ireland, and if we continue to stand aloof from the rest of the Anglophone world, it will lead to our isolation from our natural allies and from our Diaspora.

However, much of the early enthusiasm in London about easy trade deals has evaporated as these deals have proved more complex and difficult than some of the Brexiteers had anticipated. Having had a ringside seat, during my six years in Ottawa, at the detailed and torturous discussions that led to the Comprehensive Trade and Economic Agreement (CETA) between the EU and Canada, I can readily appreciate the time delays. However, given the size and affluence of the British market, I have no doubt but that the British will eventually have a wide network of future trade agreements, once they start exercising the right to an independent foreign commercial policy.

Another area in the Anglophone world where Ireland should keep a watchful eye is possible trade developments in the wider Commonwealth. The Commonwealth, or more appropriately the early Dominions including Ireland, operated the Imperial Preference system, with varying degrees of enthusiasm up to the Second World War[25]. However, in recent times, the trade aspect of the Commonwealth has fallen away, and members have tended much more towards regional trade arrangements rather than a Commonwealth-wide system.

There have been some fitful initiatives towards giving the Commonwealth a more focused trade dimension. At a meeting of the Heads of Government of the Commonwealth in Malta in 2005, and against a background of the Doha round of WTO negotiations going nowhere, the concept of pursuing trade agreements among

Commonwealth members, was endorsed[26]. However, with the largest economy in the Commonwealth, the UK, proscribed by its membership of the EU, from entering into trade arrangements on its own account, the impetus for greater free trade within the Commonwealth was in reality a futile exercise at that time.

However, with the UK freed from its previous restrictions, India becoming a major player in international trade and Canada actively looking to reduce its economic dependence on the US, it is probably an opportune time to look at a new trade initiative within the Commonwealth. Ireland, whether inside or outside the EU needs to monitor these developments very carefully as they may impinge on market conditions in some of our most valuable trading partners, e.g. the UK, Canada, Australia, India, South Africa, etc.

The obvious question arises as to whether Ireland should seek to re-join the Commonwealth. Coming from an Irish Republican background, there is an instinctive reluctance to consider that option. However, having been Irish Ambassador to three Commonwealth countries, Canada, Jamaica and the Bahamas, as well as having lived in Australia for several years, my opinion has changed over time.

Firstly, let us put a number of misconceptions to bed. Re-joining the Commonwealth does not mean that the Queen of England would have any formal role in the Republic of Ireland. I have heard people say that they could not return to the pre-1949 position of having the British monarch as the de jure Head of State for the Irish State. I agree, and the majority of Commonwealth countries are Republics, 32 out of the 54 total. Secondly the throne of England does not have an automatic right to be head of the Commonwealth, although that is the position at the moment and likely to continue for some time into the future, it is a matter for the Commonwealth nations themselves to decide.

Also, the Commonwealth has long dropped the title "British Commonwealth" to the much simpler title, Commonwealth of Nations. There is no denying the colonial origins of the institution but here again change has been occurring over a period. Several countries such as Mozambique, French-speaking Cameroon and Rwanda, who were never part of the British Empire, are now active members of the Commonwealth, helping to lessen its overt British colonial connotations. If a proud and successful country like India can be happily accommodated within the Commonwealth of Nations, then it would seem possible for Ireland to give serious consideration to re-joining the 54-nation organisation (Table 4). It should be noted that Cyprus and Malta, current members of the EU, are also in the Commonwealth.

In a post-Brexit world, it will be important for Ireland to have as many friends as possible. Re-joining the Commonwealth and by so doing greatly strengthening our links with countries as diverse as Jamaica, the Bahamas, India, Tanzania, Western Samoa, Singapore, etc. would seem to be a very sensible idea. In fact, it is only our traditional antagonism to the English royals, that has kept us out. In a post-GFA and post-Brexit world, that would appear not to be reason enough for our self-imposed exclusion.

Re-joining the Commonwealth would also send a signal to the pro-British community in the North that Ireland has matured as a State and is no longer gripped by anti-Britishness. It would be a gesture of reconciliation, at a time, when it is badly needed. Certainly, if Ireland can apply for Observer status at La Francophonie, the French equivalent of the Commonwealth, it seems perverse that it would not entertain some association with the Anglophone equivalent which is full of countries with large numbers of our Diaspora.

The reality is that the present Irish Government and elite are trying to graph a false European mainland identity onto the Irish nation, which is solidly entrenched, along with its Diaspora, in the Anglophone world. In many ways, the pro-EU group in Ireland see the country as a small State on the periphery of the EU, while those who wish for Irexit believe it is part of the world-wide Anglosphere, where tens of millions of our kith and kin live.

Table 3

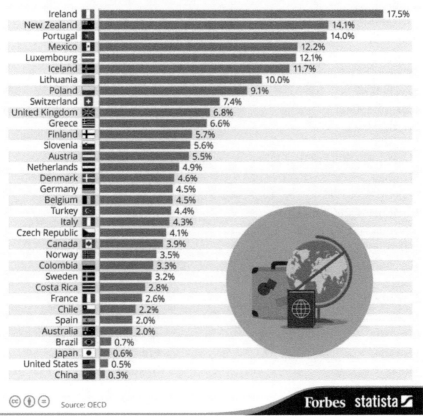

The Countries With The Most People Living Overseas
Percentage of the native-born population living abroad in 2014

Country	Percentage
Ireland	17.5%
New Zealand	14.1%
Portugal	14.0%
Mexico	12.2%
Luxembourg	12.1%
Iceland	11.7%
Lithuania	10.0%
Poland	9.1%
Switzerland	7.4%
United Kingdom	6.8%
Greece	6.6%
Finland	5.7%
Slovenia	5.6%
Austria	5.5%
Netherlands	4.9%
Denmark	4.6%
Germany	4.5%
Belgium	4.5%
Turkey	4.4%
Italy	4.3%
Czech Republic	4.1%
Canada	3.9%
Norway	3.5%
Colombia	3.3%
Sweden	3.2%
Costa Rica	2.8%
France	2.6%
Chile	2.2%
Spain	2.0%
Australia	2.0%
Brazil	0.7%
Japan	0.6%
United States	0.5%
China	0.3%

Source: OECD

Forbes statista

311

Table 4

Commonwealth Countries by region

Africa
Botswana
Cameroon
Gambia, The
Ghana
Kenya
Kingdom of Swaziland
Lesotho
Malawi
Mauritius
Mozambique
Namibia
Nigeria
Rwanda
Seychelles
Sierra Leone
South Africa
Uganda
United Republic of Tanzania
Zambia

Asia
Bangladesh
Brunei Darussalam
India
Malaysia
Maldives
Pakistan
Singapore
Sri Lanka

Caribbean and Americas
Antigua and Barbuda
Bahamas, The
Barbados
Belize
Canada
Dominica
Grenada
Guyana
Jamaica
Saint Lucia
St Kitts and Nevis
St Vincent and The Grenadines
Trinidad and Tobago

Europe
Cyprus
Malta
United Kingdom

Pacific
Australia
Fiji
Kiribati
Nauru
New Zealand
Papua New Guinea
Samoa
Solomon Islands
Tonga
Tuvalu
Vanuatu

References

1. *"Global Ireland's Footprint to 2025"*, 2018 p 23. Published by the Government of Ireland.

2. Population UK estimated the population of Northern Ireland at 1,886,788 in July 2018. The Central Statistics Office in the Republic estimated that the Population of the South of Ireland in April of the same year as 4.857,000 (CSO Statistical Release 28 August 2018) giving an overall total of 6,743,788.

3. Article 2 Irish Constitution as amended. *"Furthermore, the Irish Nation cherishes its special affinity with people of Irish ancestry living abroad who shares its cultural identity and heritage."*

4. Ireland and the Irish Abroad. Report of the Task Force on Policy regarding Emigrants to the Minister for Foreign Affairs Brian Cowen, T.D. August 2002.

5. Irish Government reshuffle after Finance Minister Charlie McCreevy was made Ireland's EU Commissioner September 2004

6. Tim Pat Coogan, *Whenever Green is Worn*, 2000, published by Hutchinson

7. American Community Survey, 2010-2015, conducted by the American census Bureau.

8. Canada, Government of Canada, Statistics. 2016 census, *https://www12. statcan.gc.ca/census-recensement/2016/dp-pd/prof/details/page.cfm?Lang=E &Geo1=PR&Code1=01&Geo2=PR&Code2=01&SearchType=Begins&Sea rchPR=01&B1=Population&type=0*

9. Canada, Government of Canada Statistics 2016 census

10. Tim Pat Coogan, *Whenever Green is Worn*, 2000, p 613

11. Rob Mullally *"A Short History of the Irish in Jamaica"*, *Jamirish@sbcglobal. net*

12. David Stanistreet and Eric Heffer *Ireland, the Anglosphere and the EU* by published by Primary Access, 14 May 2019, *https://www.primaryaccess. co.uk/spotlights/2019/ireland-the-anglosphere-and-the-eu/, retrieved*

13. https://www.cso.ie/en/index.html

14. Andrew Stoler and Geoff Raby, *The Realities of a US-UK Free Trade Agreement*, Feb 2017, Policy Exchange London, *https://policyexchange. org.uk/conservativehome-policy-exchanges-geoff-raby-considers-the-realities-of-a-us-uk-free-trade-agreement/.* Retrieved 19 Nov 2019

15. World Economic Database, International Monetary Fund, 10 April 2019, *https://www.imf.org/external/pubs/ft/weo/2019/01/weodata/index.aspx*

16. *"Trump UK visit: US committed to 'a phenomenal trade deal'* BBC News 4 June 2019, *https://www.bbc.com/news/av/uk-48517426/trump-uk-visit-us-committed-to-a-phenomenal-trade-deal.* Retrieved 9 June 2019

17. Daniel Capparelli, London School of Economics, Brexit Blog, 29, June 2017, *https://blogs.lse.ac.uk/brexit/.* Retrieved 19 Nov 2019

18. *"Nancy Pelosi warns against weakening Good Friday Agreement" Irish News* Belfast, 18 April 2019, *https://www.irishnews.com/news/2019/04/18/news/nancy-pelosi-warns-against-weakening-good-friday-agreement-1600484/*

19. Rozina Sabur and Nick Allen, *"Donald Trump and Jean-Claude Juncker agree deal to stave off trade war" Daily Telegraph* 26 July 2018, *https://www.telegraph.co.uk/news/2018/07/25/donald-trump-jean-claude-juncker-agree-deal-stave-trade-war/.* Retrieved 19 Nov 2019

20. Wolfgang Munchau *"In a Trade Way, Germany is the Weakest Link" Financial Times* 18 March 2018, *https://www.ft.com/content/ec775fea-2916-11e8-b27e-cc62a39d57a0.* Retrieved 19 Nov 2019

21. Tweet from President Trump, 11 April 2019

22. Documents on Irish Foreign Policy Volume 4 page 234

23. *"Brexit: New Zealand's Jacinda Ardern says trade deal 'a priority'* BBC Report, 21 January 2019, *https://www.bbc.com/news/uk-politics-46946692.* Retrieved 19 Nov 2019

24. Oli Smith, *"Brexit trade vow: Australia confirms HUGE trade deal will be SIGNED 'the day Brexit ends'" Daily Express*, 27 March 2018. *https://www.express.co.uk/news/uk/937395/Brexit-News-uk-eu-transition-trade-deal-australia-2021.* Retrieved 19 Nov 2019

25. Lord Beaverbrook(1963). *The Decline and Fall of Lloyd George.* London: Collins.

26. Valetta Statement on multilateral trade, 26 Nov 2005. Commonwealth Secretariat

Chapter 13

Alternative Policy Options Open to the Irish Government

"Europe's nations should be guided towards the Superstate without their people understanding what is happening. This can be accomplished by successive steps, each disguised as having an economic purpose, but which will eventually and irreversibly lead to Federation."

Jean Monnet

This is a quote from a letter written by EU founding father, Jean Monnet, to a friend in April 1952[1] and has provided the pathway to Federation for those seeking that outcome. There is an acceptance among the European zealots that too overt a promotion of this idea would inevitably lead to a backlash and hence the need for public caution and ambiguity.

For many in Ireland, including myself, such an eventual outcome would be personally anathema and a betrayal of the sacrifices of the many generations which struggled, against massive odds, to gain sovereignty for Ireland. Therefore, I cannot support a continuation of the present policy and the erosion of powers from Dublin.

There is, of course, a counterargument that the EU is never likely to go down that route and that there is very little current appetite for such an approach. However, the EU goes through periods of Constitutional stasis but there has never been a reversal in the process of political integration. Every new crisis is used as a new opportunity for Brussels to seize more power. Again, Monnet put it very well when he wrote, "I always believed that Europe would be built through crisis and that it would be the some of their solutions."[2]

Have a crisis in immigration and suddenly the EU is taking over migration policy; have a crisis in banking and we could end up with a European banking union; greatly exaggerate the threat of Putin's military and hopefully the people will support a European army; etc. In this way, the fundamental structures of the Nation States are stripped away, piece by piece. The public and the politicians are far too busy firefighting the immediate crisis to enter into any deep reflection about what is happening. In the meantime, demonise all those who oppose the onward march towards achieving Brussels control. It has been a successful strategy.

Under the current policies, the Irish State is sleepwalking into oblivion, without the bulk of our people, or even many of our politicians, ever being aware of the nature of the project. We badly need to wake up to this insidious absorption and devise a new set of policies. Ireland seriously needs to start looking for alternative options for its future relationship with Brussels. In addition, the Irish public need to be exposed to a variety of views and not just fed the existing suffocating uniformity, which sometimes passes locally as public debate on this issue.

After decades of pro-EU propaganda and a united and determined local political consensus, backed by a well-resourced EU industry, the difficulties of getting any alternative view across to the Irish public should not be underestimated. In fact, these difficulties are considerable. The establishment has essentially pushed the narrative that the economic prosperity of the country and our national identity, even our DNA, is tied up with EU membership. According to that line of argument, being critical of the EU is unpatriotic and Irexit is simply untenable. The attitude is that there is no need for reasoned argument on the issues, we simply hold them as self-evident. This represents a dangerous complacency.

However, there are considerable pressure points building against the accepted narrative and the likelihood is that these pressures will increase in the future. Ten years ago, there was virtually no political euroscepticism in Italy, yet today powerful forces in Rome are determined to resist further encroachment from Brussels. Germany now has a strong opposition to EU Federalism, as has France and many other EU States. Ireland is also likely to see a major growth in resistance to Brussels control.

However, at the outset it should be recognised that the Brexit process, which will undoubtedly make EU membership for Ireland much less attractive and hence problematic, in the short term has paradoxically made many in Ireland rally around the EU. The row over the Northern Ireland Backstop largely morphed into a traditional British–Irish spat, coupled with overtones of Green v Orange in the North. The demand to support your own "tribe", whether coming from a eurosceptical Irish Republican background or a pro-Remain Unionist, is considerable. For many these pressures can be decisive in pushing people back into the tribal camps, if only for the short term.

The Brexit process has been extremely messy, and nobody could have predicted the level of indecision and, to be frank, incompetence of the Theresa May Government. Having worked with some excellent and competent Whitehall public servants and politicians over the years, the performance of the British system, under May, was unrecognisable from previous administrations. The UK made mistake after mistake, including the fundamental error of accepting the EU's sequencing, whereby the UK had to make a number of substantial commitments in the withdrawal process, without getting concrete assurances about the future relationship. In retrospect, it would have been so much better if the withdrawal and the trade agreements had proceeded in tandem. While this may have been contrary to EU procedures, these procedures can be changed or discussions can happen informally, outside the Treaty framework, and subsequently any understandings agreed, be later adopted as a legal text at the appropriate time. Many an official "non-paper" was passed between negotiators and later became the basis of a legal agreement. This did not happen because the EU wanted to put the UK on the back foot and Theresa May very foolishly agreed. Brussels could have been more generous. After all, the European Council guidelines for the Brexit discussions explicitly states that nothing is agreed until everything is agreed[3].

While I expected the EU to be less than happy with Brexit, I never thought that Brussels would be so dogmatic and inflexible with the weak Theresa May administration. They simply decided at the outset that the UK should dance to their tune. There could be no mercy for deserters. Of course, they were assisted and even urged on this course by many

Remainers in the establishment in Britain, who simply would not accept the Brexit decision, which was mainly carried by working-class support.

Ireland has very different interests in these negotiations than EU countries such as Slovenia, Malta, Hungary, etc. In addition, the professional cadre of bureaucrats in Brussels are dedicated to establishing the ever-closer union, envisaged by Jean Monnet, which enjoys no deep support in Ireland.

As the discussions move beyond the process of withdrawal towards a longer-term agreement on how we manage EU–UK relations, strains will undoubtedly emerge between the Irish national interest of a good and harmonious friendship with London, and a more confrontational and antagonistic approach by Brussels, as it seeks to safeguard its project, namely the creation of the United States of Europe.

Ireland does not have the luxury of having any sympathy with the current sentiment inside the EU institutions that Britain needs to be "punished" for its decision to leave and that, under no account can the British be "rewarded" for Brexit. Britain needs to be made an example of "pour encourager les autres". As senior German MEP, Hans Olaf Henkel, who has served on the European Parliament's Industry, Research and Energy Committee, stated "They would seek to make sure that Brexit is such a catastrophe that no country dares to take the step of leaving the EU again."[4]

As the former leader of the Social Democratic and Labour Party (SDLP) in Northern Ireland and Nobel Peace Prize Laureate, John Hume, was fond of saying regarding this type of thinking, "An eye for an eye leaves both parties blind."

The danger for Ireland is that the EU negotiating position is based on the need to protect the European project and unbending on the sanctity of the Single Market; and on the other side with Boris Johnson as PM, the British position will become, almost certainly, equally assertive about his country's ability for independent action in economic matters. As a consequence, we may end up in a destructive stand-off between Brussels and London.

Any retaliatory action against the British is likely to disproportionally affect Ireland. It is clearly in our interest to vigorously fight that type of warped thinking. Unfortunately, all the indications from Brussels are that this impulse of being grudging to the UK, post Brexit, is deeply fixed in the mindset of the EU institutions. Ireland has played a very negative role throughout the Article 50 negotiations. The issue of the Backstop was used as a weapon against the British desire to leave the EU[5]. It is time for a change, in Ireland's own national interest. Ireland needs Brexit to be a success, not a damaging failure.

In addition, the EU is currently in some turmoil, as the popular resistance to attempts by the Federalists to diminish the role of the Nation State gathers momentum, right across the Union. Also, as outlined in Chapter 10 on ever-closer union, almost all future plans by Brussels seem to go against Ireland's national interest. On the RTÉ radio show "The Business" on 9 March 2019, former Irish Minister for European Affairs and noted pro-EU enthusiast, Lucinda Creighton, in a discussion with myself and former Taoiseach, Bertie Ahern, bemoaned Ireland's negative response to the EU's future integration plans: "We simply cannot go on saying no to everything".

Ms Creighton was pointing out an obvious development, namely that the overall drift of EU policies is seriously changing the relative balance of advantage for Ireland of remaining inside the EU. Maybe it is time for a fundamental re-examination of the future direction of Irish policy towards the EU, rather than simply accepting the Brussels-orientated direction as inevitable.

In the circumstances, any prudent administration in Dublin would start to examine its options and leave nothing off the table. Having worked inside the Irish Government system, for anybody to make such a suggestion to the current administration would be, in the words of a former senior colleague of mine, "seriously career damaging." However, we must overcome our tendency to groupthink and regularly road test the current policies.

Given the fact that the current EU problems, and especially in the Eurozone, are essentially structural, not cyclical, and will not be easily rectified, we have no other option. They are largely self-inflicted through the imposition of a poorly constructed single currency and a desire to use the Single Market as a way of imposing a top down, single size fits all type of economic management. The fault lines cannot be rectified without radical change, such as large-scale fiscal transfers between

Member States, something which would not be assented to by the Member States' democratic Governments. Hence the probability that the Eurozone experiment will end in tears.

Article 50

Therefore, if Ireland ever decided to change its relationship with the EU, very valuable lessons have been learned in the Brexit process. I believe that, on all sides, there would be no desire to repeat the British experience. This would include ensuring that a departing administration had a leader and support system, who actually wanted to achieve a successful break with the EU; not triggering Article 50 until the negotiation positions were well developed; and using the two-year time frame in Article 50 as a preparatory period; and most importantly not allowing the EU to totally dictate the sequencing of the terms and timing of the negotiations, etc.

Article 50 was included in the Lisbon Treaty without much consideration or thought that it would be actually used for a country like the UK. The Article itself is very short and simple and devoid of any great detail. The author of the article was former British ambassador to the EU and committed europhile, John Kerr, now a member of the House of Lords. Kerr has stated that "It seemed to me very likely that a dictatorial regime would then, in high dudgeon, want to storm out. And to have a procedure for storming out seemed to be quite a sensible thing to do – to avoid the legal chaos of going with no agreement."

Kerr has admitted that it never occurred to him at the time it was created that it would apply to the UK. Kerr was then Secretary-General of the European Convention, tasked with drawing up a Constitution for the EU in 2002–03.[6] Article 50, like much of the ill-fated EU Constitution, was simply transcribed, word for word, later into the Lisbon Treaty.

In the light of the experience of Brexit, there will be a need to study how this Article can be operated more effectively in the future. With so much discontent about and within the EU, it is highly likely that Article 50 will find itself at the centre of future controversies as the EU membership expands to the east and south, while contracting in the north and west of Europe. Some similarities could be drawn with the Roman Empire which eventually became centred on Constantinople (Istanbul).

Ireland should seize the initiative and propose new arrangements for those seeking to use the Article 50 escape clause.

Against that background, namely Brexit and the likelihood of further crises within the Eurozone, what are the policy options that are available to any Irish administration seeking a new way forward? Radical and innovative ways forward may have to be considered and new frameworks constructed.

Special status for Ireland within the EU (OMR)

However, before Ireland looked to a triggering of Article 50, it needs to explore whether it would be possible to stay in the EU under special conditions.

This scenario would be difficult to achieve inside the EU but given the circumstances of Brexit, which the Irish Government opposed, and our great desire to maintain the peace brought about by the GFA, a case for a special status for Ireland, inside the EU, could be credibly argued with Brussels which allowed the country to stay in a customs unions with the UK but retain unfettered access to the Single Market. I would not envisage any problem with the British side agreeing to this unusual arrangement as they have at least as much self-interest in avoiding a hard border in Ireland, as Dublin.

There are a number of possibilities but perhaps the most appropriate might be a new arrangement based on the category of the Outermost Region (OMR). This concept is recognised in the Treaty on the Functioning of the EU[7]. It allows for the EU Commission, with the agreement of the European Parliament, to propose measures for areas with particular difficulties which are remote from the European Mainland. The most notable of the OMR areas are the Canary Islands (Spain), Madeira and Azores (Portugal) and the French Overseas Departments (French Guiana, Guadeloupe, Martinique, Mayotte, and Réunion). These territories are part of the EU and subject to EU law, both primary and secondary legislation, but because of their physical separation from the European mainland, enjoy special exemptions to reflect their particular circumstances. The largest by population is the Canary Islands with 2.1m inhabitants. The islands are not part of the EU for the purposes of VAT, as outlined in Article 6 of the VAT Directive[8].

If Ireland was granted a special status and permitted a Customs Union with the UK, there would be a legitimate need for the EU to ensure that the island of Ireland was not being used as a backdoor to bring contraband goods via the open border into the rest of the EU. This could mean that Irish goods arriving in other Member States of the EU would be subject to customs procedures. However, since Irish trade direct with the EU mainland is much smaller than through the UK land bridge, this is not as big an impediment as it might appear[9]. Also, the increasing use of technology and tracking mechanisms, means that the old customs regimes are changing and becoming much more targeted and intelligence led. They are much less intrusive. Hence, an increase in custom procedures between Ireland and mainland Europe may be a price well worth paying to maintain an open trading arrangement in the longer term with the North and Britain. The issue of regulatory misalignment, between the EU and the UK, would still have to be monitored but changes here could be established well away from the border.

There is no precedent for an entire Member State of the EU being designated as an OMR but the circumstances for Ireland, post-Brexit, are unique in the EU. Soon Ireland will find itself in a difficult geographical position and, moreover, with a pressing political need to avoid a hard border. However, there is no denying that Ireland will be physically separated from the European mainland and in the circumstances will be an outermost part of the EU. Any post-Brexit arrangement for the island of Ireland needs to take account of our special circumstances.

However, there may well be severe resistance from Brussels and some Member States to Ireland taking on OMR status, as it would appear as if the country was staying inside the EU on á la carte basis. For the europhiles in Dublin, this would be anathema as it would signal that in the post-Brexit context, the country was moving away from the centre stage and was accepting that it was very much on the periphery. Also, given the hostility that our benign treatment of US multinationals arouses among other Member States, it is difficult to see them readily agreeing to Ireland getting new concessions. The imposition of custom procedures with our fellow Member States would of course be unwelcome for industry, especially the multinational sector. However, industry would soon adopt to the extra form filling.

In addition, the growing number of eurosceptics in Ireland (bound to greatly increase once Brexit is out of the way) would see OMR as a betrayal. They would argue, with some justification, that it would not protect Ireland from the negative effects of many of the EU's current and future policies, associated with the march towards ever closer union. OMR would not stop Ireland getting sucked into the further militarisation of the EU; it would not assist in moving away from using the accident-prone euro; it would not allow for the re-creation of an independent Central Bank; it would not allow the country take control of its borders in the immigration area; it would not shield Ireland from the march towards Brussels control of taxation, etc.

However, it needs to be accepted that all possible scenarios for Ireland, post Brexit, involve a suboptimal outcome to some extent. It is really a question of selecting the least bad option. However, in any solution, the political imperative must be to maintain a frictionless border and hence all scenarios which achieve that objective are worth considering, even if they contain some negative aspects.

The Norwegian model

The probability is that the EU would not be prepared to offer the Republic a special status, namely outside the Customs Union but inside the formal structures of the EU itself. It would cross far too many Red Lines and would be contrary to the whole philosophy of those in the Brussels bureaucracy, and their devotion to the concept of ever-closer political and economic union. However, withdrawing from the Customs Union may be what is required for the long term avoidance of a physical border on the island of Ireland. In these circumstances, the Irish Government should look at exiting the EU but maintaining as close as possible economic links with the Single Market.

The Norwegian model would entail Ireland agreeing to a similar type arrangement with the EU, that the Kingdom of Norway currently enjoys. Norway, while not one of the EU Member States, is a member of the European Free Trade Area (EFTA) and also participates in the European Economic Area (EEA).

EFTA is essentially for those States in western Europe who are not members of the European Union. It consists of Norway, Iceland,

Switzerland and Liechtenstein. The UK was a founder member of the organisation in 1960[10] and remained a member up to its accession to the then EEC in 1973. Ireland seriously considered joining in the discussions on its establishment in the 1950s. The then Taoiseach Éamon de Valera was sympathetic[11]. It was once considered as a rival to the then EEC but lost momentum when most of the member countries, including the UK, left and joined the EEC.

The current four Member EFTA States are among the countries with the highest income per capita in the world. The EFTA Convention regulates economic relations between the Member States and EFTA also has a network of free trade agreements, currently at 29 FTAs, with 40 partners, outside the EU[12], see Table 5. Should Ireland become a member of EFTA, it would have access to these international agreements.

Three of the EFTA members, Norway, Iceland and Liechtenstein, are also part of the EEA. The EEA was established in an international Agreement, 1 January 1994, which allows for the Single Market to be extended to non-EU members. The rules of the Single Market are essentially set by the EU and followed by these three countries[13].

Under the EEA there is currently a requirement to follow the four fundamental freedoms of the EU, namely goods, services, labour and capital. The small State, the Principality of Liechtenstein, uses clauses in the EEA agreement to restrict the movement of persons. Article 112(1) of the EEA Agreement reads: "If serious economic, societal or environmental difficulties of a sectorial or regional nature, liable to persist are arising, a Contracting Party may unilaterally take appropriate measures under the conditions and procedures laid down in Article 113." The restrictions used by Liechtenstein are further reinforced by Protocol 15 (Article 5–7) of the EEA Agreement. This allows Liechtenstein to keep specific restrictions on the free movement of labour[14].

In addition, members of the EEA are not part of the CAP or very importantly, the Common Fisheries Policy. They are not part of the drive for ever closer political union.

While Iceland, Norway and Switzerland, at different stages, applied for membership of the EU in the past, they have all withdrawn their applications[15,16]. Norway just let its application expire after the second unsuccessful referendum in 1994. Hence, none are actively seeking membership at present. There is no great popular or political support for joining the EU in these States. With the UK departure from the Union, it is unlikely that there will be any further membership expansion in the North Atlantic area. There is much more likelihood of further contraction in this geographical region than any addition of a new member. The UK and Greenland have departed, while the Faroes, Norway and Iceland do not seem keen on joining.

After the referendum result in Britain became clear, there was much discussion of the UK re-joining EFTA, post-Brexit. There were arguments in favour and against. Some felt it could be helpful as an interim measure, while the final details of the new UK–EU arrangements were being worked out. One of the strongest backers of this idea, was the Chairman of the prestigious Campaign for an Independent Britain (CIB), Edward Spalton. He argued that many Brexiteers seriously underestimated the difficulties of exiting the EU, after 40 years of convergence and that the UK should take its EU withdrawal in stages. The acrimony and ill feeling that the Brexit discussions have engendered and the election of Boris Johnson as Prime Minister essentially ended this possible option for the UK.

For Ireland, with the departure of the UK from the EU and great uncertainty with the future direction of the EU itself, there is probably an even stronger argument for Ireland opting for an arrangement similar to Norway with the EU. This could involve formal membership of EFTA or a bilateral treaty with the EU. It would allow for continued membership of the EEA. As in the case of the UK, it would allow Ireland time to consider its longer-term options, as the implications of Brexit and its consequences became clearer for the country.

In the case of the UK, the main argument in favour of re-joining EFTA and staying in the EEA was that it allowed the UK continued free trade with the Single Market and would in theory have immediate access to the benefits of the EFTA trade Agreements.

However, EEA countries are required to follow EU rules and standards and are not a formal part of the process of deciding these arrangements. For the UK, this was a big disadvantage but since Ireland has only 1% of the voting rights in the Council of Ministers, this is not as big a drawback as in the case of the UK. Ireland has always been a rule taker in the EU. For many in Britain, membership of EFTA and the EEA is essentially a halfway house type of situation and would not have represented the Clean Brexit break with the EU that they feel the referendum result demanded.

The other principal difficulty for the UK in re-joining EFTA and staying in the EEA relates to the issue of Freedom of Movement of Labour, or in other words the migration issue. This was a major theme in the Brexit referendum and there is virtual political unanimity in the UK about the need to control the numbers immigrating. Switzerland who has similar difficulties as the UK with the concept of no restrictions on the freedom of movement of workers, is covered by a number of separate bilateral agreements and has rejected EEA membership in a referendum in December 1992[17]. This issue remains an irritant in the EU–Swiss relationship.

In Ireland's case, we will need to examine all the fundamentals of our relations with London and Brussels, post-Brexit. The Norwegian model may become our preferred way forward, even as a stop gap. One of the immediate beneficiaries would of course be the UK which would be relieved of its requirement to solve the thorny border issue. Both countries could continue with the mutually beneficial arrangements currently between them. The downside would be the need for customs arrangements between the Republic and the European mainland. As mentioned already, this would only involve a very small amount of Ireland's foreign trade which goes directly to the continent.

As the value to Ireland of CAP support declines, so does the need for our agriculture to remain within the control of Brussels, also diminish. If Ireland operated the Norway model, the country would have the option to allocate more of its own resources to directly supporting rural families in an environmentally sensitive manner. There would be large savings from the annual net contribution to the EU budget. The Norway model would also allow Ireland to manage its huge fisheries resources in an environmentally sound and sustainable manner. In such circumstances, there would be a strong case for some joint management with the UK, given the shared fishery stocks. The Norwegian model would also remove Ireland from the potential danger of a Brussels imposed tax harmonisation scheme, and indeed from the obligation to engage in ever closer political union.

At the moment, Norway decides, in conjunction with Brussels, which EU programmes it decides to join and pays an appropriate sum for its participation. In any event, the overall sum remitted to Brussels annually is considerably less than Ireland's net contribution[18].

In addition, there are potential attractions to the EU for agreeing Ireland's exit to an EFTA type arrangement. Ireland was very useful in the Brexit negotiations, particularly in extracting a large financial settlement but this has largely passed. To the countries on the European mainland, Germany, France, Netherlands, Finland, etc., it is doubtful whether the continued difficulties in finding a solution to the Irish border issue is worth the candle. As the EU so amply demonstrated in the notorious forced Bailout for Ireland, it is more than willing to dispense with Ireland's vital national interest when faced with wider EU considerations. Given the small size of Ireland, relative to the EU, and the economic importance of mainland European countries ties with Britain, it is extremely unlikely that the issue of the Irish border will be allowed to continue to dog EU/UK relations in the longer run.

Better for us Irish to take matters into our own hands and seek a Norway-type arrangement with Brussels and a Customs Union with the UK.

Max Fac or the Technological Option to the border problem

The UK has clearly indicated that it does not regard a border in the Irish Sea as a long term solution to the problems arising from the need to preserve the GFA and keep the Irish border frictionless. While the EU and the Irish Government may cry foul, there is every likelihood that the UK will refuse to implement the Withdrawal Agreement, if the trade talks fail. In the circumstances, the EU and the UK may have to look to new ways of policing the Irish border in the future.

The technological solution is essentially based on the British Government paper of August 2017. In addition, there are no simple off the shelf solutions available which can be copied from places like the US/Canadian border or Norway/Sweden. Having crossed the Canadian frontier many times, it is not a simple straightforward matter and trade and individuals can be held up for hours at times. Something similar would lead to chaos and possibly civil disorder in Ireland. It should be factored in that the greatest resistance to a hard border lies in the strongly Republican districts just north of the boundary line. It would be a nightmare trying to construct and maintain any new permanent structures. Nobody wants a fixed line of confrontation in the middle of the peaceful Irish countryside.

Therefore, the authorities may have to construct something unique. It will not be perfect and will not be to anybody's 100% satisfaction. As a seasoned negotiator, the late David Ervine of the Progressive Unionist Party (PUP) said during the GFA Talks, everybody should get what they need, not what they want, and there should be parity of pain and satisfaction all round[19].

The first step is to remove any question of using the border for immigration control. The UK has already indicated that it will focus its efforts to limit immigration of EU nationals at the employment level. There is already very good cooperation between the immigration authorities, including sharing information on visa applications, informal liaison officers regularly at Belfast and Dublin airports, etc. This could continue and be enhanced.

These immigration arrangements should in theory continue as before. They can be maintained as long as the UK does not impose visa restrictions on any of the remaining 27 States. This is unlikely, especially in the short to medium term[20]. The other proviso is that Ireland stays out of the Schengen arrangements, and maintains its own mini-Schengen with the UK, Isle of Mann and the Channel Islands. The commitment to the maintenance of the Common Travel Area in the Withdrawal Agreement, and the recent bilateral memorandum of understanding (MOU) on the issue should assist Ireland to successfully ward off pressure from Brussels on Schengen.

The next area to exempt is, as indicated by the August British paper, local traffic and agriculture[21]. These make up to 80% of trade transactions on the Irish border. They are characterised by high volume and frequency of crossings but low value transactions. However, exempting these will require a level of flexibility from the EU which is not evidenced to date.

The exemptions appear to be compliant with General Agreement on Tariffs and Trade (GATT) regulations, now operated by the World Trade Organisation (WTO).

Dr David Collins, who is Professor of Law at City, University of London, and an acknowledged WTO specialist, has published a pamphlet with the prestigious British Think Tank, Politeia, on Brexit. Collins pointed out that in a free trade arrangement type, along the lines of the recent EU–Canada Comprehensive Economic and Trade Agreement (CETA)[22]:

> The land border between the UK and Ireland need not have any physical infrastructure and as such should not represent a political obstacle to a UK-EU FTA. Article XVIII of the GATT and the Trade Facilitation Agreement of the WTO require that WTO members must minimize customs procedures as far as reasonably possible. Moreover, special arrangements to streamline borders (as between Northern Ireland and the Republic of Ireland) such as those involving regular trader exemptions and technology, are permitted under the exemption for border traffic under Article XXIV of the GATT.

Also, the UK has already indicated that in a limited number of areas, including energy, animal and plant health, transport, etc., it makes perfect sense to align the regulatory requirements throughout the island of Ireland. This can be achieved, in part, through the mechanism of the North/South implementation bodies, a form of all-Ireland quangos, which have operated on an all-island basis in several sectors since 1999. They are an important element of Strand Two of the GFA.

The remaining element, which in reality means large firms with a defined number of employees or turnover, can be accommodated by a trusted trading arrangement. While any British-Irish operation on the border would be sui generis, one model which would be worth looking at is the Australian one[23].

The main features of the Australian Trusted Trader programme (ATT), which is rapidly growing, includes:

- A single point of contact between the Australian Border Service and the Trusted Trader business. Communications are normally electronic.

- A composite monthly return submitted by the Trusted Trader, rather than returns on every cargo.

- A single consolidated return for multi types of goods rather than a different declaration for different goods type.

- Regular discussions between the companies and the Australian Border Service.

- Use of a special logo, clearly designating the goods as coming or going to a Trusted Trading company.

- Extensive use of smart technology in custom clearance such as barcode scanning.

- Priority for these companies in any dealing with the Border Service.

All trusted trader systems operate on a self-assessment and self-regulation basis. Responsible companies will not wish to violate the law, and this would be backed up by a system of audits and on-site inspections, much as the present VAT system operates.

In addition, there could be a further requirement that all HGV operators on the island of Ireland install a special tracking device in their vehicles so that the customs authorities could check whether any company returns tallied with the physical evidence of the tracking device.

These types of arrangements could be modified over time as experience is gained in where snags arise and where it works well. However, if operated with a coordinated mutual recognition programme by the two customs services, it may be sufficient to facilitate all parties desire to avoid a hard border.

There would, of course, still be a need to have some monitoring of vehicles crossing the border on the main routes but this could be achieved through technology and backed up with the use of cameras. There are already cameras installed on the main Dublin–Belfast highway, just south of the border city of Newry. These are unobtrusive, and taken with the other arrangements, might be adequate enough to avoid any new installations.

There may also have to be some limited checks at ports connecting Ireland, both North and South, with Britain. These would constitute a similarly unobtrusive arrangement to ensure that areas which remained aligned on an all island basis, and where there was some divergence with Britain, were also monitored. It is also likely that this system would require some spot checks at mainland European ports on vessels, engaged in direct Irish trade from these ports, to ensure the system was not being abused as a backdoor into the EU.

As with the present EU–Swiss model, a supervising committee[24] comprising expert representatives of the EU and the UK, could meet regularly to monitor its operation and advise authorities on the need for any changes.

There have been doubts raised about the viability of a purely Max Fac solution and critics have pointed out that there is no such working model around the world. The same could have been said about attempts to draw up the GFA. In examining different models for that Agreement, no existing arrangement met the needs of the situation and new concepts and designs were constructed. The Max Fac solution to the Irish border will be the same.

Much of the criticism of the technological approach came from politicians who, apart from having no real knowledge of customs arrangements or technology, had a vested interest in discrediting this approach. They were trying to undermine the Brexit referendum result. On the other hand, I have been struck by the consistent private advice of current and former customs officials who believe that the Max Fac approach is entirely viable, even if it would be expensive and take some time to implement. They claim that this is the way customs procedures in developed economies will go in the future[25].

In support of this view, the Policy Department for Citizens' Rights and Constitutional Affairs of the European Parliament heard testimony from Lars Karlsson, former Director of the World Customs Organisation, to the effect that Max Fac could ensure an open border in Ireland. Karlsson helped prepare "Smart Border 2.0, avoiding a hard border on the island of Ireland for customs control and the free movement of persons."[26]

This study provides background on cross border movement and trade between Northern Ireland and the rest of Ireland and identifies international standards, best practices and technologies that can be used to avoid a 'hard' border as well as case studies that provide insights into creating a smooth border experience. The technical solution provided is based on innovative approaches with a focus on cooperation, best practices and technology that is independent of any political agreements on the UK's exit from the EU and offers a template for future UK-EU border relationships.

This view would appear to have the support of Niall Cody, chairman of the Irish Revenue Commissioners, who in testimony to an Irish Parliamentary Committee stated, "I'm practically 100% certain we will not be providing new trade facilitation bays in whatever parts of Donegal, Monaghan or Cavan." He further confirmed that most cross-border trade related to the food and construction industries and could be documented online and cleared via an automated e-border[27].

The suspicion is that objections to Max Fac are essentially political not practical.

Table 5

EFTA's 38 FTA partners (excluding EU) are: Albania, Bosnia and Herzegovina, Canada, Central American States (Costa Rica, Guatemala and Panama), Chile, Colombia, Egypt, Georgia, the Gulf Cooperation Council (GCC; comprising Bahrain, Kuwait, Oman, Qatar, Saudi Arabia, United Arab Emirates), Hong Kong China, Israel, Jordan, Republic of Korea, Lebanon, Macedonia, Mexico, Montenegro, Morocco, Palestine, Peru, the Philippines, Serbia, Singapore, Southern African Customs Union (SACU; comprising Botswana, Lesotho, Namibia, South Africa, Swaziland), Tunisia, Turkey and Ukraine.

References

1. Extract from a letter written by Jean Monnet to a friend 30 April 1952, quoted by Philip Jones in blog, 12 September 2009. The end of the Nation States of Europe, (The Irish referendum on the Lisbon Treaty October 2nd, 2009)

2. Jean Monnet *Memoirs* 1976, p 417

3. European Council (article 50) Guidelines for Brexit Negotiations, Press Release 29 April 2017, Brussels, *https://ec.europa.eu/commission/publications/european-council-article-50-guidelines-brexit-negotiations_en.* Retrieved 19 Nov 2019

4. Thomas Hunt *"BREXIT REVENGE: Brussels chiefs 'desperate to PUNISH the UK' to save EU, German MEP says"* Express 19 July 2017, https://www.express.co.uk/news/uk/830334/brexit-michel-barnier-guy-verhofstadt-Hans-Olaf-Henkel-mep-eu-talks-lord-livingston. Retrieved 19 Nov 2019

5. Ray Bassett, *Brexit: Options for the Irish Border* p 11, 2018, Politeia

6. Andrew Gray *"Article 50 author Lord Kerr: I didn't have the UK in mind"* Politico.eu 28 March 2017. https://www.politico.eu/article/brexit-article-50-lord-kerr-john-kerr/. Retrieved 19 Nov 2019

7. The Outermost Regions are recognised by the Maastricht and Lisbon Treaties. In addition, the Treaty on the Functioning of the Eu 2007, Article 349 allows for specific measures to be undertaken in favour of the outermost regions due to remoteness, insularity, difficult topography and climate or economic dependence which severely restrain their economic development

8. European Commission. *https://ec.europa.eu/* Turnover taxes in the Canary Islands, accessed 25/April 2019

9. John Whelan, *"EU as a bigger home for Irish exports than the UK is a pipe dream"*, Irish Examiner 2 January 2018, https://www.irishexaminer.com/breakingnews/business/eu-as-a-bigger-home-for-irish-exports-than-uk-is-a-pipe-dream-820899.html. Retrieved 19 Nov 2019

10. EFTA Through the Years, Main events in the History of EFTA 1960 until Today. EFTA Website accessed 26 April 2019, https://www.efta.int/About-EFTA/EFTA-through-years-747

11. Documents on Irish Foreign Policy, Volume 10, p749

12. Global Trade Relations, EFTA Website retrieved 26 April 2019. https://www.efta.int/free-trade

13. European Economic Area (EEAS). Website of the European External Action Service, retrieved on 26 April 2019, https://eeas.europa.eu/diplomatic-network/european-economic-area-eea_en. Retrieved 19 Nov 2019

14. Robert Oulds *"Freedom of Movement between EEA (European Economic Area) States and the EU"* 17 November 2015, published by the Campaign for an Independent Britain. *https://campaignforanindependentbritain.org.uk/freedom-of-movement-between-eea-european-economic-area-states-and-the-eu/*. Retrieved 19 Nov 2019

15. Hortense Goulard, "Switzerland withdraws its application to join the EU , Politico.eu, *https://www.politico.eu/article/switzerland-withdraws-application-to-join-the-eu/*. Retrieved 26 April 2019

16. *"Iceland Drops EU Membership Bid, Interests Better Served Outside the Union"* Guardian, 22 March 2015, *https://www.theguardian.com/world/2015/mar/12/iceland-drops-european-union-membership-bid.* Retrieved 19 November 2019

17. Alan Riding, "Swiss reject tie to wider Europe" *New York Times,* 7 December 1992 *https://www.nytimes.com/1992/12/07/world/swiss-reject-tie-to-wider-europe.html.* Retrieved 19 Nov 2019

18. Norway EU payments. Full Facts, independent fact checking charity, https://fullfact.org/europe/norway-eu-payments/. Retrieved 3 March 2020

19. Ray Bassett, *Brexit: Options for the Irish Border,* 2018, Politeia

20. European Parliament Website *"Brexit: reciprocal visa-free access for EU and UK nationals"* Press release 4 April 2019, *https://www.europarl.europa.eu/news/en/press-room/20190403IPR34819/brexit-reciprocal-visa-free-access-for-eu-and-uk-nationals.* Retrieved 26 April 2019

21. Northern Ireland and Ireland – position paper, published by the British Government 16 August 2017, *https://www.gov.uk/government/publications/northern-ireland-and-ireland-a-position-paper.* Retrieved 19 Nov 2019

22. David Collins *Negotiating Brexit, The Legal Basis for EU and Global Trade,* 2018, Politeia London.

23. Austrade, Australian Trade and Investment Commission,*"Australian Trusted Trader program commences"* Press Release, I July 2016, Canberra, *https://www.cbfca.com.au/CBFCA/News/NNF/2016/NNF_2016_109. aspx*

24. ec.europa.eu, Agreement between the European Economic Community and the Swiss Confederation, entry into force 1/1/1973, summary on website of the European External Action Service, *http://ec.europa.eu/world/agreements/prepareCreateTreatiesWorkspace/treatiesGeneralData. do?redirect=true&treatyId=73.* Retrieved 26 April 2019.

25. *Trading Across Borders, Technology gains in trade facilitation. https://www. doingbusiness.org/content/dam/doingBusiness/media/Annual-Reports/ English/DB17-Chapters/DB17-CS-Trading-across-borders.pdf.* Retrieved 15 March 2020

26. Smart border 2.0. Avoiding a hard border on the island of Ireland for customs control and the free movement of persons – Study. Publications Office of the European Union, 18.1.2018. *https://www.europarl.europa.*

eu/thinktank/en/document.html?reference=IPOL_ATA(2018)604946. Retrieved 19 Nov 2019

27. *Belfast Telegraph* "*No new customs points planned for Irish border after Brexit, says Revenue chief*"25 May 2017, *https://www.belfasttelegraph. co.uk/news/northern-ireland/no-new-customs-points-planned-for-irish-border-after-brexit-says-revenue-chief-35754851.html.* Retrieved 19 Nov 2019

Chapter 14

Conclusion

Irish attachment to the EEC and subsequently the EU, in reality, has been almost wholly superficial and largely ignorant of the long-term objectives of the disciples of Jean Monnet, who have persistently shaped long-term developments. Apart from a few ardent europhiles, our political class is unaware of the fundamental process which is underway. Any person raising serious questions about the erosion of Irish sovereignty, salami slice after salami slice, is normally portrayed by the mainstream, as a maverick or some type of deranged dissident. Yet it is extremely doubtful if a dozen members of the Dáil could be found who could speak authoritatively about the implications of creeping Federalism. Most would be unaware of the huge democratic deficit at the heart of the European project. Ministers are far too occupied by the day to day business of Government to be in a position to read and digest all the various activities, which are taking place in their names. Countless working groups and technical meetings in Brussels are taking place every week, with the EU Commission providing the secretariat, all of which are pressing in the same direction, towards the creation of a single Federal European State which will be a global power.

For Ireland, the experience of being a member of the EEC and then the EU was initially beneficial. The financial transfers from Brussels, over the years, were very welcome and certainly helped Ireland make the quantum leap to a much more successful economy. The erosion of powers from the democratic institutions at national level was slow and to many almost imperceptible. Hence, with the grants flowing from membership, there was no need to delve any deeper.

To those who raised the sovereignty flag, such as redoubtable Anthony Coughlan, the pro-EU elements answer had a perverse logic. By surrendering part of the country's sovereignty, Ireland had actually become more sovereign because this was a huge contrast with attitudes in our neighbouring island. It was not so much surrendered as shared, yet nobody could point to a single instance where a shared power had been returned to a national capital. It is clearly a phony piece of euro spin. The shared sovereignty concept is rarely articulated in the larger countries.

Much of the so-called Irish attachment to Brussels has also been a form of old-fashioned Anglophobia, masking itself as a modern europhilia. The more the English were uncomfortable with the EU, the more the Irish liked it. But now the Brits are leaving, and we no longer have that motivation. In addition, the European largesse has dried up. Ireland has become a net contributor to the European budget to the tune of circa €1bn in 2019. The traditional mainstay of our receipts, the CAP, stands to be reduced further, increasing even more the net outflow of funds.

Hence, the landscape is changing in a negative direction as is the relative attractiveness of EU membership to Ireland.

Ireland now faces difficult choices in the post-Brexit landscape. Brexit has been an extremely unwelcome development for the country, compounded by Dublin's failure to assist former PM David Cameron extract any meaningful concessions from Brussels. Our adherence to the Backstop, ensured the failure of the Theresa May administration and the arrival of a committed Brexiteer, Boris Johnson, as Prime Minister in London. Apart from alienating our most important trading partner, the nature of the EU may also change and in a similarly unwelcome direction. It will be much harder to resist the EU centralist tendencies, coupled with bureaucratic overregulation, without the support of the second largest economy in the EU.

There are other unmistakable trends and growing unrest in mainland Europe. Any thought that the citizens of the various countries are simply going to allow their governing elite to effortlessly lead them along the road to European Federation can be safely dismissed. There is conflict everywhere. The days of passive acquiescence on Europe in the general population appear over. Citizens in mainland Europe are waking up to the enormous implications of policy positions that those with whom they have entrusted stewardship of their States have been taking behind closed doors. Divisions in societies all over the continent are opening up between those who have benefitted from the EU and those who have been left behind.

Apart from the democratic deficit, the EU, or more particularly the Eurozone, has been performing very poorly economically in comparison with other regions of the world, including North America. Discontent is rising in almost every Member State. Sometimes the EU can look like an experiment of trying to construct a State around an unstable currency.

The euro, the most extreme form of a fixed currency rate mechanism, is exasperating economic difficulties. There are huge imbalances being created with underperformance in southern Europe and massive surpluses for Germany. France has traditionally coped with the different economic performance with Germany through repeated devaluations. This course of action is not open to Paris under the common currency. Italy, the third largest economy in the Eurozone, has also been economically damaged by its continued membership of the common currency.

Somehow, we have ended up with a German hegemony in a centralised and top-down undemocratic system, with no real means of changing the rules. Even Berlin is uncomfortable with the role that has been thrust upon it. The Government of the EU is run by unelected officials who are required to forsake their national allegiances and plough ahead with ever closer union. The Project regularly gets stalled for a period, as today, but it is never reversed.

Many of the European elite react to the current difficulties by reaching for their preferred option to every problem, namely more Europe. However, this is the type of approach which is one of the fundamental causes of the current instability. A whole raft of new policies, which all centralise functions and powers in Brussels, are in various stages of preparation. None of these are to Ireland's liking. In fact, it is difficult to identify a single new EU policy which is helpful to Ireland.

A post-Brexit Britain is likely to align itself much more closely with its transatlantic cousins, Canada and the United States. Tensions are rising between Washington and Brussels, and Ireland, heavily reliant on the Anglosphere world, will find itself in an uncomfortable position.

In the meantime, Ireland has been existing in a little beneficial ecosystem of its own, which is dependent on using a simple tax avoidance regime. This has allowed the country to swim against the current of economic poor performances that characterises much of the Eurozone. This little sweet spot is also unlikely to survive in its current form because it has led to major distortions in the marketplace.

Ireland has facilitated the multinational digital companies in getting an unfair advantage over more conventional firms through our corporate tax policy. This has led to a heavy overdependence on these firms that pay a tiny rate of tax relative to their turnover but given Ireland's small economy, the inflow of these tax revenues has transformed the Irish Government's fiscal situation.

Apart from the damage it has done to other companies and the corporate tax take in larger jurisdictions, it is morally difficult to justify. Therefore, there is little sympathy in other European countries to allow this to continue. Ireland needs to adjust its policies and business model before changes are forced on it.

There is little appreciation in the wider Irish public on how vulnerable the country is to outside changes, not only in Brussels but also in the United States. Ireland has essentially established itself as an offshore haven for US investment in Europe. With the changes in attitudes in the US, especially under President Donald Trump, the climate for offshore investments may be turning cooler.

In fact, international stats are already picking up these trends. The United Nations Conference on Trade and Development estimates that global FDI fell by 23% in 2017, continuing a trend discernible in 2016[1]. Among developed economies the fall was much bigger. This is worrying for a country, like Ireland, which is so heavily dependent on FDI.

For Ireland, the initial attraction of membership of the EEC was access to markets for its agricultural products. Over the years, the emphasis switched to access to the Single Market for US companies based in Ireland. The changes in the external environment call for strategic long-term thinking on Ireland's part, the type of which has often been absent in the past. We need a long hard look at our EU membership and pose the question, is it worth the price?

The billionaire businessman, George Soros, an ardent europhile, has accepted the inevitable and predicted that unless the EU reforms it will perish. The pipe dreams of Emmanuel Macron and his proposals for even a more centralised EU are vanishing against the cold reality of the desire for the citizenry of EU Member States for national sovereignty. The disastrous showing of the establishment centre right and centre left parties in the 2019 European Parliament elections demonstrated this in a very direct way. Voters, and particularly young voters, flocked to the anti-status quo parties, including the Greens.

Against the changing external environment, Ireland, in my view, handled the Brexit process very badly. Dublin lined itself squarely behind those who simply would not accept the referendum result. These Remainers have done everything to sabotage the UK's departure. The border in Ireland has been described as a weapon in this process and was cynically used to try to reverse the Brexit decision. This was quite successful in the short term but has stored up huge problems for the future. If Ireland has antagonised large sections of the British political system, how long will it be before there are calls to retaliate in areas like the CTA, Irish food imports, etc.

Ireland needs a real debate on its future direction. Too many of our leaders, whether political, media or in big business, have a vested interest in the status quo. They have grown too close to Brussels. They seem incapable or unwilling at looking at the wider perspective and a changing external environment. Groupthink dominates the local narrative. This has been a recurrent and extremely debilitating aspect of Irish public life for generations.

Other trends will affect the future direction and again there is a lack of a long-term vision. Demographic changes in the North, as well as the growing disparity with the economic performance of the Republic means that for many in Northern Ireland, the reunification of the country is increasingly attractive. There is likely to be a majority for a change in the Constitutional status of the North in the not too distant future. The Brexit process was an ideal opportunity for the Government in Dublin to demonstrate that it was capable of governing in the interests of all its potential future citizens.

This new all island State would have a sizeable minority who have identified themselves as British or at any rate pro-British. This group would constitute just over 15% of the overall Irish population. These people would have genuine concerns about any Government in Dublin looking after their interests, including their links with the UK, after the Government of Leo Varadkar adopted such an antagonistic attitude to the UK, and to the interests of those pro-Brits, during the Brexit discussions.

Any Irish Government must begin the process of healing the Dublin–London divide, not just to assuage Unionist concerns in Northern Ireland, but for the overall good of the country. We will be geographical neighbours forever and our futures, just as our pasts, are hugely intertwined. While we cannot change our troubled history, we can write a new more cooperative and mutually beneficial chapter for the future.

In my view it is time for a long hard look at where or long-term interest lies. I believe that Ireland would be better off recognising that its geography, its ethnic links, and its indigenous industries all would be better served by leaving the EU's institutions but staying in the EEA. This is the Norway model, even if as an interim measure. It would mean that we could preserve a free border with the UK, while maintaining our access to the Single Market. Since agricultural products are not included in the EEA arrangements, it means we could use much of the present EU net contribution on directly supporting rural families. We would also become an independent coastal State again, with the ability to manage our valuable fish resources, in conjunction with our neighbouring island.

If we decide on going down the Norway model, we need to look at unhitching ourselves from the euro. The decision to join was a purely political one and it brought about the great Irish financial crash and the infamous Bailout. We need to regain control of the most important economic levers available to a State. Our small size and our attachment to the Anglophone world means that the ECB is never going to take our particular economic circumstances into account when deciding macro-economic measures.

In addition, this is a good time to ditch the euro. If a country leaves a common currency from a position of weakness, then it will suffer heavily in the currency markets and its foreign debts will be much harder to service with a depreciated currency. However, given Ireland's strong economic credentials at the moment, there is little likelihood of that happening. Since we would not have been forced out of the Eurozone group, it should not destabilise the system for the remaining members of the common currency.

Whatever the decisions taken about our future direction, we need to ensure that we promote genuine debate and contests between ideas. The Irish media seem to believe that it fulfils its commitment to diversity by having panels, made up of equal numbers of male and female contributors, all of the same view. This was particularly acute during the Brexit debate. It is the antithesis of balance. Unfortunately for some organisations, diversity and equality issues, have been reduced to a form ticking exercise on gender.

Those in Ireland and elsewhere who unthinkingly supported treaty after treaty – the Single European Act, Amsterdam, Nice, Maastricht, Lisbon, etc. – without having the faintest idea what were in them, bear a very heavy responsibility for the sorry state Europe is in at present. They treated the average citizen with contempt and broke the connection between the ordinary citizen and the State. They must accept their responsibility for Brexit and future departures from the EU and the Eurozone.

The motivation for many who oppose further European integration is a desire for the Nation States to regain sovereignty. Of course, modern interdependence makes it impossible for any State to enjoy a reasonable standard of living unless it is prepared to share control of specific economic and trade areas with like-minded States. However, this should not mean that we run up the white flag on efforts to determine as much as possible of our future by ourselves or that we reverse the efforts of many generations of Irish people to establish a sovereign State and Parliament on the island of Ireland.

For those who espouse Irexit, the image in Ireland of British Brexiteers as portrayed in the Irish media, is a major drawback. There is very little nostalgia among most Brexiteers for a return to old Empire attitudes, yet Irish commentators try valiantly, and often in vain, to conjure up such a picture. It tells much about the desire of our chattering classes to delegitimise those who disagree with them. Brexit is very much an anti-establishment movement, which draws its support base from the British Midlands and North.

There is, in truth, some element of racism among some Brexiteers but that should not blind us to a cold and logical assessment of the arguments. The EU will increasingly become a cold house for Ireland, and we need to seriously consider Irexit as the most logical position for our country.

This is not to deny that there are extremely positive aspects to our association with the other Members States of the EU, including the Erasmus programme, high environmental standards, mutual recognition of qualifications, etc. In any further negotiations, it would be important to preserve as much of the beneficial elements of close cooperation as possible.

There are valid arguments on both sides of the debate regarding future Irish membership of the EU. Just summarily dismissing the viewpoint of those we disagree with does a disservice to us all. We should also be prepared to look past the terrible mess that ex-British Prime Minister, Theresa May, made of the earlier part of Brexit, which should not blind us to the fundamental arguments. Brexit may look much better in retrospect than at present.

References

1. "Foreign Direct Investment" 2018 e-Handbook of Statistics UNCTAD publications. *https://stats.unctad.org/handbook/EconomicTrends/Fdi.html.* Retrieved 28 May 2019

PART IV

Chapter 15

Epilogue

At the outset, it is important to understand that the Irish diplomatic Service traditionally has harboured a major divide between those who worked with multilateral organisations, such as the United Nations, European Union, etc.; and those who worked on issues relating to peace in Northern Ireland, Irish communities overseas or citizens welfare abroad. This was true since the day I first walked into Iveagh House in February 1978, as a raw new Third Secretary, the entry grade for Irish diplomats. I was switching from clinical biochemistry in the Mater Hospital to the more refined environment of Ireland's Foreign Service. Its HQ is the palatial former town house of the Guinness Brewing family. It is hard to think of a greater contrast between the marble statues, ballroom, etc. of Iveagh House and the cramped workspaces of the clinical laboratories in the busy Mater Hospital, where blood and other bodily tissues were being analysed.

To be quite honest, it was not something for which my previous experiences had prepared me. I was required to learn a whole new set of skills and expertise, especially mastering Civil Service English. It has its own unique method of expression and jargon. If you were to be accepted and contribute, it was necessary to learn the code. The work was very interesting, and I persisted, despite my initial weaknesses.

Even though the pay was less than the Mater, and the staff in the hospital were a joy to work with, I jumped at the chance of joining Ireland's Foreign Service. I had always wanted to work directly in promoting Ireland's national interests. My old school, O'Connell's on North Richmond Street in Dublin, had been a hotbed of Irish Nationalism. Its former students had provided much of the backbone of the 1916 Insurrection in Dublin. In fact, on 8 May 1916, three former students, Con Colbert, Seán Heuston and Éamonn Ceannt, were all executed by the British. The school maintains a roll of honour of the 100+ students and ex-students who participated in the 1916 Uprising. These included former students Seán Lemass, a future Taoiseach, and Sean T. O'Kelly, a future President of Ireland. Kevin Barry, executed by the British when he was just 18 years of age, was another member of the school's alumni. Ernie O'Malley, who became one of the most effective fighters during the War of Independence and later a renowned writer, is also on that list.

In the 1960s, the school prided itself on inculcating a sense of patriotism among its students, as well as a strong tradition of Irish language teaching. As with all Irish schools of the era, it had a strict regime but from which I benefitted enormously, especially from the great work and support of many of the teachers there. I know that many did not have as positive an experience of that school as I did, and I accept fully the authenticity of their accounts. However, I can only reiterate my own more positive recollections. My old school friends have remained my closest associates throughout my adult life.

Hence, I was delighted to be given the opportunity to serve my country. I expected all those who were so privileged to sit behind the name Ireland to be similarly enthused. After several hundred years of colonial rule, we were finally free to have a separate and independent role in world affairs. I was deeply conscious of the sacrifices, including for some the ultimate sacrifice of life itself, that had enabled us to take our place among "the nations of the Earth."

However, some others did not share my views and regarded joining Iveagh House as a stepping-stone. Ireland was not the primary focus of their ambitions. From day one, my interactions with the multilateral side of that divide were not encouraging. These people, who liked working with large multinational organisations, generally fitted into what was the more classic idea of a diplomat, well dressed, articulate and a passion for international issues. However, their contact, and indeed empathy, with the average Irish citizen was often fairly minimal. They existed in their own world and enjoyed the company of their own counterparts in other foreign ministries and international civil servants. They sneeringly described working with Irish communities overseas as engaging in Paddywhackery. It held no great attraction for them.

Nationalism and patriotism were nineteenth-century concepts. They could just as easily work for another foreign service or multinational organisation. They had no difficulty at all in switching their allegiances from the national Government to the EU. In fact, on more than one occasion, I was told by an Irish diplomat that they felt more European than Irish. By the way, this type of attitude was not confined to the Irish Foreign Service but can be found in other foreign services and especially among the Brussels bureaucracy. I often wondered, in the middle of meetings, just how representative of the average citizen some of these foreign diplomats were.

This elitist distain for the will of the ordinary voter is also seen in their vocabulary which pours such scorn on phrases like populism, nationalism, etc. There is a concerted attempt by the more liberal elements in society to demonise these words, which in the past were regarded as associated with noble sentiments.

This attitude extends into many areas but is especially prevalent in matters relating to the European Project. There is a stream of thought inside the EU that matters relating to Europe are just too complicated for the average Joe Soap and really should be kept out of the hands of elected politicians. Hence the most powerful body is the unelected and independent European Commission, which operates as the executive power in supranational fashion. It alone can, in reality, initiate new policies and laws. The European Commission is not the Civil Service of the EU but rather the unelected Government.

This is the body with which we have placed our future in the post-Brexit negotiations. As events have demonstrated so clearly in the past, the Commission has its own agenda, and should we show any signs of independence then our alliance will be over immediately. The Bailout, where the interests of European banks, and in particular the vulnerable German financial institutions, were given precedence over the rules of the ECB and natural justice, demonstrated this in no uncertain manner.

Despite that experience, some of my former colleagues appeared to have more loyalty to the EU than to the average Irish citizen. That attitude was a world foreign to a Christian Brothers educated Northsider. I always felt it had a snobbish element to their distaste for our more practical work.

I also felt that much of their work was pointless. I actually worked for three years in the International Political Division, early in my career. It soon dawned on me that working for a small west European nation, inside a Brussels imposed framework, meant that we had little real influence over the events that we were covering. The work, which was within the then European Political Cooperation (EPC) framework, usually involved countless meetings and interactions with other foreign ministries, the end product was often a statement by the then EEC on some particular issue. The statement usually involved the condemnation of a particularly nasty dictator in Africa/Asia which was promptly ignored by the target. The statement itself became the objective of the exercise, not doing something concrete about it. The ability to draft a beautifully worded statement, which essentially meant nothing, was the highest achievement, an art form in itself. Also, the choice of target usually needed to be acceptable to the former colonial powers, France and Britain, so only pro-Soviet ones were fair game.

The years working in the Political Division almost convinced me to leave Iveagh House and head back into the world of science.

However, I discovered that on the other side of Iveagh House, there were much more interesting and relevant things going on. There were also more colourful characters involved. It was my natural home and it is where I spent the bulk of my career. I have never regretted the decision to specialise in the more practical areas or to stay on in the Department.

That side of Iveagh House developed a different style where there was much greater need for local political skills, working under pressure, dealing with bereaved families, etc. While our multilateral colleagues were frequently attending esoteric conferences in places like Bali and Mauritius, we often spent our (usually wet) weekends in Newtownbutler, Maghera, etc., observing a Black Preceptory march or standing in a community centre in the Lower Ormeau, getting abused about being from the Free State. I was once told by a leading Republican that being called a Free Stater was the lowest insult she could possibly imagine.

The diplomats in the multilateral area often disparagingly referred to the Anglo-Irish part of Iveagh House as the Department of Fenian Affairs and regularly complained about what they considered too great a sympathy with the Nationalist community in the North. However, the great advantage in working in this area was that you could sometimes see the effect of your actions on the ground, e.g., making representations for a new peace wall in Newington, North Belfast; the end of unfair harassment of an individual; etc., which often made a huge difference to the lives of local residents, especially in interface areas in Belfast. There was a great deal of job satisfaction which made up for the loss of sunshine.

Throughout my years of working on issues relating to Northern Ireland, I had always had a healthy degree of scepticism about some of my colleagues' blind devotion to the European Union. They regularly used the term "communautaire" to justify anything that came from Brussels, as if this was a reason, in itself, to accept everything which carried the EU label.

There was no logic to their devotion. I remember one of the DFA officials, involved in the preparation of the Lisbon Treaty, giving a briefing to senior officials about the outcome. He had no hesitation in stating that there was nothing positive in the Treaty for Ireland, in fact the opposite, our influence was to be greatly diminished. I asked him why we should accept it. He replied, in all seriousness, that anything that was good for Europe was good for Ireland. This was something I simply could not comprehend. He and the people who worked alongside him had no compunction about putting the needs of the European establishment above those of Ireland. In fact, there was a certain distaste for the ordinary Irish voter. Of course, they would never put it as bluntly to the politicians, rather they would confuse them with jargon and pleas for European solidarity.

I also recalled that after the unsuccessful Nice Treaty referendum in Ireland, I was asked, along with my colleague Gerry Staunton, by a very senior official, for ideas, within days of the negative result, on how to overcome the democratic vote. I protested when I saw that there was no intent at all in accepting the outcome. It was this lack of respect for the people who voted No that persuaded me to vote against the Lisbon Treaty on two occasions. The lack of respect for democratic referenda is a recurrent theme inside the EU. My colleagues on the EU side enthusiastically conspired, almost from the moment that the results of the first Nice and Lisbon referenda were declared, to suborn the rejections. The idea that this was somewhat unethical never seemed to occur to them. The whole thrust of their motivation was that they needed to deliver a positive Irish endorsement to Brussels for the Treaty. The actual content was of secondary importance.

In line with the view that the average citizen could not possibly understand the European project, there was a feeling that "something" needed to be done about having referenda on EU treaties. I have listened to countless fruitless discussions about how to overthrow the Crotty, Coughlan and McKenna judgements which ensured fair play in Irish referenda. The Supreme Court came in for huge criticism. I always expressed my opinion that this type of thinking would lead to alienation, but the short-term imperatives always won out. People like Anthony Coughlan were regarded as the enemy for trying to assert the primacy of the Nation States. While I obviously did not agree, at that time, with what the Irish anti-EU lobby were saying, I could never understand the deep hostility of the official reaction. A more confident State would have been much more tolerant of dissenting views. They should have welcomed such challenges as a way of testing the mettle of their own arguments.

However, in Ireland undue deference to sacred cows is a tradition and one which has served us very poorly in the past. Elements in the Catholic Church abused their unchallenged positions to destroy the lives of many thousands of innocent children, medical professionals covered up their mistakes, banking executives wrought economic havoc to the economy with their greed and hubris, etc. All these misdeeds occurred because there were not enough people with the courage and ability to challenge these untouchables. In any democratic society, as in any business concern, ideas and plans should be rigorously tested. Unfortunately, the questioning of fundamentals and generally accepted "truisms" has not been a strength of Irish society. As my late mother would say, "Sunlight is the best antiseptic." Trying to nobble open discussion is a sure indicator that there is "uisce faoi thalamh", an old Irish saying, literally meaning water underground, namely that something underhand is taking place.

The Irish diplomatic service badly needs to have a broader vision of Ireland's place in the world. Too many are completely wedded to the concept of serving the EU, rather than their own country. We need to ensure that it becomes more broadly reflective of Irish society and not just recruited from those third level institutions, which have programmes that are essentially EU propaganda schools.

Annex 1

Letter from the President of the ECB, Jean-Claude Trichet to Brian Lenihan, Irish Minister for Finance on the Bailout

Mr Brian Lenihan, Tánaiste and Minister of Finance

Frankfurt, 19 November 2010

Dear Minister,

As you are aware from my previous letter dated 15 October, the provision of Emergency Liquidity Assistance (ELA) by the Central Bank of Ireland, as by any other national Central Bank of the Eurosystem, is closely monitored by the Governing Council of the European Central Bank (ECB) as it may interfere with the objectives and tasks of the Eurosystem and may contravene the prohibition of monetary financing.

Therefore, whenever ELA is provided in significant amounts, the Governing Council needs to assess whether it is appropriate to impose specific conditions in order to protect the integrity of our monetary policy. In addition, in order to ensure compliance with the prohibition of monetary financing, it is essential to ensure that ELA recipient institutions continue to be solvent.

As I indicated at the recent Eurogroup meeting, the exposure of the Eurosystem and of the Central Bank of Ireland vis-a-vis Irish financial institutions has risen significantly over the past few months to levels that we consider with great concern. Recent developments can only add to these concerns. As Patrick Honohan knows, the Governing Council has been asked yesterday to authorise new liquidity assistance, which it did.

But all these considerations have implications for the assessment of the solvency of the institutions which are currently receiving ELA. It is the position of the Governing Council that it is only if we receive in writing a commitment from the Irish government vis-a-vis the Eurosystem on the four following points that we can authorise further provisions of ELA to Irish financial institutions:

1) The Irish government shall send a request for financial support to the Eurogroup;

2) The request shall include the commitment to undertake decisive actions in the areas of fiscal consolidation, structural reforms and financial sector restructuring, in agreement with the European Commission, the International Monetary Fund and the ECB;

3) The plan for the restructuring of the Irish financial sector shall include the provision of the necessary capital to those Irish banks needing it and will be funded by the financial resources provided at the European and international level to the Irish government as well as by financial means currently available to the Irish government, including existing cash reserves of the Irish government;

4) The repayment of the funds provided in the form of ELA shall be fully guaranteed by the Irish government, which would ensure the payment of immediate compensation to the Central Bank of Ireland in the event of missed payments on the side of the recipient institutions.

I am sure that you are aware that a swift response is needed before markets open next week, as evidenced by recent market tensions which may further escalate, possibly in a disruptive way, if no concrete action is taken by the Irish government on the points I mention above. Besides the issue of the provision of ELA, the Governing Council of the ECB is extremely concerned about the very large overall credit exposure of the Eurosystem towards the Irish banking system. The Governing Council constantly monitors the credit granted to the banking system not only in Ireland but in all euro area countries, and in particular the size of Eurosystem exposures to individual banks, the financial soundness of these banks and the collateral they provide to the Eurosystem.

The assessment of the Governing Council on the appropriateness of the Eurosystem's exposure to Irish banks will essentially depend on rapid and decisive progress in the formulation of a concrete action plan in the areas which have been mentioned in this letter and in its subsequent implementation.

With kind regards,

Jean-Claude Trichet

Annex 2

Footnote on the Common Travel Area

Freedom of movement between the islands of Britain and Ireland has existed in different forms for hundreds of years. This was carried over into membership of the EEC. The arrangements are reflected in three Protocols annexed to the Treaty on the Functioning of the EU.

Protocol 19, which relates to the Schengen open borders zone, provides that Ireland and the UK are not automatically covered by Schengen rules, or by proposals to develop them.

Protocol 20 allows the UK and Ireland to "continue to make arrangements between themselves relating to the movement of persons between their territories ('the Common Travel Area')."

Protocol 21 provides that each of the UK and Ireland may unilaterally choose to opt in to immigration or asylum legislation other than Schengen rules, or to discussion of proposals relating to such legislation

Joint British/Irish Statement on the Common Travel Area

Recognising the deep and enduring relationship between our two countries, the Governments of Ireland and of the United Kingdom of Great Britain and Northern Ireland have today entered into a Memorandum of Understanding reaffirming our joint commitment to the Common Travel Area (CTA), and to maintaining the associated rights and privileges of Irish and British citizens under this longstanding reciprocal arrangement.

The Memorandum of Understanding was signed for Ireland by the Tánaiste and Minister for Foreign Affairs and Trade, Simon Coveney T.D. and for the United Kingdom by the Chancellor of the Duchy of Lancaster and Minister for the Cabinet Office, the Right Honourable David Lidington CBE MP.

The CTA involving Ireland, the United Kingdom, the Channel Islands, and the Isle of Mann facilitates the ability of Irish and British citizens to move freely within the CTA. Flowing from this right to move freely are associated reciprocal rights and privileges that are enjoyed daily by British citizens in Ireland, and Irish citizens in the UK. These include access to employment, healthcare, all levels of education, and social benefits on the same basis as citizens of the other State, as well as the right to vote in local and national Parliamentary elections.

In entering into this Memorandum of Understanding, the two Governments today reaffirm the standing of Irish and British citizens in each other's countries by virtue of the CTA. For generations, Irish and British people have moved seamlessly between our countries and developed deep and lasting ties. Although predating it, the CTA has also underpinned the Belfast / Good Friday Agreement. The CTA has and will continue to enhance and nurture bilateral relations between our countries.

Both the Government of Ireland and the UK Government are committed to maintaining the CTA in all circumstances, recognising it pre-dates Irish and UK membership of the European Union and is not dependent on it. Neither Irish citizens in the UK nor British citizens in Ireland are required to take any action to protect their status and rights associated with the CTA. Both Governments are committed to undertake all the work necessary, including through legislative provision, to ensure that the agreed CTA rights and privileges are protected.

In entering into this Memorandum of Understanding, the Governments of Ireland and of the United Kingdom of Great Britain and Northern Ireland reaffirm the immensely important and enduring nature of the relationship between our two countries and the unique ties between our citizens.

8 May 2019

Annex 3

The British Irish Intergovernmental Conference – Extract from Strand 3 of the GFA

- There will be a new British-Irish Agreement dealing with the totality of relationships. It will establish a standing British-Irish Intergovernmental Conference.

- The Conference will bring together the British and Irish Governments to promote bilateral co-operation at all levels on all matters of mutual interest within the competence of both Governments.

- The Conference will meet as required at Summit level (Prime Minister and Taoiseach). Otherwise, Governments will be represented by appropriate Ministers. Advisors, including police and security advisers, will attend as appropriate

- All decisions will be by agreement between both Governments. The Governments will make determined efforts to resolve disagreements between them. There will be no derogation from sovereignty of either Government.

Bibliography

Ahern Bertie (2009) *The Autobiography*, Hutchinson, London

Barrett Gavin *Building a Swiss Chalet in an Irish Legal Landscape? Referendums on European Union Treaties in Ireland and the Impact of Supreme Court Jurisprudence. European Constitutional Law Review* vol 5 no 1 pp 32–70

Barrett Gavin (2011) *A Road less Travelled, Reflections on the Supreme Court Rulings in Crotty, Coughlan and McKenna,* (No 2) Dublin

Bassett Ray (2017) *An Irish Perspective on the Brexit Talks So Far,* Policy Exchange, London

Bassett Ray (2017) *After Brexit will Ireland be Next to Exit,* Policy Exchange, London

Bassett Ray (2017) *The EU is becoming less hospitable for Ireland, it is time it joined Britain in leavin,* Policy Exchange, London

Bassett Ray (2017) *No threat to the Common Travel Area from the UK,* Policy Exchange, London

Ray Bassett (2018) *Time for Political game-playing over the Irish border to stop,* Policy Exchange, London

Bassett Ray (2018) *Brexit and the Border, Where Ireland's True Interests Lie,* Politeia, London

Bassett Ray (2018) *Brexit: Options for the Irish Border 2018,* Politeia, London

Beck Gunnar (2018) *The Court of Justice of the EU, Imperial, not Impartial,* 2018 Politeia, London.

Benn Tony (1995) *The Benn Diaries*, Random House, London

Booker Christopher and North Richard (2005) *The Great Deception Can the European Union Survive?* Continuum, London

Bootle Roger (2014) *The Trouble with Europe. Why the EU Isn't Working, How It Can Be Reformed, What Could Take Its Place*, Nicholas Brealey Publishing, London

Carswell Simon (2011) *Anglo Republic, Inside the Bank that broke Ireland*, Penguin, Dublin

Collins David (2018) *Negotiating Brexit, The Legal Basis for the EU and Global Trade*, Politeia, London

Collins Jude (2019) *Laying it on the Line, The Border and Brexit*, Mercier Press

Connelly Tony (2017) *Brexit and Ireland, The Dangers, Opportunities and Inside Story of the Irish Response*, Penguin, Dublin

Connolly, Bernard (1995) *The Rotten Heart of Europe*, Faber and Faber, London

Coogan Tim Pat (2000) *Wherever Green is Worn, The Story of the Irish Diaspora*, Hutchinson, London.

Coogan Tim Pat (1993) *De Valera: Long Fellow, Long Shadow*, Arrow Books, London

Coogan Tim Pat (2012) *The Famine Plot, England's Role in Ireland's Greatest Tragedy*, Palgrave Macmillan, New York.

Coughlan Anthony J. (2015) *Tackling the EU Empire. Basic Critical facts on EU/Eurozone*, National Platform, EU Research and Information Centre, Dublin.

Coughlan Anthony J. (2019) *The EU, Brexit and Irexit – A Handbook for Irish and European Diplomats, Whether Politically Centre, Left or Right*, National Platform, EU Research and Information Centre, Dublin.

Denham Roy (1997) *Missed Chances: Britain and Europe in the Twentieth Century*, Indigo

Devine Karen (2008) *A Comparative Critique of Irish Neutrality in the 'Unneutral' Discourse*, Royal Irish Academy

Documents on Irish Foreign Policy Volumes 1 – X1, published by the Royal Irish Association 1998–2018

Gallagher Frank (1957) *The Indivisible island. The story of the Partition of Ireland*, Victor Gollancz, London

Gillingham John R (2016) *The EU, an Obituary*, Verso, London

Greaves Desmond C. (2018) *The Life and Times of James Connolly*, Manifesto Press, London

Gudgin Graham and Bassett Ray (2017) *A Triumph of Ambiguity. What the EU deal means for the UK-Ireland border*, Policy Exchange, London

Gudgin Graham and Bassett Ray (2017) *Perspectives on the Irish Border and Brexit Negotiations*, Policy Exchange, London

Gudgin Graham and Bassett Ray (2018) *Don't Listen to the Doom Mongers – Why the UK (including Northern Ireland) can leave the Customs Union, avoid a hard border and preserve the GFA*, Policy Exchange, London

Gudgin Graham and Bassett Ray (2018) *Getting Over the Line: Solutions to the Irish Border*, Policy Exchange, London

Gudgin Graham and Bassett Ray (2018) *The Irish Border and the Principle of Consent*, Policy Exchange, London

Halligan Liam and Lyons Gerald (2017) *Clean Brexit: Why leaving the EU still makes sense*, Biteback Publishing Ltd. 2017

Harkness DW (1969) *The Restless Dominion, The Irish Free State and the British Commonwealth of Nations*, Macmillan, London

Heath Edward (1998) *The Course of My Life: The Autobiography of Edward Heath*, Hodder and Stoughton, London

Howe Martin (2018) *The Cost of Transition: Few Gains, Much Pain?* Politeia, London.

Kelly Morgan (2009) *The Irish Credit Bubble*, Working Paper Series WP09/32

Lane Philip R. (2015) *The Funding of the Irish Domestic Banking System during the Boom*, Trinity College Economics Papers, TEP working Paper No 0515

Lawlor Sheila (2018) *Deal, No Deal? The Battle for Britain's Democracy"*, Politeia, London.

Legrain Philip (2014) *Aftershock: Reshaping the World Economy After the Crisis*; and *European Spring: Why Our Economies and Politics are in a Mess – and How to Put Them Right*, Published USA

Lucey Cormac (2014) *Plan B. How Leaving the Euro Can save Ireland*, 2014, Gill and MacMillan

Keoghan Frank, O'Donnell Ruan and Quinn Michael(eds) (2018) *A Festschrift for Anthony Coughlan, Essays on Sovereignty and Democracy*, Iontas Press, Maynooth

MacCormaic Ruadhán (2016) *The Supreme Court, the Judges, the Decisions, the Rifts and Rivalries That Have Shaped Ireland*, Penguin Ireland

McKittrick David, Kelters Seamus, Feeney Brian, Chris Thornton and David McVea (2001) *Lost Lives: The Stories of the Men, Women and Children Who Died as a Result of the Northern Ireland Troubles*, Mainstream Publishing

Mansergh Nicholas (1934) *The Irish Free State: Its Government and Politics*, George Allen & Unwin, London

Mansergh Nicholas (1952) *Survey of British Commonwealth Affairs: Problems of External Policy 1931–39*, Oxford University Press, Oxford

Major John (1999) *The Autobiography of John Major*, HarperCollins, London

Mitchel William and Fazi Thomas (2017) *Reclaiming the State, A Progressive Vision of Sovereignty for a Post-Neoliberal World*, Pluto Press, London

Mody Ashoka (2018) *EuroTragedy a Drama in Nine Acts*, Oxford University Press, Oxford

O'Toole Fintan (2009) *Ship of Fools, How Stupidity and Corruption Sank the Celtic Tiger*, Faber and Faber, London

O'Toole Fintan (2018) *Heroic Failure, Brexit and the Politics of Pain*, Head of Zeus Ltd.

Oxfam Report *Blacklist or Whitewash?* (2016), Oxfam

Phoenix Eamonn (2008) *Northern Nationalism, Nationalist Politics, Partition and the Catholic minority in Northern Ireland, 1890–1940*, Ulster Historical Association, Belfast

Podmore Will (2018) *Brexit, The Road to Freedom*, i2i Publishing

Rogers Ivan (2019) *9 Lessons in Brexit*, Short Books Ltd

Ross Shane (2009) *The Bankers, How the Banks Brought Ireland to its Knees*, Penguin Dublin

Singham Shanker A. (2016) *Cost of EEA Membership for UK*, Legatum Institute Special Trade Commission Briefing

Singham Shanker A. (2017) *A Blueprint for UK Trade Policy*, Legatum Institute Special Trade Commission Briefing

Spencer Graham (2020) *Inside Accounts, The Irish Government and Peace in Northern Ireland, from Sunningdale to the GFA, Volume 1*, Manchester University Press, Manchester.

Spencer Graham (2020) *Inside Accounts, The Irish Government and Peace in Northern Ireland, from the GFA to the Fall of Power Sharing Volume 2*, Manchester University Press, Manchester

Stiglitz Joseph E. (2016) *The Euro: And its Threat to the Future of Europe*, W W Norton and Co Inc. New York.

The Anglo-Irish Agreement, November 1985, published by the Irish Government

The Good Friday (Belfast) Agreement 1998, published by the Irish Government

Name Index